OTHER BOOKS BY PETER FARB

FACE OF NORTH AMERICA: *The Natural History of a Continent*
LIVING EARTH
THE LAND AND WILDLIFE OF NORTH AMERICA
THE ATLANTIC SHORE: *Its Human and Natural History*
      (with John Hay)
THE LAND, WILDLIFE, AND PEOPLES OF THE BIBLE
ECOLOGY
THE FOREST
THE STORY OF LIFE

PETER FARB

MAN'S RISE TO CIVILIZATION AS SHOWN BY THE INDIANS OF NORTH AMERICA FROM PRIMEVAL TIMES TO THE COMING OF THE INDUSTRIAL STATE

E. P. Dutton & Co., Inc.

New York · 1968

ILLUSTRATION CREDITS

Peter Farb: pp. 5, 88, 166, 167, 184, 217, 218
Riverside Museum, New York City: pp. 87, 91 (bottom), 93, 241, 272, 287
Smithsonian Institution Office of Anthropology: pp. 21, 39, 80, 84. 96, 105, 116,
    121, 123, 132, 157, 252, 284
Museum of the American Indian, Heye Foundation: pp. iv, 1, 23, 46, 51, 58, 62, 91
    (top), 109, 136, 144, 162, 186, 189, 222, 223, 231, 282, endpapers
Museo Nacional de Antropologia, Mexico: pp. i, 170, 180, 183
Museum of Anthropology, University of British Columbia: p. 258
Museum of Navaho Ceremonial Art, Santa Fe: p. 269
Rare Book Division, N.Y. Public Library: pp. 4, 171
Victoria, B.C., Provincial Archives: p. 146
William Gedney: p. 294

All maps and charts were prepared by William Sayles

Designed by The Etheredges

A20325

For Oriole

Acknowledgments

When 'Omer smote 'is bloomin' lyre,
He'd 'eard men sing by land an' sea;
An' what he thought 'e might require,
'E went an' took—the same as me!
—RUDYARD KIPLING

It is a pleasant duty to enumerate here the debts I have accumulated, both intellectual and personal. I am conscious of having appropriated freely the thoughts of three contemporary anthropologists: Elman R. Service and Leslie A. White of the University of Michigan, and Julian H. Steward of the University of Illinois. I realize that in some ways this book departs from or takes exception to specific points in their writings, and that occasionally some of my inferences go beyond their original intentions.

Elman Service, Betty Meggers, and Clifford Evans did me the great kindness of reading the manuscript in its entirety, submitting both my facts and my interpretations to conscientious scrutiny.

Personal encouragement, advice, and stimulation were received at one time or another during the years I have been working on this book from: George Agogino, Director, Paleo-Indian Institute, Eastern New Mexico University; Ignacio Bernal, Director, Museo Nacional de Antropología, Mexico; Lewis Binford, Department of Anthropology, University of California at Los Angeles; George F. Carter, Department of Geography, Johns Hopkins University; John Corbett, Chief, Archaeology Branch, National Park Service; Clifford Evans, Office of Anthropology, Smithsonian Institution; the late James L. Giddings, Department of Anthropology, Brown University; Esther S. Goldfrank; Shirley Gorenstein, Department of Anthropology, Columbia University; Marvin Harris, Department of Anthropology, Columbia University; Phyllis Jay, Department of

Anthropology, University of California at Berkeley; Paul S. Martin, Chief Curator of Anthropology, Field Museum of Natural History; Betty Meggers, Office of Anthropology, Smithsonian Institution; James Officer, Associate Commissioner, Bureau of Indian Affairs; Harry L. Shapiro, Chairman, Department of Anthropology, The American Museum of Natural History; Albert H. Shroeder, Assistant Southwest Regional Archaeologist, National Park Service.

I am acutely conscious of the tremendous debt I owe those field workers on whose findings I have drawn so heavily. Rather than list them here by name, I have called attention to their most enduring monuments, their publications, in the Notes and Sources.

My acknowledgments would be incomplete without mention of Jack Macrae, my editor, whose countless wise and helpful suggestions were of great aid in this book, and whose patience and sympathy have endured through several previous books. Amy Clampitt once again has been of great assistance in the final preparation of the manuscript, and Marjorie Weinstein in checking proofs.

I would also like to thank Louis and Nettie Horch for their unwavering faith and encouragement over many years.

All of the above people are to be absolved from blame for failings in this book. Such failings are the inevitable result of my being all too human.

P. F.

January, 1968

Contents

Illustrations

Foreword

BY PROFESSOR ELMAN R. SERVICE

This book has two great virtues. It is the best general book about North American Indians that I have ever read and it also does a fine job of illustrating an important use of cultural evolutionary theory.

The North American Indians, of course, are subjects of an enormous amount of fiction. Unfortunately, however, they are largely a genre, like our romanticized cowboy, rather than a reasonable depiction of the aboriginal reality. There is, to be sure, a fairly large body of specialized anthropological theses and monographs, but these are not literature. Most are academic, pedantic, unreadable. La Farge's *Laughing Boy* is a fine book, but it is also a grand exception.

Man's Rise to Civilization . . . is not a novel like *Laughing Boy,* however, but a scientific work designed to be informative in a very general way. I believe it is scientifically accurate. But it departs strikingly from the standard works, such as Wissler's classic in anthropology, *The American Indian,* by being readable. Peter Farb studied his subject hard for years, but he writes like a breeze, and the reader is thus not conscious of the labor.

Such a wonderfully interesting subject, the American Indians, yet how demeaned by the mediocre literature, both literary and academic. But I am not saying that Peter Farb's book is merely the best of a poor lot. It is a very good book in an absolute sense.

Equally important is the other virtue of the book, its contribution to the theory and practice of cultural evolutionism. For over half a century American and British academic ethnology has been actively antievolutionary, or at best, passively nonevolutionary. The antievolutionary phase seems over and a few articles and fewer books have recently appeared with proevolution arguments. But they are, naturally, mostly general and theoretical arguments with little actual application that demonstrates the intellectual potentiality of the theory.

Evolutionary theory, basically, is about the rise of complexity, whether of the movement from simple to complex biological organisms or simple to complex cultures. The American Indians are highly variable in cultural complexity, ranging from simple hunting-gathering bands of only a few hundred people, through intermediate tribes like the Iroquois, to the affluent chiefdoms of the Northwest Coast, and finally the flamboyant empire of the Aztecs of Mexico. The average White American is not at all conscious of the tremendous cultural differences that are related to these vast differences in size and complexity.

The Indians of both North and South America are one race. Yet no cultural similarity, however general, can be discerned that is ascribable to that fact. On the other hand, literally hundreds of diverse language *families* (not just separate languages) are found among them. But here again there is no important sociocultural characteristic attributable to a language family. Some of the simplest bands, the Shoshone of Nevada, are of the same language family as the imperial Aztec!

Evidently a theory of cultural evolution is a substitute for racistic and language-family accounts of the origin of cultural diversity. It holds that the origin of the major divergent forms of culture are functional concomitants of the rise of societal complexity—that is, of the evolutionary process itself. But evolution is not a simple, one-way process. The key to modern evolutionary theory lies in the concept of adaptation: every society has a culture that adapts, more and less successfully, to an environment. Some of the Indian societies reached a dead end of adaptation, while others continued adapting in ways that made for (or allowed) the rise of greater complexity. This interesting book illustrates clearly the uses of the theory.

Many American readers are Boy Scout types like me, who refuse to grow up, who romantically love the American Indians and will never stop. This is a great book for them (us). But some of us are also, perhaps unexpectedly, would-be intellectuals: interested in science, theory, logic, history, abstractions, data, art and literature, among other things remote from adventurous Indian scouts. Here for once is the romantic subject we love, and the intellectualism we love, served up at the same time by one single author. Peter Farb is plainly one of us.

PART ONE

THE EVOLUTION OF COMPLEXITY

I

A Laboratory for Modern Man

THE FIRST AMERICANS

"They all go naked as their mothers bore them, and the women also, although I saw only one very young girl," reported Christopher Columbus in his journal for October 12, 1492, after making his landfall in the West Indies. "Some of them paint their faces, some their whole bodies, some only the nose. They do not bear arms or know them, for I showed to them swords and they took them by the blade and cut themselves through ignorance."⇕*

Columbus was certain that he had arrived at an island off the mainland of Asia, or even in the fabled Indies themselves. The name he gave these people, Indians, has remained in use to this day. Among themselves, of course, the American Indians had no name to distinguish their race from any other, and they had no knowledge that other varieties of mankind might exist. Usually an Indian group called itself simply "the people," although sometimes a descriptive adjective was added. Such descriptive names—*Chiluk-ki* (Cherokee), "the cave people," and *Hopitu* (Hopi), "the peaceful people"—were sometimes later adopted by European settlers. Most of the names, though, came from epithets given one Indian group by another. The Sioux Indian's contemptuous description of one of its neigh-

---

* I have avoided burdening the text with footnotes, yet I realize that some readers will want to pursue further the subjects discussed. The appearance of the symbol ⇕ indicates that a comment, a source, or a further amplification appears in the "Notes and Sources" section that begins on page 295, arranged by chapter and by page. This section is cross-indexed with the Bibliography that begins on page 308 and lists my principal sources.

3

Uneasy encounters: The first attempt by Europeans to portray the inhabitants of the New World is this engraving (LEFT) from Columbus' letters, published in 1493. A small boat from one of Columbus' ships is making a landfall to barter with the natives, who, Columbus wrote, were as "naked as their mothers bore them." An Indian view of the Spaniards is that of the Pueblo Indians living near the present-day Cochiti Reservation in New Mexico. Their cave painting (RIGHT) shows what impressed them about the invading Spaniards. Amid the older and more traditional Pueblo symbols, designs, and kachina masks are Spaniards on horses and a church with a cross.

bors as *sha hi'ye na,* "speakers of an unintelligible language," resulted in our calling these people Cheyenne.‡

As the Spanish explorers probed the contorted shoreline of the North American continent, and finally penetrated inland, they were bewildered by the great variety in the Indian societies they encountered. In the West Indies and in the Southeast most Indian groups lived under the rule of powerful chiefs. When Cortés conquered Mexico he came into contact with a glittering culture and elaborate systems of government that much resembled those found in Europe. As Coronado's expedition of 1540–42 pressed northward into the Southwest and the high plains, eventually reaching Kansas, still other kinds of Indian societies were encountered: small bands of impoverished hunters in northern Mexico; Pueblo Indians living as tribes in large and compact villages; seminomadic bison hunters.

The Spaniards observed the diversity of customs, laws, beliefs, tools, and crafts between neighboring Indian groups, as well as the resemblances between widely separated ones; and the Spaniards did not know how to explain what they saw. Some Indian groups produced sophisticated art, irrigated their fields by an extensive system of canals, lived in permanent villages, and performed elaborate ceremonials; whereas others living nearby wandered about in bands no larger than a family, collected what-

ever food was available whether grasshoppers or lizards, produced no art, and had hardly any ceremonials at all. One group appeared remarkably democratic, whereas another had a rigid system of classes based on wealth. A few groups were leaderless; some paid attention to a headman; other groups appointed temporary leaders, and still others carried a semidivine chief around on a litter. As a succession of Spaniards, Frenchmen, and Englishmen explored the length and breadth of North America, the differences and similarities became even more bewildering. The Iroquois practiced torture; the Choctaw took heads as trophies; the Kwakiutl enslaved captives. The Mandan lived in earth lodges, the Sioux in bison-skin tipis, the Choctaw in cabins. The Sac and the Fox lived close to each other in what is now Wisconsin, and they were very similar in language, customs, traditions, and religion; yet, inexplicably, Whites* clearly found the Sac much easier to deal with.

* There is great difficulty in finding a fitting word to describe the various peoples, mostly from Europe but also from parts of Asia, who came to the New World, made contact with the native inhabitants, and ultimately destroyed their cultures. Some writers describe the explorers and settlers as "Europeans," but such a word would include such people as the Swiss who obviously were not a European colonial power; the use of "Europeans" also ignores the important influence of Asiatic Russians who made early contacts with Eskimo bands and Indians from Alaska southward to California. Other writers have used the word "white" (spelled with a lower case "w"), but that is unsatisfactory also. In this book I am not pointing an accusing finger at all the members of a particular race; that would be

Most people attributed such diversity among Indian cultures to stubborn chance, and they were willing to leave it at that. They saw merely a continent to be won and its inhabitants to be pacified. There was little time to speculate about the exotic Indian customs, or even those customs that so uncannily seemed to mirror European ones. But later it became clear that the multitudes of different Indian groups in North America, the thousands of them, could be fitted into categories that ranged from the simple to the extraordinarily complex, from a condition of "savagery" to that of "civilization." The important thing about all these speculations, though, is that long before Darwin and Wallace brought biological evolution to the attention of the world in 1858, observers of the American Indian had recognized that evolution occurs in cultures.

Various attempts were made to plot the Indian's cultural evolution. One well-known sequence was by Lewis Henry Morgan,‡ who saw seven stages through which all societies must inevitably progress: lower savagery, middle savagery, upper savagery, lower barbarism, middle barbarism, upper barbarism, and finally civilization. Morgan believed that each of these stages was ushered in by the evolution of some new advance; a group went from upper savagery to lower barbarism, for example, when it learned the art of pottery. Karl Marx in 1857 proposed an evolutionary theory that began with Primitive Communism and proceeded through Pagan Society, Ancient Classical Society, Feudalism, and two kinds of Capitalism, up to the ultimate—Communism. Aside from the fact that Primitive Communism probably never existed, these stages are much too bound by the egocentric ideas of Western civilization.

Another commonly accepted evolutionary sequence was based on the increasing complexity of family life. This theory stated that the family originally centered around the mother, and the father served merely for the role of fertilization. But as societies rose toward civilization, the father spent more and more time with the family until, as in the European

---

quite unfair to the Caucasoid population of Ceylon, for example, who of course played no part in the conquest of North America. So, with much reluctance (and with an avowal that no racism is intended), I have settled upon "White." I hope the fact that I have spelled it with a capital letter imparts to the reader that I am really not talking about any particular Caucasoids but about an abstraction—a composite of social, political, and economic attitudes by certain people, whose skin is usually whiter than most of the world's population and who behaved in a certain way toward primitive peoples wherever they were encountered around the globe. The White is a colonizer who early developed an advanced technology; he is an exploiter of human and natural resources; he has destroyed, often intentionally, almost every alien culture he has come in contact with; and he has imposed an iron rule on the remnant peoples of these cultures.

civilizations, a child inherited his or her father's name. The whole question of whether a family or a group is oriented toward the male or the female is much more complicated than that. The Great Basin Shoshone, among the most primitive peoples in North America, based their descent on the father and not the mother. Among the peasants of Guatemala, the Indians are strongly patrilineal—yet the families of mixed-bloods or ladinos, who are also peasants, are most often headed by women. And the whole problem is further complicated by economics. In some modern societies, particularly among the lower classes, the father is unable to contribute much income or prestige to the household. As a result, the major influence in the family is maternal; such a situation exists among the people of East London, England, and particularly among Negro families inhabiting the ghettos of North America.

An evolutionary sequence that has been popular from time to time shows human groups progressing from hunting to agriculture and finally to civilization. But such a broad sequence is too generalized to be meaningful, as a comparison of the Northwest Coast Indians with the neighboring Eskimo demonstrates. They lived close to each other and the societies of both were based on hunting—but that was about all they had in common. The Northwest Coast Indians were organized as wealthy and elaborate chiefdoms, whereas the Eskimo lived as impoverished and very small bands. The two groups differed also in settlement patterns, social organization, religion, crafts, and practically everything else. So lumping two such diverse cultures into the single broad category of Hunters explains nothing.

Although these and other theories‡ have been shown to be inadequate, the very fact that they were proposed in such number and variety demonstrates the intense interest of Europeans in the cultures of primitive peoples. Many of the great philosophers of the Enlightenment (Rousseau, Turgot, Condorcet), like the earlier English theorists (Hobbes and Locke, to name only two), were all thinking in terms of American Indians as proofs for their theories. It soon became obvious that those cultures could shed much light on the customs and behavior of modern man.

North America is the place in the world most nearly ideal to observe the evolution of human societies and customs, institutions and beliefs, for these are revealed there with all the clarity of a scientific experiment. The story of the Indians in North America provides modern man with a living test tube, in which the major ingredients that went into the experiment, the intermediate reactions that took place, and the final results are largely known.

For hundreds of millions of years the North American continent was there; but no species of man had ever trod it before the ancestors of the Indians arrived tens of thousands of years ago. They are the ingredients that went into this experiment in the evolution of man's institutions. Surprisingly, a good deal is known about them from archeological investigations. They brought only meager cultural baggage with them when they migrated to North America: a social organization at the level of the small band, crude stone tools, no pottery, no agriculture, no domesticated animals except possibly the dog. Most of what the Indian would become he would invent for himself in the New World, for once he arrived in North America he was in most part isolated from the Old World. He could evolve unfettered his social and political institutions, his religion and laws and arts.

The major steps by which these interactions took place are now known; and, finally, so is the outcome of the experiment itself. At the time of Columbus' discovery of North America in 1492, the cultures of American Indians existed at all stages of development. As the explorers made their landings on the rim of the continent and then penetrated deeper into its forests and deserts and grasslands, they discovered all the stages of human society from the simplest kind of band up to the complex state. It was eventually realized that the American Indian spoke more than five hundred languages in North America alone, some of them as different from each other as English is from Chinese. Every category of religious system known to man, including monotheism, had been evolved somewhere on the continent. More than two thousand kinds of plant food had been put to use, and economies had been developed for harvesting the products of the seas and the lands.

Here, in the Indian societies, was the experimental evidence by which man might be explained as a social being—his complex relations with other men and with the environment itself, his political and social institutions, his religious systems and legal codes, his often strange ways of behaving, and his apparently curious customs. The perplexing problems that have bewildered thinkers since the earliest human speculated about himself might find an answer in the living laboratory of North America. And that is exactly what has happened. The evolution of the Indians' culture has shown that human societies around the world are something more than patchworks or haphazard end products of history. The study of the tribal organization of the Iroquois, for example, gives hints about the ancient Hebrews at the period when they, too, were organized as tribes.

What is now known about the total power of the Aztec state tells modern man much about why the Assyrians acted the way they did. The varying responses of the North American Indians to the invading Whites sheds light on today's questions about colonialism in Africa and Asia, and its aftermath.

HOW CULTURES CHANGE

The foremost influence in anthropology today is cultural evolution—as stated by Elman R. Service and Leslie A. White of the University of Michigan, and Julian H. Steward of the University of Illinois—and this book is written with their general viewpoint. These three scholars, although they differ as to details, believe that cultural evolution is as much a fact as biological evolution has been shown to be. They do not, though, hold with the previous theorists who maintained that societies evolved from matriarchy to patriarchy, from hunting or pastoralism to agriculture, from savagery to forms of barbarism and then to civilization. Nor do they regard cultural evolution as steady "progress" toward some inevitable goal. Impoverished bands of hunters in Mexico ten thousand years ago did not know that their descendants would someday be part of the sophisticated Aztec culture, any more than a primitive reptile knew that its descendants would someday evolve into birds.

How, then, do cultures evolve? Why have some progressed from small bands to larger tribes, while others have become different kinds of tribes or chiefdoms or states? The answers to questions about different human societies usually cannot be found solely by looking at the environments they inhabit, nor by noting great historical events or the arrival on the scene of great men. Rather, an analysis must be made of the structures of the cultures themselves. Every culture is composed of multitudes of cultural elements such as different kinds of baskets, religious beliefs and social practices, tools, weapons, and so forth. Some cultures, like Modern America, have millions of such elements, whereas Great Basin Shoshone bands, which lived between the Rocky Mountains and the Sierra Nevada of California, possessed only about three thousand elements at the time of their first encounter with Whites.

These cultural elements are in a continual process of interaction; new syntheses and combinations are constantly being produced. But whether or not the new combinations survive in a human group depends on whether or not they work in the existing cultural context. An invention or new combination can be successful only if all of the elements necessary for the recombination are present in the culture. An excellent example of a new combination of several previous inventions is Leonardo da Vinci's plan for the submarine—which never materialized because his culture did not yet possess the technology to produce it.

The Cheyenne Indians of the plains demonstrate how a new combination and a new synthesis may take place in a culture. Just before the arrival of Whites, the Cheyenne had migrated from Minnesota to the plains where they practiced a primitive agriculture. All around them thundered bison, but the Cheyenne lacked the technology to substitute hunting for agriculture as the base of their economy. In the eighteenth century, though, the Cheyenne obtained Spanish horses, which resulted in a new combination for their culture. The horse was the element, the precise tool, that had previously been lacking in Cheyenne culture. Once the Cheyenne began to exploit the abundance of the bison, changes swept through their culture. New styles of dress and ornamentation were adopted. Village life was abandoned in favor of wandering in pursuit of the migratory bison herds. Social stratification based on wealth in horses arose in a society that had previously been egalitarian.

These were only a few of the more apparent changes that occurred in the Cheyenne way of life, solely because of a new cultural element, the horse. It may seem obvious to a modern observer that the Cheyenne would recognize instantly the superiority of the horse for use in killing bison, but that is not necessarily true. The Cheyenne culture possessed many special aspects that permitted it to accept the horse and to integrate it into its culture. After all, the Paiute of the Great Basin also obtained horses from the Spaniards. But instead of using the horses for hunting, the Paiute ate them.↕

Every culture is similarly made up of shreds and tatters from other cultures. Consider that this book is printed by a process invented by a German, on paper invented in China. Its written symbols are a Roman-Etruscan variant of a Greek form of the alphabet, in turn obtained from the Phoenicians, who originally got the idea from Egyptian hieroglyphics. Our "American" culture of today is composed almost entirely of such imports and borrowings from every continent. Nevertheless, despite the borrowings, our culture *is* distinctly American. The important point is not so much the borrowings as the particular ways the culture has combined the home grown and the imported into a harmonious whole—and as a result evolved to a different level of complexity.

DIFFERENCES AND SIMILARITIES IN THE CULTURES OF MANKIND

Are the apparent differences and similarities in man's cultures merely the result of random changes, or does some pattern exist that will explain them? Most social scientists do not believe that cultures are haphazard. But they disagree considerably about the patterns they detect. One commonly heard explanation is based on the biology of man. It seeks to interpret human culture on the basis of man's brain, adrenal glands, muscular responses, and nervous system. But the fallacy in logic here is that behavior common to all people cannot explain why particular kinds of behavior exist among some groups of people but not among others. A theory that explains eating by man's digestive system cannot explain also why different societies obtain and prepare food in different ways, or why some have food taboos and others do not. Men in all societies possess the biological equipment to remove their hats or shoes, but it is the birth within a particular culture that decides that a Jew will keep his hat and his shoes on in his place of worship, a Mohammedan will take off his shoes, and a Christian will keep his shoes on but remove his hat. Sweeping changes took place in most areas of English culture between 1066 and 1966, yet in that time the English people as biological organisms underwent no appreciable changes. So there is nothing in biology to explain culture changes and differences between societies. As a logician might state it: You cannot explain a variable (in this case, culture) in terms of a constant (the biological makeup of man).

The psychological explanation, as popularized by Ruth Benedict in her *Patterns of Culture,*‡ is a variant of the biological. To Ruth Benedict, the Pueblo Indians of the Southwest were a placid, nonaggressive people, whereas the people of the Northwest Coast chiefdoms were warlike. When she wrote this book, she had virtually no field experience in observing American Indian societies and her interpretations were based on observations by others, which she either misinterpreted or romanticized. The psychological description of a culture in terms of its ethos or world view fails to answer really basic questions. How did such a world view originate in the first place? Why did one society embrace a particular world view but a neighboring society did not? No one denies that the human personality is shaped by the culture into which it is born. But no one has ever demonstrated the reverse—that a culture itself is created by the personality or temperament of the individuals who compose it.‡

A goodly amount of data has been collected about the Yurok Indians of California; an interpretation of this data permits us to see if psychology can offer really basic insights. The Yurok inhabited an earthly paradise with equable and invigorating climate, salmon in the rivers, and acorns in the forests. In fact, the Yurok had so much food available that their population density was greater than most other groups living in primeval California. Yet, if the Yurok society were an individual, it would be labeled paranoiac. Psychologically trained observers have described the people as being pessimistic, hypochondriacal, extremely superstitious, full of fear. A Yurok did not drink strange water because it might be poisoned; he did not mix the meats from deer and whale at the same meal; nor did he eat at all while he was in a boat on the ocean. After eating deer meat he washed his hands, but he did so in a stream and not in a container of water. His bow had to be made from wood cut from a certain side of a particular species of tree. From the moment he opened his eyes in the morning, the life of the Yurok was circumscribed by all sorts of prohibitions and magic.

And it is precisely at this critical point that the psychologically oriented anthropologist drops the matter. He has described how a typical Yurok individual behaves. If pressed for an explanation as to why the Yurok behaves that way, the psychologist might answer that the Yurok learned to behave that way from his parents, who in turn learned it from theirs. Still, the anthropologist has failed to explain what it was that caused the very first Yurok ancestor to became "paranoiac."

A much more satisfactory explanation than the psychological exists. Anyone who examines closely Yurok economy can see that it was organized at the uncomplex level common to bands that collect for food any seeds or insects they stumble upon. The Yurok society functioned at the economic level of the impoverished Shoshone, even though an abundance of food, due to an accident of geography, led it to organize itself politically at the much higher level of a chiefdom. Because of an insufficient integration between the political and economic levels, Yurok society was exposed to a great many stresses and strains that revealed themselves in interpersonal fears. The society simply did not possess the built-in checks and balances found in the more successful neighboring chiefdoms of the Northwest Coast. The Yurok reach had exceeded its grasp. It was stuck with a complex social structure that it could not manipulate. Unconsciously recognizing this fact, the people sought in magic, ritual, and taboos what their social institutions were unable to provide.

So if the differences and similarities in cultures are not due to man's biology or to his personality, what then is left? There remains a third characteristic of man—his sociality, for like the ant, man cannot survive alone. It is in the social and political institutions that the explanations for differences and similarities will be found.

MAN AS A SOCIAL ANIMAL

All men everywhere exist as members of social groups, however small. A group of men is much more than a random collection of individuals who accidentally happen to share particular customs. The mystifying variety of Indian societies that greeted the explorers of North America can be understood by examining their social structures—that is, the web of relations among people, groups, and institutions. Social organization is an indicator; it is the common denominator of the group, the integrator. Social organizations are simple or complex, with many gradations in between, for the reason that a culture composed of many elements has more parts and requires a more effective degree of integration than a culture with few elements. A complex society is not necessarily more advanced than a simple one; it has just adapted to conditions in a more complicated way.

In arriving at their varying ways of life, societies do not make conscious choices. Rather, they make unconscious adaptations. Not all societies are presented with the same set of environmental conditions, nor are all societies at the same stage when these choices are presented. For various reasons, some societies adapt to conditions in a certain way, some in a different way, and others not at all. Adaptation is not a conscious choice, and the people who make up a society do not quite understand what they are doing; they know only that a particular choice works, even though it may appear bizarre to an outsider.

Often, the adaptation seems to be irrational conduct that jeopardizes the very society that practices it. An adaptation of the Koryak of Siberia, distant relatives of the Eskimo, is likely to strike an outsider as extremely curious. Their religion demands that every year they should destroy all of their dogs, an apparently suicidal step that jeopardizes their survival as herders of reindeer and hunters. Why, then, does their religion make things even more difficult for them in their already harsh environment?

The truth is that they are not in jeopardy, for they immediately replenish their supply of dogs by purchasing them from nearby tribes that impiously breed dogs instead of killing them. The relationship between the Koryak and their neighbors now becomes much clearer. The neighbors are content to breed dogs and to trade them for the Koryak's meat and furs. If the Koryak ever halted their annual dog-kill, then the neighbors would be faced with an eroded market. They would have to go out and hunt on their own, in that way destroying a peaceful trade relationship with the Koryak and substituting one that competes for game.‡

By examining the ways in which men have organized themselves socially, it is possible to explain why certain culture elements appear in one kind of society but disappear in another. It is also possible to place societies into evolutionary stages of increasing complexity. Each stage incorporates some of the traits of a simpler stage before it, and it also adds some unique features of its own. An examination of the stages of cultural evolution explains many of the mystifying aspects of Indian cultures: why Indians living at one stage broke their promises to Whites, and why those living at a different stage did not; why one group of Indians seemed peaceful and another group warlike; why certain groups appeared to waste their resources while others conserved them. Private property, division of labor, the presence or absence of priests, and many other characteristics of societies are not found at random, but rather exist only at particular stages.

Several words of caution. The previous paragraph does not state that every *people* must pass through the same evolutionary sequence, as was once believed by those who tried to track mankind's tortuous journey from savagery to civilization. A people may pass directly from hunting wild game to agriculture without ever having flocks and herds, as happened with all North American Indians except the Navaho, who stole their sheep from the Spaniards. A people may even seem to retrogress in giving up agriculture to return to hunting; many Plains Indian agriculturists who obtained horses from the Spaniards and then hunted bison did exactly that. No stage must necessarily precede or follow any other stage when particular groups of *people* are being discussed. Cultural evolution predicts major trends, and not necessarily the history of a particular group, in much the same way that a life-insurance company's mortality figures predict life expectancies for whole groups of people but cannot tell a particular policyholder when he will die.

More is known about the American Indian than any other major aboriginal group in the world. He has been observed, described, catalogued, and cross-compared. This book will not examine the Red man with a romantic eye, not regard him as one of nature's noble savages or as some unspoiled child of the land. The romance of primitive cultures lies in a different direction—revelations about our own roots and significance. It is now possible to use all the information about Indian societies, to arrange them into a taxonomic classification that will reveal important relationships, differences, and similarities. This taxonomy, which will be followed in the next ten chapters, will examine Indian groups at every level of social organization in an attempt to make sense out of the intricate web of relationships that makes up the whole fabric of people, groups, and institutions. This taxonomic classification‡ is:

1. THE BAND
    a. *The family*
    b. *The composite band*
    c. *The patrilocal band*

2. THE TRIBE
    a. *The lineal tribe*
    b. *The composite tribe*

3. THE CHIEFDOM

4. THE STATE

Part II examines the roots of the Indian cultures back to the original peopling of North America, and it looks at the evolution of man's body and speech. The concluding Part III investigates what happens to societies undergoing starvation and disease, economic exploitation, the pressure of religious conversion—all of which were a part of the White conquest of North America. The answer to why certain societies survived while others became culturally extinct will be found, in many cases, in the varying levels of cultural evolution they had attained.

THE BAND

II

Great Basin Shoshone: Cultural Impoverishment

OF APES AND MEN

Speaking about the "Digger Indians" of the Great Basin, the explorer Jedediah Smith opined in 1827 that they were "the most miserable objects in creation." Actually many different Shoshonean-speaking groups shared this disdainful name given them by Whites who saw them half-starved, grubbing for roots. Mark Twain, riding the overland stage west of Great Salt Lake in 1861, reported coming across "the wretchedest type of mankind I have ever seen up to this writing." He went on to describe the Gosiute, one of those groups commonly called Diggers, who "produce nothing at all, and have no villages, and no gatherings together into strictly defined tribal communities—a people whose only shelter is a rag cast on a bush to keep off a portion of the snow, and yet who inhabit one of the most rocky, wintry, repulsive wastes that our country or any other can exhibit. The Bushmen and our Goshoots are manifestly descended from the self-same gorilla, or kangaroo, or Norway rat, whichever animal-Adam the Darwinians trace them to."↕

From the moment that the first explorers encountered them, there was no doubt that the Shoshonean-speaking Indians, who inhabited one of the driest and least hospitable areas on the continent, led a miserable existence. They pried roots out of the ground with a digging stick. They made simple nets to snare rabbits. The Whites watched with disgust as the Diggers de-

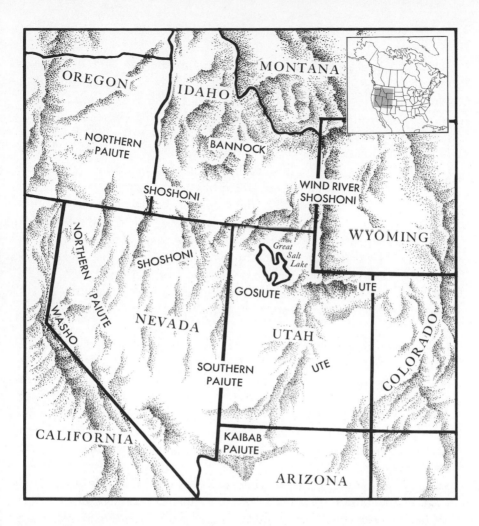

voured grasshoppers. Their clothing was sparse: The men wore a breech-cloth; the women, a double apron woven from plant fibers. An early historian, Hubert Howie Bancroft, even put forward the idea that they hibernated: "Lying in a state of semi-torpor in holes in the ground during the winter, and in spring crawling forth and eating grass on their hands and knees, until able to regain their feet; having no clothes, scarcely any cooked food, in many instances no weapons, with merely a few vague imaginings for religion, living in the utmost squalor and filth, putting no bridle on their passions, there is surely room for no missing link between them and the brutes."⬦

To the Whites, here were people who lived at the lowliest state of humankind, no better than the apes. And here, it was thought by some, would be found the earliest customs of mankind surviving into the present. Others thought that the Shoshone might be, if not the missing link, then some sort of transition between the societies of apes and men. The researches of anthropologists have left all such thoughts unsupported. Neither the Great Basin Shoshone nor any other group of primitive peoples has ever revealed itself as a society that knows no laws, that consists of unfettered humans free to do what they want when they want. Instead, the Great Basin Shoshone are circumscribed by customs, rules of behavior, and rituals that in comparison make the Court of Versailles or the Kremlin appear unusually permissive. At every moment of his life the Shoshone must be careful to observe the complicated folkways of his group, to do reverence to superhuman powers, to remember the courtesies and obligations of family, to pay homage to certain sacred plants, or to avoid particular places. And at those critical times of life called the rites of passage—birth, puberty, death—an elaborate etiquette regulates his behavior.

The belief that the lowliest human is only a notch above the highest ape and forms a continuum is an old, respected—and erroneous—idea. Darwin was assuredly in error when he declared flatly that "there is no fundamental difference between man and the higher mammals in their mental faculties."‡ Numerous psychologists, sociologists, and anthropologists have continued from time to time to parrot this view. The truth is that man is different from the apes; he belongs to a separate category of being altogether. The social life of a nonhuman primate is governed by its anatomy and physiology, whereas human society is ruled by culture.

"Culture," unfortunately, is a word with too many connotations, but it is the best one available for the subjects being discussed in this book. The word can mean good breeding or it can describe a love for the more elevating aspects of human life; it may refer to the tillage of the land, the raising of oysters for their pearls, the training of the physique, and the propagation of microorganisms. In this book, though, the word is used solely in its anthropological meaning. The earliest definition, and probably still the best, was stated in 1871 by Edward B. Tylor, the founder of the modern science of anthropology: Culture is "that complex whole which includes knowledge, belief, art, law, morals, custom, and any other capabilities and habits acquired by man as a member of society." Culture is all the things and ideas ever devised by humans working and living together. It is what it takes to be human, and without it man would be simply an animal. A troop of baboons, for example, has several organizational features in common with a human society at a primitive level. But there are essential differences, one of which is that the behavior of baboon society is largely instinctual while that of man is almost completely learned.

The digging stick of the Shoshone, one of the simplest tools used in primitive human societies, demonstrates how culture makes man. Even though some apes and monkeys have been observed to use sticks for digging, a digging stick represents something much more complex for a Shoshone. To an ape a stick is merely an object, but to man the stick is an item of culture, an idea as well as an object. It is not just any stick, but a *digging* stick; it is intended for the special purpose of digging plant roots out of the earth and not for some other use such as digging out rocks. When a Shoshone wants to pry out a rock he uses a different kind of stick, not a digging stick. Moreover, the digging stick is instantly recognized by all members of his band as a digging stick and as no other category of stick. The stick is also the focal point for traditions and proper usage. There may be a ritual connected with its manufacture; everyone in the band manipulates it in a particular way when digging out roots; some sticks are adjudged to have been fashioned better or more attractively than others. The digging stick is none of these things to an ape, to whom one stick is very much like another.

A Digger Indian may appear to a White to be living on a level no better than an ape; but the Digger can classify his relatives, distinguishing his cousin from his sibling, and he can set up rules about which relatives he will marry and which he will not. No nonhuman primate can do that. Economic teamwork is nonexistent among the nonhuman primates, but the Diggers hold cooperative rabbit hunts, share food during famines, and have complicated rules of hospitality and exchange. Prestige among the Diggers is based on who gives away the most, precisely the reverse of the test for dominance in ape and monkey society. The Digger, unlike the ape, is conversant with spirits and witches, knows holy places and magical procedures, and is awed by death. It is not a case of the Digger having merely a "better" conception of myth, the supernatural, and death than the apes. It is, rather, a case of either-or. Either the ape knows about death, the supernatural, and the soul—or it does not. There can be no question of degrees of belief by an ape in the origin myths of its society; either it possesses such beliefs or it does not. Apes and monkeys are utterly incapable of having any such conceptions. No other living creature can enter the world of human beings and experience what the human experiences, no matter at how primitive a level that human seems to be living.‡

The cultural impoverishment of the Diggers (who hereafter will be called the Shoshone; they include Ute, Paiute, Northern Shoshoni, and Gosiute bands) is explained instead by two factors, one not very important and the other vital. The unimportant one is that the Shoshone inhabited one of the bleakest places on earth, a stern environment that afforded only limited opportunities. The Great Basin is a land of dry soil, high evaporation, low rainfall. Native plants that can resist drought, such as greasewood and sagebrush, are of little value to humans. Native plants bearing edible seeds or roots do occur in abundance around streams, but streams are few and far between.

Much more important than the environment in explaining Shoshone impoverishment is that the Shoshone lacked a technology that allowed them to rise above these limitations. The soil and the climate around Salt Lake City today are no different from what they were in aboriginal times; only the cultures have changed. Yet today Utah is inhabited by many wealthy White farmers who produce not only an adequate supply of food for themselves, but even a huge surplus that is exported to other places. The technology of modern Whites has allowed them to nullify the environmental limitations by the use of irrigation, drought-resistant crops, farm machinery, and so forth; White culture is based on an economic system that encourages the production of a surplus and has provided ways to store and distribute it.

How poorly equipped the Shoshone were to cope with this environment can be seen from the number of their cultural elements, such as their tools and social institutions and even religious practices, which totaled about three thousand. In comparison, the United States armed forces invading North Africa during World War II unloaded five hundred thousand elements of *material* culture alone.‡ No one could hazard a guess as to the large number of cultural elements possessed by a wealthy White farmer near Salt Lake City today, to say nothing of the enormous number of elements of Modern America, which surely would run to many millions.

But take caution not to misinterpret this comparison between the impoverished Red man and the technological White. No claim for the superiority in intelligence of one race over another has ever withstood scientific scrutiny. Nor does a greater number of biological mutations occur in some races or cultures than in others. Actually, biological mutations produce humans with the potential to grow into geniuses at a steady rate at all times and among all peoples. That virtually no geniuses are recorded for a thousand years in ancient Athens does not mean that they were not

Paiute Woman, making a basket outside of her brush shelter, was photographed near Grand Canyon during the Colorado River Expedition of Major John Wesley Powell in 1871–5. Note at bottom center the basketry jar coated with pitch to make it watertight.

produced. Nor does the astonishing cluster of geniuses (Socrates, Plato, Aristotle, Sophocles, Hippocrates, Pindar, Phidias, and many others) that appeared in the fifth and fourth centuries B.C. in Athens mean that biological mutations were produced in greater number at that time. The rate of mutation remained the same; what changed was the culture, which allowed great men to flourish.

Culture operated no differently in Indian societies. Biological mutations leading to genius no doubt took place per unit of population among the Great Basin Shoshone as often as among Athenians. Shoshone culture, though, was different from Athenian. It simply was not receptive to inventions. At various times Shoshone geniuses must have invented permanent shelters. But the Shoshone populace always rejected living in houses because their local food supply was precarious, and the family continually had to abandon its shelter and move on to new foraging territory. The White settlers should not have condemned the Shoshone for living under mere piles of brush; they should have applauded the Shoshone for having had the intelligence not to be tempted by anything so ostentatious, yet so useless for their culture, as a house.

Even a very advanced culture may reject an invention that does not fit in with its way of life. All the high cultures of Mexico lacked a characteristic of the ancient civilizations of the Near East: the wheel. Contrary to what most people believe, though, the Indians of Mexico *did* invent the wheel also. In 1944 archeologists unearthed, near Tampico, wheeled toys (or possibly cult objects) made of pottery. Clearly, the principle of the wheel had been understood in Mexico just as well as it had been understood in the Near East. Yet the Mexicans constructed no wheeled vehicles. What they made for play or for cult use, they rejected when it came to utility. One reason why Mexican societies rejected the wheel is apparent. They lacked horses, donkeys, oxen, or other Old World domesticated beasts capable of being trained to pull wheeled vehicles. The wheeled toys of Mexico document the principle that a cultural novelty's encounter with existing conditions is what determines whether or not it is adopted, and if so in what form.

THE IRREDUCIBLE MINIMUM OF HUMAN SOCIETY

Because of the simplicity of their culture and the limitations imposed by the environment, the Great Basin Shoshone over much of their range lived at the density of one person to fifty square miles, and in some places only one every hundred miles. No more than a few families could remain together for any length of time; there simply was not enough food to go around. A few families might come together for cooperative hunts or live in small winter settlements, but they soon dispersed to their individual hunting grounds. It is no wonder, then, that the Shoshone existed at the simplest level of human organization known, the irreducible minimum of the family. The social organization of some Shoshone groups ranks among the most primitive ever discovered by anthropologists and may recapitulate the early life of our remote ancestors more than a million years ago.

No human organization can be simpler than the family, which is a stable association of a man, a woman, and their children. It is as basic as it is possible to get in interpersonal relations, but simple as it is, the family is the foundation upon which larger bands and more complex social organizations have been built. That is because of the several relationships involving the female: A married female is in conjugal relationship with her husband, in biological relationship with her children, and in social relationship with the family into which she was born and which she left to get married.

An isolated human in a primitive society is usually a dead human, and that is why unmarried or widowed relatives always attach themselves to some family. A Shoshone family was a self-sufficient unit that carried out all the economic activities from production to consumption. There was division of labor: Women gathered plant food, made baskets, prepared meals; men hunted, not only for meat but also for hides and furs needed for winter clothing. The male head of the Shoshone family was its entire political organization and its whole legal system. The family offered almost all that the Shoshone needed, which is not to say that this is what the Shoshone wanted. His lot would have been much easier were he able to exist in larger social units. As a matter of fact, the nuclear family probably never existed outside of theory, for a tendency was constantly at work to unite several families into a higher level of social integration, a loose band. That was done by marriage alliances. As families wandered about seeking rabbits or seeds ripe enough for harvest, they occasionally came into contact with other families. Most usually these families were ones into which their relatives had married or which were potential providers of spouses for their children.

Wheeled toys from Mexico, a dog and a cayman, demonstrate how a culture may reject an invention. The peoples of Mexico obviously understood the principle of the wheel as well as did the peoples of the Near East. But the Indians constructed no wheeled vehicles because they possessed no domesticated beasts of burden to pull them.

All of which brings up the thing which Western civilization calls love. The Shoshone, and those peoples around the world who still survive at the least complex levels of social organization, are aware of romantic love. They know that it exists. But they also recognize it for what it is—in their case, a form of madness. Explorers' journals are full of accounts of Shoshone men fleeing at the arrival of the Whites, leaving their women to the latter's mercy. Most primitive peoples joke about the carryings on of their youngsters enmeshed in romantic love; they regard the participants with tolerance and patience, for they know that the illness will soon go away. They treat a youth involved in romantic love with all the tolerance we would devote to a retarded person in our society. For to the primitive, only someone mentally backward would base an institution so important to survival as marriage on romantic love.

To a Great Basin Shoshone, marriage is nothing to write sonnets about; it is a life-and-death business. It offers benefits that include division of labor, sharing of food, protection and education for the children, security in old age, succor in sickness and in accidents resulting from the hunt. It includes everything meaningful in life, but it does not necessarily include romance. And the interesting thing is that most of the world—except for Western civilization, which is definitely in the minority—feels exactly the same way about it. Western man in his industrial society is nowadays making another departure from the view of the family held by the rest of the world. No longer does he need the partnership of the family to supply his material needs. A solitary male in Western society now survives very well without marriage, whereas in primitive society he would be unable to live. He sends his shirts to the laundry and gets them back the same day; he dines out or buys prepared frozen dinners; a service company even comes in several times a week and cleans his apartment. Once upon a time, a man had to enter into marriage to receive all these benefits. Now he can save himself the bother and preserve his energies for romantic love. He does, however, give up the economic benefits of marriage—an estimated $6,000 to $8,000 a year that a single man must pay specialists for services he would otherwise receive free from his wife.⏍

INCEST

Relatives are important in a primitive society such as that of the Shoshone. It is pleasant to see them a few times a year, to sit around the campfire with them and swap stories; they also can be counted upon to avenge wrongs and to share food in times of acute shortage. The importance of relatives also helps us to understand the reason for prohibitions against incest.

Incest is banned in almost every human society known about on earth, no matter how primitive or how advanced (the major exceptions being the royal families in ancient Hawaii, Peru, and Egypt). Most people confidently explain this prohibition by stating that all humans possess an instinctive aversion to incest. This is, of course, an inadequate explanation— for if the aversion to incest were instinctive, then there would be no reason for such elaborate and explicit rules prohibiting it in almost every society. Furthermore, despite this supposed instinctual aversion, which is reinforced by the prohibitions of law and custom, cases of incest have been reported among many peoples, including "advanced" as well as primitive ones. Incest apparently occurs with some frequency in the United States, for, at this writing, several states have passed laws that make abortion legal for one of these three reasons: pregnancy that results in danger to the mother, or that results from rape or incest. A psychologist has recently estimated that one case of incest may occur for every one thousand people in the United States. And he estimated that at least forty percent of the women who kill their children were involved in incestuous relations with them.‡

Another explanation often presented is that the incest taboo eliminates the deleterious effects of inbreeding, but this is not satisfactory either. For one thing, it is by no means certain that inbreeding is always biologically deleterious. Gibbons, for instance, have practiced it for millions of years, and they still survive. The avoidance of incest has no roots in the biological nature of man, for possibly the only other animal that avoids incest is the Canada goose; man's closest relatives, the great apes, seem to have no way of recognizing siblings.‡ Nor is it conceivable that primitive peoples, some of whom do not understand completely the physiology of reproduction, put incest taboos into operation because they understood the modern genetic principles of the inheritance of recessive defects. The upholders of this explanation sometimes qualify it by stating that general inbreeding is not the thing prohibited but only relations between too-close relatives.

This argument, too, is untenable because it cannot explain why in one society incest consists of marriage between particular kinds of cousins, whereas in another society, marriage is explicitly urged between those same kinds of cousins but forbidden between other kinds. Nor can it explain why some incest taboos apply to people who are not even biologically related. A survey was once made of 167 Indian groups living between Vancouver, British Columbia, and Mexico, and then eastward to Colorado and New Mexico. About seventy-five percent of the groups frowned sternly upon marriage with a stepdaughter; only five percent of them regarded it as proper conduct.‡ Yet marriage between a man and his stepdaughter is not a case of too close a relationship; there is no relationship in blood at all.

Incest taboos obviously have nothing to do with blood kinship. If man rejects the notion of incest, it is solely because he himself dreamed up the notion in the first place. The reason that psychological and genetic explanations explain nothing is that the problem is not psychological or genetic; it is cultural.

Edward B. Tylor in 1888 recognized the truth about incest taboos, but his statement is usually overlooked or ignored. He wrote:

Among tribes of low culture there is but one means known of keeping up permanent alliance, and that means is intermarriage. Exogamy, enabling a growing tribe to keep itself compact by constant unions between its spreading clans, enables it to overmatch any number of small intermarrying groups, isolated and helpless. *Again and again in the world's history, savage tribes must have had plainly before their minds the simple practical alternative between marrying-out and being killed out.* [Italics supplied]‡

Tylor made it clear that incest represents a threat to the entire band because it prevents alliances gained through marrying-out. The more primitive the group is, the more of a threat it is, which explains why the concept of incest is‡ most sharply defined and violations most drastically punished among the very primitive groups. The prohibition against marrying a stepdaughter, who is not related by blood, now becomes understandable. There is no advantage in it, since a man would be marrying into a kin group with whom, because of his previous marriage to the mother, he already maintained good relations. If a man marries his own sister, he gives up all possibility of obtaining aid in the form of brothers-in-law. But if he marries some other man's sister and yet another man marries his sister, he has then gained two brothers-in-law to hunt with or to avenge his death in a quarrel. The primitive looks upon incest more as something threatening than as something repulsive. Incest establishes no new bonds between unrelated groups; it is an absurd denial of every man's right to increase the number of people whom he can trust.

So it is clear that marriages in primitive society are alliances between families rather than romantic arrangements between individuals. Primitive peoples appear anxious about the permanence of the alliance, for they often try to bolster it. One way is to have several marriages between children of the same two families; another is to have the man marry several sisters from the same family.

Marriage as a political system of alliances explains two institutions that are widespread around the world, particularly at the band level of social organization. They are the levirate and the sororate. Levirate (derived from the Latin *levir,* which means "husband's brother") is the rule that obligates a man to marry his brother's widow. Sororate (derived from the Latin *soror,* "sister") obligates a woman to marry her deceased sister's husband. Both institutions function to preserve the marriage alliance even after the death of one of the partners; they clearly show marriage to be an alliance, because by the operation of these rules many marriages outlast the particular partners to it. The levirate was one of the laws of the ancient Hebrews, particularly before they achieved a complex social organization under King David. Witness the law stated in Deuteronomy (25:5): "If brethren dwell together, and one of them die, and have no child, the wife of the dead shall not marry without unto a stranger: her husband's brother shall go in unto her, and take her to him to wife, and perform the duty of an husband's brother unto her." The story is also told in Genesis (38:8–10) of Onan who refused to marry his brother's widow, and instead spilled his seed on the ground "lest that he should give seed to his brother." The upshot was that God slew Onan in punishment, and the word "onanism" entered our dictionary.

Among the Shoshone, marriage alliances were undoubtedly a great source of comfort and assurance. Shoshone marriages on the whole were enduring, and the alliances between families were maintained during the very long periods in which the families never saw each other. Each family spent approximately ninety percent of its time isolated from other families as it wandered about in quest of food. Yet, when families did meet, marriage alliances served to make interfamily relations less haphazard, for kin cooperated with kin wherever possible.

THE MOST LEISURED PEOPLE

Much has been written about the precariousness of the Shoshone food supply. Indeed, the occurrence of both their plant and animal food was unpredictable from year to year because of the variations in rainfall. A particular area might be wet one year—allowing plants to grow, which in turn nourished animal prey—but be dry and sparse for several years thereafter. Almost no localities provided a dependable food supply, and so the

Shoshone families spent a good deal of time moving about from place to place. Each family knew thoroughly its terrain and the exact weeks when the various foods were expected to become available. The Shoshone had a remarkable amount of knowledge about plants and animals. They harvested some one hundred species of plants; they knew when rabbits would be most plentiful, when pronghorn antelopes would be in the vicinity, when grasshoppers would be abundant.

Most people assume that the members of the Shoshone band worked ceaselessly in an unremitting search for sustenance. Such a dramatic picture might appear confirmed by an erroneous theory almost everyone recalls from schooldays: A high culture emerges only when the people have the leisure to build pyramids or to create art. The fact is that high civilization is hectic, and that primitive hunters and collectors of wild food, like the Shoshone, are among the most leisured people on earth.

The Shoshone had nothing but time on their hands, which is what made them appear unusually lazy to White settlers. Their leisure is explained not by laziness but by an absence of technology to store and preserve food. They might cache some seeds or nuts for the winter, but a bonanza in rabbits did them no good because they did not know of any way to preserve the meat. Once a Shoshone caught a fish he had to consume it immediately before it spoiled, because he had never learned to dry and smoke it. He had no way to cope with a surplus. There were times of the year when the Shoshone were surrounded by an incredible abundance of game animals, but they derived no benefits from it. Even though pronghorn antelopes might suddenly become abundant, the Shoshone ceased further hunting until they consumed what they had already killed. The inability to cope with a surplus is true of hunting societies everywhere, with the sole exception of the Eskimo. They inhabit a natural deepfreeze that preserves the surplus, and so they manage to survive the harsh Arctic winter.

Even when their food supply was nearly exhausted the Shoshone still did not work very hard. Since they consumed a wide variety of foods, they had the choice of going after whatever was most readily available at the time. If fish were migrating upstream, the Shoshone merely went out and harvested that resource. If not, then they probably knew some place where a supply of seeds was ripening. They might have to trudge many miles for their supply, but there was nothing haphazard about the undertaking; they knew exactly what was available and in which direction it lay. Despite the theories traditionally taught in high-school social studies, the truth is: the more primitive the society, the more leisured its way of life.

Also helping the Shoshone to lead a leisured life was his "caloric balance." For a Shoshone or any other human to carry on his physiological functions, he needs about 2,500 calories a day (although the diet of about half of the world's population falls below that). Such a daily intake of calories from food is balanced by the expenditure of calories necessary to produce not only the food but also the culture. A primitive hunting culture in a tropical forest, a much more hospitable environment than that inhabited by the Shoshone, might produce nearly two calories for each one expended on hunting, which leaves somewhat less than a calorie free for all other aspects of culture. But as cultures become more elaborate, the ratio of calories produced to the effort involved must rise very much more. The modern Maya of Guatemala who practices intensive agriculture must produce more than enough maize and other food for his family. He must set aside seed for the next crop and also for feeding his farm animals; he needs a further surplus of calories to give him energy to make metal tools, to build storage bins and a house, to chase off predatory birds and mammals, and of course to sell or barter. A study of Mayan farmers has indicated that they produce an average of thirty-three calories for each one expended. (A Kansas wheat farmer, with his much greater technological efficiency, produces about three hundred calories for each one spent in raising wheat.)↕

So it is apparent that man does not need surplus production for physiological reasons, but for cultural ones. The Shoshone, though, were not saddled with an elaborate culture that they had to support with a high caloric ratio. They did not have to spend calories on making a variety of tools, building houses and storage bins, caring for farm animals; they did not have to give away valuable calories to support the work of artisans or full-time priests. When a Shoshone wanted a drink of water, his cupped hands did as well as a cup that would have required calories to manufacture. The Shoshone was able to replace his caloric expenditure by working only a few hours a day, and also by keeping the cultural demand for calories low.

COOPERATION

The tendency was always present among the Shoshone for several families to unite and to form a more complex order of social organization, a band. An important unifier was the cooperation necessary for a rabbit or a pronghorn-antelope hunt. Four elements were essential before a cooperative hunt could be organized: a large supply of game, several families (preferably related), nets, and a leader. If just one of the elements was lacking, then the hunt could not be held. But when all elements were present, the cooperative hunt yielded more game than the same individuals could kill acting separately.

In a typical cooperative rabbit hunt, several nets, each about the same height as a tennis net but hundreds of feet long, were placed end to end to form a huge semicircle. Then the women and children frightened the rabbits into the semicircle, where the animals were clubbed or became entangled in the nets. The most experienced hunter, given the name "rabbit boss" by Whites, was in charge of all aspects of the cooperative hunt. He selected the locality, decided where the nets should be positioned, and divided the game (giving the net owners a somewhat larger share than the rest of the hunters).

Although several families cooperated closely during the hunt, there were good reasons why such cooperation established only temporary bonds. Neither the time nor the place for the next cooperative hunt could be foretold; it was held when the game was abundant enough to make the hunt worth the effort, and when families, nets, and a rabbit boss all came together at the same place and time. No one could anticipate which families would happen to be near each other when all essentials for a hunt were present. Since families wandered about a great deal, it was rare that even two families might hunt together for several years in succession. Nor did the several families, the rabbit boss, and the owners of nets all arrange to be at the same place the following year—for there was no guarantee that game would be available then.

In some areas of the Great Basin a more reliable food supply permitted several Shoshone families to remain together and to cooperate. In these areas, both the larger population and the need to maintain peaceful relations with non-Shoshone neighbors created a role for leadership. The first White explorers to arrive in such parts of Nevada were delighted to find leaders with whom they could make treaties. The Whites, however, understood nothing about the band level of social organization, and so they made the mistake of attributing to this leadership more power than it actually possessed. The leader of a Shoshone band possessed nothing like the political power of a chief. Agreements the Shoshone leader made with Whites in good faith were not kept by other Shoshone, because in band society no mechanism existed to enforce the leader's agreements.

Before the coming of the Whites, the Shoshone, pitiful and impoverished as they were, had nevertheless achieved one of the noblest aspirations of civilized man. They did not engage in warfare. The explanation lies not in some superior Shoshone ethic or in their being Noble Red Men, but in more practical matters. The Shoshone did not wage war because they had no reason to. They had no desire to gain military honors, for these were meaningless in their kind of society. They had no territories to defend, for a territory is valuable only at those times when it is producing food, and those were precisely the times when the Shoshone cooperated, rather than made war. Even if they had wanted to steal from richer neighboring Indians, they lacked both the weapons and a society sufficiently complex to be organized for concerted action. Whenever other Indians invaded their lands and attacked them, the Shoshone did not fight back but simply ran away and hid.

But when that new culture element introduced by Whites, the horse, spread northward from New Mexico into Shoshone lands, it was greeted in various ways, depending upon the degree of impoverishment of the different Shoshone groups. The horse made evident the subtle cultural differences between the slightly wealthier Shoshone and their poorer relatives. The Shoshone living at the lowest subsistence level in the arid portions of the Great Basin found no value at all in horses. In fact, horses consumed the very plants upon which these Shoshone fed.

Farther north there was more grass—and, more important, bison herds. There, too, Shoshone families had already developed more permanent ways of cooperating than the occasional rabbit drives. The coming of the horse was the catalyst that enabled families to unite into predatory bands of mounted horsemen. The Ute, for example, obtained some horses by about 1820, and almost immediately they began to raid neighboring Indians, later attacking Mormons and other White settlers in their lands. The mounted Ute even made it a practice each spring to raid their Shoshone relatives in Nevada who were weak after a winter of hunger; the Ute then fattened them for sale as slaves to the Spaniards in Santa Fe.

The Bannock and the Northern Shoshoni bands, who obtained their horses by theft and by trade about 1800, went even further in changing their culture from aboriginal Shoshone ways: They practiced the same sort of bison hunting from horses as did the Plains Indians. So successful were they that by about 1840 they had already exterminated the bison in the Great Basin; they then took to hunting the eastern side of the Rocky Mountains. Although some of the mounted Shoshone bands took on the trappings of the Plains tribes with whom they were in contact, that was all show. The mounted Shoshone adopted the material culture of the Plains Indians, such as horses, feather bonnets, and hide tipis. They failed to adopt what was really important for survival: a more complex social organization. The mounted Shoshone, despite their sudden acquisition of wealth, were still organized basically at the family level. Their leaders had almost no authority, and they could not coordinate attacks or defense. Most Plains Indians, on the other hand, were organized at the much more complex level of the tribe, and they found the Bannock and Northern Shoshoni bands easy prey for their raiding parties.

ADJUSTING TO A WHITE WORLD

For more than ten thousand years the Shoshone and their ancestors had scratched out a precarious living that changed very little. Then for perhaps fifty years some of them became the temporary lords of an immense region between the Rocky Mountains and the Sierra-Cascade ranges. By 1870, though, their burst of splendor had been extinguished. They had been defeated by other Indians and finally by the United States Army. Their lands were quickly filling up with White settlers, who built ranches at oases in the desert and let livestock graze on the Shoshone's food plants. Miners threw up boomtowns in the midst of Shoshone foraging grounds. In 1872 Major John Wesley Powell, explorer of Grand Canyon and founder of the Bureau of American Ethnology, described the effect of the White settlement on the Shoshone: "Their hunting grounds have been spoiled, their favorite valleys are occupied by white men, and they are compelled to scatter in small bands to obtain subsistence . . . They are in an exceedingly demoralized state; they prowl about the mining camps, begging and pilfering, the women prostituting themselves to the lust of the lower class of men."↕

Shameful as the conditions of the Shoshone were—and to a great extent still are—these people were spared the complete disruption experienced by other Indian groups that possessed more elaborate social organizations. The Shoshone had little to lose. They were united in no complex fabric of culture, meticulously woven strand by strand, to be ripped apart suddenly by the invasion of Whites. As White families settled the lands that had once been theirs, the Shoshone went on as they had before, except that they attached themselves to White families instead of to Indian ones. Few Shoshone had ever known anything beyond an intolerably low standard of living, so they easily made do with the low wages the Whites paid for their occasional labor. When they were forced to move about, either to find work or to be herded onto reservations, they did not suffer the extreme anguish many other Indian groups did under similar conditions; the Shoshone had never been tied to any particular localities in the past. There was little for the Whites to disrupt—no bonds of community, no elaborate ceremonial societies, no complex political organization.

The Shoshone continued to maintain themselves as they always had, on the family level. All their family customs—kinship relations, child-rearing, belief in magic, and even games—continued as before. Their leaders easily switched over to a role not much different from organizing a cooperative rabbit drive: They negotiated for several cooperating families in dealings with Whites. For all these reasons the Shoshone made a comparatively smooth transition to White society, surviving the wars, epidemics, famine, and humiliation that destroyed numerous other Indian societies. Relations between Whites and Shoshone have been amiable, on the whole, and these Indians today do not seem to bear the deep-seated resentment toward Whites that most other Indian groups do.

III

Eskimo: Environment and Adaptation

THE FAR-FLUNG PEOPLE

The Eskimo were the first inhabitants of the New World to be seen by Europeans, for the Vikings encountered them at least as early as 1005, probably on the southeast coast of Labrador. Surprisingly, the numerous Norse sagas made little mention of them at first. But within another two centuries the Eskimo were already being described with the exaggeration and lack of understanding that later came to typify the European's view of the natives of the New World. The anonymous author of the thirteenth-century *Historia Norvegiae* wrote: "Hunters have found some very little people, whom they call Skraelings, and who, when they are wounded with weapons while still alive, die without loss of blood, but whose blood, when they are dead, will not cease to flow."‡ Nor does much reliable information exist about the numbers of Eskimo. The population probably never was very high, perhaps 100,000 or so at its maximum, but soon after contact with Whites the Eskimo numbers plummeted because of epidemics of measles, smallpox, and other European diseases that they had not previously encountered and therefore had not developed an immunity to. (In the same way, syphilis, probably contracted by Columbus' sailors from Indians, was brought back to Europe, where an epidemic quickly spread across the continent.) The Eskimo population is believed to have risen again in this century to an estimated 73,000, living from extreme northeastern Siberia across Alaska and Canada to Greenland.‡

The Eskimo inhabit the broadest stretch of land of any primitive people on earth. They circle nearly half the globe along the Arctic coast, a distance of some six thousand twisting and turning miles. This is a considerably smaller area than they inhabited in aboriginal times, for in the seventeenth century the Eskimo were reported as far south as the Gulf of St. Lawrence, and there is archeological evidence of their once having inhabited a large part of eastern Siberia (about fifteen hundred or so Eskimo still live in Soviet Russia). No other primitive people has ever shown an equal uniformity in physical type, language, and culture over such a wide area. No matter where they live, most Eskimo are readily identifiable by their stocky build, long heads and short faces, and the narrow slanting eyelids with the Mongoloid fold. Their dialects, with the exception of a few in Siberia and in Alaska, are mutually intelligible; a new song or joke introduced into Alaska makes its way from one scattered camp to another and may turn up in Greenland a year or so later. All Eskimo base their economy on hunting. They everywhere refer to themselves as *inuit,* which is simply the plural of *inuk,* "man," in that way emphasizing their own identity in contrast to the Indians around them, who differ in physical type, language, and culture. The White man's name, Eskimo, was coined in 1611 by a Jesuit who heard them called *eskimantsik,* which means "eaters of raw meat," by neighboring Indians.‡

A common thread that runs through all Eskimo cultures is adaptation to the stern Arctic environment. The latitudes in which the Eskimo live are marked by enormous differences between summer and winter. During the winter the sun does not shine for weeks; during the summer it never sets. Summer is the only time in which mean daily temperatures rise above freezing, but it is also the season of biting flies and of melted water lying over the tundra without draining away, forming an impenetrable morass. Tree growth is impossible under such conditions, and only in a few places occupied by the Eskimo do even low tangles of willow and alder grow. For his supply of wood, the Eskimo must rely on the drift brought into the Arctic Ocean by rivers that drain the interiors of North America and Asia.

Despite these unpromising conditions, the material culture of the Eskimo shows a more complex development than that of any other primitive people living on such a simple level as the family. They are operating at very nearly one hundred percent of the potential of the environment. Everyone has heard of at least some of their adaptations. The igloo, or snow house, is the best possible structure that can be built with the materials available; it is strong, it is easily constructed, and it is durable. Some Eskimo use the dog sled and the kayak, and they tailor their clothes

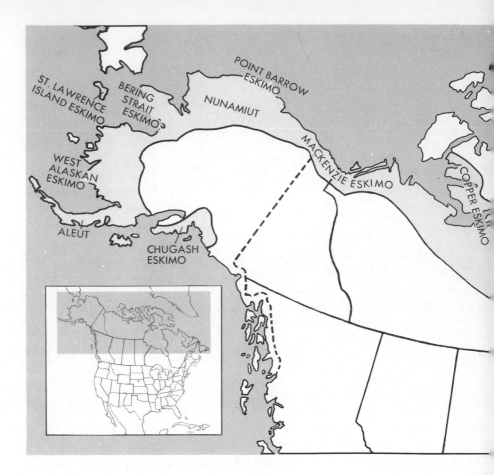

so that the seams are waterproof. Slit goggles are made from ivory to protect against the blinding sun reflected from the snow. Deprived of wood for heating and light, they invented the smokeless stone lamp that burns seal oil. They have even devised a beater to remove snow and thus prevent fur clothing from deteriorating in the humid atmosphere of the igloo.

Anyone who has seen the tools and weapons of the Eskimo in a museum knows how carefully, and often beautifully, they are made. That fact has interesting implications for theories about the beginnings of art. In the far north, where man must face the constant threat of starvation, where life is reduced to the bare essentials—it turns out that one of these essentials is art. Art seems to belong in the basic pattern of life of the Eskimo and the neighboring Athabaskan and Algonkian Indian bands. Samuel Hearne, an eighteenth-century Hudson's Bay Company trader, in midwinter in the desolate Canadian tundra came upon the tracks of a snowshoe with a

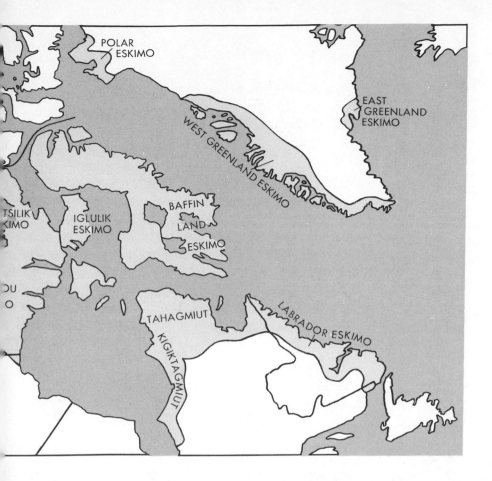

strange shape. He followed the trail to a little hut; inside he found a lone woman who explained she had been kidnapped by another band but had escaped seven months previously. Since that time she had lived alone, supporting herself by snaring what small game she could. "It is scarcely possible to conceive," observed Hearne, "that a person in her forlorn situation could be so composed as to contrive or execute anything not absolutely essential to her existence. Nevertheless, all her clothing, besides being calculated for real service, showed great taste, and no little variety of ornament. The materials, though rude, were very curiously wrought, and so judiciously placed as to make the whole of her garb have a very pleasing, though rather romantic appearance."‡

An inventory of Eskimo technology and inventiveness could be extended for pages and chapters. One can measure, describe, photograph, and make a diagram of a kayak, and he can even transport it to a museum. But no matter how perfect his kayak specimen is, he still has not captured the reality of kayak-ness. A kayak is not an end in itself; rather, it was manufactured to achieve an end. The physical presence of the kayak in a museum cannot be regarded as a substitute for the idea of kayak-ness, for there are parts of a kayak that no one can ever transport to a museum. These parts, every bit as much belonging to it as the wooden frames and skin cover, include who owns it, who is allowed to ride in it, taboos concerning it, rituals connected with its launching and its use, and so on. Only when these and many other things are known can anyone understand what the kayak truly means to an Eskimo. And the same principle applies to all other aspects of Eskimo material culture.

The Eskimo used to be put forward as evidence of a people molded by their physical environment. Although now rejected as fallacious by almost all anthropologists, this old theory of "environmental determinism" nevertheless has subtly entered our way of thinking. You still hear some educated people maintain that Massachusetts has produced more scholars than Alabama because New Englanders have long winters for snowbound study, whereas it is too hot in the South for study anyway. It is true that Massachusetts has produced many more scholars than Alabama, but not because of the climate or any other aspect of the physical environment. Other factors—the superior educational system in Massachusetts, the earlier founding of its schools, the intellectual receptivity of its settlers, and so forth—are much more important than the long winters. And if any connection did exist between long winters and scholarship, then the Eskimo surely should have produced even more scholars than the people of Massachusetts.

Of course the natural surroundings do influence the broad outlines of a culture: An Eskimo inhabitant of the Arctic ice could no more become an agriculturist than a Pueblo Indian of the Southwestern desert could ever base his economy on harpooning walruses. The environment does not determine man's culture; it merely sets the outer limits and at the same time offers opportunities. The advance and the retreat of the ice sheet in North America did not determine that the ancestors of the Indians *had* to act in any particular way; it merely provided them with a particular set of choices from which they selected, unconsciously of course, the ones that worked best. The limits and opportunities of the physical environment are felt in varying ways by different peoples, depending upon their level of culture. Drought represented a disaster to a Great Basin Shoshone band. But inhabiting an equally arid environment in Mexico were the Mixtec, a culturally advanced people who had largely liberated themselves from their

This earliest surviving picture of an Eskimo, dated 1577, was probably drawn by John White at Frobisher Bay.

environment by the construction of irrigation works. To the Mixtec, drought was no more than a hardship from which they soon recovered.

The Arctic demonstrates with almost textbook clarity the fallacy of environmental determinism—for if man has been able to make different kinds of adjustments there, then it is clear that environment influences cultures only in the most general way. The North American Eskimo has exploited the Arctic environment with all the ingenuity of the igloo, sled, harpoon, snow goggles, and so forth. In the Siberian Arctic, just across the Bering Strait, the environment is exactly the same and the land is inhabited by close relatives of the Eskimo known as the Chukchi—yet the Chukchi have evolved quite a different kind of culture. The Chukchi do not make igloos; instead dwellings are built by attaching skins to wooden frameworks, even though wood is as scarce in the land of the Chukchi as it is in the land of the Eskimo. Nor are the Chukchi very proficient hunters, unlike the Eskimo. Before the coming of Whites, the Eskimo hunted caribou (reindeer), whereas the Chukchi herded them. The fact that the Chukchi have survived shows that they adapted to the Arctic environment just as successfully as the Eskimo—but they did so in a different way. Clearly, other factors besides the environment must have influenced the different kinds of cultures the Eskimo and the Chukchi developed.

SOCIALITY AND SURVIVAL

Interest in the environment of the Eskimo and the drama of his response to it has blinded us to other important things the Eskimo can reveal about man. The material technology of the Eskimo, sophisticated as it is within narrow limits, may obscure the primitive reality of the Eskimo's life and what it may reveal about the simpler stages of society. Less dramatic, and ultimately more important, are the Eskimo's *social* adaptations, his customs and laws and religion.

The Eskimo's precarious existence has placed certain demands upon him. The primary one is that he had to find a way to survive in small and isolated groups and at the same time lead a nomadic life. Because the Eskimo feeds mostly on migrant animals rather than stationary plants, every morsel that enters his mouth must be sought out, often over great distances. (He has been able to dispense with plant food because he eats at least half of his meat raw, and that half includes the fat and the internal organs of the animal. With such a diet, he obtains from the meat every vitamin and mineral, as well as all the protein, necessary for human nutrition.) The Eskimo has improved upon the lot of most primitive hunters by devising sleds to carry his possessions, but even so, the amount that he can transport is small. Because of the extremely low population density, contacts between families are rare; the local group that comes together during the winter is usually composed of fewer than a dozen families, perhaps related, although actual kinship is not emphasized.

The only leadership in these groups of families is that of a headman (whose title in the Eskimo language means "he who knows best"). He obtains his position solely by achievement; he does not campaign for it, nor can he pass on the office to his sons or other relatives. In a republic of equals, he is only slightly more equal than others. The family group usually does not have definite marriage or residence rules. Among some Eskimo groups, the older sons might live with the father and the younger sons might live with their wives' families. Religious ceremonies are rarely concerned with the group as a whole, but rather with the rites of passage of the individual and his immediate family: birth, puberty, and death.

Yet certain factors tend to unite families. Among the Copper Eskimo of Canada, for example, the inhabitants of a settlement are all connected by blood or by marriage. Each owes special duties to the others: to care for them in sickness, to feed the aged and the infirm, to protect widows and orphans. In this way, a group of separate families takes on a corporate unity. It eventually is referred to by a common name, which is usually the suffix *miut* added to the name of a prominent topographical feature in the region it inhabits. *Kogluktokmiut,* therefore, is the name of the group that frequents the Kogluktok, or Coppermine, River. Physical propinquity, a similarity in habits and dialect, and intermarriage have given them a sense of closeness that sets them off from neighboring Eskimo groups—but that nevertheless has failed to unite them into a tightly knit band.

WIFE-LENDING AND OTHER EXCHANGES

Marriage is at the center of Eskimo life, even though some explorers have maintained that because of wife-swapping and other sexual irregularities the Eskimo does not much revere the institution. But the Eskimo is enthusiastically in favor of marriage. A man marries just as soon as he can hunt with sufficient skill to feed a wife, and girls often marry before they reach puberty. A man is destitute without a wife. He has no one to make his clothes or to cook for him. A woman without a husband must live like a beggar, for she has no one to hunt game for her. Marriage is simply an economic necessity, and so there are no elaborate courtship displays or marriage celebrations among the Eskimo. A man and a woman arrange to live together with less pomp than a modern American displays when he contracts with a carpenter.

The thing that most bewilders a prudish White about the Eskimo's connubial eccentricities—wife-lending, wife-swapping, polyandry, and polygyny—is the good nature with which the arrangements are made. Occasionally an Eskimo man will beat his wife for being unfaithful—not because she had sexual intercourse with someone else, but because she took it upon herself to grant rights that are the husband's privilege to bestow. The next week he himself may lend her to the same man. Wife exchange exists to some extent in all Eskimo groups that have been studied; the explanation is that such an exchange is one of the best ways to formalize an economic partnership or a social alliance. With so few opportunities existing to create bonds between families, the Eskimo must use ingenuity, and one of the best methods is exchanging sexual rights.

So wife-lending and wife exchange must be looked upon not as examples of sexual license, but as clever social mechanisms that function to unify small groups. Further, wife-lending is a wise investment for the future, because the lender knows that eventually he will be a borrower. Perhaps he has to go on a long journey, and his wife cannot accompany him because she is sick or pregnant; then he borrows his friend's wife. He is not a lecher who wants a woman, but a man who needs such essential services as cooking and serving. While he is out hunting, his friend's wife makes the igloo habitable, lays out dry stockings for him, makes fresh water from melted ice—and is ready to cook the game he brings back. Similarly, polyandry and polygyny are essential, for a lone Eskimo cannot survive. He or she must become attached to some family, even though there already is a spouse.

Wife exchange usually is an essential ritual in the formation of an economic partnership between hunters. When two men agree to become partners, they have symbolically extended the bonds of kinship to each other. They become in effect related by marriage when they then exchange wives for a while. In northern Alaska in particular, wives were exchanged as a sort of attestation to the formation of a partnership. The wives rarely objected, since, among other reasons, each stood to profit economically because of her husband's new economic bond. The partnership arrangement also extended to the children. A child called his father's partner by a special name, which freely translated means "the man who has had intercourse with my mother." The child also used a special name—*qatangun*—for his father's partner's sons, who might be his half brothers. He knew that if he was ever in trouble he could call on his *qatangun* for help and his request would be honored.

Exchange is a necessity of Eskimo life that applies to other things besides wives. The explorers of North America made much of what seemed to them an inordinate preoccupation by the Eskimo and the Indian with gift-giving. Over and over the explorers related their disillusionment when the Eskimo or Indian failed to have the "courtesy" to thank for gifts. And the explorers invariably expressed amazement that their unacknowledged gifts were remembered and later repaid in full. The explorers merely regarded gift-giving as a quaint Eskimo custom and did not recognize it as an aspect of exchange.

When one Eskimo gives to another in his band, he is usually giving to a relative or to a partner. An exchange among those in close relationship is not a gift, and that is why the receiver does not offer thanks. An Eskimo praises a hunter for the way he hurled the harpoon but not for the way he shared the meat from the seal the harpoon killed. Sharing is a kinsman's due, and it is not in the category of a gift. The Arctic explorer Peter Freuchen once made the mistake of thanking an Eskimo hunter, with whom he had been living, for some meat. Freuchen's bad manners were promptly corrected: "You must not thank for your meat; it is your right to get parts. In this country, nobody wishes to be dependent upon others . . . With gifts you make slaves just as with whips you make dogs!"‡

An important thing about exchange in the life of the Eskimo is that he alternates between feast and famine. One Eskimo hunter may be successful in killing seal after seal while another hunter is having a long streak of bad luck. Anyone who has been molded by a capitalistic culture knows what he might well do in similar circumstances—if he were the fortunate hunter and the others were in need. He would jack up prices. Such a thing could never happen in Eskimo society—not because an Eskimo is innately nobler than you or I, but because an Eskimo knows that despite his plenty today, assuredly he will be in want tomorrow. He knows also that the best place for him to store his surplus is in someone else's stomach, because sooner or later he will want his gift repaid. Pure selfishness has given the Eskimo a reputation for generosity and earned him the good opinion of missionaries and of all others who hunger and thirst after proof of the innate goodness of man.

The Eskimo male from time to time engages in conflicts, often violent ones, and surprisingly enough, the apparent cause in his sexually lax society is adultery. It is not considered adultery when a husband lends his wife to a friend. Nor is it considered adultery when a husband and wife join other couples in the game known as "putting out the lamp"—during which period of darkness they pick at random a partner of the opposite sex. Adultery exists only when a woman has sexual intercourse without the express approval and prior knowledge of her husband. Since such approval can usually be had for the asking, adultery has a significance other than sexual gratification. It is one man's unspoken challenge to another. And the offended husband must respond to the challenge or else he will live out the rest of his years in shame.

Homicide is almost always the outcome of such a challenge to status. When the Arctic explorer Knud Rasmussen visited a community of fifteen Eskimo families in the early 1920's, he found that every one of the adult males had committed homicide at least once, and in every case the apparent motive had been a quarrel about a woman.‡ It would, however, be a mistake to think that an Eskimo is more preoccupied with usurpation of sexual rights than other people are. The Eskimo's problem lies in his society, which possesses no clear-cut laws governing marriage and divorce. Marriage is simply living together; divorce is simply ceasing to live together any longer. In arrangements as informal as these, no way exists to determine when someone is trespassing on another's rights. Since in Eskimo society things are always being borrowed, there is no definition of where borrowing of a wife ends and appropriation of her begins. When a wife is borrowed, she does not leave the premises with a return date like a library book. Judgment and good taste—and probably an undercurrent of hostility toward the husband on the part of the borrower—determine how soon she will be returned.

FEUDS AND DUELS

The murder, either of the interloper or of the injured husband, must be revenged by the kinsmen of the murdered man, and this in turn may result in further retaliation. There is no chivalry or bravery involved in blood revenge: In all Eskimo communities, except those of western Greenland, it is carried out by stealth. Since a murderer is required to care for the widow and the children of his victim, blood revenge sometimes creates a ludicrous situation. A murderer rears as his own stepson the son of his victim—and when this boy grows to manhood he may be the very one to exact delayed blood vengeance upon his foster father.

Several mechanisms serve as checks on the proliferation of killings and revenge. The Eskimo realize that feuds are potentially dangerous to their existence, and families are quick to punish the wrongdoers in their own ranks. Every attempt is made to prevent a quarrel from leading to murder. As soon as a quarrel becomes public knowledge, other people in the group seek out a kinsman common to both parties to adjudicate. A man who has murdered several times becomes an object of concern to the entire community. An executioner obtains in advance the community's approval—including that of the family of the inveterate murderer—for doing away with this social menace. No revenge can be taken on the executioner, for he is acting in the name of all the people.

Other outlets for ending quarrels short of actual murder are buffeting, butting, wrestling, and song duels. In buffeting, the opponents face each other and in turn give forceful blows until one is felled. In butting, the opponents strike at each other with their foreheads, and the one who is upset is derided by the onlookers. Wrestling seems safe enough, but it occasionally has a deadly outcome, and it is one of the subtler ways of carrying out blood revenge. Such contests are announced in advance, and they take place before the whole group, which regards them as festive occasions. Regardless of the underlying justice of the case in dispute, the winner is the one who possesses the greatest strength. Justice is irrelevant to the outcome, and the victor wins not only the case but also social esteem.

In Alaska and in Greenland all disputes except murder are settled by a song duel. In these areas an Eskimo male is often as acclaimed for his ability to sing insults as for his hunting prowess. The song duel consists of lampoons, insults, and obscenities that the disputants sing to each other and, of course, to their delighted audience. (Incidentally, the West Indies calypso, now sung as an entertainment for tourists, similarly originated as a song of ridicule.)‡ The verses are earthy and very much to the point; they are intended to humiliate, and no physical deformity, personal shame, or family trouble is sacred. As verse after verse is sung in turn by the opponents the audience begins to take sides; it applauds one singer a bit longer and laughs a bit louder at his lampoons. Finally, he is the only one to get applause, and he thereby becomes the winner of a bloodless contest. The loser suffers a great punishment, for disapproval of the community is very difficult to bear in a group as small as that of the Eskimo.‡ Prestige is a precious thing to an Eskimo, as the following incident emphasizes. Among the Chugach Eskimo, a thief once entered a house in which an old woman was eating. She began to sing:

> *Old Shit, Old Shit.*
> *He makes me ashamed.*
> *He was looking at me when I was eating.*
> *Old Shit, Old Shit.*

This song may not appear particularly clever, but it was sufficient to make the thief leave the house without taking anything. Soon the children in the band sang the song whenever they saw him. The result was that he was cured of stealing.↕

A COMMUNISTIC SOCIETY?

The absence among the Eskimo and other primitive peoples of our conventional concepts of property has been the source of some theories that communism is a basic condition of mankind. But do the facts really warrant such a conclusion? The Eskimo have two kinds of property: communal and personal—but they lack private property. The natural resources on which the band depends—the rivers filled with fish, the tundra where the caribou feed, the shores of the sea in which seals live— are communal and are open to use by all members of the band. Personal property consists of things made by individuals: weapons, tools, ornaments, fetishes, and so forth. These items are not really private property, because they belong not to the individual himself but to his *role* in Eskimo society. It is preposterous that an Eskimo woman, who has a specific role in society, should own a harpoon, even though she may have been foolish enough to devote her energies to making one. Nor is the concept of personal ownership very far-reaching: It is unthinkable that one Eskimo should possess two harpoons while a less fortunate kinsman lacks even one.

Eskimo hunting scenes are depicted on a pipe carved from walrus ivory. It was collected at Little Diomede Island, between Siberia and Alaska in Bering Strait, and shows the influence of the shape of old Russian pipes.

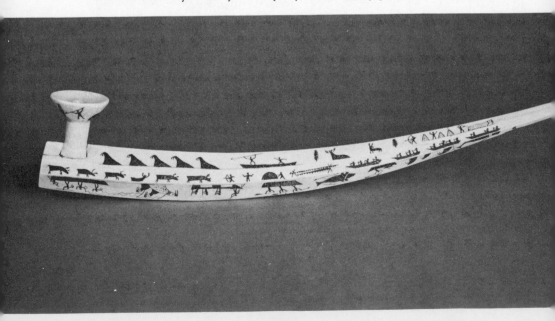

Since no private property exists among the Eskimo, it would appear that they are communistic. But to believe so would be to miss an important point about primitive society. Communism, as the word is understood in modern society, refers to ownership by *all* the citizens of the means of production and an absence of exploitive relations. In modern communism, the "all" refers to the entire population, related or not. But who are the "all" in Eskimo society? Almost everyone is related by blood or by marriage or as an economic partner. The Eskimo group is really one big family that includes also close friends (in the same way that an American child might call his parents' friend "aunt," even though she is not a relative). Even in capitalistic United States, most families practice this same sort of "communism" of the family: They are generous to children, indulgent to nephews and nieces, hospitable to cousins. So before you rush to praise the generosity of primitive peoples, remember that we act some of the time—in our relations with kin and close friends—the way primitive peoples act all the time.✦

THE BIRTH OF THE GODS

Someone reared in the context of Western civilization will also find the spiritual beliefs of the Eskimo considerably different from the religions he is used to. Eskimo belief is among the simplest known, and it incorporates the two common denominators of all religions everywhere: spirits and magic. It completely lacks all the other ideas of religion found in advanced societies: revelation, a redeemer, a priesthood, orthodox rituals, articles of faith, and so on. Probably the Eskimo spiritual beliefs do not differ much from man's earliest gropings toward religion, but that will never be known for sure.

The debate as to where "magic" ends and "religion" begins is an old one that seemed settled some decades ago when scholars concluded that there was no discernible boundary between them. As a result, the two were often lumped together as "magico-religious," in much the same way that the compromise word "socio-cultural" originated. Nevertheless, at least one distinction must be made between magic and religion. In magic, the practitioner believes that he can directly affect other humans and nature, either for good or for ill, by performing certain steps. Magic is therefore instrumental—and some of these instruments are witchcraft, sorcery, oracles, divination, and various kinds of curing. Although many "religious" people do use religion for instrumental ends, the primary emphasis in religion is on broad social and cosmological relationships.

Eskimo magic differs from Christianity, Judaism, Mohammedanism, and Buddhism in that it does not attempt to regulate behavior in the society as a whole or to propagate a code of conduct and belief. It is not interested in the totality of the invisible world, but is instead limited to the individual's relationship to his food supply and to his physical environment. The Eskimo's magic operates through an elaborate system of hundreds of taboos that constrain his every action. A wise Iglulik Eskimo once told Knud Rasmussen: "What do we believe? We don't believe; we only fear." This sums up the attitude of Eskimos as well as of other peoples in simple societies. They live in a world of anxiety, frustration, inadequacy, and vulnerability, in which the spirits control everything that cannot be explained rationally. The modern American, of course, does not suffer the same kind of anxiety, since he has exerted technological control over many of the things that make the Eskimo fearful. In place of science, the Eskimo has only magic to bridge the gap between what he can understand and what is not known. Without magic, his life would be one long panic.

The taboos must be scrupulously observed. To violate one is a sin, and the most notable thing about the Eskimo attitude toward sin is that it lacks the holier-than-thou atmosphere. The group does not revel in an upwelling of indignation; there are no righteous lectures, no public stonings of the miscreant. Instead, the community unites in compassion and tolerance around the sinner. He is encouraged to purge his sin, and he does so by hiring a part-time religious practitioner known as a shaman who draws forth from the sinner's mouth the exact details of each taboo violation. The villagers sit in the background, chanting cries of forgiveness for this pitiful sinner.

Illness in the soul of the wrongdoer usually is the result of sin—but the Eskimo feels that illness might also result from the witchcraft of a malevolent shaman. Witchcraft is not head-to-head butting or even murder by stealth, but evil worked in the privacy of one's own igloo. Social scientists used to think that witchcraft was correlated with the food supply: the more precarious a group's food supply, the more prevalent the fear of sorcery. But this is not true. Compared with the Eskimo, the Navaho of Arizona and New Mexico live in luxury, yet they are even more haunted by witchcraft. When an Eskimo falls sick and attributes his sickness to witchcraft by a hostile shaman, he feels that he has probably done something to the shaman that cannot be settled publicly by a song duel or even by murder. In such a case, the ill person must fight poison with poison, so he hires a friendly shaman to locate the secret attacker and nullify his power.

Now we come to grips with what witchcraft is really all about: It is aggression for which a society has not provided channels. In fact, an examination of witchcraft in primitive societies around the world shows that it appears when people attempt to handle their vital problems in the absence of legitimate social controls. What is surprising about witchcraft in Eskimo society is not that it exists, but that it is not much more prevalent. This is due to the various social constraints mentioned earlier: public ridicule, prestige, the use of kinsmen in settling quarrels, a public executioner, and so forth. Although these are not our familiar social controls of laws, courts, and the police, they serve somewhat the same function.

An understanding of witchcraft in primitive societies helps us explain a well-known witch scare in a more complex modern society: the Salem, Massachusetts, witch hunt. By 1692, when Salem was subjected to the witchcraft hysteria, there had been almost a complete breakdown in governmental controls. After James II was deposed in 1688, Sir Edmund Andros was forcibly removed as governor of the Dominion of New England. Two years later an attempt was made to re-establish colonial government, but the new charter was unworkable and unpopular. Upheavals in the colonial administration resulted in much internal dissension between the Puritans and the government; there was also the disruption and anxiety caused by wars with Indians. Aside from the general collapse of the theocracy in the colony, the village of Salem in particular suffered also from a breakdown in judicial controls. Accepted rules of evidence and accepted legal practices of questioning the accused were ignored by the Salem courts. Conditions degenerated into social chaos, and hysterical girls were allowed to accuse hundreds of citizens; nearly thirty people were executed before social controls were reasserted.‡

THE SHAMAN, DEALER IN THE SUPERNATURAL

The only division of labor in many Eskimo bands is by age or by sex—except for the part-time shaman. The word "shaman" comes from the Tungus language of Siberia, but the shaman is important among all the Eskimo bands and among many American Indians, particularly in the West, where he has usually been called a "medicine man" by Whites. Wherever he exists, the shaman moves with ease in the supernatural realm. He is in the business of going to the invisible world and contending with the spirits on their own ground. An Eskimo believes that spirits must be coerced, and a widespread Eskimo myth tells how the sea spirit Sedna had to be harpooned to force her to release sea mammals for the hunt.

There is a vast difference between a shaman and a priest. A priest is a legally constituted specialist; he belongs to a special group set apart from the rest of the social organization. An Eskimo shaman, on the other hand, dresses no differently from anyone else, and he lives like the rest of the community. He hunts, or he joins a whaling crew; he may be married and have children. He has no special privileges or insignia, except the tambourine, a skin drum open on one side, that all Eskimo shamans use while singing.

There are, however, ways to recognize him. Search out the least skilled hunter in the group, one who is also physically or mentally handicapped and who makes nervous movements with his hands or feet. You have probably located your man. The shaman actually is different from everybody else, and the Eskimo is smart enough to recognize this and put it to work in his society. Some Eskimo maintain that they can identify a future shaman, even while he is still a child, by certain signs. He is meditative and introverted; he may have fits or fainting spells; he is disturbed by dreams and suffers from hallucinations and hysteria. The shaman is a psychological type known as the neurotic, borderline schizoid‡—which is perfectly all right with the Eskimo, since he believes the shaman needs extraordinary abilities in his traffic with the supernatural. The shaman comes to the fore because Eskimo culture encourages his hallucinations, creates such situations as the curing ceremonies in which he can flourish, and even pays him when his symptoms appear.

Some anthropologists have stated that the shaman fills an important function by draining off the potential "Arctic hysteria" of the group. But it is not so simple as that, and the shaman may actually represent the element of hostility in Eskimo culture. The person who becomes a shaman is almost always more misanthropic, more covertly aggressive, and less physically skilled than the ordinary man. The things the shaman himself hates—the successful hunter, the virile man with many women, the boatowner with his prestige—are also things the rest of the group envies. Unlike the ordinary Eskimo, the shaman can do something about his malevolence: He can call

Wooden mask of Alaskan Eskimo represents the spirit of cold weather and storms. The Eskimo believe the sad expression is because he must leave the people in the spring. The mask is carved from driftwood, the only source of wood in this timber-poor country, yet it is burned each year after use and a new one carved for the following spring. As the mask is usually too fragile to be worn, the dancer holds it in front of his face to identify himself to the other participants in the ceremony.

down sickness upon the envied one. A skilled hunter may suddenly no longer find game—and he attributes his misfortune not to chance but to the malefic influence of some shaman or other. He employs his local shaman to perform an emotional ceremony that removes the evil influence. The hunter emerges from the experience a more humble man; he is careful in the future not to boast of his hunting skill, to leave game for others, to share more. The shaman and the rest of the Eskimo group have had the satisfaction of seeing the mighty brought low.

In any discussion of shamans, the question naturally arises: Are these people frauds? Shamans use many tricks to heighten the effects of their performances: ventriloquism, hypnosis, legerdemain, and general stage magic. Houdini-like escapes are a specialty. A shaman often impresses his audience by vomiting blood; he does this by previously swallowing a bladder filled with animal blood, then breaking it with his stomach muscles at the appropriate moment. Although the shaman is perfectly aware that he is at times merely performing tricks, he nevertheless is firmly convinced of his power to deal with spirits. When he falls into a trance, it is a real trance; when he has a fit, it is a real fit. He regards his ultimate purpose as an honest one, and if he can intensify the supernatural experience by slightly hoodwinking his audience, then he goes ahead and hoodwinks them. So convinced of their own efficacy are the shamans that, like psychiatrists, when they are sick in spirit they call in a fellow practitioner to administer treatment.↕

TABOOS: HANDICAPS TO SURVIVAL?

The life of the Eskimo is hedged in by numerous taboos that appear ridiculous to us and that seem to handicap the Eskimo in his struggle for survival. One taboo, for instance, prohibits any work during a time of mourning; so if someone dies during the long winter of privation, hunger inevitably results. A taboo prohibits using whaling tools for more than one season, despite the scarcity of raw materials. Such prohibitions appear to run counter to the best interests of the Eskimo. Is there some hidden value in these ridiculous taboos, or has the Eskimo managed to survive despite them?

No doubt many of the Eskimo's religious observances work to his detriment. Yet they continue to be observed because they afford certain social benefits that cannot be achieved by other methods, although the Eskimo himself undoubtedly has no conscious understanding of these benefits.

Note that all the taboos are concerned with rather ridiculous matters, and they are all very demanding, just as the hazing of freshmen on some college campuses demands scrupulous attention to trivial observances. Both taboos and hazing have the same result: They promote cooperation because all the people are made to suffer together. In the simple society of the Eskimo, the sharing of fears and the scrupulous attention to details of conduct create a social bond. The Eskimo's compliance with folkways, no matter how seemingly foolish or trivial, has afforded him a better unifying social mechanism than he probably could have devised rationally.

Today the life of the Eskimo has changed, for the Whites brought him a technology that has resulted in a new relationship to the environment and to other bands. Commercial fishing has encouraged small Eskimo groups to merge into large villages. The Eskimo now imports canned and preserved foods from the temperate and tropic zones to help him through the winter. He has switched to a cash-and-credit economy: He earns money by working at a fish-canning factory or by turning out soapstone carvings for tourists. Yet, despite the apparent changes in his culture, the first of the native Americans to encounter the Whites has managed to salvage more of his culture than any other aboriginal group in North America.

IV

The Sub-Arctic: Living with Expediency

THE COMPOSITE BAND

South of the tundra domain of the Eskimo, from Newfoundland westward nearly to Bering Strait, lies the thick green carpet of the Sub-Arctic coniferous forest. Game of all sorts abounds in the forests: deer, elk, moose, bears, and a variety of fur-bearing mammals. Herds of caribou live along the tundra-forest border, while the woodland caribou are, or at least used to be, plentiful in the forests. Fish swim through the cold glacial lakes and fast streams. Late each spring the sky fills with birds. Almost everywhere this forest grows there used to be Indians who belonged to two large language families, the Algonkian and the Athabaskan; to this day numbers of these Indians still inhabit their ancient lands. Those living to the south and east of Hudson Bay speak Algonkian and include such bands as the Montagnais and Naskapi of Labrador, the Micmac of New Brunswick, the Penobscot of Maine, the Chippewa or Ojibway of Ontario. The Indians to the west of these speak Athabaskan and include the Yellowknife, Chipewyan, Kaska, Slave, and Beaver.

Despite the differences between the two language families, the Indian cultures over this immense area have many things in common. In primeval times both Algonkians and Athabaskans hunted a variety of mammals, fishes, and birds, but with the establishment of French and British trading posts, they soon switched to trapping. Although their environment is no less rigorous for them than for the Eskimo, the Sub-Arctic Indians differ from the Eskimo technologically in many ways. They build conical skin tents (wigwams) rather than igloos; they use toboggans instead of dog sleds; their feet are shod with moccasins rather than sealskin boots; they use the birchbark canoe instead of the kayak.

Only a meager amount of information about the culture of the Northern Algonkians and Northern Athabaskans in primeval times exists, for it was altered very rapidly and very early by the arrival of fur traders. The Whites also brought with them diseases, the severity of whose ravages is difficult to imagine today. Lacking any immunity to smallpox, the entire Indian population of Canada was very nearly eradicated by a single epidemic occurring about 1780. A Hudson's Bay Company explorer reported that this epidemic alone wiped out nine tenths of the population of Chipewyan Indians, and this was only one of many epidemics. The Ojibway, originally one of the largest Indian groups north of Mexico, met with such a succession of disasters that as early as 1670 their numbers had dwindled to about one hundred and fifty. In addition to disease, depopulation was caused by increased warfare among Indian groups, by starvation, and by migrations to other areas.

The arrival of the Whites radically disrupted the Indians' true bands, which had been organized on the basis of kinship and had strict rules about residence after marriage. In aboriginal times, male societies for hunting and for defense, strict marriage alliances, and many other rules gave structure to the bands. Within a mere few decades after the arrival of the Whites, though, the band organization was ripped apart almost everywhere in the Sub-Arctic. Those Indians who had survived the warfare, famine, disease, and migrations ended their hostilities toward each other and their remnants merged into the "composite band," an expedient confederation of families in which rules of marriage, kinship, and residence become blurred.

The composite band is more complex than the social organization of the Eskimo and the Shoshone, but less complex than the patrilocal bands of some California groups described in the following chapter. The important thing about the composite band is that it is an aggregate of families, sometimes numbering a few hundred people, that is based on cooperation rather than on actual kinship. Any man and woman can marry so long as they are not closely related; after marriage there are no rules as to whether they should live with the husband's family or the wife's family—or with neither. The headman is acknowledged to be an outstanding hunter, as well

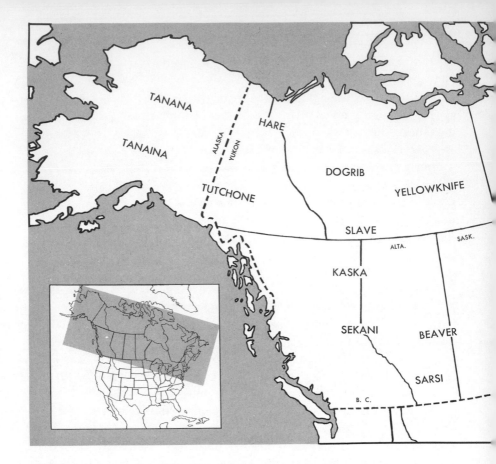

as a sharp bargainer; he usually represents the entire band in its sale of furs to the Hudson's Bay Company. There does not exist, though, any political or legal mechanism in the composite band for enforcing his wishes.

CAPITALISM: INNATE OR ACQUIRED?

The composite band usually controls in common the principal resources in its hunting territory: the herds of caribou, the fishes, the birds, even the maple trees, which are tapped for sugar. Alongside communal ownership, though, there exists small-time capitalism—family ownership of territories for trapping small fur-bearing mammals, particularly beaver, but also marten, otter, and lynx. No one can at will cross another's territory; permission first must be obtained and reciprocal right of passage assured. The territories are fairly rigid, and their boundaries known to all the inhabitants of an area. As recently as early in this century, it was still possible to map the hunting territories claimed by the twenty-two surviving families of the Penobscot Indians of Maine, even though their lands

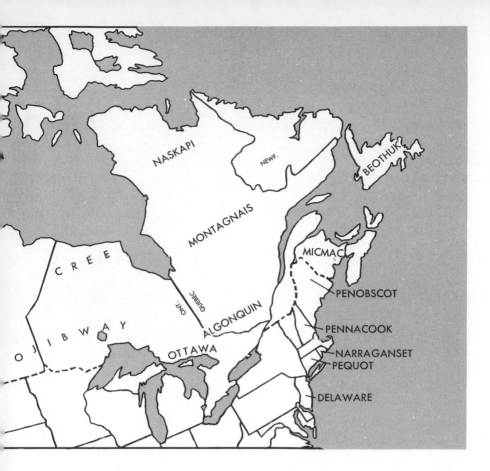

had been taken over by Whites centuries earlier. Such ownership among primitive hunters appears to demonstrate that capitalism may, despite the absence of private ownership in the Shoshone and the Eskimo, after all be a primitive urge of mankind. But is such really the case?

Those who seek in these Indians some instinct toward a pure form of capitalism will be disappointed. In the first place, it is doubtful if such hunting territories ever existed before the arrival of Whites. The Sub-Arctic Indians were among the earliest on the continent exposed to White culture, long before the formation of the Hudson's Bay Company in 1670. French companies had been founded during the sixteenth century, and as early as about 1550 French ships were sent to Canada with the sole purpose of trading with the Indians. Indian bands near Quebec and Tadoussac were already acting as middlemen in the trade with isolated bands farther north and west.

Even at this early date, the French scramble for furs had given the Indians a brief course in capitalism. Champlain in 1611 wrote that the Indians were becoming canny, for they "wanted to wait until several ships had arrived in order to get our wares more cheaply. Thus those people are

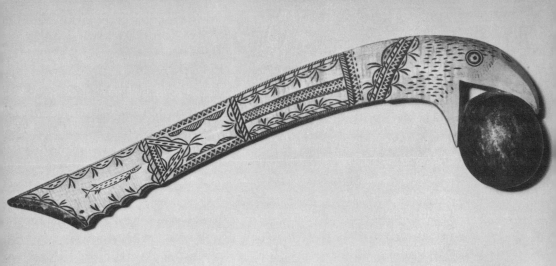

This Ojibway tomahawk, although carved about 1900 and somewhat more decorated than those made in primeval times, remains faithful to the traditional form and shape of the Northern Algonkian war clubs.

mistaken who think that by coming first they can do better business; for these Indians are now too sharp."✝ In 1632 the Jesuit Paul Le Jeune observed : "Now that they trade with the French for capes, blankets, cloths, and shirts, there are many who use them."✝ The displacement of native crafts by European kettles, axes, knives, and iron arrowheads was just about completed by 1670. Trade had become so much a way of life that the Indians were already largely dependent upon the supplies obtained from the trading posts. So it is clear that the native economic system was early disrupted by Whites who introduced the paraphernalia of European capitalism. The traders economically seduced the Indians by displaying their wares and in many other ways fostered capitalistic drives.

THE HUNTING TERRITORY

The Whites caused an upheaval in the Sub-Arctic economy when they encouraged the Indians to produce for *trade* rather than for *use*. The Indian's attention switched from the ancient concern with the products of the land to the real estate. Before the arrival of Whites, a typical Algonkian band hunted cooperatively and shared its game. Because the hunt was uncertain, a system grew up whereby several families looked out for one another; such a system represented primitive insurance, guaranteeing security when hunting was poor. But a shift in economic traditions took place when the Algonkians started to produce for trade rather than for use. The most important economic ties were no longer within the band; they now reached outside the band to the White trader. Rather than being in a cooperative relationship with the rest of the band, the band members began to compete. Neighboring families no longer were insurance against hardship, but instead they became hindrances to the acquisition of limitless furs. No longer were other families welcomed, for each was a potential competitor in the collecting of furs.

In times of shortage, an Indian could always obtain a loan from the trading post. To repay his loans, and also to obtain the alluring merchandise on display, he merely had to increase his take of furs. If the Northern Athabaskan and Northern Algonkian Indians husbanded the land and its wildlife in primeval times, it was only because they lacked both the technology to kill very many animals and the market for so many furs. But once White traders entered the picture, supplying the Indians with efficient guns and an apparently limitless market for furs beyond the seas, the Indians went on an orgy of destruction. As far back as the early seventeenth century, Father Le Jeune complained of the wholesale slaughter: "When the savages find a lodge of them [beavers], they kill all, great and small, male and female. There is danger that they will finally exterminate the species in this region, as has happened among the Hurons."‡

Despite the capitalistic economy introduced by the trading post, the Sub-Arctic Indians managed to hang on to at least part of their communal ways. The leader of the band, who in primeval times allocated hunting areas to groups of families and who kept the various families distributed more or less evenly, now had a new function. He became the one who helped the families to swing sharp bargains with White traders. He also probably served an important function in helping groups of families stake out their individual hunting territories. These hunting territories resulted in increased efficiency in trapping, for the families got to know their own areas very well.

Considering their lack of experience with a capitalistic market and individual ownership of land, these Indians adapted well to the changed conditions. Their societies did not become nearly so capitalistic or so competitive as anthropologists once thought. Every family had the right to trap on land of its own, and if its allotment of land was insufficient it could petition the headman to make an adjustment. Such petitions were almost invariably honest and justified, for there was no advantage for an Indian family to claim more territory than it could patrol or trap. No institution existed for the buying and selling of real estate, so there was no reason for anyone to try to enlarge his holdings or to aggrandize the land of a neighbor.

A truly impressive aspect of the adaptation to capitalism and land ownership was how well these Indians maintained the band's traditional cooperation. Trespass was now defined as someone entering another's territory—but only with intent to obtain *furs to sell*. It was not trespass if he entered another family's territory to fish, to collect berries, or to strip bark from trees for a canoe. The products of the land were still owned communally. Trespass applied only to those items—the fur of beaver and other mammals—that were desired by the White trader. An Indian might even kill a beaver on someone else's land if he were hungry, but he had to give the fur to the owner of the territory. So it appears that the hunting territory is less significant in some ways than was once thought, and more significant in others. The territory is not proof that the urge to ownership, the pride of possession, is innate in man even at the primitive level of the band. What it does demonstrate is the way in which a social organization with rather loose strands, and thus resilient, can meet a new challenge and adjust to it.↕

THE SOCIAL FUNCTION OF ANXIETY

The question arises why these Indians so respect the others' territories, why they engage in such courtesies toward each other—whereas we would be likely to capitalize on the fact that such a society lacks a fear of God, police courts, jails, or any other control. True, the Northern Athabaskans and Northern Algonkians have no religious or civil institutions to coerce them, but something else serves to regulate their personal conduct—anxiety. All primitive peoples are extremely anxiety-ridden, and every day they must worry about performing a multitude of little observances, which often appear ridiculous to us. (Many of our anxieties appear equally absurd to them: to name just one, our anxiety not to be late for an appointment.)

The social functions that anxiety performs were studied carefully—by A. I. Hallowell of the University of Pennsylvania Museum—among the Salteaux branch of the Ojibway, who live east of Lake Winnipeg in Manitoba, Canada. To the Salteaux, the major sanction regulating conduct is fear of disease. A headache or a raspy throat may cause mild anxiety, but anything even slightly more serious brings with it trauma that is out of all proportion to the possible dangers resulting from the illness. Every disease is the penalty for what the Salteaux call "bad conduct." The deeds that can cause illness are many, and they include failure to share with others, insults, insufficient attention to the dead, cruelty to other humans or to animals, incest, sexual perversions, homicide.

Bad conduct usually does not cause illness right away. The transgression may lie around quietly for years, ready at any time to unleash its punishment, and a man may commit a deed in his youth that will cause illness decades later in his children. Whatever the cause, the ill person can never be certain how serious the sickness may become. It may be only a passing indisposition, but on the other hand the sick one's life may be in jeopardy. He suffers an anxiety reaction: A feeling of helplessness comes over him that cannot be alleviated until the precise cause of the illness is discovered.

The illness can be combated in only one way—by confession. But it is a different idea of confession from what we are used to. We assume that any confession made to a priest, psychoanalyst, friend, or lawyer will be held in strictest confidence; it is a private matter. But among the Salteaux, the whole point of confession is that it must be public; the transgressor must suffer all the shame of self-exposure. By confessing his guilt and telling the members of the band exactly what he did wrong, the sinner deters others from making the same mistake in the future. And he reinforces the whole system of belief, because his confession quickly spreads through the band. The young hear it discussed endlessly, and in that way they learn the kind of conduct that is expected of them.↕

AN EXPLANATION OF REINCARNATION

Neither the Great Basin Shoshone nor the Eskimo believe in reincarnation, but many of the Northern Algonkian and Northern Athabaskan bands do. Clear proof that a person has been reincarnated comes when he has a dream about events in an earlier life. One young man among the Parry Island Ojibway of Lake Huron dreamed that a grave contained something valuable for him. When the grave was uncovered and a gun found there, his people regarded him as the reincarnation of the Indian who had been buried there a century before.↕ Reincarnation is considerably different from the mere belief in spirits that both the Eskimo and the Shoshone have. Unlike reincarnate beings, spirits do not assume corporeal forms, nor do they come back to earth as personalities in a new shape. The question arises: Why does the belief in reincarnation appear at the level of the composite band but not at the lower level of the family? The answer lies in the different ways of life. In the composite band, several families live together in relative isolation and share a code of conduct. Such a small group forms a world in itself. Each individual becomes well known for special personality traits. One may be known to shirk work, another to be a lecher, a third to possess dexterity in fashioning hunting bows; individuals become known for a way of dressing, for a characteristic physical gesture, even for a particular tone of voice.

There is a second requirement for a belief in reincarnation to appear in this population: These families must continue as a community from generation to generation. There must be something, such as the ownership of hunting territories in the Sub-Arctic, that binds succeeding generations to the same lands. The influence of an individual in that way extends beyond the kin and neighbors of his own generation to future generations. A grandchild may hear stories about his peculiarities or personality traits, and when such a peculiarity crops up again a generation or so later, the simplest explanation is to attribute it to reincarnation.

The conditions that lead to a belief in reincarnation may exist in large and complex societies as well as in simple bands. Many large chiefdoms

Witchcraft doll of the Ojibway Salteaux was part of the medicine bundle of a headman and was used to bewitch an enemy. Carved from native wood, the figure has eyes made from brass tacks obtained from White traders.

and even states are actually made up of numerous small isolated hamlets and settlements. How, then, is it possible to explain the widespread belief in reincarnation among the teeming masses of India, who usually do not live in small settlements but in large villages, towns, and cities? In one important aspect Asian Indian society resembles that of the people of the Canadian Sub-Arctic. The key is the caste system of India. Each large village is actually segmented into many castes. Members of the same caste tend to live near each other, to intermarry, to join in ritual observances, to laugh at jokes that may be intelligible only to members of that particular caste. A large town in India is really a collection of small and separate communities based on caste that perpetuate themselves from generation to generation. For example, one village in India, with a population of eight hundred—much too large for the intimate knowledge of personality traits necessary for a belief in reincarnation—was really made up of thirty-five separate caste communities. Each of these caste communities was isolated from the others; each perpetuated from generation to generation the knowledge about personalities that allowed a belief in reincarnation to persist.↕

TOTEM AND TABOO

One of the most intriguing beliefs of the people of the Sub-Arctic centered on the totem. Each family had a particular animal as its emblem, and personal names were often derived from these animals. Descent was claimed either directly from the animal or from a legendary ancestor associated with that animal. The very word "totem" is derived from the Algonkian language of the Ojibway; their expression *ototeman* means, roughly, "he is my relative."

A branch of the Penobscot that lived near the Maine coast demonstrates the complex set of beliefs connected with totemism. Groups of families claimed association with certain aquatic creatures that fit into two categories: saltwater totems (Whale, Sculpin, Crab, Sturgeon, Perch, and Lobster) and freshwater totems (Frog and Eel). All the Penobscot, regardless of their own totem, explained their association with the particular animals by the same origin myth. A giant frog swallowed all the world's water, causing a universal drought, but a mythical hero slew it and in that way released the water. Some of the people were so thirsty that they foolishly rushed into the water, where they were transformed into the various aquatic animals. Relatives who escaped the transformation then assumed the names of these animals and became the founders of the various Penobscot families. As time passed, the descendants of these founders gradually assumed some of the characteristics and peculiarities of their totems. Those, for example, whose totem was the Sculpin—a spiny, large-mouthed, and unattractive fish of the New England coast—were generally regarded as being ugly, even though an objective observer would consider some of them quite comely.

Each group of Penobscot believed that the particular animal whose name it bore was especially abundant in its territory. The totemic animal was killed and eaten, although certain rituals often had to be performed. Permission first had to be asked of the animal to kill it, and apologies later were made to it. Many Penobscot Indians also believed that each totemic animal offered itself more willingly to hunters and fishermen of the group bearing its name.‡

Before anyone ridicules these beliefs, he should first be certain that equivalent ones do not occur in our society. As a matter of fact, they do, as was demonstrated by a study of the development of totemism in the 42nd Division of the United States Army during World War I. The soldiers in this division came from so many states that the regimental colors were as varied as those of a rainbow. The simile stuck, and by the time the 42nd arrived in France, the soldiers, when asked to what unit they belonged, promptly replied, "I'm a Rainbow." Shortly thereafter, most of the men in the Rainbow Division became convinced that the appearance of a rainbow in the sky was a good omen for them. Most stated with conviction that a rainbow appeared every time the unit went into action, even though the evidence of meteorology showed it was impossible for rainbows to form at those times. The unit soon took to painting its vehicles with a rainbow emblem and to wearing a rainbow patch on the shoulder. Use of the rainbow emblem by outsiders was resented—and punished—by those entitled to wear it.‡

Probably no anthropological subject has had so much ink and paper expended upon it as has totemism, for it appears around the world in many kinds of cultures. Psychologists, sociologists, anthropologists, folklorists, and others have all had a crack at it. Not only is there no agreement, but most theorists throw up their hands and wish the troublesome aspects of the subject would simply go away. Freud's lengthy and well-known study, *Totem and Taboo* (1918), demonstrates the lengths to which theorists have gone to find an explanation. Freud stated that each male child innately wishes to have sexual intercourse with his mother and so wills the death of his father, his rival. In the Primal Horde, murder of the father by his jealous sons actually took place. Ever since, though, such murder has been vicarious. The ritual slaughter of an animal was substituted for the original act of patricide. In that way, reconciliation with the father is achieved through a father substitute, the totemic animal. Examination of cultures around the world has failed to substantiate Freud's theory, either in whole or in part. Anthropologists today totally discredit it, the one thing about totemism they all seem able to agree upon.‡

Claude Lévi-Strauss, the distinguished anthropologist at the Collège de France, has examined totemism around the world in an attempt to discover its common denominator in many cultures. He has isolated such a common denominator: Totemism always deal with dualities or opposites.

The duality of the totems may be as close as two species of the same animal, or, as among the Haida of British Columbia, it may be two birds that are known to be rivals, like the Eagle and the Raven (or Crow). The crow usually attempts to get its food by subterfuge or theft from the eagle, which nevertheless is much stronger. No matter where in the world totemism is examined closely, it always consists of opposites that share at least one characteristic that allows comparison. The crow and the eagle are both birds, but the habits of one will never become the habits of the other.

All the totems of the Penobscot belonged to a single set of aquatic animals, within which were the opposites of saltwater animals and freshwater animals. The Ojibway Indians of Parry Island who took birds as their totems divided them into the opposites of aerial birds (such as the Eagle) and aquatic birds (such as the Loon); those who selected mammals for their totems divided these into terrestrial (Moose, Wolf) and aquatic (Beaver, Otter).

Totemism, when looked at in this way, begins to take on significance for the understanding of human societies. Claude Lévi-Strauss states: "The animals in totemism cease to be solely or principally creatures which are feared, admired, or envied: their perceptible reality permits the embodiment of ideas and relations conceived by speculative thought on the basis of empirical observations. We can understand, too, that natural species are chosen not because they are good to eat but because they are 'good to think.' "‡

Anthropologists misunderstood totemism for so long because they thought primitive man was concerned only about filling his stomach. The primitive, though, is not thinking about the single totemic animal but about the duality. A single, isolated totem is meaningless; it becomes important only when it can be related to one or more other totems that are generally similar but particularly different. So when the Indian talks about two species of totemic animals, he is not stressing their animality—rather, their duality.

There is only one valid reason for accenting such a duality, and that is a social, not a psychological one: Totems serve to define the important marriage relationships. Particularly in a composite band, where there has been disruption and merging of the remnant bands, blood relationships are often forgotten, and there is the danger of incest. Some method must be found for a man to determine whether he is related to a woman who is a potential wife. He cannot rely on memory alone, for disease and famine caused too many deaths among the old people who might have been able to recall relationships. But he can rely on the woman's allegiance to a totem. If both a man and a woman owe allegiance to the Eagle totem, then they are considered related (even though in actual fact they may not be) and they cannot marry. But if one is an Eagle and the other a Loon, then the duality of the totems guarantees that they are of different blood—and so permitted to marry.↕

The societies of the Shoshone, the Eskimo, the Northern Algonkians, and the Northern Athabaskans—simple as they seem to be—nevertheless possess many characteristics that give them unity, that lift them above the level of the mere family. Also constantly at work is a tendency toward stability and permanency, a tendency for cooperating families to formalize their relationships. The family organization possesses a potential to grow and to become more complex: the patrilocal band, which is discussed in the next chapter.

Southern California:
The Potentialities of the Band

THE PATRILOCAL BAND

In southern California, southwestern Arizona, and most of the Baja California peninsula of Mexico there lived the Serrano, Cahuilla, Luiseño, Diegueño, and similar groups. That was before the Spaniards totally disrupted their way of life by gathering them into missions, the first of which was founded in 1769 and later grew into the city of San Diego. All these Indians inhabited environments that had in common a limited food resource which was evenly scattered and was usually no more abundant at one time of the year than at another. One limitation such an environment imposed on its inhabitants was that the band's population remained low, usually numbering only about fifty people. Another was the lack of opportunity for various bands to come together occasionally, as the Great Basin Shoshone families did. The Shoshone were blessed with the seasonal abundance of a crop of piñon nuts or a herd of pronghorn antelopes. Because of the sudden bounty of the piñons or the pronghorns, families of the Great Basin Shoshone could gather, cooperate in the hunt or in collecting seeds from the same groves, then wander off again in different directions.

Among the southern California Indians, however, each group had to become expert in exploiting a particular territory, no more than a few hundred square miles, that it knew well. Families tended to remain in the same areas from generation to generation, harvesting the resources they were familiar with. Their game was small and nonmigratory, and they could best exploit it by staying in their own hunting territories. The absence of herd mammals, like bison and caribou, explains why the southern California groups did not organize themselves into large composite bands, as did the Canadian Athabaskans, to hunt these mammals cooperatively.

The interaction of all these factors produced the patrilocal band, which is distinguished from other kinds of bands because rules clearly dictate that the married couple must reside with the husband's family. The male child therefore grows up in his father's geographical area—his hunting territory—and has little relationship with the family from which his mother comes. The married woman is an outsider, for she had to leave her own family whose totem was the Coyote, for instance, to go live with her husband's father's family whose totem may have been the Wildcat.

Modern American culture lacks strict rules about residence after marriage and considers it unimportant whether a couple lives with the husband's family, the wife's family, a grandparent, or in a house of its own. But to people who have organized themselves along the lines of the patrilocal band, such rules are of overwhelming importance. There are several explanations for these rules, among them that at this level of society the male is tremendously important as a hunter. If the male hunter were to live with his wife's family after marriage, he would then be hunting in territory unfamiliar to him. He is apt to be much more successful by continuing to live with his father and hunting on lands he has known all his life.

A second rule of the patrilocal band is reciprocal band exogamy, whereby marrying-out as an alliance is carried to its logical extension. Several bands align themselves into two "sides," known as moieties, which intermarry. In several southern California groups, all the people were either Coyotes or Wildcats. A male Wildcat could not marry a female Wildcat, even though she was from another band; he must marry a Coyote. This marriage rule created a whole set of new relationships between neighboring patrilocal bands: It separated them in some ways, but it also united them because they had to maintain marriage relationships.

The primitive mentality often seems obsessed by concerns of kinship. If a stranger arrives in another band's territory, he is usually greeted with elaborate politeness while he sits on the outskirts of the camp and talks with the old men about possible family relationships. If the stranger can trace any kind of relationship to someone in the group, then he is accepted into it; it is known just where he fits into the society and how to behave toward him. Otherwise, he would represent a danger. The old men might chase him away or simply kill him—for he would be similar in status to a madman in our society.

Our society has asylums for such misfits, but primitive societies do not. Edward B. Tylor long ago pointed out that, in English, the words kinship and kindness have the same root, "whose common derivation expresses in the happiest way one of the main principles of social life."‡ Such a derivation is true in many other languages as well. In East Africa, the same word can mean "kinship" or "peace." In Polynesia, "to be relatives" is the same word as "to live in peace"; for the Fijian, "not related" can also mean "enemy," someone you are permitted to eat. For a band to survive, some sort of relationship among its members must exist. If it does not exist by blood relationship or if such relationship has been forgotten, then the fiction of it must be created to reinforce the solidarity of the band. So the patrilocal band retains its unity by accenting other things—secret insignia, mythology, totems, ceremonies —in place of any actual determination of kinship.

LINEAGES, MOIETIES, AND SACRED BUNDLES

The political and social organization of the patrilocal bands of southern California was based upon the lineage. A lineage, technically speaking, is a

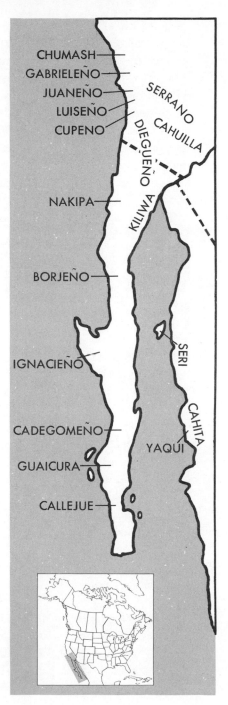

group of blood relatives in which kinship is stronger in one line of descent than in another. In the lineages of a patrilocal band, sons are closer relatives than daughters (who eventually go off to live with a husband from some other lineage). Each California lineage had a leader—the headman—who, despite this title given him by Whites, possessed only a small degree of authority. As in other kinds of bands, he did not rule but merely advised; he could neither command nor punish. When a headman died, one of his sons usually succeeded him to the office. If his sons were unqualified because of some defect in hunting skill or in character, another man, often a brother of the deceased headman, took over. The leadership was then passed on to *his* sons, unless they, too, were unqualified.

The ceremonial duties of the headman served to reinforce his social function in the band. His house served as the focus for the band's religious activities. The lineage's religious paraphernalia were usually entrusted to his care. He also determined the religious calendar: He announced when the religious rituals should be held, and he played a leading part in their performance. Group solidarity was fostered in other ways also. Some lineages were bound together by more than kinship alone, since they lived near each other and jointly claimed a particular territory, which they defended against interlopers. The lineages also formed parts of larger kinship units, the moieties.

Somewhat more is known about the Serrano than most other southern California bands, as a few hundred of them maintained their identity into this century; for that reason, they serve as a good example of a typical patrilocal band. The Serrano bands centered in the San Bernadino Mountains, northeast of Los Angeles, but they also extended deep into the Mohave Desert. The people who spoke the various Serrano dialects were never united into a single political organization, even partially, but instead existed as localized lineages. These small groups were autonomous and they occupied definite territories. All members of each lineage traced their descent through the males back to a common ancestor. Upon marriage, the Serrano woman was incorporated into her husband's lineage; she also put aside the ceremonial ties that were hers by birth, to take up those of her husband.

In all the southern California patrilocal bands, each moiety was in a reciprocal relationship with another because both moieties had to exchange marriage partners. The Serrano extended the moiety idea one step beyond that of the neighboring patrilocal bands and made even more of a unifying factor of it. The Serrano band divided ceremonial functions between its two moieties. One moiety possessed the ceremonial leader and the ceremonial house. The opposite moiety possessed the ceremonial assistant and the sacred bundle, which was a mat made of plant fibers in which ceremonial equipment was wrapped, and which was carefully preserved and venerated. The Serrano bundle included eagle feathers, bands of woodpecker feathers worn by dancers, ceremonial wands, and strings of shells. So both moieties had to cooperate to perform a ritual. The sacred bundle, by the way, shows how a cluster of important and abstract ideas can be attached to seemingly valueless objects—in much the same way that some people venerate a jar of water from the River Jordan.

Originally, each Serrano lineage belonged either to the Coyote or the Wildcat moieties, and marriage between members of the same moiety was strictly prohibited. As the generations came and went, the recollection of actual marriages and kinship affiliations became clouded and then faded out altogether. But people could easily enough remember whether they were members of the Coyote or the Wildcat moieties, and consequently either marriageable or taboo. After the coming of the Whites, lineages were broken apart, and the fragments of Serrano bands were uprooted from their territories; populations decreased sharply as a result of disease, hunger, and warfare. It became nearly impossible to maintain the marriage taboos, because there usually were too many Coyotes to Wildcats or vice versa. The Serrano continued to recognize the existence of the rules they were forced to break. An anthropologist who studied the remnants of the Serrano bands several decades ago reported that whenever two Coyotes married they were deprecatingly called *wahimaiam,* which means "Coyotes that do not know each other."↕

PUBERTY RITES

The religious rituals of the southern California bands lacked the institutionalization of worship found in more complex cultures. Puberty rites were observed for both sexes, although those for girls were considerably shorter and the proceedings much less elaborate than those for the initiation of boys into manhood. Among the Luiseño, for example, several youths of puberty age were gathered at night into a special enclosure where they drank a concoction prepared from the roots of Jimsonweed. The effects of the drug lasted from two to four days. During that time the initiates experienced visions of spirits, which they believed gave them supernatural powers. Later the initiates had to descend into a pit dug in the ground, symbolic of death, and then climb out again, supposedly indicating rebirth. Inside the pit they had to jump from one flat stone to another, and if a boy stumbled, that clearly indicated a short life for him. They were put through several physical ordeals; the severest one was to lie motionless while being bitten repeatedly by hordes of angry ants. As ordeal passed to new ordeal throughout the ceremony, the candidate received long lectures on proper conduct, on how to become a man of value, and on the religious practices of his band.

Civilized man is often contemptuous of the primitives and their cruel puberty rites. He also is apt to wonder what possible benefits a California band finds in making a youth suffer the fury of biting ants. The puberty rites of the southern California Indians become much more understandable after one looks at another society that makes its pubescent youths suffer even more extreme ordeals.

The Australian aborigines known as Aranda are also organized as patrilocal bands, and they independently developed many of the same institutions, customs, and practices as the southern California Indians. The Aranda puberty rites, though, are much more elaborate, and they go on for weeks instead of only for days. The initiate is led from one ordeal to another; he is circumcised, lacerated, and made to suffer terrible pain in many ways. One night he is suddenly thrown spread-eagled on top of a human operating table formed by his kinsmen kneeling on their hands and knees. Other kinsmen stretch him on his back while the ritual surgeon seizes the boy's penis, inserts a long thin bone deep into the urethra, and slashes at the penis again and again with a small piece of flint used as a scalpel. He cuts through the layers of flesh until he reaches the bone, and the penis splits open like a boiled frankfurter. The boy is then led to a fire over which he squats while his blood runs out into the embers. This operation, known technically as subincision, is the final step in his becoming a man in the Aranda band.

. What possible use can such a horrible ordeal serve? Most scholars are of the opinion that the operation has something to do with sex, but they do not agree in what way. Freud, for example, interpreted subincision in terms of castration and the conflict of the Oedipus complex. But Dr. Bruno Bettelheim rejected Freud's outrageous theory—only to substitute an outrageous one of his own. He concluded that subincision developed because males are envious of the female's sexual organs. These ritual operations, he believes, serve as both symbolic and surgical attempts by males to achieve not only the female organ but also the female's menstrual flow of blood. He offers no plausible explanation of why Australian males should suffer so seriously from vagina envy.

Recently an anthropologist and a psychiatrist jointly proposed an even more outlandish theory: kangaroo-penis envy. The kangaroo has a bifid-shaped penis which the subincised human penis somewhat resembles. The fact that the subincised male must squat to urinate, as Bettelheim pointed out a woman does, is used to support this theory, for the kangaroo squats also. This theory even proposes a motive for the Australian aborigine. He is envious of the kangaroo's virility, whose single copulation lasts up to two hours.↕

The most sensible explanation is the one offered by anthropologist John Greenway of the University of Colorado, who has done field work in Australia. He interprets subincision and other puberty ordeals as mnemonic devices.↕ He compares the Australian subincision rites to the soap tycoon in *The Hucksters* who disgusted a conference of advertising executives by spitting on the polished mahogany table. But he achieved his aim: The executives remembered what he said to them. If an act is unforgettable, then whatever is associated with that act is unforgettable also. The Australian Aranda youth will never forget what was done to him at his initiation, nor will he ever forget the lore of the band that he was told at the same time. Nor will you, male reader, probably ever forget what you have just read about subincision.

Associating information with trauma is an ancient technique in education. Until recently, schoolboys learned their lessons under the threat of the birch rod. Punishment is still the basic way to train an animal, whether it be an electric shock for a rat that makes a wrong turn in a maze or a bit in a horse's mouth. Greenway adds the interesting thought that such rites are most severe in societies where survival is most precarious, and they become less painful (and therefore less memorable) as life for the group becomes easier. Other Australian aborigines, who live along the coast where the environment is less harsh, do not practice subincision; instead they submit the youth to the somewhat milder ordeal of having a tooth pounded out. The rites become steadily less memorable—and consequently less meaningful—in more affluent human societies, where they are reduced to fraternity initiations, Catholic confirmation, or Jewish bar mitzvah. The Australian aborigines are a long distance from the bands of California, but everything said about them applies to the American Indians also. A Luiseño youth whose flesh has been lacerated by ants does not forget the lessons about responsibility to the band that he was taught on the day he became a man.

CULTURAL HYBRIDS

Of the various kinds of bands, only the patrilocal band possesses the potentiality for growth, for reaching a higher level of complexity. That is because a common mythology, ritual, and totems all produce unity, and also because moieties promote new relationships in which ceremonies are shared and marriage partners exchanged. The most important factor, though, is the unique position of women in a patrilocal band. Every wife is an alien, often so much so that she speaks a different language and has different customs. The very presence of women from other groups represents a tendency for differences among bands to become less meaningful.

In Baja California, as an example, the patrilocal bands spoke three languages, each of which was subdivided into several regional dialects. The bands were also isolated geographically, because the varied topography of Baja California allowed each to settle in a particular kind of environment: seacoast, low desert, a higher desert lying at about 4,000 feet, semialpine conditions at about 7,000 feet, oak forests, and so forth. Because each band spoke its own dialect and each was faced with different problems in exploiting its particular environment, one would expect that each band had its unique culture.

Instead, each patrilocal band was an assemblage of cultural and linguistic bits and pieces. The reason is that a Coyote man could not select his marriage partner from among relatives—and a relative was every woman who was also a Coyote. The chances were slight of finding in one of the small neighboring bands a female of the right age who was a Wildcat. So the Coyote male had to look much farther afield; and that often meant selecting a Wildcat woman from another band that differed a great deal in both culture and language. Some males of a Paipai band, for example, had to go far afield and marry Kiliwa or Diegueño females. As a result, the Paipai band contained male speakers of Paipai and their wives, who usually spoke a different language such as Kiliwa or Diegueño. Furthermore, the culture in which a Kiliwa or Diegueño female had grown up was slightly different from the culture of her Paipai husband.

Because the patrilocal band's rules of exogamy demanded marriage with women different in language and culture, and the rules of residence brought all these women together in the father's territory, the children were likely to grow up not as "pure" Paipai, but as bilingual and bicultural. Culturally speaking, the child of a Paipai father and a Kiliwa mother was a hybrid. And he was also a slightly different kind of hybrid from the child who lived next door, who may have had a Paipai father and, say, a Diegueño mother. Each child, therefore, was the receptor not of a single cultural system but of several, which he probably perceived inaccurately and confusedly.✥

Such a situation was not crucial for the female child; she would leave the band anyway when she married. But it was serious indeed for the male children, the transmitters of the patrilocal band's culture. At this point, the puberty ordeals discussed earlier assume new importance. Previous to the ordeals, the male child had been influenced by the alien culture of his mother. As he approached the age of responsibility, he had to have impressed on him his "real" culture, not the foreign culture of his mother. The ordeals and rituals all functioned to teach him that from then on he existed within the cultural context of his male relatives.

Even though these ordeals and ceremonies were usually performed at an age close to puberty and are usually referred to as puberty rites, Greenway points out that they had nothing to do with sex. They took place at a time just before the young male was obligated to marry and to carry the cultural burden of his own patrilocal band. If these cultural rites, as they should more properly be called, did not exist, then all neighboring cultural systems of patrilocal bands would probably have merged into a monotonous sameness. As it was, most of the southern California bands appeared the same to the casual eyes of the Spanish friars, and differences among them did not become apparent until they were studied by anthropologists. Other patrilocal bands around the world—the Bushmen of South Africa, the Negritos of the Philippines, the aborigines of Australia, the Indians of Tierra del Fuego and Patagonia in South America—similarly offset the tendency to merge culturally by giving prominence to ordeals.

The Spaniards first encountered the southern California bands in the early years of the seventeenth century, and they could not believe that such a blessed people existed. "The women are very beautiful and virtuous, the children are fair and blonde and very merry," recorded the chronicler of the Vizcaíno expedition. But, as the Franciscan missions were established, the California Indians changed quickly. Their light-colored skin and hair disappeared under the dirt of toil for Whites. They no longer were allowed their cleansing sweathouses, nor the cosmetic practice of washing their hair with urine, which probably bleached it. The diseased and hungry women were no longer beautiful and certainly not virtuous. Once-proud hunters were set to work as laborers on mission lands.

Conditions did not improve under the government of the United States, which succeeded the Mexican rule. Debased and uprooted, the southern California Indians fell into drunkenness and were regularly jailed every Saturday night. They were bailed out promptly every Monday morning by Whites, who got a week's free labor out of the prisoners just by paying the two-dollar fines. The few Indians who managed to survive epidemics and famine were crowded onto wasteland reservations that every year grew smaller as land-hungry Whites swallowed up the acreage. Any hope that the Indian bands might somehow survive was dashed by the statement of a government official who, in 1858, opined that these Indians were sacrifices offered up to the "great cause of civilization, which, in the natural course of things, must exterminate Indians."

That prophecy proved too true. Few of the Indians of southern California survive today, and their cultures not at all. Thousands of healthy and proud Luiseño were herded into missions in the late 1700's; today, possibly a few hundred, almost all of mixed blood, survive. The complex web of their social, religious, and political life has been irreparably torn apart. As a viable kind of culture, the Luiseño are as extinct as the passenger pigeon, and the same thing applies to most other southern California Indians.

VI

Zuni: Unity Through Religion

THE PUEBLO INDIANS

The Pueblo Indians include the Hopi and Zuni tribes in northeastern Arizona–western New Mexico and the Eastern Pueblo (such as Taos, San Ildefonso, Isleta) along the Rio Grande River in central New Mexico. Only about thirty pueblos (Spanish for "villages") still survive out of some seventy inhabited at the time Don Francisco Vásquez de Coronado made contact with them in 1540 while in search of the mythical Seven Cities of Cíbola. The ancestors of the Pueblo Indians once occupied an extensive territory in Utah, Colorado, Arizona, and New Mexico, but the Spaniards cannot be given the entire blame for their attrition. Before the Spaniards arrived, a drastic shrinkage in territory and a great reduction in the number of villages had taken place. A prolonged drought in the thirteenth century and changes in the patterns of river flow accounted for the abandonment of hundreds of villages; others were evacuated or destroyed because of inter-Pueblo warfare and because of the depredations by Ute, Apache, Navaho, and Comanche groups.

Although the villages today number fewer than in Coronado's time, no other North American Indians have survived with so much of their culture intact. Despite pressures by the Spaniards and later by Mexicans and Americans, the Pueblo have clung tenaciously to their traditions. The really important aspects of their life continue with remarkably little alteration: Their clans still function; their social structure is largely intact. Although the world around them has changed markedly in the past four centuries,

they have remained insulated against these changes and have stubbornly maintained their culture. Some of their dances are open to White spectators, but most of the ceremonials are not; even the "open" ones possess much esoteric lore of which the White onlookers are ignorant. Not only are Whites often denied entrance, but even Pueblo Indians not members of participating clans are excluded from the secret rites, much as a sergeant-at-arms will bar anyone who is not a member from a Masonic meeting. Most of the villages have kivas, secret ceremonial chambers that are usually built partially or sometimes completely underground, although the six at Zuni are all aboveground.

All of the Pueblo Indians are organized as tribes, which at first look may seem very much like bands. A tribe is still based largely on the family; it is egalitarian; there are still no full-time specialists such as soldiers, artisans, priests, or political office-holders. There are differences as well; the most apparent one is that a tribe is much larger than a band. It has merged the local, exogamous lineage into a more complex social and political entity composed of several lineages. Not only is the tribe composed of a greater number of groups than a band, but there are also specialized functions among the groups.

The tribe is an inherently fragile structure; it possesses no strong political organization or permanent office of control that might give it stability. Instead, the tribe is regulated by a variety of social institutions, among them clans, secret clubs, and specialized societies that carry on warfare or perform ceremonials. The tribal "chief" belongs to no political hierarchy or dominant group; he is merely a sort of consultant, an adviser who may or may not be listened to. In the absence of political authority in the tribe, the households take unto themselves the right of self-protection. As in the band, disputes tend to be perpetuated as feuds, with each act of revenge generating a reprisal.

No anthropologist has ever actually witnessed a band grow into a tribe, but it is possible to imagine how such a transition might be achieved. First, there existed a partrilocal band, with its low population density and its scattered lineages inhabiting particular territories. Once agriculture developed, or if in some way the environment was better exploited, greater productivity resulted in a denser population—and either more people occupied the same amount of territory, or the same number of people needed less territory. In either event, land became available for new lineages to form and to find food in the immediate area of other lineages, resulting in a still greater population density. At first a continued respect for kinship relations was sufficient to unite several lineages into a tribe; but when the population grew larger, exact kinship relations were no longer remembered. Nevertheless, the *fiction* of kinship had to be maintained to create solidarity; and in the case of what are called lineal tribes, this was done largely by clans. Clans stress the common ancestry of the group. They are also ceremonial societies, land-holding corporations, recruiters for war—but above all, they police their own members and maintain good relations with other clans in the tribe. Among the better known lineal tribes are the Zuni and the Hopi, the Navaho, the Iroquois, and several other groups that lived just south of the Great Lakes.

THE CLAN

Some 2,500 Zuni still live near the Arizona–New Mexico border, in their brown, sunbaked pueblo of adobe and stone that the chronicler of the Coronado expedition described as "a little crowded village, looking as if it had been crumpled together." The people of Zuni are organized into thirteen clans, each one named for a different totemic animal or plant; marriage between members of the same clan is prohibited. There is no taboo against eating the totem, nor must any special observances usually be paid to it. Both the marriage prohibition and the ignoring of the totem as a food source serve to reinforce the theory discussed earlier that totemism really is concerned with marriage and not with the food supply. The members of a clan cooperate in the harvest and help each other in building houses; each clan possesses its own sacred fetish, which is kept in one of the clan households.

The clan was foreshadowed in the band when hunting groups cooperated and held joint ceremonies. In the patrilocal band, such cooperating groups were by-products of residence with the father. Clan membership, though, is based not on one's place of residence but on who one's parents are. Rather than accenting the territoriality of groups, the clan is pantribal; it cuts across boundaries and emphasizes common ancestry. The most important ways this is done are by special insignia and ceremonies, the use of the same name, and a shared mythology and clan history. The very fact that two Zuni belong to the same clan is sufficient to prove their kinship, even though their actual blood relationship might not be known. No distinction is drawn between a close relative in the clan, such as a first cousin, and someone who is not a blood relative but with whom the fiction of kinship is maintained. The situation is not much different from a college fraternity where one's blood cousin who belongs to the same fraternity is no closer a "fraternity brother" than any other member, even one totally unrelated by blood who belongs to a chapter at a different campus.

Pueblo village of Zuni, when photographed in 1879, still looked much as the chronicler of Coronado's expedition described it—"as if it had been crumpled together." A Spanish innovation is the beehive oven in the foreground.

Clans emphasize the alliance of various families, and in that way they reinforce the solidarity of the lineal tribe. Many of their methods are the same as those found in the Masons, the Elks, the Shriners, and other fraternal organizations. Each clan possesses an assortment of secret paraphernalia—costumes, fetishes, and sacred altars. There may be esoteric insignia, such as face decoration and clothing designs, and even symbolic patterns painted on houses. Each clan has its own rituals, and great secrecy is maintained; punishment for disclosure to an outsider is severe, often flogging or even death. The influence of the clan reaches into other areas as well: It controls agricultural fields, maintains burying grounds, and preserves peace among its members. A clan may specialize in a particular duty for the entire tribe, or it may be responsible for performing a ceremony. Various clans hold the rights to particular offices and to certain rituals. For example, the Priesthood of the North is always a member of the Dogwood clan and the Priesthood of the South a member of the Badger clan; the head of the Kachinas comes from the Deer clan. Each clan is therefore essential to the welfare of the whole tribe, and all clans are bound together by their dependence upon one another.

THE WOMAN'S ROLE

The Zuni kinship system is matrilineal and matrilocal. The husband goes to live with his wife's family who may add an extra room for its daughter's new family. The constant addition of rooms is one of the reasons the Zuni village looks like a jumble of houses. The household is really an extended family, sometimes numbering twenty-five people, that includes the grandmother, her unmarried daughters, her married daughters with their husbands and children, and her unmarried brothers and sons. The women own the house, and all the men except the unmarried brothers and unmarried sons are outsiders. The fields also belong to the matrilineal clans, with the women possessing the rights to what the land produces. The men labor in the gardens, but whatever they harvest goes into the common storage bins of the household's women.

Marriage at Zuni is best described as "brittle monogamy." A wife can divorce her husband at any time simply by placing his possessions outside the door. The ease and frequency of divorce are explained by the security of the woman in her own lineage and her own household. There are no property claims to be resolved since she and her lineage own almost everything; her sons, her unmarried or divorced brothers, and her sisters' husbands can easily enough provide the necessary manual labor until she remarries. Similarly, the divorced man can always expect a welcome if he returns to his mother's and his sisters' household; they are happy to receive the windfall of his labor. The husband feels that his real home is in the household of his mother and his sisters. He interests himself deeply in their affairs; he is concerned with the rearing of his nephews and nieces; and he returns to their household on ceremonial occasions.

Matrilineal descent and matrilocal residence present a problem that did not exist in the patrilocal band: the change in the husband's authority role in the family. He has married into his wife's lineage and he lives with her family; he is the one who is the stranger. In Zuni and in many other matrilineal societies the wife's brother (her closest male relative who is a member of her lineage) takes over the authority role from the biological father of the child. Subtle readjustments in family roles result: The biological father is much less likely to be as domineering and as authoritative as he is in a patrilineal tribe; his wife's family is always prompt to remind him that he is, in every sense, "out of line." He is in a competitive situation with his wife's brother for the affection of his own children, particularly of his sons. As a result, he is apt to be mild in the treatment of his sons and lavish in giving them presents.

Although many tribes trace descent through the father and have rules providing for residence with the father's family, many other tribes have become matrilineal in the way the Zuni, Hopi, and Iroquois have. One likely reason for residence with the father among bands of hunters was that brothers could cooperate in hunting a territory they had known all their lives. An emphasis on cooperation among women also seems to explain why some tribes have become matrilineal. Most of the matrilineal tribes known about around the world have one thing in common: They practice gardening based on natural rainfall rather than on the building of irrigation works, which would have required male labor to build and to maintain. As the primary food producers, women tend the gardens, collaborate in processing the food, have common storage places, and sometimes even cook together. Irrigation somewhat changes the picture, as the responsibility for the success of agriculture then depends upon the men who must cooperate to keep the water flowing.

Even in areas where rainfall gardening is practiced and matriliny may be expected, warfare sometimes alters conditions. Because of the accent on male cooperation for offense and defense, the tribe may become patrilineal, as has been seen among the Mundurucú Indians of the Amazon jungles of

Brazil. This tribe also seems to confirm the theory that the type of cooperation necessary is the reason why some tribes reckon descent through the
mother and others through the father. Before the influence of many
Whites on their jungle domain, the Mundurucú women collaborated in
growing manioc and in processing flour from these plants, but this activity
was overshadowed by the unremitting warfare between the Mundurucú and
their neighbors. Male cooperation in warfare served to emphasize the
patrilocal marriage rules instead of the matrilocal ones that might have been
expected. Then the Whites who settled the area became a profitable market
for the sale of manioc flour produced by the Mundurucú women; at the
same time, the Whites prohibited warfare between tribes. Within a period
of about fifty years, female participation in Mundurucú society became
paramount, and the tribe switched from patrilineal to matrilineal rules.✡

ZUNI RELIGION

A Pueblo Indian spends about half his waking hours in religious activities,
and practically everything he does is hedged about with religious strictures.
Each village is governed by a council made up of the leaders of the various
religious societies. The priestly underpinnings of Pueblo society were
immediately recognized by the chronicler of the Coronado expedition:
"They do not have chiefs . . . but are ruled by a council of the oldest
men. They have priests, who preach to them, whom they call 'elder
brothers.' They tell them how they are to live, and I believe that they give
certain commandments for them to keep, for there is no drunkenness
among them, nor sodomy, nor sacrifices, neither do they eat human flesh
nor steal, but they are usually at work." Hardly a week goes by in a village
in which some ceremonial event is not enacted to bring rain, to keep the
crops growing, to bring blessings to the village and health to the individual.

Of all these religious Pueblo Indians, the Zuni are the most devout.
They have been characterized as "one of the most thoroughly religious
peoples of the world" by Ruth L. Bunzel, a Columbia University anthropologist, who several decades ago made an extensive study of their
ceremonialism.✡ Zuni is a thoroughgoing theocracy: Control is vested in a
council composed of three members from the principal priesthood, plus the
heads of three other priesthoods. The priests also have the power to appoint
the officers of the secular government, for the priests are concerned
primarily with matters of ritual and leave the day-to-day affairs of the

Kiva scene in Zia pueblo shows priests conducting a curing ceremony. This photograph was taken in 1890, just before the Pueblo Indians began to enforce strict prohibitions against Whites inside their ceremonial chambers.

village to the tribal council. This secular arm is concerned with settling disputes within the village, with nonreligious crimes and their punishments, and with conducting external relations, which nowadays means dealing with the various bureaus of the United States government.

The Zuni religion extends its influence into the clan, as well as into the household and the government of the village, in a variety of ways. There are six specialized religious cults: the Sun, the Uwanami ("rain makers"), Kachinas (also spelled Katcinas), the Priests of the Kachinas, the War Gods, and the Beast Gods. Each cult possesses its own priesthood, its own fetishes, its own kiva. Each devotes itself to particular rituals in its own cycle of ceremonies, and each is dedicated to the worship of a particular set of supernatural beings. It is difficult for outsiders to realize how very complex the ceremonials of these cults are. Every color and every piece of material in the dance costume, every step and every gesture—all are replete with significance. Each of the six kiva groups dances at least three times during the year, and the preparations may take several weeks or even months. Membership in a kiva is not hereditary, but rather each youth is sponsored by a ceremonial "father" whose kiva he joins. In this way, the bonds of the boy to his biological father are further weakened: He is emotionally and socially attached first to his mother's lineage, then to his uncles on his mother's side, next to his ceremonial sponsor into a kiva, and only last to his biological father.

The most vigorous cult at Zuni, and the one most Whites have heard about, is devoted to the kachinas, the nearly two hundred happy spirits who live beneath the surface of the waters. The Zuni believe that the kachinas visit the village each year, at which time they are impersonated by Zuni men wearing costumes and large masks. The masks are treated with great reverence, for once a dancer dons one it is believed that he becomes temporarily transformed into the kachina itself. The owner prizes his mask above all else, and it is usually burned at his death. The kachina dolls often purchased by White tourists along roadsides in the Southwest have no spiritual significance at all, contrary to the usual belief. They are pedagogical devices to educate the young in the identification of the numerous kinds of kachinas. There is nothing sacred or divine about them, even though the proprietor of the roadside curio shop may make such a claim. What are sacred are the masks used in the dances, and that is why one can almost never buy a mask from a Zuni no matter how much money is offered.

The solidarity of Zuni culture, obvious even to the casual observer, is due to the interlocking relationships of clan and religious societies. A person is born into his household, lineage, and clan affiliations, and he can choose to belong to various social and religious groups as well. Many loyalties serve to integrate the entire village by linking people in all directions: A person might belong to household A, kinship B, clan C, society D, kiva E, priesthood F, and so on. Nearly every Zuni in an entire village is linked in some sort of formalized relationship with his fellow citizens.

In bands the shaman performs for the individual alone. But at the level of the lineal tribe religion is an activity for the entire tribe. The individual is no longer a lonely soul in quest of the spirits; he becomes part of a social group that has specific methods for dealing with the supernatural. That does not mean that all the showmanship has gone out of religion. The Zuni cult of the Beast Gods, for example, is made up of twelve medicine societies, and each society has developed its own secret tricks of swallowing swords or walking over hot coals. But in the tribe such prestidigitation is controlled by society and not by religious entrepreneurs. Nor does a Zuni humble himself before the supernatural. He dickers with it. The Zuni priest tells the supernatural agencies exactly how he has fulfilled his part of the bargain by the performance of the ceremonials. Now, he says, it is up to the spirits to deliver. The Zuni often conceive of the spirits as being human and therefore susceptible to emotional appeals. So the Zuni not only bargain; they also flatter and appeal to the pity of the spirits.

Something else also appears in religion at the level of the lineal tribe. In the band, various classes of spirits controlled particular places and people, perhaps a spirit of the house or of the fishing boat or of a hunting territory. But in the lineal tribe, a new concept emerges—superior gods who control more than only a certain area or a territory. They control ideas, and each god is in charge of his particular idea, whether it manifests itself in a boat or on a mountain or in a person's house. The superior gods of the Zuni are not much different from the gods of the ancient Greeks and Romans: Mercury or Hermes, the winged messenger; Neptune or Poseidon, ruler of the sea; Mars or Ares, god of battle. Nor are they much different in function from the patron saints of the Roman Catholic Church. Each superior god is important, although no one god is all-powerful. Each reigns over a specific activity and, by extension, therefore protects all people who engage in that activity. Among the Zuni, the water serpent Kolowisi is the guardian of springs wherever they may exist; Chakwena Woman aids in rabbit hunts; each of the medicine societies possesses its own Beast God, which assists it in the practice of its specialty, whether it be curing colds or removing bullets.

The superior gods of Zuni are not as clearly delineated as are the superior gods in the more complex societies of the chiefdom and the state. At Zuni, all men work in the fields and hunt, and there is little occupational specialization. Therefore, the superior gods of the fields and the hunt are not very sharply distinguishable from one another. But in the more complex societies of the chiefdom and the state, occupations become increasingly more specialized. Some men hunt only particular kinds of game, others farm, and still others may devote themselves to creating art. In the chiefdom and the state, human society with its various specializations provides a model for the superior gods, who then possess distinct personalities and very specific areas of responsibility.

In the Eskimo or Shoshone band, a man is considered poor if he lacks kin whose aid he can count on. In Zuni, the poor man is the one who lacks a place in the religious rituals or who does not own ceremonial property. Wealth among the Zuni is equated with ceremonial activities: Only the wealthy man has the time and resources to participate to the fullest in religious ceremonies. Masks are always kept in certain wealthy households. Also, particular families vie to entertain the Zuni, masked as kachinas, both during the ceremonies and for several days afterward when the dancers go into retreat. Once again, wealth becomes a factor, for not every family can afford the large expenditure necessary for food or the cost of adding a separate wing for the housing of the dancers.

RITUAL AND MEMORIAL DAY

Zuni ceremonial observances, for all their primitive strangeness to a modern American, really do not differ very much from the annual round of religious-secular holidays in the United States that includes Easter, Memorial Day, Thanksgiving, and Christmas. All are legal holidays, and all have their holy and their secular aspects; all are celebrated both in places of worship and in the social and economic sphere. In the specific case of Memorial Day, an American family may go to church in the morning to lament the dead and to the Memorial Day doubleheader at the baseball park in the afternoon to cheer on the living. On this day, Americans, no matter where they live or how rich or poor they may be, express stylized sentiments and platitudes. The common heritage of all Americans is accented, even though it is largely a myth—for the ancestors of many people alive in the United States today immigrated to the United States

Kachina dance inside an Isleta kiva was clandestinely recorded in this painting by an Indian of the pueblo. You can detect the very faint pencil notations he made for a Columbia University anthropologist to explain the amazingly complex symbolism of the ceremonies.

after the first Memorial Day was observed, following the Civil War. Nevertheless, many American towns reel off their rosters of war dead, and they try hard to find among the names a Jones, a MacNamara, a Goldberg, a Russo, a Solinski. In the same way that the Zuni village is composed of cults, the United States settlements have their places of worship, each claiming great authority and each with its own set of symbols, whether they be two crossed pieces of wood or two triangles, one inverted, that form a star.

Like a ceremonial at Zuni, Memorial Day occupies much more than the single day of its observance. Plans for it begin right after department stores

Rain dancer at Santa Clara pueblo, New Mexico, is symbolism in motion, from the evergreen sprigs on her arms to the intricate designs on her headdress, from the kinds of feathers that adorn her to the colors of the material in her skirt.

have taken down their "Easter Sale" signs. Each participating group immediately sets to work to organize meetings, to publicize the parades, to arrange for the feeding of marchers; merchants order stocks of flags and bunting well in advance; gravestones and landscaping that have been neglected during the year are put into repair; the American Legion turns out poppies and canisters by the hundreds of thousands for the solicitation of coins. Look objectively at Memorial Day and you can see its true nature: a cult of the dead that cuts across boundaries of religions, national origins, and social and economic classes to achieve national unity. The common theme of all speeches made in observance of that cult is the obligation of the living to be worthy of the sacrifices made by the dead. Memorial Day also serves as a catharsis for personal anxieties about death. "There is no death," thunders the Memorial Day orator—and that seems confirmed by the massive assault upon it by the marchers bearing the mystic crossed sticks and colorful bunting, by the pilgrimages to the shrines of heroes like the Unknown Soldier, by the number of different organizations wearing distinctive insignia and carrying their own totems.‡

THE "PEACEFUL" PUEBLO?

A myth about the Pueblo Indians in general and the Zuni in particular has arisen largely as a result of the popularity of the book *Patterns of Culture* (1934) by Ruth Benedict. According to her study, Zuni represented the ideal human society, one of "Apollonian" noncompetitiveness. Everyone was devoted to religion; sobriety and inoffensiveness were highly valued; there was equality in wealth; life was orderly, pleasant, unemotional. If someone regularly won races, he withdrew in the future so as not to spoil the contest for others. Everyone was sexually adjusted and no more attention was paid to sex than it deserved. Children grew up as unfettered spirits without strictures or discipline.

Ruth Benedict's view of Zuni is totally misleading; in fact she never did sufficient field work there to justify her conclusions. Most anthropologists who have studied the Zuni close up have come away with far different conclusions. Esther Goldfrank found the Zuni (and the nearby Hopi as well) to be anxiety-ridden, suspicious, hostile, fearful, and ambitious.‡ Florence Hawley Ellis has effectively demolished Ruth Benedict's view of the "peaceful" Pueblo: "Pueblo people are endlessly bickering, with covert expressions of hostility against anyone who does not quite fit into the Pueblo pattern, who has more or different possessions. Like any other human beings, these people are subject to jealousies, angers, and the desire for retaliation."✠ The Pueblo Indians may appear peaceful on the surface, but their history belies appearance. Every village had—and most still have—a war priest, with rank equal to the leading civil priest, and a warrior society, which served as a military force outside the village and as a police force within it. Each village was always mobilized. No recruitment or special preparations had to be made for war; the war priest and the warrior society stood ready to meet violence at any time. Other anthropologists have learned that Ruth Benedict's assertion that drunkenness is "repulsive" to the Zuni is ridiculous. By far the most common crimes at Zuni are drunkenness and drunken driving.✠

Chinese scholar Li An-che, in reporting✠ on his three months at Zuni, raised the obvious point that we should not rely too much on appearances. He replied to Ruth Benedict's belief that a Zuni eschews ambition and is afraid of becoming a leader lest he be accused of sorcery:

The problem is not the contrast between leadership and its denial, but the valuation of the ways and means of achieving it. In any face-to-face community, it is safe to assume that no individual with common sense will try to make himself ridiculous by seeking what is obviously beyond his reach, and that even the most eager and legitimate aspirants to high position will make the ordinary official declination of an offer. Modern societies have asylums to take care of the insane, but a primitive community would have to charge the mentally dangerous with sorcery in order to follow the policy of "safety first" for the communal welfare.

Further, Li An-che finds in the very presence of so many secular and religious functionaries at Zuni clear evidence that ambition is not lacking.

Li also believed Ruth Benedict had been much deceived about the subject of sex, for promiscuity seemed triumphant over fidelity. Liaisons were arranged in the afternoon as young men slunk against fences or darted around houses, wearing large hats that masked their identities. After a quick supper, the young men made the night calls arranged for that afternoon. Li did not consider it an idle boast when one youth told him that he could have intercourse with any woman at Zuni whose husband happened to be away or who was not married.

Finally, Li did not find Zuni child-rearing as worthy of emulation as Ruth Benedict did. She praised the permissiveness of Zuni parents, and she maintained that as a result Zuni children were rarely disobedient. Once again she was misled. Responsibility for discipline of Zuni children falls heavily on no one in particular, because the authority of the biological father is weakened in a matrilineal society. The end result, though, is the opposite of permissiveness: Instead of being subjected to authority merely from his one biological father, the Zuni child finds himself disciplined by

Myth of the "peaceful" Pueblo Indians is disproved by the figure of the Zuni war god (TOP), which was placed at a shrine following ceremonies for war. The carved stick emerging at a right angle is not a phallus but rather the umbilical cord which in Zuni mythology represents the center of life. A secret Isleta painting (BOTTOM) portrays part of the war ceremony and proves that the Rio Grande Pueblo were as much inclined to war as the Zuni. The painting shows the portion of the ceremony during which the scalp dancers withdraw into the kiva, leaving a single member of the war society to watch over the scalp tied to the kiva ladder.

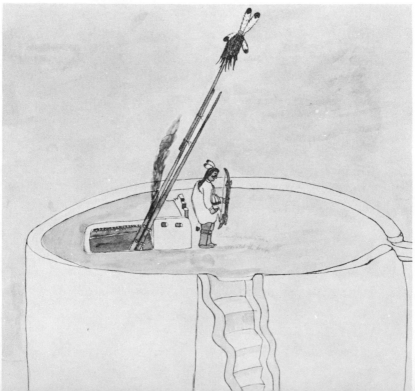

everyone in his household, and that may amount to more than twenty-five people. And almost every adult in the village, even those not in a kinship or in a ceremonial relationship to the child, takes pains to correct any slight misbehavior he happens to note. Wherever the child turns, the adults of Zuni present a united front against him. If he gets out of line he is immediately hushed by a glance from some adult. At Zuni the preferred method of chastisement, which the people consider more effective than physical punishment, is ultimately much more cruel to the child: It consists of constant ridicule and belittling.

RITES OF REBELLION

Even though Ruth Benedict drew the wrong conclusions, some of her observations about Zuni are true: Its society is structured, overtly un-emotional in behavior, controlled in its obedience. But can people continue to survive in a society from whose psychological strictures they cannot escape? Or are there hidden mechanisms in Zuni society that allow repressed aggressions to be worked off?

There assuredly are. Before the enforced peacefulness brought by Whites, the Pueblo Indians had enthusiastic war cults that channeled aggression into socially acceptable paths. Before the coming of the Span-iards, and even for some time thereafter, considerable internecine warfare took place between various Pueblo tribes, a common excuse being a suspi-cion of witchcraft. The war cult, which nowadays functions solely as an internal police force, in pre-White times must have safely evaporated a tremendous amount of aggression. To become a member of the Bow Priests, for example, a warrior had to bring back an enemy's scalp. The war ceremonies in recent times have of necessity become more symbolic than real. The ceremonies make do with one of the old scalps still kept in the Zuni kivas, instead of one from a fresh victim. The scalp is kicked into the village by four aunts of the "warrior" while the onlookers whoop it up and shoot off guns. If a mere symbolic dramatization produces such a frenzy today, imagine what must have been the commotion when a warrior returned with the actual scalp of a Navaho or a Ute. In those days, dances continued for twelve nights around a scalp pole erected in the plaza.

Rebellion against conventional behavior nowadays shows up in certain rites that mock the gods, ridicule the ceremonials, revile conventional be-havior, and merge obscenity with religion. During these rites of rebellion, hostility that Zuni society represses during most of the year comes to the surface in a socially approved fashion. The prime agents of these rites are

Ceremonial clowns of the Rio Grande Pueblo, similar to the Mudheads of Zuni, act as intermediaries between the Indians and the gods, but also are privileged beings who can express the rebellious thoughts of the people. This painting was made about 1920 by the well-known San Ildefonso pueblo artist Tse Ye Mu.

members of the cult of Kachina Priests known as Koyemshi, or Mudheads. They are sacred clowns, grotesque in appearance, wearing mud-daubed masks in which the nose and eyes are bulging knobs, the mouth a gaping hole, the face covered with large warts.

The Mudheads are believed to have been born of an incestuous union; they are therefore excused from conventional behavior while they utter obscenities or mock things held in reverence. They cavort around the serious dancers, speaking whatever their unconscious throws out about the ceremony or the audience. Their antics are funny in the same way a circus clown is funny and partly for the same reason, both being excused from conventional behavior. A Mudhead may satirize the dancers by a too-meticulous attention to ceremony; he may keep dancing long after the conventional dancers have finished, focusing attention on himself until he finally realizes his "mistake." One routine, reminiscent of vaudeville or television, is the Zuni clown who uses an imitation telephone to carry on an imaginary conversation with the gods.

Some observers have thought that these routines originated only in recent decades, perhaps inspired by movies or by television—but one account of clowning at Zuni in 1881 reveals there is nothing new about them.‡ The account states that twelve members of a religious society dressed themselves in odd bits of clothing that allowed them to caricature a Mexican priest, an American soldier, an old woman, and several other types. The principal performance of the evening was a devastating parody of Roman Catholic ritual. The dancers rolled on the ground, and with extravagant beating of the breast mocked a Catholic service. One bawled out the paternoster; another portrayed a passionate padre; a third mimicked old people reciting the rosary. The dancers then started to eat such things as corn husks and filthy rags. One called out, in the same way that a diner might summon a waiter in a restaurant, for a portion of dog excrement. Instead of sacramental wine, several of the dancers drank long draughts of human urine, smacked their lips, and pronounced it very tasty indeed. The account reports that the audience of men, women, and children howled with uncontrolled merriment.

What do these rites of rebellion indicate? Are they as infantile as they seem, or is some more complex social mechanism at work? Obviously, they release the audience emotionally by permitting it to tread, in a socially acceptable manner, in forbidden areas. Comic relief, though, is probably only part of the answer, for these rites assuredly are not solely negative. They are of positive value in supporting the Zuni social order and in resolving conflicts. On one level, burlesque is negative because it undermines convention. Contrariwise, though, it emphasizes through contrast and the very enormity of the obscenity exactly what everyone in the audience knows all along—the proper social behavior.

An examination of those American Indian societies that had ritual clowns reveals an interesting fact: Clowns were prevalent only in societies that possessed an unchallenged and established social order, those societies that were sure of themselves.‡ Modern American society has little place for institutionalized rites of rebellion, because it is a democratic society; it is characteristic of a democratic society always to question and to challenge, never to be certain of itself. Modern Americans cannot conceive of a television comic parodying sacred ritual or eating excrement; such conduct would be adjudged the symptoms of a nervous breakdown rather than an expression of rebellion. Modern American society is so unsure of itself that it has not been able to endure even the rebellious humor of the "sick comedians," and as outcasts of Modern America they were hounded until they retired, escaped into the fantasy world of narcotics, or committed suicide. Most Americans seem unable to endure anything stronger than the mild television barbs of a Bob Hope or the buffoonery of the circus clown.

VII

Iroquois: Primitive Democracy

"THE GREEKS OF AMERICA"

At the time the Whites arrived in northeastern North America, the most powerful Indians in the region were centered in New York State—various groups that spoke dialects of the Iroquoian language. They were immigrants from the general direction of the south and west, but there is great uncertainty as to exactly where they originated. At first they suffered reversals in war. They went into training, grimly and systematically, to equip themselves for warfare in the woodlands; and they grew quickly in population, prosperity, and in the complexity of their culture. Eventually they drove a wedge into the almost solidly Algonkian hunting cultures of the Northeast. Some American romantics have called the Iroquois "The Greeks of America"—but it would probably be more accurate to label them, as the historian Francis Parkman did, "the kinsmen of the wolves," or to regard them as the Prussian Junkers among the Indians.

The culture of the Iroquois tribes differed considerably from the neighboring Northern Algonkian bands. The Iroquois constructed a village on flat land alongside a stream or a lake, and they surrounded it by a palisade of logs for protection. The village became a permanent fixture of the landscape; around it the forest was cleared to plant gardens and to increase the number of deer that browsed on fresh growth. Inside the palisade were rectangular longhouses, each occupied by a matrilineal extended family.

The Iroquois were much admired by the Jesuits of New France, particularly when the fathers contrasted these sedentary agriculturists with the

95

nomadic Algonkian bands. The Jesuits approved of the settled villages, which sometimes numbered several hundred people; the extensive cultivated fields of maize and other vegetables; and the dignified governmental council. One of the Jesuits underscored the differences between the Iroquois and the Algonkians: "The Iroquois and Hurons [also an Iroquoianspeaking people] are more inclined to practice virtue than the other nations; they are the only savages capable of refined feelings; all others are to be set down as cowardly, ungrateful, and voluptuous."‡

Despite their many virtues, the Iroquois were noted for the havoc they spread among the Algonkians and other Indians as far south as Virginia and Tennessee and westward to Michigan. The fiercest of the Iroquois were the Mohawk (the name means "cannibals") who lived along the Hudson River of New York. West of them were the extraordinarily fierce Oneida, and then came the Onondaga, a relatively peaceful tribe; farther west were the Cayuga, a small group. The most westerly Iroquois, and the most numerous, were the Seneca, who harassed the Indians living along the Ohio River and its tributaries. These five tribes formed the *Hodesaunee* or League of the Five Nations (later the Six Nations when the remnants of the Tuscarora were admitted in 1722). During the English colonial rule, several other groups, such as the Delaware, were brought under the protection of the Iroquois. The League eventually might have extended its control from the western Great Lakes to the Atlantic Ocean by subjugating the Algonkians—had not the White colonists checked them.

THE DEMOCRACY OF THE LEAGUE AND MARXISM

The name Iroquois usually refers to the five (later six) tribes that united in the confederacy. These were located near several other tribes (such as the Huron, Erie, Susquehanna, and Neutrals) who also spoke Iroquoian languages, as did the Cherokee in the South. The emphasis of this chapter, though, is upon the League members. The story of the origins of the League has been pieced together from numerous sources, a good many no doubt fictional. It seems that about 1570 a saintly prophet named Deganawidah, the son of a virgin mother whose face was pure and spotless, put an end to warfare among the five tribes and established "The Great Peace." Deganawidah was supposedly inspired by a dream in which he saw a huge evergreen tree reach through the sky to the land of the Master of Life. This sturdy tree was the sisterhood (not brotherhood, for the Iroquois were a matrilineal society), and its supporting roots were the five Iroquois tribes.

Portrait of a Mohawk "king" was engraved in London in 1710 when four Iroquois were brought to visit Queen Anne. His totem, the bear, is in the background.

The teachings of Deganawidah were brought down to practical reality by his councilor Hiawatha, a Mohawk. The Iroquoian Hiawatha was said to have paddled his white canoe from tribe to tribe, urging peace among them, and his efforts resulted eventually in the formation of the League. Longfellow's noted poem has caused much confusion about the historical Hiawatha. Longfellow used as his source a number of legends of Ojibway bands; casting about for a main character to tie together these legends, he chose the name Hiawatha, who was the real hero of Iroquois tribes.

The impetus for Iroquois confederation might be found in the probings of French ships into the Gulf of St. Lawrence early in the sixteenth century rather than in any vision of Deganawidah. Although there is no record of direct contact being made with the Iroquois at this time, the Iroquois could hardly have been unaware of the Whites just beyond their borders. Cartier, for example, had sailed up the St. Lawrence River, and probably reached the vicinity of Montreal, thirty-five years before the League was formed. Again and again in North America the Indians, challenged by White invasion, either ran away (as did the Great Basin Shoshone), or they settled their petty differences and confederated (as did the Pueblo Indians when they rebelled against the Spaniards in 1680). The very practical matter of Iroquois defense against the alien Whites may have been given religious sanction by the visions of Deganawidah.

The League deeply impressed the White settlers, and some historians believe that it was one of the models on which the Constitution of the new United States of America was based. The League did somewhat resemble the union of the Thirteen Colonies in organization, but it could more accurately be compared to the United Nations. It did not deal with the internal problems of the member tribes but solely with external affairs of war and peace. The League had a constitution, orally transmitted, but it could not levy taxes, and it lacked a police force to carry out its decisions. The hereditary leaders, the Council of Sachems, could not interfere in the affairs of the individual tribes, a situation similar to the small influence the United States federal government once had over the internal affairs of the thirteen states. Each tribe had its own sachems, but they also were limited in their powers; they dealt with the tribe's relations with other tribes and not with clan matters.

There were inequities in the tribal representation in the Council of Sachems, but these were more apparent than real, for the Iroquois worked out their primitive democracy in a way that modern Americans are not used to. Of the fifty hereditary sachems, the Onondaga had fourteen; Cayuga, ten; Mohawk and Oneida, nine each; and Seneca, even though the most numerous, only eight. Before any vote was taken, the sachems of each tribe met in private so that each tribe could speak with one voice, just as in a presidential election in the United States each state casts its entire electoral vote for one candidate. The major difference in the Iroquois system was that all decisions reached by the Council of Sachems had to be unanimous. If four of the tribes were in favor of a motion, but the fifth against it, then they would argue until the fifth gave in—or until the single recalcitrant tribe won over the other four. So any inequality in representation between the numerically superior Seneca, with only eight sachems, and the Onondaga, with fourteen, was meaningless.

Democratic as the Iroquois system might have appeared to the early settlers, after the Iroquois were more scientifically studied it was learned that such was not the case at all. The fifty sachem titles were rigidly controlled. Only males belonging to certain matrilineages within each tribe could hold the sachem titles. When a sachem died, his successor could be selected from only the matriliny holding that title, and the women were the ones who did the choosing. The headwoman of the lineage assembled all the women of her household and her clan and discussed with them her choice for a successor sachem. Then she went to both moieties and got their approval. The women's control over the sachem did not end with his selection. If he failed to perform his duties as they liked, the headwoman gave him three stern warnings, after which he was removed and his badge of office given to a new candidate. So even though the women did not themselves rule, they had the sole power to appoint and to remove from office.

All of which only emphasizes the control exerted by women among the Iroquois. All property and goods were inherited through the female line. The women owned the longhouse, the garden plots (even though they were cleared by the men), and the tools used to cultivate the land. Peace and order in the longhouse were maintained by the women. Husbands came and went, either through losses in warfare or the simple process of divorce, and the children of these unions belonged to the mother's lineage. In the political sphere, women appointed the sachems, named their successors when they died, and might even act as a regent for a sachem too young to rule. For all these reasons the Iroquois are usually regarded as having come as close to being a matriarchate as any society in the world.

By a strange irony, the League of the Iroquois has become a model for Marxist theory. The twisting trail that leads to Friedrich Engels begins with Lewis Henry Morgan, a Rochester lawyer and lobbyist for railroads. His interest in the Iroquois was aroused because he wanted to use their rituals in a rather sophomoric fraternal organization he and several business friends were setting up. As a result, he studied the Iroquois deeply and in 1851 published one of the classic works in anthropology, *League of the Ho-De-No-Sau-Nee or Iroquois.* That study only whetted his appetite for Indian lore, and he began to study the societies of other Indians and primitives around the world, relating their differences and similarities to what he knew of the Iroquois.

He was a thoroughly conventional man, unquestioning in religious orthodoxy, and also a staunch capitalist. But he published his theories in *Ancient Society* in 1877, at the very time that Karl Marx was working on the final volumes of *Das Kapital.* Marx was enthusiastic and made notes about Morgan's findings, which by accident fitted in with his own materialistic views of history. Marx died before he could write a book incorporating Morgan's theories, but Engels used them as the cornerstone for his influential *The Origin of the Family, Private Property and the State* (1884). This volume has become the source book for all anthropological theory in Soviet Russia and most other communist countries. Engels was ecstatic about what he had learned, or thought he had learned, of the League of the Iroquois from Morgan: "And a wonderful constitution it is . . . in all its childlike simplicity! No soldiers, no gendarmes or police, no nobles, kings, regents, prefects, or judges, no prisons, no lawsuits." Engels found it the ideal society: "There cannot be any poor or needy—the communal household and the gens [the lineage] know their responsibilities towards the old, the sick, and those disabled in war. All are equal and free—the women included." Engels died before learning the truth about his American primitives, and later communists have chosen to ignore it. That bourgeois gentleman Morgan is to this day enshrined in the pantheon of socialist thinkers. The Marxists have chosen to ignore some of Morgan's more embarrassing theories, such as his view of poverty: "I can hardly see why there should be any poor in the United States except such as may be poor from misfortune, or owing to causes where the blame rests entirely with themselves."⇕

GREAT MEN AND GREAT EVENTS

This would seem to be a good place to pause and to speculate about what might have happened to the Iroquois League had no Hiawatha been born.

Would the League itself ever have been established—and if it had, would the great events that followed have been any different? The question really being asked is: Do great men and great events determine the major course a culture will take?

People who believe that the answer to these questions is in the affirmative usually point to sudden spurts in the histories of cultures around the world. The culture of ancient Greece lasted for about 1,250 years, but most of its glory was concentrated in the 150 years around the fourth century B.C. and was seen primarily in the small area of Athens. During this brief time Greek democracy developed, the population increased, military ventures were almost always successful, the arts and sciences flourished. Similarly, much of the grandeur of Rome was compressed into the few decades of the reigns of Julius Caesar and Augustus. Similar bursts of cultural energy took place in the Chou and Han dynasties of China, the Pyramid Age and the Middle Kingdom of Egypt, the Renaissance in Florence and the England of Elizabeth I.

Most of us learned in school to explain such climaxes in cultures by the birth of great men or by great historic events. If the logic of such an explanation is carried to its conclusion, then Shakespeare must have been inspired to write his plays by the reign of Elizabeth I and the defeat of the Spanish Armada; and Rome's burst of creativity in architecture, road building, sculpture, and literature occurred because the Gauls were conquered and because Augustus succeeded Julius Caesar. Of course such explanations are nonsense. A close examination of Elizabethan England and Augustan Rome reveals that the creative bursts had already begun *before* the onset of the great events or the arrival of the great personages.

We are in the habit of thinking in terms of great men, largely because the great men themselves want it that way. The pharaohs ordered that their accomplishments be carved on stone; medieval nobles subsidized troubadours to sing their praises; today's world leaders have large staffs of public-relations consultants. There is no way in which any culture can be explained in terms of one or more of its great men, whether they be Pericles, Augustus, Charlemagne, Genghis Khan, Franklin Roosevelt, or Hiawatha. The great man is not the culture's prime mover; he is its manifestation. If Newton had spent his life being a lowly tavernkeeper instead of going to Cambridge, it is certain that someone else would have discovered the law of gravitation—because the culture of the time demanded that such a discovery be made and because the intellectual groundwork for the acceptance of that discovery had already been laid. No great intellectual leap was required for the invention of the steamboat: Steam is a principle known to ancient man, and knowledge of the boat also goes back thousands of years. The combination of steam and the boat took place at a time when European civilization was receptive to new ideas and when its technology was sufficiently advanced for a workable steamboat to be made. If the actual inventors had not performed the cultural synthesis of these two ancient ideas, then other people would have done it.

This is proven beyond doubt by the several hundred known instances of inventions and scientific discoveries that were made simultaneously by two or more people working independently and completely ignorant of each other's efforts. Some of them are:

TELESCOPE:	Jansen, Lippershey, and Metius, 1608
SUNSPOTS:	Galileo, Fabricius, Scheiner, and Harriott, about 1610
NITROGEN:	Rutherford, 1772; Scheele, 1773
OXYGEN:	Priestley and Scheele, 1774
TELEGRAPH:	Morse, Henry, Steinheil, Wheatstone, and Cooke, about 1837
PHOTOGRAPHY:	Daguerre and Talbot, 1839
PLANET NEPTUNE:	Adams and Leverrier, 1845
ANESTHESIA BY ETHER:	Jackson, Liston, Morton, and Robinson, 1846
NATURAL SELECTION:	Darwin and Wallace, 1858
TELEPHONE:	Bell and Gray, 1876
AIRPLANE:	Wright brothers and Dumont, 1903
HUMAN-HEART TRANSPLANTS:	Barnard, Shumway, and Kantrowitz, 1967–1968 (within a period of six weeks)

How can the great-man theory possibly explain why a discovery like the telescope was made not by one man, but by three—all in the same year, and all working without knowledge of the others' investigations? To reply that it is "coincidence" explains nothing and puts a great strain on the laws of chance. And to say that the invention "was in the air" or "the times were ripe for it" are just other ways of stating that the great men did not do the inventing, but that the cultures did. Such is in fact the probable explanation.

All three inventors of the telescope worked in Holland, no doubt because lens manufacture had progressed the farthest there. For the same reason, the compound microscope also was developed in Holland, and the major early discoveries in microscopy were made by two other Dutchmen, van Leeuwenhoek and Swammerdam.‡ The great-man theory cannot possibly explain this fact: It became known in 1958 at the International

Congress of Zoology that zoologists in Britain, Holland, Germany, and Austria, all working independently, had gotten the same startling idea of encouraging nonhuman primates to paint abstract pictures.‡ Human-heart transplants were the culmination of heart surgery that began before World War II, the development of the heart-lung machine, the new artificial pumps that assist failing hearts—and finally the discovery of drugs that can suppress the human body's natural tendency to reject a foreign organ transplant.

The seventeenth-century Iroquois, as described in detail by Jesuit missionaries, actually practiced a dream psychotherapy that was remarkably similar to Freud's discoveries two hundred years later in Vienna; there is no evidence whatever that Freud ever knew of these reports or could possibly have had any inkling of this aspect of Iroquois culture. There are, of course, some differences between the psychotherapeutic systems of the Iroquois and of Freud, but they are no more marked than the differences between, for example, the Freudian and Jungian schools of psychoanalytic theory.

The Iroquois explained their concept of dreams to the Jesuit fathers in terms remarkably similar to the words that Freud used:

In addition to the desires which we generally have that are free, or at least voluntary in us, [and] which arise from a previous knowledge of some goodness that we imagine to exist in the thing desired, [we] believe that our souls have other desires, which are, as it were, inborn and concealed. These . . . come from the depths of the soul, not through any knowledge, but by means of a certain blind transporting of the soul to certain objects.

The Iroquois believed also that a person's natural wish was often fulfilled through his dreams, "which are its language"—and the Iroquois were sufficiently intuitive to realize that a dream might also mask rather than reveal the soul's true wishes.

All of which is a remarkably sophisticated grasp of what we in a different culture have evolved as modern psychiatry. The Iroquois recognized the existence of an unconscious, the force of unconscious desires, how the conscious mind attempts to repress unpleasant thoughts, how these unpleasant thoughts often emerge in dreams, and how the frustration of unconscious desires may cause mental and physical (psychosomatic) illnesses. The Iroquois knew that their dreams did not express facts but rather symbols—which then had to be brought to "certain persons, more enlightened than the common, whose sight penetrates, as it were, into the depths of the soul." And one of the techniques employed by these Iroquois seers to uncover the latent meanings behind a dream was free association, a technique employed by psychiatrists today. The Iroquois faith in dreams, by the way, is only somewhat diminished after more than three hundred years. The Iroquois still pay attention to hints given in dreams when they have to choose a curing ceremony, select a friend, or join a particular association; they still bring their more vivid dreams to a clairvoyant, usually a woman, for interpretation.‡

The conclusions are inevitable: Had Freud not discovered psychotherapy, then someone else would have. Had Hiawatha not united the five Iroquois tribes, then someone else would have. The culture of the Iroquois tribes was sympathetic to such a possibility; its level of social and political organization at the time made confederation possible; and the arrival of the Whites made it imperative.

WARFARE IN THE WOODLANDS

No sachem position was named in honor of the founder, Deganawidah, as the Iroquois felt he had no interest in worldly office. Instead, the title of "Pine Tree" was instituted for him, and, unlike the inherited sachem titles, this honor had to be earned. The main route to becoming a Pine Tree was by courage and success in war, and no shortage of such opportunities existed. The Iroquois were surrounded by traditional Indian enemies, who afforded targets for raiding parties, and later the warriors preyed on White settlers. The Pine Tree upstarts presented a problem in rebellion to the Council of Sachems, which was traditionally concerned with peace.

Iroquois war parties carried bows and arrows, but these were used only for ambushes. The Iroquois preferred close-in fighting with the club that the Algonkians called a tomahawk. The Iroquois warrior also carried a wooden shield, and he wore a sort of armor made of sticks laced together by buckskin. The Iroquois method of warfare, as described by terrified White settlers, was to sneak up on the enemy like foxes, fight like lions, and disappear into the woods like birds. The object was both to kill and to obtain captives. Some captives, especially the young ones, were adopted into the Iroquois tribes to substitute for the husbands, brothers, and sons lost in battle. Most of the others, though, were reserved for orgies of torture that were distinguished by their ferocity and their organization. The

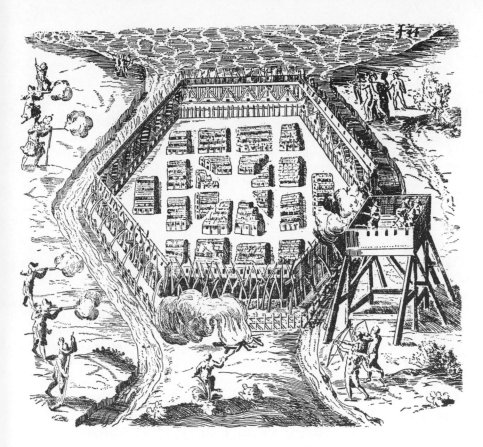

Champlain's attack on an Onondaga fort in 1615 is depicted in a contemporary French engraving. Note the elaborate fortifications typical of Iroquois villages: the moats, a double stockade, and a location near water. The platform on the right was erected by the French so they could shoot down on the terrified Iroquois. Attacks like this cost the French their empire in North America, for the Iroquois supported the British in the French and Indian War.

torture continued for as many days as the victim could be kept alive. He was refreshed with water and even given long periods of rest so that he might regain his strength—and also feel the pain more exquisitely. The Jesuit Le Jeune describes one torture he witnessed:

One must be there to see a living picture of Hell. The whole cabin appeared as if on fire; and athwart the flames and dense smoke that issued therefrom, these barbarians, crowding one upon the other, howling at the top of their voices, with firebrands in their hands, their eyes flashing with rage and fury—seemed like so many demons who would give no respite to this poor wretch. They often stopped him at the other end of the cabin, some of them taking his hands and breaking the bones thereof by sheer force; others pierced his ears with sticks which they left in them. One of these butchers having applied a brand to his loins, he was seized with a fainting fit . . . As soon as day began to dawn, they lighted fires outside the village, to display there the excesses of their cruelty, to the sight of the Sun. There they began to burn him more cruelly than ever, leaving no part of his body to which fire was not applied at intervals . . . Therefore, fearing that he would die otherwise than by the knife, one cut off a foot, another a hand, and almost at the same time a third severed the head from the shoulders, throwing it to the crowd, where someone caught it to carry it to the Captain Ondessone, for whom it had been reserved, in order to make a feast therewith.‡

This excerpt actually represents one of the less gruesome descriptions of what Western civilization regards as barbarism (although there is no century in the history of Western civilization in which equivalent or worse tortures have not been practiced). Some psychologists have found in these tortures an emotional release for a people who spent a good deal of their waking hours obedient to rigorous standards of conduct, and who lived under the stressful conditions of several families crowded into a longhouse.

Such explanations of torture, of course, possess degrees of truth, but one other explanation should not be overlooked. A tribe is by its very nature a fragile organization; it lacks institutions that promote unity *within* the tribe. For a tribe to survive, it must find some way to achieve internal unity—and that way usually is external strife. The tribe exists at all times in a state of mobilization for war against its neighbors. The slightest incident, or often merely a desire to increase prestige, is enough to set off a skirmish, and such strife with external enemies was unremitting in aboriginal times.

The explanation for the brief skirmishes is that neither a tribe's social organization nor its economy could sustain warfare as practiced in more complex societies. No specialized class of soldiers existed to devote itself full-time to warfare. Nor could male labor constantly be diverted from the needs of clearing fields and building houses. Acquiring new land was of no benefit, for the Iroquois lacked both the political machinery and the manpower to administer occupied territory. The best they could achieve was a kind of stalemate in which they obtained captives and other booty. That explains why soon after an enemy was defeated it was back again spoiling for a new battle. The emphasis was not on building a mighty war machine but on becoming expert in psychological warfare. Rather than face-to-face combat, the Iroquois and their neighbors fought a war of nerves whose weapons were torture, ambush, ruthless massacre, and even the howl in the night. The Iroquois did in one way improve on the warfare practiced by most tribes. They adopted some of the conquered peoples to replace their own losses. More than half of some Iroquois tribes—particularly in the sevententh century when warfare had increased—consisted of adopted Huron and Algonkians who had been trained to equal in ferocity any native-born Iroquois.

THE GREAT SPIRIT AND MONOTHEISM

The Iroquois theogony was probably complex to begin with, and it survives only in a form garbled further by the explorers and early settlers. There seem to have been three classes of supernatural phenomena: spirits, ghosts of the dead, and the gods. In addition there was a Great Spirit, together with his satanic counterpart. At a man's death, his spirit departed for the afterlife—not for some "happy hunting ground," which was the White conception of the Indian afterworld. (An Iroquois did not believe he ate food after death and therefore he had no reason to hunt.) The dead man's ghost maintained an interest in the tribe. Special wintertime feasts were held for the ghosts, who were thought to participate unseen in the dancing and the games; they also accompanied raiding parties, even though they could only watch and not fight.

The Iroquois represent the least complex social organization in North America in which monotheism existed. Monotheism, contrary to what most people believe, goes beyond simply a belief in one god. It signifies rather the belief in a supreme being who, himself uncreated, nevertheless is responsible for creating clusters of other supernatural and sacred beings, whether they be angels, demons, or saints. Judaism, Christianity, and Mohammedanism are monotheistic beliefs not because Jehovah or God or Allah is the *only* supernatural being, but because each is the *first cause* and creator of the world. Our modern fundamentalists in religion often ignore the references in the Old Testament to immortals in addition to the supreme being Jehovah. In the King James Version the Hebrew words are often translated "sons of God"—but "divine beings" is more accurate.‡ The Iroquois worshiped their Great Spirit for himself—and also for bringing the other gods into being.

The Iroquois raise an interesting question about the origins of monotheism. Many scholars have assumed that monotheism arises whenever people have experience with the powerful human rulers who hold sway over empires or kingdoms; a supreme god then becomes a celestial reflection of some supreme ruler on earth. That was probably true in Egypt, where the worship of the high god Aton lasted for a time under the fanatic Pharaoh Ikhnaton. Christianity increasingly came to reflect the political society of the Roman Empire in which it arose by developing a hierarchy of God, Jesus, the Pope and priesthood, angels, and saints. Eventually, there were nine orders of the celestial hierarchy, and they were supposed to number 266,613,336 angels.‡ The Iroquois, on the contrary, lacked not only a single strong ruler but even any powerful government. The Council of Sachems, which limited itself mostly to external questions of war or peace, was unable even to control its own young Pine Tree warriors. The case of the Iroquois is in some ways similar to the ancient Israelites in the time of the Judges when a potent Jehovah controlled human affairs, yet the earthly government was that of a weak council of elders. These Israelite elders merely expressed the consensus of their communities and could not even enforce their views; they did not represent any strong, independent policies of their own.

The monotheistic societies of the Iroquois and other cultures, past and present and around the world, reveal one common characteristic: A hierarchy of numerous allegiances extends from the individual to the outermost boundaries of his society. Among the Iroquois, the individual was part of a nuclear family, which belonged to a household, which lived with other households in a longhouse, which constituted part of a clan, which belonged to a moiety, which made up a tribe, which in turn was part of the League of the Iroquois. The individual Iroquois was ensnared in a morass of allegiances; the only way to make sense out of it all was to postulate an orderly environment over which rules prevailed even at the ultimate, supernatural boundaries. The connection that has long been noted between monotheism and societies that practice agriculture now can be explained. Only under agriculture does a society become sufficiently complex for the hierarchy of groups and allegiances to appear that allows the birth of monotheism.

FALSE FACES

Despite the sophistication of much of Iroquois society, its religious rituals were still shamanistic—with the difference that they were not carried on by a religious free-lancer but by an organized shamanistic group. The individual shaman's songs, dances, and other hocus-pocus were restricted to the False Face society, whose members cured with the aid of large wooden masks.✠ These distorted facial nightmares consisted of twelve basic types—crooked mouth, straight-lipped, spoon-lipped, hanging mouth, tongue protruding, smiling, whistling, divided red and black, long nosed, horned, pig, and blind. There were also some additional local types, such as the diseased face, as well as color variations. A catalog of all combinations probably would number several dozen kinds. The society members always

The false face mask of the Iroquois was first carved into the trunk of a living tree (LEFT), then cut out and painted. The Onondaga mask (RIGHT) depicts one of the most important Iroquois supernatural beings, the Humpbacked One. The distorted features portray the pain he suffered when, according to Iroquois mythology, he struck a mountain. The knobbed chin, though, has nothing to do with the accident; it merely allows the wearer more easily hold to the mask in front of his face.

functioned as a group, and they put on a frightening performance at the house of the sick person. They lurched, humped, crawled, and trotted to the house, grunting and issuing weird cries from behind their masks. They danced around the sick person, sprinkled him with ashes, shook their large rattles made from the carapaces of turtles, and sang out their incantations.

In 1751 the pioneer American naturalist and a friend of the Indian, John Bartram, described what it was like to encounter one of the members of the False Face society:

He had on a clumsy vizard of wood colour'd black, with a nose 4 or 5 inches long, a grinning mouth set awry, furnished with long teeth, round the eyes circles of bright brass, surrounded by a larger circle of white paint, from his forehead hung long tresses of buffaloes hair, and from the catch part of his head ropes made of the plated husks of *Indian* corn; I cannot recollect the whole of his dress, but that it was equally uncouth: he carried in one hand a long staff, in the other a calabash with small stones in it, for a rattle . . . he would sometimes hold up his head and make a hideous noise like the braying of an ass.↕

The false faces really should not be regarded as masks, since they were not intended to hide anything. There has been considerable discussion and dispute about them, and a common explanation is that they represent merely a form of idolatry. It is true that in addition to the large masks intended to be worn, there were much smaller "maskettes," often only two or three inches long. They were kept partly as charms, much as some people keep a lucky stone, but they were primarily compact substitutes for, and reminders of, the larger masks, similar to the Saint Christopher statuettes some drivers place on their automobile dashboards. If the word "idolatry" is pronounced with a condemnatory tone, as many good White Protestants often do, then the Iroquois must be defended. The Iroquois worshiped—and they, the few that are left, still worship today despite the inroads of Christianity—their supernatural beings and not idols. They regarded their masks as portraits into which the supernatural has made itself manifest. The wearer behaved as if he were the supernatural being whom he impersonated. He had obtained the mask by carving in the trunk of a living tree the vision he had of a False Face, and then cutting the mask free. During this ceremony, the spirit revealed itself to the maker, who then finished carving the features and painted the mask. The Iroquois did not worship the images themselves, only what they signified. Iconism is undoubtedly a better description than idolatry.

Historians can speculate endlessly about the Pax Iroquoian that might have spread over much of the East and resulted in one of the greatest confederacies the world has ever known had not the Whites arrived. It is true that the Iroquois never had the opportunity to reach full flowering, but even if the Whites had never intruded, the Iroquois probably would not have achieved it. In addition to the fragility inherent in any tribal organization, there was the unresolved friction between the hereditary sachems and the military opportunism of the Pine Trees. Rivalry between the British and the French—and later the British and the Americans—for the loyalty of the Iroquois served only to accent this basic problem and was not the cause of it. The League, formed in 1570 and not discovered by Whites until about 1640, had very nearly disappeared by 1851 when Lewis Henry Morgan wrote:

Their council-fires . . . have long since been extinguished, their empire has terminated, and the shades of evening are now gathering thickly over the scattered and feeble remnants of this once powerful League . . . The Iroquois will soon be lost as a people, in that night of impenetrable darkness in which so many Indian races have been enshrouded. Already their country has been appropriated, their forests cleared, and their trails obliterated. The residue of this proud and gifted race, who still linger around their native seats, are destined to fade away, until they become eradicated as an Indian stock. We shall ere long look backward to the Iroquois, as a race blotted from existence; but to remember them as a people whose sachems had no cities, whose religion had no temples, and whose government had no record.‡

VIII

Plains: Equestrian Revolution

THE GREAT AMERICAN EPIC

To many people, the typical Indian was the Plains Indian, a painted brave in full regalia, trailing a war bonnet, astride a horse which he rode bareback, sweeping down upon a wagon train, in glorious technicolor. In actual fact, the picturesque culture of the Plains Indian was artificial, not aboriginal, and it did not last very long. The amalgam known as the Plains culture was not fully accomplished until the early 1800's—and like the spring grass of the high plains, it withered quickly.

This culture emerged almost inconspicuously in the middle of the eighteenth century as its catalytic agent, the horse, spread northward from Spanish settlements in New Mexico. Within only a few generations, the horse was found throughout the central heartland of the continent, and Indians from all directions spilled onto the plains. They originally spoke many different languages and had various customs, but they all found in the horse a new tool to kill greater numbers of bison than they had ever believed possible. They became inconceivably rich in material goods, far beyond their wildest dreams, and like a dream it all faded. By about 1850, the Plains culture was already on the wane as the "manifest destiny" of a vigorous United States to push westward shoved them aside. The fate of the Plains Indians had been sealed with the arrival of the first miners and the first prairie schooner. The battles of extermination between Plains Indians and United States cavalry represent America's own great epic—its *Iliad,* its *Aeneid,* its Norse saga—but this epic was no more true than any other.

Despite the surrounded forts, the saving of the last bullet for oneself, the occasional acts of heroism, and the frequent acts of bestiality on both sides—despite this picture portrayed in the Great American Epic, there was remarkably little formal combat. Deaths and hardship there were in plenty as the Plains Indians met their catastrophic end, but most deaths were due to starvation, exposure, disease, brutality, and alcoholism, and not to bullets. In all the actual battles between White soldiers and Indian braves, only several thousand deaths on both sides were due to bullets and arrows. The wars of the plains were not epics but mopping-up operations. In the process, the millions of bison very nearly vanished without leaving any survivors, the plains were turned into a dust bowl, and the once-proud Indian horsemen were broken in body and spirit.

The famed Plains Indian culture did not exist in all its glory when Coronado first explored the plains. Lured on by tales of rich lands, where kings were supposed to be lulled to sleep by the chimes of golden bells, Coronado eventually reached Kansas in 1541. Here the Spaniards saw the beast they had been hearing so much about: the remarkable "cow," actually a bison, as large as a Spanish bull, but with an enormous mane and small curved horns. They also met some impoverished Indians who lived in conical tipis "built like pavilions," according to the chronicler of the expedition. He was particularly impressed by the way the bison seemed to provide most of the materials needed by the Indians: "With the skins they build their houses; with the skins they clothe and show themselves; from the skins they make ropes and also obtain wool. With the sinews they make threads, with which they sew their clothes and also their tents. From the bones they shape awls. The dung they use for firewood, since there is no other fuel in that land. The bladders they use as jugs and drinking containers."↕

Hunting bison on foot was not productive, and it certainly could not support large numbers of Indians. Such hunting was practiced largely by the wretched nomads who moved around in small groups and who lived off the occasional weakened bison they could kill or those they could stampede over bluffs. Most of the aboriginal cultures on the plains and prairies were based on the cultivation of maize, beans, and squash. Agriculture had spread westward from the eastern Woodlands, and it followed the finger-like extensions of rivers throughout the arid Dakotas, Texas, and virtually to the foothills of the Rockies. Hunting bison, for these people, was only incidental to the primary subsistence based on agriculture. They went on a hunt about once a year to supplement their vegetable diet and to obtain hides, sinew, bone, and other raw materials.

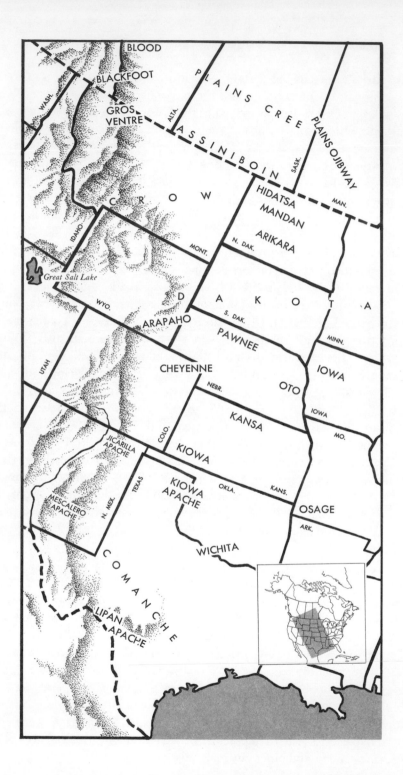

Once the horse arrived on the plains, that way of life changed. The nomadic bison hunters became ascendant over the farmers, who either were driven off their lands or abandoned agriculture to become bison hunters themselves. Indians had never seen the horse until the Spaniards brought it to the New World, for sometime during the great glacial melt it had become extinct in North America. The Indians obtained the first horses after the Spaniards settled New Mexico in 1598. (Contrary to previous belief, the Indians captured no horses from de Soto, Coronado, or other early explorers, for these horses either died or were taken home again.) The Spaniards prohibited the sale of horses to Indians, but the revolt of the Pueblo Indians between 1680 and 1692 threw some of the animals on the Indian markets of North America. The Spaniards restocked their herds, which proliferated, but they were unable to prevent further horse stealing by Indians. Horses were bartered—or stolen—from Indian group to group. Soon a whole new Indian profession of horse merchant grew up, and the animals—as well as the knowledge of how to break and train them— spread northward from New Mexico. In addition, some Spanish horses had gone wild and roamed the plains in herds. The Spaniards called them *mesteños* ("wild"), from which the English word "mustangs" is derived.

By the first half of the eighteenth century, enterprising Indian merchants had already sold the horse to Indians as far north as the Northern Shoshoni of Wyoming and taught them its management. The Shoshoni slowly built up their herds and learned to ride as if they had been born to the saddle. No longer did they have to remain impoverished and secretive inhabitants of the Rocky Mountains, at the mercy of more powerful Indian groups. They swooped down the eastern flanks of the mountains and onto the high plains, where they found a bonanza in bison and a way to even the score with their traditional persecutors, the Blackfoot. From all over, other Indian groups converged on the plains and quickly adapted themselves to an economy based on the bison. The lands of the agriculturists were usurped, and the plains became a maelstrom of varied and often conflicting cultures.

A LIVING EXPERIMENT IN CULTURE CHANGE

The stolen, bartered, bought, or captured horse was a new cultural element in the heartland of North America, and it changed the entire way of life there.‡ The whole of the plains, from Alberta to Texas, became peopled by groups of great diversity who had come from all directions and often from

The make-believe Indians: Rocky Bear of the Dakota poses in the full regalia of a typical Plains Indian of the end of the last century.

great distances. There were Athabaskans from the north (Kiowa-Apache), Algonkians (Cree, Cheyenne, Blackfoot) and Siouans (Mandan, Crow, Dakota) from the east, Uto-Aztecans (Comanche, Ute) from the west, Caddoans (Pawnee, Arikara) from the south. The plains became a melting pot for more than thirty different peoples, belonging to at least five language stocks. It has given anthropologists a living laboratory of culture change. Culture change is the way in which a group alters because of new circumstances, or the way it borrows traits from other cultures and fits them into the configurations of its own.

By about 1800 the gross differences in culture among all these peoples had disappeared; the Sun Dance ceremony, for example, was eventually observed by virtually every tribe. Of course differences apparent to the trained eye of the anthropologist still existed; yet it is remarkable that a people from the eastern forests and another from the Great Basin of the west, two thousand miles away, should within only a few generations have become so nearly identical. Even more remarkable, this homogeneity was achieved with great speed, was not imposed on unwilling people by a more powerful group, and was done in the absence of a common tongue—save for "sign language," the lingua franca of the Plains tribes.

The Plains Cree demonstrate how a people originally distant from the plains in both culture and geography eventually could become so typical of it. The Cree were first recorded in the *Jesuit Relations* of 1640, but at that time they had nothing to do with the plains at all. They inhabited the forests between Hudson Bay and Lake Superior, and they were roving hunters and gatherers of wild rice. Their culture was typical of the Northern Algonkian bands, and after the Hudson's Bay Company was founded they turned to trapping. The demand by Whites for more beaver pelts led them to push westward; because they had obtained guns from White traders, they were able to dispossess the previous inhabitants. By about the middle of the eighteenth century, some of the Cree had already penetrated to the west of Lake Winnipeg. Their culture had changed considerably. It was now parasitic on the White trader for weapons, clothing, and cooking utensils—and sometimes even food, because the Cree spent his time trapping rather than hunting. Then the Cree living farthest west discovered the resource of the bison. Historical records reveal that as early as 1772 they had developed primitive ways of hunting bison, although they still did not possess the horse. Within only a generation, though, the Plains Cree had emerged—a typical equestrian Plains tribe, very different in customs and outlook from the Cree that still inhabited the forests, although both groups continued to speak the same language.

And all this was due to the horse. No longer were just stray or stampeded bison taken, but the herds were pursued on swift horses and the choicest animals killed. No longer was the whole animal utilized for raw materials, which had so impressed the chronicler of the Coronado expedition, but the Indians could now afford the luxury of waste. They stocked the tipi with supplies for the future: meat dried in the sun (jerkee), or else pounded and mixed with fat and berries to become pemmican. Even though most of the Plains Indians never saw a White close up until their swift decline, his influence was felt profoundly as his goods and trade articles flowed westward across the plains by barter from one tribe to another. Tipis almost twenty-five feet in diameter were filled to overflowing with new-found riches. An economic revolution, for which the Indians' traditions had not prepared them, took place. The women no longer toiled in the fields—for gardening was not as profitable as hunting, nor could it be practiced in the presence of nomadic horsemen—and they stopped making pottery because brass kettles were obtained from Whites. Permanent villages disappeared, and with them went the elaborate customs and crafts, rules for marriage and residence.

After the Indians discovered the effectiveness of rifles, an armaments race began on the plains. Just as Indians earlier had realized the value of horses, and those lacking them were driven to obtain them by any means, the acquisition of rifles upset the entire balance of power. As soon as one tribe acquired firepower, the competition for others to obtain equal armaments became fierce. Not only the rifles had to be acquired, but there was also a continuing need for powder and for lead. The Indians were driven to take ever greater chances in raids to steal horses which they might barter for guns and ammunition. For a period of nearly fifty years, the plains became an arena of turmoil in which the status quo changed from year to year, as successive groups became supreme in supplies of horses or guns, or in the powerful allies they could muster.

THE MAKE-BELIEVE INDIANS

The Plains Indians in their heyday were a study in hyperbole, and as make-believe as the set for a western movie. They sprang from greatly differing traditions, from farmers and from hunters and from collectors of wild plants. Each contributed something of its own that created almost overnight a flamboyant culture whose vigor was for a time unequaled. In this world of hyperbole, many traditions that existed in non-Plains Indian societies became wildly exaggerated. Other Indians also possessed clubs and associations, but none were so extravagant in ritual and insignia as the Plains warrior societies. Indians elsewhere also believed in the reality of visions, but none so relentlessly pursued the vision quest and were so caught up in the emotional excesses of religion as the Plains tribes. Other

Indians tortured captives, but none evoked pain so exquisitely in their own bodies.

A special kind of social organization developed on the plains that is known as the composite tribe. Wherever the composite tribe is found, it always signifies a breakdown in culture with a subsequent readaptation. Sometimes the breakdown is due to population loss through migration or increased warfare, as occurred to the Pueblo Indians around the Rio Grande River of New Mexico. Sometimes it is due to the disturbance of the resource base through economic exploitation by outsiders, as has been characteristic of primitive African societies. Occasionally, as happened on the North American plains, it is due to the loss of old culture traits and the borrowing of new ones. Whatever the cause, composite tribes usually arise after an alien culture appears; and almost everywhere Whites have penetrated around the world their presence has resulted in the formation of the composite tribe.

A distinguishing characteristic of the composite tribe is that descent reckoning is unspecific: It can be through either the father's or the mother's line, or both. Marital residence rules also are unspecific, and the newly married couple lives with whichever relatives expediency suggests. The composite tribe of the Plains Indians was much more a collection of bands than were the Zuni or the Iroquois lineal tribes. During most of the year the bison lived scattered in small herds, but during the late summer rutting season they came together in huge herds that blackened the plains. The Indians responded with a parallel social cycle. Most of the year a number of Plains Indian families lived together as a band, uniting only at the time of the summer encampment with other bands for tribal ceremonies and a communal hunt. Furthermore, band membership tended to change, and many Plains Indians belonged to several bands during their lifetimes. One cause of the changing membership within bands was the constant feuding, which often became so oppressive that the only way to preserve any peace at all was by fragmentation of the original band. The Plains Indians appear to have been no more complex in their social organization than the Eskimo and the Great Basin Shoshone bands, but that is not really true. They became functioning tribes at least during their summer encampments, and they managed to maintain that identity the rest of the year, even though they broke up into small bands.

The primary way in which identity was achieved was not through clans but through non-kinship sodalities. The word "sodality" is derived from the Latin *sodalis,* which means "comrade" or "associate," and in a modern society it is equivalent to fraternities and sororities, political parties, service clubs like the Rotary or the Lions, and religious organizations. It is an association that binds people together around a single interest. It may be the burial association of the Irish-American immigrants in the last century, credit associations in medieval Europe, even the crop-watching societies in Chinese villages. When the Plains tribes united in the summer, they were crosscut by a bewildering variety of sodalities with ceremonial, social, and military functions. There were dance societies and feasting societies, and even societies based on a common supernatural experience. Some societies were only for women, like the craft guilds of the Cheyenne. Others were open to both men and women, like the tobacco societies of the Crow which revolved around the raising of special kinds of tobacco for ceremonial use.

The Cheyenne, as just one example, had six military societies that somewhat resembled the dueling societies of German students. A youth was permitted to join any one of them if he could demonstrate his courage, but he usually chose to go into the one his father belonged to. These societies served not only as the tribe's military force but as its police as well. And each of the six had a particular area of responsibility, such as protecting the movement of the encampment from one place to another, or enforcing the rules against individual hunting that might scare away the bison. Only the bravest of the brave warriors could belong to the elite military society known as the Contraries. Somewhat like the Zuni Mudheads, they were privileged clowns. They did the opposite of everything: They said *no* when they meant *yes;* went away when called and came near when told to go away; called left *right;* and sat shivering on the hottest day.

A special development in the warrior societies was found among the Mandan, Hidatsa, Arapaho, and Blackfoot, which had a hierarchy of societies. The societies were arranged in order of the age of their members, and as the members grew older they moved up a step. In this way a warrior society existed for every male from the youngest to the oldest, with the exception of the effeminate male known as a berdache. No scorn was attached to his position; he was regarded with pity and with a degree of sacred awe for being the victim of a condition that was not of his own doing. Even the berdache found his place in Plains Indian society. He permanently adopted woman's clothing and woman's role; he became skilled in the female tasks of beadwork or skin-tanning, and he was eligible to join the women's societies.

The richness and diversity of the Plains sodalities is explained by the

The Bison Dance of the now-extinct Mandan was pictured in all its primeval splendor and fury by the artist Carl Bodmer, who accompanied Prince Maximilian on his expedition to the plains in the early 1830's. The dancers portrayed both the game animals and the hunters, and through ceremonials such as this one they hoped to gain power in the hunt.

lack of lineal residential groups. The need for non-kin sodalities was so great on the plains because they filled the social void caused by the absence of clans. Had these non-kin sodalities failed to develop, with their complexity of rules and regulations that often seem so ridiculous to us today, the tribes would have been reduced to mere collections of bands. The sodalities brought unity to one of the most diverse collections of people on earth.

COUPS AND SCALPING

Almost all the sodalities had religious aspects, and almost all were concerned with war in one way or another. The various cultures had engaged in warfare even before they migrated onto the plains and obtained horses, but with the emergence of the Plains Indian culture during the nineteenth century, warfare became as ritualized as medieval knighthood. Only during the very twilight of the Plains culture did large battles take place that pitted Indian against Indian or Indian against the United States Army, with each group seeking to exterminate the other. Previous to that, tactics consisted of forays and raids by small war parties; the conflicts were brief and usually indecisive.

The Plains Indians fought not to win territory or to enslave other tribes, but for a variety of different reasons. One was the capture of horses, which had a high economic value. Another reason, already discussed in reference to the Iroquois, was that external strife served to unify the tribe internally. A tribe, especially one as fragile as the composite tribe unified only by non-kin sodalities, needed a common enemy as a rationale for its existence. A third reason was that war was regarded as a game in which the players might win status. In this game, exploits were graded according to the dangers involved. The exploit itself was known as the *coup,* from the French trapper's word for "blow," because originally it signified that the brave had struck the enemy's body with a special stick that was often striped like a barber pole. Later, "counting coups" referred to the recital by the brave of all his war deeds; as he immodestly proclaimed each one he gave a blow against a pole with his ax. These recitals went on endlessly. Each time a young man accumulated a new honor, he used it as an excuse to recount his old exploits. If he lied about his exploits, though, or even shaded the truth a bit, he was challenged immediately by someone who had been along on the same war party.

Each Plains tribe had its own ranking for coups. Among the Blackfoot, stealing an enemy's weapons was looked upon as the highest exploit. Among some other tribes, the bravest deed was to touch an enemy without hurting him. The least important exploit usually was killing an enemy, but even that deed was ranked according to the way it was done and the weapons that were used. The whole business of counting coups often became extremely involved. Among the Cheyenne, for example, coups could be counted by several warriors on a single enemy, but the coups were ranked in the strict order in which the enemy was touched by the participants; it was immaterial who actually killed or wounded him. Like a sort of heraldry, these deeds were recorded in picture writing on tipis and on bison robes. They gave the warrior the right to hold public office. Among many tribes, each coup earned an eagle's feather, and the achieving of many coups accounts for the elaborate headdresses of some of the Plains war leaders.

Exploits of a Plains warrior were painted on bison skins for all to see—and envy. This Pawnee skin from about 1870 shows in picture writing the principal accomplishments of a leading warrior.

Scalps taken from dead or wounded enemies sometimes served as trophies, but they were insignificant when compared with counting coups. Many Plains tribes did not take scalps at all until the period of their swift decline, which began in the middle of the last century. Most people believe that all Indians took scalps, and that scalp-hunting was exclusively a New World custom. Neither idea is true. Herodotus, the ancient Greek historian, mentioned the taking of scalps by the Scythians, for example. In South America scalp-taking as a custom was practically unknown; in North America it *may* have existed before the arrival of Whites, but only in a few areas in the eastern Woodlands. Many historians still question whether scalp-taking was an aboriginal Indian practice or rather one learned quite early from the White settlers.

Whatever its exact origins, there is no doubt that scalp-taking quickly spread over all of North America, except in the Eskimo areas; nor is there any doubt that its spread was due to the barbarity of White men rather than to the barbarity of Red men. White settlers early offered to pay bounties on dead Indians, and scalps were actual proof of the deed. Governor Kieft of New Netherland is usually credited with originating the idea of paying for Indian scalps, as they were more convenient to handle than whole heads, and they offered the same proof that an Indian had been killed. By liberal payments for scalps, the Dutch virtually cleared southern New York and New Jersey of Indians before the English supplanted them.‡ By 1703 the colony of Massachusetts was paying the equivalent of about $60 for every Indian scalp. In the mid-eighteenth century, Pennsylvania fixed the bounty for a male Indian scalp at $134; a female's was worth only $50. Some White entrepreneurs simply hatcheted any old Indians that still survived in their towns. The French also used scalp-taking as an instrument of geopolitics. In the competition over the Canadian fur trade, they offered the Micmac Indians a bounty for every scalp they took from the Beothuk of Newfoundland. By 1827 an expedition to Newfoundland failed to find a single survivor of this once numerous and proud people.‡

Among the Plains tribes, apparently only the Dakota and the Cree placed any value on scalps; both tribes were late immigrants to the plains from the East, where they probably learned the practice from Whites. Nor was there as much torturing of captives by Plains tribes as was once believed. The tradition of the White settler's saving his last bullet for himself to avoid a horrible death was a needless precaution. Unlike the Indians of the eastern Woodlands, the Plains Indians killed swiftly. They looked upon the White custom of hanging, for example, as cruel and barbaric.

CAUSES OF WARFARE

The Great American Epic has traditionally regarded the Plains Indians as the most "warlike" on the continent. Indeed, history does confirm that the heartland of the continent was an arena for continual strife. Yet, stating that a Blackfoot, for example, was "warlike" reveals nothing. The entire Blackfoot tribe did not habitually engage in war because individual members possessed "warlike" personalities. Individual men go to war for individual reasons: for social prestige, for economic rewards and for booty, because of religious convictions—even to escape from frustrations at home. Entire societies, though, do not go to war for such personal reasons. The fact is that the individual Blackfoot was warlike simply because his whole cultural system obliged him to be that way.

All the various theories as to why groups of people go to war fall into four general categories. The first states that it is the very physical nature of man to be pugnacious and aggressive. Such a view of man holds that a warlike urge is biologically inherent in him. This is an old theory, and it keeps popping up from time to time in new presentations, most recently in Konrad Lorenz' *On Aggression* (1966). But there is no evidence in the physical makeup of man to suggest that he has been fashioned as a warlike animal. Man, in truth, is a puny creation, lacking fangs, claws, thick skin, speed, or other adaptations for combat. The whole idea of the innate belligerency of man is laid to rest by evidence that warfare is virtually absent among the most primitive of men, those whose "true" biological nature might appear to be closest to the surface. The Great Basin Shoshone, for example, never waged war, nor did most other very simple societies before the arrival of Whites.

The second explanation is an affront to logic: Men are warlike because they are warlike. Such an explanation is ridiculous, but even so noted an anthropologist as Ralph Linton wrote that the Plains Indians would not have been so interested in war if "they had not been warlike."‡ Similar statements exist in Ruth Benedict's *Patterns of Culture*. Obviously, such logic is akin to explaining obesity in middle-aged males by saying that many middle-aged males are obese.

The third explanation is a psychological one, and it probably boasts the most adherents—which is understandable, for these people can bolster their case by surveys, personality tests, statistical analyses, and other impressive tools of modern scholarship. Even before the widespread use of such tests and surveys, Freud, in an exchange of correspondence with Einstein in 1932 about the causes of war, agreed that "there is an instinct for hatred and destruction . . . which goes halfway to meet the efforts of the warmongers."‡ All of these psychological studies, though, can explain only the motivations behind why *individuals* go to war. The real point is that although individuals slug each other in a barroom brawl or drop napalm from airplanes over Vietnam, individuals do not go to war. Only societies do that.

That leaves the fourth explanation, which states simply that the causes for war are to be found within the cultures of the contending groups. This explanation avoids confusing the issue with related problems, such as individual motivations or the kinds of warfare practiced. The Plains

Indians confirm this cultural explanation. For one thing, the composite tribes of the Plains Indians could not have survived without external enemies, real or imagined, against whom their warrior associations could unite. For another, the Plains culture was artificial, brought into being by the reverberations sent across the continent by the arrival of the Whites. The Whites upset delicate adjustments the Indians had made to each other over very long periods of time. As just one example, the French encouraged warfare between the Ojibway and surrounding groups; the Ojibway spread westward and displaced Siouan tribes, which migrated westward and southward to the plains; there the Sioux displaced Hidatsa and Mandan, who in turn stirred up the Cheyenne and others. The whole unreal situation was very much like a series of balls caroming off one another and resulting in new rebounds.

Most important, once all these groups were on the plains and had altered their cultures by acquiring horses and guns, their whole make-believe world had to be kept in motion or it would collapse. Horses had to be stolen so they could be bartered for more guns to aid in the stealing of more horses. Many White traders encouraged the strife to capitalize on it by selling guns, liquor, and kitchenware. The herds of bison, once thought limitless, dwindled, and as they did there was additional cause for strife over hunting territories. In any event, there were good cultural—that is, social, political, economic, and technological—reasons why the Plains Indians were warlike. They were that way not because of their biology or their psychology, but because their new White-induced culture demanded it.‡

THE NEW RICH

Among the Mandan, Hidatsa, Arapaho, and Blackfoot, a member of a war society purchased his way up the ladder of age-grades until he arrived at the topmost grade and was thereupon entitled to wear the famous feathered bonnet. At each step, he selected a seller from the next older brotherhood, and then purchased his rights. A buyer was free to select any seller he wanted, but he usually chose someone from his father's family. Often, as part of the payment, the purchaser had to relinquish his wife to the seller for a time; if the purchaser was unmarried, he had to borrow a wife from a relative. The whole business of joining an age-grade brotherhood was accompanied by an elaborate etiquette that was also somewhat sophomoric and not unlike the mock seriousness of today's Masonic initiation.

Membership in other kinds of societies was also often purchased, and in fact many things were for sale among the Plains tribes: sacred objects, religious songs, and even the description of a particularly good vision. The right to paint a particular design on the face during a religious ceremony might cost as much as a horse. Permission just to look inside someone's sacred bundle of fetishes and feathers was often worth the equivalent of a hundred dollars. A Crow is known to have paid two horses to his sponsor to get himself invited into a tobacco society, and the candidate's family contributed an additional twenty-three horses. A prudent Blackfoot was well advised to put his money into a sacred bundle, an investment that paid him continued dividends. The investment was as safe as today's government bond is; and it was readily negotiable at a price usually higher than the purchase price. By permitting the bundle to be used in rituals, its owner received fees that were like dividends. As the Plains tribes became richer, the price of sacred bundles continued to rise, much as the price of a stock-exchange seat goes up during prosperous times.

Until they became horsemen, almost none of these tribes had ever known wealth. The Comanche, for example, had been an impoverished Shoshonean people from the Great Basin before the nineteenth century. Most of the other tribes only a few decades before had been marginal hunters, all of whose possessions could be dragged along by a single dog. But the Plains tribes learned the laws of the marketplace rapidly, both from each other and from the White trader. The accumulation of wealth became important, but it was not incorporated into the societies in any meaningful way. Perhaps it would have been in time, and the Plains tribes might have served economic theorists as the very models of the steps by which societies become capitalistic.

Anthropologists can do no more than guess what might have happened to the concept of wealth had the Plains culture endured for another century, or even for a few more decades. Some indication is given by tribes such as the Kiowa, who learned how to use wealth to create more wealth. A Kiowa warrior was forced by custom to give away some of his wealth, but he also learned to hoard it, not only for himself but also to keep it in his family through inheritance. Classes based on wealth arose in what had once been an egalitarian society. The wealthiest classes could afford to give their sons certain benefits. They equipped them with the best horses and guns and sent them down the road to military glory at an early age. And when the son of a wealthy Kiowa achieved an exploit, everyone heard about it, for the wealthy controlled the channels of publicity through their ability to give gifts. Such publicity paid further economic benefits: The scion of a wealthy Kiowa, with his well-publicized exploits, could increase his wealth even more because he easily obtained followers for a raiding party.

Not knowing what to do with the new-found wealth that crammed their tipis, the Plains Indians regarded it as materially unimportant, but valued it as a status symbol. It became another way to count coups, to get one up on a neighbor. And since the primary way to acquire wealth was to steal horses from someone else, wealth became a validation of bravery. The warrior also could be sure that no one forgot his prowess by the constant reminder of gifts. Gift-giving emphasized that the giver was brave enough to go out and steal more wealth any time he felt like it.

The sudden wealth achieved by the mass slaughter of bison changed customs in other ways also. It took only a moment for a man on horseback to kill a bison with a bullet, but it still remained a long and arduous task for his wife to dress the hide for sale to the White trader. As a result, a shortage of women arose and a premium was placed on them to the extent that eventually "bride price" was paid. Men always needed the hands of extra women to dress the skins, and the parents of a healthy girl could negotiate her marriage from a position of strength. At the same time, polygyny, which probably had existed in some tribes to a limited extent, became widespread, for a good hunter needed as many wives as he could afford. There are even instances known of berdaches being taken on as second wives, not for any sexual variety they might offer, but merely because they performed women's tasks.

VISION QUESTS

Most North American Indians greatly respected visions, but few immersed themselves so deeply in them as did the Plains tribes. Sometimes a spirit might come of its own accord in a vision, just to befriend a mortal, but usually the Plains Indian had to go in active pursuit of his vision. He did this by isolating himself, fasting and thirsting, and practicing self-torture, at the same time imploring the spirits to take pity on his suffering. The youth gashed his arms and legs, and among the Crow it was the custom to cut off a joint from a finger of the left hand. Cheyenne vision-seekers thrust skewers of wood under pinches of skin in the breast; these skewers were attached to ropes, which in turn were tied to a pole. All day the youth leaned his full weight away from the pole, pulling and tugging at his own flesh while he implored the spirits to give him a vision.

Mortification of the flesh has always held a fascination for religious fanatics everywhere, for it is the most obvious way that this too, too human flesh can break its link with the world of men and approach the threshold of the gods. Among those who have groped toward deities in this way are the Jewish Essenes around the Dead Sea, the many ascetic orders of Christian monks, the Whirling Dervishes of Islam, and the hermits of Buddhism.

The spirit might at last take pity on the Plains Indian youth—actually it was dehydration, pain, and delirium taking their effects—and give him supernatural guidance. A successful vision supported the youth for the rest of his life. He always had a guardian spirit on whom he could call for help and guidance, although from time to time he had to repeat the self-torture to renew his familiarity with the spirit. During his vision, the youth usually learned what items—such as feathers, a stone pipe, a piece of skin, maize kernels—he should collect for a sacred medicine bundle and put in a small pouch. A particularly lucky youth might also receive his own songs, which when sung served as a call to supernatural aid; that they sounded like gibberish to everyone else only reinforced the belief that he had received a unique vision. A few youths failed to receive any visions at all, even though they tried repeatedly. Those who could not obtain a vision on their own could sometimes purchase one, as well as a replica of the successful visionary's sacred medicine bundle.

What is remarkable about such visions is that they were not invariably experienced, since the entire Plains culture worked toward producing them. Every Plains youth grew up believing firmly in the reality of the vision, so no resistance to the idea had to be overcome. Secondly, the youth worked himself into an intense emotional state by starvation, thirst, self-torture, exposure to the sun, and isolation—all of which are known to produce hallucinations. Thirdly, the shape in which the vision came to him was predetermined by the structure of the myths and visions he had heard about since childhood. Finally, in retelling his vision, he unconsciously reconstructed it and filled in gaps, adapting it to the norms of behavior of his culture—much as we do in reporting an incoherent dream, no matter how sincerely we believe we are not distorting it.

Plains Indian visions were clearly recognized as differing from person to person and from tribe to tribe. Some of the individual differences were biological and psychological. An Indian with an auditory personality might hear loud calls of birds or gibberish songs, whereas a visual type would be apt to see a horse with strange markings. Probably some individual fears and anxieties went into the vision. Despite the Plains warrior's attitude of fearlessness, a common vision was the sudden transformation of rocks and trees into enemies; but the youth was made invulnerable to their arrows by his guardian spirit. Often the vision involved the visit of some animal. An eagle might fly by, the flapping of its wings sounding like crashes of thunder; and bison, elk, bears, and hawks appeared quite often among the nobler beasts. Among the Pawnee (who, alone of the Plains tribes, had worked out an orderly system of religious beliefs, including a supreme being), the stars and other heavenly bodies entered quite freely into visions.

The desire for a vision existed among most of the Indians of North America, and it seems to have developed in two different directions. Among some Indians, it led directly to shamanism, for shamans were believed to be recipients of particularly intense visions and to have the power to summon up new visions at will. The other line of development led to visions of more limited power that had to be sought after. In this second category, there was a great range of variation, from the Plains youth, who suffered ordeals, to the Great Basin Shoshone, who passively waited for the spirit to find him.

Before the contrasting attitudes of the Plains tribes and the Great Basin Shoshone can be explained, the vision must first be recognized for what it is: a resort to supernatural aid in a dangerous undertaking, in which individual skill alone is not enough to guarantee success. The Plains culture provided numerous such dangerous undertakings, such as riding among a herd of stampeding bison or stealthily entering an enemy camp. For the Plains warrior, the rewards of such undertakings were certainly great enough to compensate for the few days of self-torture and fasting required to obtain a guardian spirit. The arid country of the Great Basin Shoshone, however, provided no such rewards. There the land yielded a bare minimum, and the rewards went not to the man who showed courage and daring, but to the one who simply exerted industry in collecting seeds or grasshoppers. Any yearning for visions that existed among the Great Basin Shoshone was not for protection in the dangers of the hunt or in warfare, but for the cure of snake bites or sickness.↕

The various responses of different cultures toward visions partly explains why some Indians took enthusiastically to the White man's alcohol and others did not. The use of firewater was particularly intense among the Plains, as well as among the nearby forest Indians, who were the ancestors of many Plains Indians. Alcohol was promptly recognized by the Plains Indians as a short-cut method of producing derangement of the senses and hallucinations. In primeval North America the Plains tribes had been remarkably free from the use of hallucinogenic plants such as peyote and mushrooms. The Plains vision-seekers were not even fortunate enough to have *Datura* or Jimsonweed, for its original range in the West was probably in only portions of the Southwest and southern California. Nor had the Plains tribes learned that tobacco, which they smoked in a few ritual puffs, could be swallowed to produce considerable discomfort and emotional upset, the way many Central and South American Indians used it.

Only when the Plains culture was disintegrating rapidly after about 1850 did a hallucinogenic cactus known as peyote take hold. Peyote is native to northern Mexico, but it spread like a grass fire from tribe to tribe as far north as the Canadian plains. Although peyote is used elsewhere in North America to a limited extent, it was most widely and promptly accepted by the Plains tribes. Peyote afforded a way to seek visions; it also provided an escape from the humiliation of the complete defeat by Whites in the latter part of the last century.

THE END OF A CULTURE

After the Civil War, a tide of White settlers streamed westward, and they sealed the fate of the Plains tribes. Treaty after treaty was broken by Whites as the Indian lands were crisscrossed by easterners covetous of acreage and precious metals. At first the Whites tried to restrict the Plains Indians to valueless territories, but that policy soon changed to a war of extermination. Said General William Tecumseh Sherman in 1867: "The more I see of these Indians, the more convinced I am that they all have to be killed or be maintained as a species of paupers." To help clear the Indians from the Plains, the Whites struck at their food base, the bison. They themselves not only destroyed the animals, but they also contrived to get the Indians to collaborate with them by offering to buy vast quantities of such delicacies as bison tongue.

Tensions between the Whites and the Plains Indians increased during the 1870's. On July 5, 1876, newspapers reporting celebrations of the young nation's Centennial reported also the news of a humiliating defeat. The elite Seventh Cavalry, a tough outfit of 260 men, which was organized specifically for killing Plains Indians—and led by Lieutenant Colonel Custer—had been annihilated on June 25 by a combined force of Sioux and Cheyenne in the battle of Little Bighorn. But for Sitting Bull and Crazy Horse, the victory over Custer had been empty, and only marked the beginning of the end for the Plains Indians. From that time on troops pursued them mercilessly from waterhole to waterhole; their women and children were slaughtered before their eyes, their encampments and their riches burned. The glory and the poetry had gone out of the Plains Indians. Mighty chiefs emerged from hiding as miserable fugitives, hungry and without bullets for their guns. The survivors, like so many cattle, were herded onto reservations, where rough handling, cheap whiskey, starvation, exposure, and disease severely depleted their numbers.

The very end of the Plains culture can be dated exactly. In 1890 the surviving Plains Indians enthusiastically listened to a native messiah who foretold the return of dead Indians and the magical disappearance of the Whites. Alarmed, the United States government sent out cavalry to suppress this Ghost Dance, as it was called. While being placed under arrest, Sitting Bull was accidentally killed; and some three hundred Sioux, mostly women and children waiting to surrender at Wounded Knee Creek, South Dakota, were massacred by trigger-happy troops. Wounded Knee marked the end of any hopes the Plains Indians still cherished. The Ghost Dance had proven as make-believe as the rest of their improbable culture.

Custer's last stand is seen in this drawing by an Indian veteran of the battle of Little Bighorn. Custer and about 250 men of the elite Seventh Cavalry were massacred in 1876, which resulted in the final White assault upon the few Plains groups that still held out.

THE CHIEFDOM

Northwest Coast: Status and Wealth

THE AFFLUENT SOCIETIES OF THE PACIFIC COAST

Northwest Coast culture refers to the Indian groups of diverse languages and physical stocks inhabiting the narrow strip of land between the continent's westernmost mountains and the Pacific Ocean, from eastern Alaska to northern California, a distance of some fifteen hundred miles. The subsistence pattern of all these Indians must technically be regarded as hunting-and-gathering. Yet, because of a fortuitous combination of environmental factors, their food supply was more like the abundance reaped from intensive agriculture. So rich are the products of the sea and the land along this coast that the Indians "harvested" them much as agricultural Indians living on fertile soils harvested their fields.

Much of the wealth along this coast is—or was, before the building of big dams and the effects of pollution destroyed the rivers—in huge salmon that swarm up the inlets and rivers on the way to their upstream breeding grounds. They used to be so numerous that at places they filled the rivers from bank to bank, and an early explorer averred that "you could walk across on their backs." The Indians learned to harvest this crop with ingenious traps, nets, and weirs. And since several different species of fish returned from the ocean to the rivers at different times of the year, the Indians could often count on five to seven major runs during the summer and fall. Salmon was only one of the products of the sea. In the spring there was the candlefish, so rich in oil that all the Indian had to do was run a wick through it. Cod and halibut swarmed in unbelievable numbers just

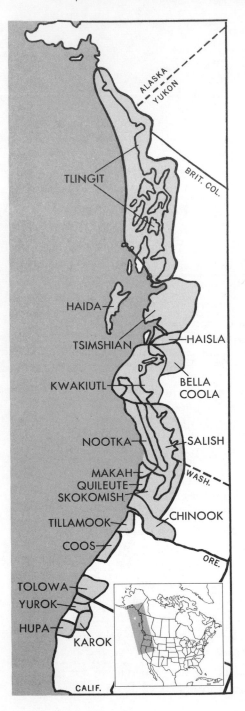

offshore, smelt sparkled in the surf, shellfish could be gathered all along the beaches and rocks. A little farther offshore the wealth in sea mammals could be harvested from large canoes: humpback whales, hair seals, sea lions, and the sea otters, whose pelts first attracted Whites to this coast. And all this abundance was for the taking.

Although the environment does not determine the kind of culture that will arise in any particular place, it nevertheless provides limitations and opportunities. The abundance of food on the Northwest Coast led to a population that was basically sedentary. The incredible yield of the seas, together with the discovery of ways to preserve fish by smoking and drying, resulted in the piling up of vast surpluses, which in turn gave rise to large populations, much larger than might be anticipated in a hunting economy not located in such a favorable environment. The Northwest Coast Indians might have developed any one of several different kinds of societies. But they handled this large population, which possessed a surplus of food, by developing elaborate institutions based largely on wealth, status, and rank.

A COMPLEX SOCIAL ORGANIZATION

A particular kind of social organization arose here—the chiefdom, which transcends the tribe in two important ways. A chiefdom usually has a more dense population; and the chiefdom is better integrated in its economic, social, and religious life. Chiefdoms arise most often in environments where an abundance of food and materials is obtained from a variety of sources such as the sea, beaches, forests, rivers, mountains. A lowly band exploits this kind of environment by moving from place to place, first fishing the river, then going to the forest to pick berries, later moving up the slopes to hunt big game, and so on. But a chiefdom can exploit such an environment differently and much more efficiently. In the chiefdom, the people do not move around. One group lives most of the time near the river, and it fishes; another resides in the forest, and it specializes in hunting game; a third gathers plant food. Each group channels the food and raw materials to a central authority—the "chief"—who then redistributes them to all.

Two areas exist in the New World where such environments prevail and where chiefdoms arose: the Northwest Coast and the Circum-Caribbean area (southeastern United States from Virginia to Texas, Central America south of Guatemala, the large islands of the West Indies, and Venezuela). In other parts of the world, chiefdoms were most abundant in the myriad islands of Polynesia, Micronesia, and Melanesia; among the steppe nomads of central Asia (including the Turkic and Mongol hordes of less than a thousand years ago); and in West Africa among the Ashanti, Benin, and Dahomey—before Whites taught them to become slavers.‡

Other places in North America also were blessed with an environment with the potentiality to yield a surplus, yet their hunters and gatherers remained at the band or tribal levels and never reached the level of the chiefdom. These people were unable to create a surplus because they never learned to preserve and to store food, and so there was no need for a central authority to redistribute goods. The Plains tribes were surrounded by the summer abundance of bison, but all they ever learned to do was to save some of the meat as jerkee or pemmican. For the rest of the year they were mostly at the mercy of the environment, living off their meager supplies and hoping to find stray bison during the winter. Lack of a technology of food storage places severe limits on how complex a society can become culturally, for the society has no way to sustain its social, economic, and political links during the long periods of scarcity. The Northwest Coast people, on the other hand, were remarkably efficient in developing a technology of food preservation; and they developed it for fish, a food that is notorious for spoiling very rapidly. Salmon were dried, smoked, and pressed together into bales. The roe from the females was

Abundance of the sea off the Northwest Coast was harvested by fishermen and harpooners in seagoing canoes. This Haida carving, made in the last half of the nineteenth century, shows a canoe filled with oarsmen. The Haida alone carved from argillite slate, which is comparatively soft while being carved, but which hardens after exposure to the air.

stored in seal bladders, or else it was smoked to produce what White settlers called Siwash cheese.

The chief was basically the group's economist. It was his responsibility to lay aside sufficient supplies of food and raw materials and to distribute them as needed. But he was also every bit as much a figurehead for his people as is the monarch of England today. The Tsimshian who lived on the coast opposite the Queen Charlotte Islands in British Columbia were bound together by loyalty to their chief and by participation in his activities. They took extravagant care of him from the cradle to the grave. They built his grandiose house, saw that he did no manual work, and financed his elaborate feasts given to demonstrate his superiority over a neighboring chief; and when it was all over they buried him with much mourning. If a member of another chiefdom even accidentally caused the slightest inconvenience to their chief, the Tsimshian rose as one to vengeance. Since the reputation of the Tsimshian among their neighbors depended upon the reputation of the chief himself, he could demand support and assistance in warfare.

The chief, though, had no political power and no way to back up his decisions. His control over the lives and property of his people existed only because of the prestige of his position and through the force of his own personality. The weakness inherent in the chiefdom was the chief's lack of legalized force to carry out his wishes. Those who live in complex modern society think in terms of political authority enforced overtly by the policeman on his beat or covertly by the Central Intelligence Agency acting through secret agents. A modern American assumes that political decisions made by his government will be enforced by specialists with legally sanctioned police powers. The chief lacked any such monopoly of force. He was the central authority, but if his personality lost its charm, then he no longer could function as chief. The Tsimshian chief, for example, always needed to court the favor of the heads of powerful lineages who served as his cabinet and advised in all affairs of importance. If they did not approve of his plans, they simply withheld their support, and he become politically paralyzed. Sometimes a strong chief successfully overruled opposition; but in most cases the chief realized that his powers were not as limitless as the horizon of the gray Pacific.‡

RANK AND STATUS

Once a man has been elevated to the position of chief, his whole lineage at the same time is elevated in rank and status. That is why, in the evolution of culture, rank appears for the first time at the level of the chiefdom; bands and tribes, on the other hand, are egalitarian. Every member of the chief's family becomes a little better than any member of any other family, a situation somewhat equivalent to Europe in the Middle Ages, when each new king created a new nobility of his family and descendants. In the case of the first Northwest Coast Indian to be made chief, his immediate family was his nobility. But as the generations passed and the family proliferated, the number of people related to the reigning chief became very great indeed, and their varying relationships formed an intricate web of connections with other lineages.

Once a society starts to keep track in this way of who is who, there is no telling where such genealogical bookkeeping will end. In Northwest Coast society it did not end until the very last and lowliest citizen knew his precise hereditary rank with a defined distance from the chief, and he knew it with exactitude. There is a record of a Kwakiutl feast in which each of the 658 guests from thirteen subdivisions of the chiefdom knew whether he was, say, number 437 or number 438. Such a situation is similar to the order in which a state or local government assigns its license plates, the numbers of which are usually based on rank and status but not necessarily on salary scale. The mayor may get number one and the head of the city council number two. But the head of the Department of Welfare may get number six while the equally salaried head of the Department of Sanitation may get number nine. Here is dramatized an essential difference between the hereditary chiefdom and the egalitarian tribe, where, at best, some headmen were slightly more equal than the people they led.

Because of concern with succession to power and with order of rank, which begin at the level of the chiefdom and continue into the primitive state and the modern industrialized state, people learn to keep track of their genealogies. In a band or a tribe, people usually cannot trace back their genealogies more than about three generations. But in a chiefdom, particularly among the higher ranks, the game of genealogies assumes great importance. Some Polynesian chiefs, for example, are supposed to have been able to reel off their genealogies going back fifty generations.

In most chiefdoms around the world, the emphasis on rank and status has resulted in a class system of chiefs, nobles, and commoners. But the Northwest Coast lacked classes, and instead there was a continuous gradation from the topmost chief down to the lowliest citizen. Each man was graded as evenly as the one-sixteenth-inch marks on a yardstick, equidistant from the man above him and from the man below him. Such precise ranking was similar to the ranking of the aristocracy in feudal Europe, the major difference being that the Northwest Coast had no mass of peasants under the aristocrat. A specialist in the Northwest Coast has wisely stated: "To insist upon the use of the term 'class system' for Northwest Coast society means that we must say that each individual was in a class by himself."‡

That is quite different from class equality, for no two people belonged to precisely the same class—and even identical twins were ranked in the order of their birth. The only equality lay in every man's knowledge that he had a place in the rank order. Although no distinct class of nobles was set off against a class of commoners, some individuals were generally recognized as "high" and others as "low," but it was impossible to define exactly the line between them. Unquestionably, someone at the top of the scale wore costly ornaments and strutted before everyone else at ritual occasions; unquestionably, someone at the bottom wore meaner garb and brought up the rear. But there was no precise point in the scale of gradations above which certain ornaments were acceptable and below which they were in poor taste.

The whole question of ranking in the Northwest Coast became of crucial importance at the potlatches, those extravagant feasts at which gifts were distributed to every guest. Gifts had to be given out in some kind of order to avoid a chaotic scramble, and the most logical way was to give the most important man his gift first; then the next highest ranking individual was given a somewhat lesser share, and so on down the line until the lowliest citizen received his pittance. By the time all gifts had been distributed, each knew the exact number of his rank; he knew also that this number had been announced to everyone at the potlatch, and that it would soon be known throughout the chiefdom.

Such a method of announcing rank to the world exists in Soviet Russia on the reviewing rostrum of the May Day parade. American political analysts join the Soviet citizens in carefully noting the distances of the dozens of officials from the center of the rostrum. From year to year, some officials rise in rank and move closer to the center while others fall in rank and stand farther away.

Each Northwest Coast Indian achieved his precise rank partly through birth and inheritance, partly through accident, and more rarely through social maneuvering. Opportunities for social mobility were few. Every parent wanted his child to marry someone of a greater rank; all these ambitions nullified each other, and so most marriages were between men and women of roughly equivalent rank. Inheritance and accident were much more important. Much as with European laws of primogeniture, the Northwest Coast Indians were reluctant to divide up inheritances. So a man usually passed on his estate intact to his eldest sister's eldest son if he belonged to the matrilineal Tlingit, Haida, Tsimshian, or Haisla—or to his own eldest son if he belonged to one of the patrilineal Northwest Coast societies.

Rank and status were important in all things, even in adultery. If the adulterous male belonged to a very high rank, the offended husband was the one who had to be quieted down; his clansmen gave him gifts, for if he sought revenge against a man of high rank, retribution might be brought against his entire clan. But adultery was handled much differently if the man were of low rank and the married woman of high rank. First, the wife's clan had to show to the world that it was offended, and it did that by killing two of the offending male's clansmen of a rank midway between the ranks of the two adulterers. Next, the adulterous male's clan was expected to offer for slaying one of its men equal in rank to the high rank of the woman. If this was done, the woman's clan was satisfied. As for the adulterous male himself, he usually became a debt-slave to his own clan to repay the losses that resulted from his being caught at adultery with a woman of high rank. Throughout all of these complicated maneuvers and compensations, the offended husband remained indoors until the entire affair had been settled. Then he grandly emerged and accepted lavish gifts from the adulterer's clan; translated into English, these gifts were known as "they wipe the shame from my face."↨

SUMPTUARY LAWS

Beginning at the level of the chiefdom and continuing up to today's industrialized state, society has had to cope with the problem of making clear its distinctions in rank and class. On the Northwest Coast, the *position* of chief had to be invested with its own dignity, in addition to the mere personality of the human who happened to occupy the post at that time. Similarly, all the world had to be told somehow that one man held a high rank while another held a low one. The simplest way for a society to set apart high offices, or even whole upper classes, is by sumptuary laws, which apply to differences in dress, ornamentation, and deportment allowed to privileged people. The Northwest Coast chief lived in the largest village, in the most ornate house, and the crests carved on it were the most ostentatious. Certain types of dress were appropriate only to the chief and to those with the highest rank. Most often the laws were concerned with dress and ornamentation: Only heads of lineages were allowed to wear ornaments made from abalone shell or to have their robes trimmed with sea-otter fur.

Sumptuary laws have arisen in other societies also. In the Aztec state, a commoner who built a stone house was punished by death. In Tudor England, only men entitled to be addressed as "lord" were permitted to wear sable fur. Sometimes sumptuary customs have resulted in different vocabularies and pronunciations—and even the use of a completely different language, such as the French spoken in Czarist Russia or Mandarin in China.

Somewhat similar are the status symbols of Modern America. During the years of the Great Depression in the United States, women tried to maintain pale complexions to show they did not rank so low that they had to labor outdoors. There were definite class distinctions in speech, both in pronunciation and in choice of vocabulary, and in dress. But in the more egalitarian society that followed World War II, the American upper class found its status barricades crumbling. A suntan sported in winter showed that a person had the leisure to follow the sun. However, those who did not have the leisure achieved the same results by investing in a sunlamp. Speech differences became less pronounced. Returning GI's from the slums took advantage of federal aid to go to Harvard, Yale, and Princeton. Within a few months after a high-ranking woman purchased a thousand-dollar dress from an Italian designer she might see a close imitation of it worn by her husband's secretary, who purchased it for only $24.95. The American of rank has constantly had to devise new sumptuary customs to protect his status. The rise of a "jet set," which flies to Paris for dinner and the opera and then home the next morning, is only one method being used currently to push back the assault by the middle classes.

PRIMITIVE SLAVERY

Only one gap existed in the orderly ranking of Northwest Coast society: the division between free men and "slaves." The latter were not really part of the society; they were usually war captives from some other chiefdom, were not related to anyone with rank in the society, and had no rank of their own. Unlike the true slaves of Western colonialism, they were not a productive part of the economy. They performed only menial tasks around the village, the same tasks that might be performed by a free man of very low rank. In most cases they did not produce enough even to earn their keep. They were merely tangible evidence that helped their owners validate rank. The "slave" was more a trophy of war and a prestige item than a producer of economic wealth. There is no justification for calling the Northwest Coast cultures "slave" societies, and in the rest of this discussion these people will be referred to as "captives."

Some White apologists have claimed that it is in man's nature to enslave other men; as evidence they have pointed to the Northwest Coast Indians or to Africans who formerly put other Africans in chains. The truth is that slavery has never been proved to exist in any primitive society beneath the level of the state, except where the primitives learned slave making from a more complex culture. Primitive peoples in West Africa and in the Philippines were taught the slave trade by the Spaniards; they were responding to the economic incentives of Western civilization and not to those of their own cultures. The closest any American Indian society ever came to slavery was the "debt slavery" practiced in some parts of the Northwest Coast, particularly in California and Oregon. Debts might be incurred in a variety of ways, most commonly by gambling. A man rescued from drowning also owed a debt to his rescuer, and if he could not pay it then he became his rescuer's debt-slave until the obligation was worked off, or, as was more likely, his kinsmen ransomed him. In every case, the master owned only the slave's economic services and was not allowed to harm him physically.

The Northwest Coast captive was an object of contempt, and he lacked any rights at all. Marriage was allowed only with other captives. A captive's only hope was to be ransomed by his kinsmen; usually his family made every effort to buy his return. Once back with his own people, he gave many face-saving feasts, but he never fully recovered his former rank. The stigma attached to having been a captive was so great that sometimes his relatives refused to ransom him because they did not want their family's shame back in their village.

A Northwest Coast captive could be killed at the whim of his master. Among the Tlingit, for example, it was the custom to put the body of a captive in the bottom of the hole dug to secure the heavy post for a new house. This was not intended to sanctify or to bless the house in any way, but just to show that the builder was of such high rank he could not only put up a house, but he could also dispose of one of his assets. For similar purposes of gaining prestige, sometimes the bodies of dead captives were used as rollers over which a visiting chief could slide his canoe to beach it. When a Northwest Coast Indian killed a captive, even one who had been living in his house for years, he undoubtedly did not consider such an act barbarous. To all intents and purposes, that person had been a dead man from the moment he allowed himself to be captured; killing him a few years later merely represented a delay in the execution of the sentence. However, captives were seldom put to death; an owner might just as easily free one as kill him, since in that way also the owner could show off his prestige.

SPECIALISTS IN RELIGION AND ART

Occupational specialization occurs to a minor degree in tribes, and even on rare occasions in bands, where the Eskimo owner of a whaling boat is a kind of specialist. A great leap forward occurs at the chiefdom level. Specialization becomes an integral part of the economic system, and it exists at every step from production through redistribution. The man who spends his time creating art needs berries, and the man who knows where to find berries usually does not know how to produce art; and both of them need fish from the sea and game from the forest. The central authority of the chiefdom can satisfy all these requirements, with the result that craftsmen, fishermen, berry pickers, and hunters can be specialists in their own occupations, yet also be assured of receiving through redistribution the other necessities of life.

Specialized work, such as hunting whales or seals, making canoes, carving totem poles, netting fish, tended to be perpetuated in families in the Northwest Coast, with the skills increasing from generation to generation. Certain families eventually assumed the roles of guilds in medieval times. In addition to the manual skills passed on from father to son (or from uncle to nephew), something else was needed—and that was ritual knowledge. A young man must first dream that he could perform the work he was destined for. Even though he came from a long line of wood carvers, he nevertheless still needed a vision as assurance that he could perform adequately as a wood carver. That is why the Northwest Coast youth was enthusiastic in his search for a vision. He flayed his body with thorns and immersed himself in cold lakes. Visions came to the youths almost in proportion to their rank. A ranking man's son quickly found the spirit helper who had helped his ancestors to become specialists in a particular kind of work. A poor youth usually had only weak or uninteresting visions, so he ended up in a less specialized occupation, perhaps performing only the menial task of gathering wood. Apparently the Northwest Coast culture did not encourage dreams of glory by those born at the lower levels of society. Captives were nonpersons and were not supposed to have any visions at all.

Religion was a specialized occupation also. In the chiefdom it may not appear much different from the shamanistic practices in many bands and tribes, but in reality several shifts in emphasis did occur. In a band a shaman cures only one particular person at a time, but in a chiefdom he has a broader role. He participates in ceremonials and rituals that have strong social functions rather than merely satisfy individual needs. He also operates within a cosmogony in which the supernatural beings are arranged in a genealogical rank that reflects the rank of the chiefdom's social system.

The greatest difference, though, is that in a chiefdom the shaman comes closer to the role of the priest—that is, one who is the permanent holder of a specialized religious office. In Eskimo society, anyone might become a shaman, particularly if he was distinguished by certain psychotic personality traits. In a Northwest Coast chiefdom, though, shamans tended to come from certain families that specialized in shamanism. In that way, the Northwest Coast shaman foreshadowed the permanent priesthood that emerged in the Aztec state. There also tended to be collusion in the chief-

The complexity of Northwest Coast art can be seen in this shaman's rattle, which shows a large raven with a human reclining on its back. The human is sucking on a frog's tongue to draw out a poison that the shaman believed to be of help in working spells. The frog's body itself emerges from the back of a hawk's head.

dom between the secular leader (the chief) and the spiritual leader (the shaman). They usually collaborated in matters of policy, and both offices occasionally descended in the same family line. And sometimes the same person even held both offices.

The results of specialization among the Northwest Coast Indians were most apparent in their art. The art of the Haida, Tlingit, and Tsimshian in particular produces a dramatic effect by its sheer size and power. But all Northwest Coast art has a more or less uniform style that is instantly recognized by the museum viewer. Figures of animals and mythical beings were carved or painted—usually with almost unvarying symmetry and with a tendency, approaching agoraphobia, to fill every inch of the surface—on totem poles, house fronts, canoes, wooden boxes, eating utensils, in fact practically any surface. All the art was produced in the context of a status society. A Northwest Coast Indian would have regarded as ridiculous the thought that a house-front carving served to make the house more attractive. Such a carving had only one justification: It glorified the social and economic position of the house owner and aroused the envy of his neighbors. Much of the Northwest Coast art took the form of intricate crests, because certain beings, both mortal and supernatural, were associated with particular lineages. To display such crests was to announce one's status, as was the display of crests in Europe in past centuries.

TOTEM POLES

The most dramatic and best known manifestation of Northwest Coast art was the huge totem pole—a quite misleading name given these carvings by

Whites. A pole that displayed a bear, an eagle, and a beaver, with a few mythological beings thrown in for good measure, represented not a totem but simply a crest, a pride in one's ancestry and a glorification of high rank.

The person who paid to have the pole carved and painted also had this same combination of figures painted or carved elsewhere: on a mortuary pole alongside the grave of a relative, on his household furnishings, on the posts and beams of his house, and on the family's canoes. Probably the best way to understand the totem pole is to regard it as similar in function to a cattleman's brand in Texas. This also is an artificial emblem, often composed of the family's initial, together with arbitrary symbolic elements such as a bar or a circle. Say that the Johnson family burns the Circle-J brand on all of its cattle to show ownership. But the Johnson family probably will not stop there. The brand will also be carved over the front gate and over the entrance to the corral. The brand may also be carved on the house door, cast in metal for the door knocker, painted on the mailbox, and etched on crystal ash trays in the living room. It may be carved into the leather of the boots worn by members of the family; and some families may even display their brands on bathroom fixtures.

Many reasons have been given for the production of art in different cultures: religious adoration, magic, esthetics, and so forth. But probably no other culture besides the Northwest Coast had ridicule and boasting as its incentive for art. A totem pole was intended to outface and browbeat the neighbors by telling how distinguished its owner and his ancestors were. Among the great events that a chief might want recorded in a new pole was the way in which he outwitted another chief, and for that reason some poles are nothing more than billboards that advertise the humiliation inflicted upon someone else. Several of the carved beings on one pole in the Haida village of Old Kassan are undoubtedly Russian priests. The owner of the pole was extremely proud of having successfully resisted attempts by the priests to convert him in the nineteenth century. He had defeated the priests in a contest of wills, in the same way that he might have defeated a neighboring chief in warfare. So he felt entitled to record the event and to ridicule the priests on his pole.

Seeing the weathered and cracked poles, either in a museum or still in place in Alaska and British Columbia, one is likely to consider them to be of great antiquity. The truth is that almost all are quite recent—most of them less than a hundred years old, with only a few as old as a hundred and fifty years. So a question arises: To what extent are totem poles an indigenous art? The first totem pole was not described by a White explorer until 1791; yet, more than a hundred vessels from Europe and the United States had already visited the Northwest Coast to trade during the twenty years before that. Some of these ships had in their crews Filipinos and Hawaiians who might have passed on the art to the Indians; indeed, the closest approximation to totem poles anywhere in the world exists in the islands of the Pacific Ocean. It is possible also that some ships from Asia might have reached the Northwest Coast even before the Whites arrived, bringing with them the idea of totem poles.↕

The question of whether totem poles are indigenous or resulted from alien contacts is not an idle one, for the answer may help to explain how cultures change. First, the fact is inescapable that the *idea* of the totem pole was indigenous to the Northwest Coast culture: One function of the totem pole was its connection with the mortuary rites for a chief, and this tradition existed long before the arrival of the first Whites. Second, although the earliest White explorers did not report any large totem poles, they did report that the custom of painting a crest for a house or a grave was an

Totem poles at the abandoned Kwakiutl village of Alert Bay, British Columbia, boast of real and fictitious events in family histories.

ancient and honored one on the Northwest Coast. But it is also true that previous to the coming of the Whites, these Indians possessed no metal tools, and the carving of the huge totem poles was impossible without them. So the conclusion is that when one looks at a totem pole in a museum, he sees both a fascinating concept as well as a mere object. The *idea* of a totem pole had been part of the Northwest Coast culture for perhaps thousands of years, yet the idea could not be executed because the technology of iron tools was not available. Then the Whites arrived with cheap iron and released a tendency that had been bottled up for all that time.

THE ECONOMICS OF PRESTIGE

The Northwest Coast culture was one in which social rank was exemplified by economic wealth. The two went hand in hand. Common to almost the entire Northwest Coast was wealth in the form of dentalia shells. Shells of the same size were strung on strings of a specified length, and the value of a string increased markedly in proportion to the size of the shells strung on it. Early in the nineteenth century, a string with eleven large shells was worth about $50. A string of the same length that contained fifteen smaller shells was worth a mere $2.50. But to interpret dentalia as money is to misunderstand the culture of the Northwest Coast Indians. They did not translate the cost of something into a certain number of shells, as a modern American does with coins or bills, then decide whether or not it was worth the purchase price. Actually, in the prolific environment of the Northwest Coast, with its abundant resources and its chiefs to ensure redistribution, there was no need to purchase the essentials of subsistence. An Indian did not need money to buy food or clothes, but he did need it to purchase social recognition. Ownership of a large number of shell strings was not a way to improve his diet or his haberdashery, but it did confer prestige. When one village had to humble another for an insult to its chief, it often demanded that compensation be paid in the form of dentalia. If someone was entitled to a reward, dentalia strings enhanced his prestige more than its equivalent value in a small canoe.

Status, as demonstrated by economic wealth, constantly had to be reaffirmed in the Northwest Coast. The modern system of tipping usually represents only a petty annoyance to the tippers (although it does function in our society in helping to redistribute wealth). Tipping reached astounding proportions in the Northwest Coast, and a man who wanted to maintain his rank was almost constantly handing out small gifts. If invited to a feast, he had to tip whoever invited him. If someone mentioned his name with reverence, the immediate reward was a gift. If he stumbled at a ceremonial—which exposed him to possible ridicule, with its resultant loss of status—he had to give presents to the onlookers to restore his dignity. For these reasons he left his house in the morning wearing several blankets that he could give to people who performed important services for him during the day; he also carried many lesser presents that he tossed away as casually as a modern American tips a delivery boy.

The really amazing thing about the Northwest Coast economic system was that it worked without laws to enforce it. It was kept going by vanity, prestige, and ridicule. Economic products were assembled in vast surpluses, and they flowed in the direction of the chief via his nobles and their even lowlier satellites. Such a flow was neither tax nor tribute, as it was in the Aztec state. Perhaps the reason the system worked was that the participants sensed that sooner or later they would get back a comparable amount of goods at a feast known as a "potlatch." The word originally came from the Nootka *patshatl*, "to give," but as Whites penetrated the Northwest Coast a sort of pidgin English developed that was basically a jargon of the Chinook language. The Chinook altered the word *patshatl* into the one that Whites came to use: "potlatch." (The Chinook jargon also called home-brewed liquor *hootchenoo*, which is, of course, the origin of the American "hootch.") Potlatches were given as soon as a group of people could amass enough property to serve as hosts; but the memorable potlatches were those given by the chiefs. The chiefdom gathered surpluses from the whole population, and then its chief feasted another chief. Everyone understood that in a year or two the guest chief would reciprocate, at which time his surplus goods would be given as presents to the chief who had been his host.

This whole bizarre system differed from what we, trained in a market economy, are used to. We would be inclined to handle such a series of transactions competitively. We would try to get the better of the bargain at each step as goods changed hands. The competitive attitude of the Northwest Coast Indians, though, was just the opposite. Their competitiveness lay in trying to give away more than was received, in order to humble someone else. And what to us is simply an economic transaction, to the Northwest Coast Indians was gift-giving. Their potlatches produced incidental benefits that our system of trade does not. The participants got a lavish feast as a dividend, plus the occasion for good fellowship and for building up peaceful relations with neighbors. By means of the seating arrangement at the feast and the order in which gifts were distributed, the feast also filled the important social function of validating the rank of each participant.

As soon as plans for a potlatch were announced, vast quantities of oil, carvings, blankets, iron tools, and other valued items were assembled; sometimes, for a really memorable potlatch, years of preparation were necessary. Everyone contributed willingly to the potlatch, for it was an opportunity once again to validate rank. If anyone lagged in participation, he might find himself dropped down several notches. A potlatch also offered an opportunity to humiliate another lineage or another chief by hosting a grander potlatch than had been received previously. The competition grew to such an extent that given away at one Kwakiutl potlatch were eight canoes, six captives, fifty-four elk skins, two thousand silver bracelets, seven thousand brass bracelets, and thirty-three thousand blankets —and the guests consumed about fifty seals. (My discussion of the potlatch has been in the past tense, for the lavish potlatches belonged to the last century. But it is also true that so deeply embedded was the idea of the potlatch in the Northwest Coast culture that even today the remnant populations of these chiefdoms exchange gifts. Sewing machines, refrigerators, bedspreads, bolts of cloth, and similar goods keep changing hands far in excess of their actual use or need.)

At its very end, the potlatch degenerated into such an orgy of waste and competitive destruction that the system devoured itself. The Northwest Coast chiefdoms had originated the potlatch as one way to redistribute the surplus with which their seas and forests had endowed them. But the Whites, in their scramble to obtain sea-otter and fur-seal pelts, pumped vast amounts of fresh wealth into a system already trying to cope with a surplus. The potlatch simply could not handle the new flood of mass-produced fabrics, guns, metal kitchen utensils, cheap jewelry, steel tools, and other products of industrialized Europe and the United States. So one cause for the explosion of the potlatch was the deluge of White wealth that the Northwest Coast surplus economies did not need.

A second factor was that diseases introduced by the Whites' trading ships and the deadly warfare due to the Whites' guns caused Northwest Coast populations to plummet. Fewer Indians were available to share the fantastic abundance. Furthermore, the numerous deaths left open more noble titles and crests than there were persons of high rank to bear them. The humble man who had been among the last to receive his small present at the previous year's potlatch suddenly found himself, through the death of those ahead of him, a contender for the role of heir presumptive to the chief. He was not the sole contender, however; probably half a dozen other humble men had also risen for the same reason.

A bitter competition developed to give potlatches of unprecedented lavishness. The sole rationale for these potlatches was to allow one man to claim prestige over another so he could fill a vacant high rank. No longer did the potlatch serve its traditional functions of redistributing wealth, validating rank, and making valued alliances. The wealth of these new rich seemed limitless, more than they could ever consume at a potlatch. So they instead destroyed vast amounts of wealth before the horrified eyes of the guests, as well as the other contenders, to dramatize the extent of their holdings. Fortunes were tossed into potlatch fires; canoes were destroyed; captives were killed. The competing claimants had no alternative but to destroy even more property at *their* potlatches.

Competitive potlatching went wild, particularly so among the Kwakiutl, where an intricate system of credits to finance the feasts developed. Despite the belief of early anthropologists, there was no fixed rate of interest. A typical interest charge for a loan of less than six months was about twenty percent or so; for six months to a year, forty percent; for one year, a hundred percent. But if the borrower had poor credit, the rate might rise to two hundred percent for less than a year. The borrower then promptly loaned out what he had borrowed to someone else, at an even higher rate of interest if he could get it. Within only a few decades, everyone was in debt to everyone else. In one Kwakiutl village, the population of somewhat more than a hundred people possessed only about four hundred actual blankets. Yet, so pyramided had the system of debts, credits, and paper profits become that the total indebtedness of everyone in the village approached 75,000 blankets.

We, trained in a capitalistic society, are horrified by the financial panic that would have resulted if just one person called in his loans. But it never occurred to a Northwest Coast Indian to do that. The point of his loans was not to make a profit, but rather to validate the higher rank he was reaching for. If he called in his loan, it would stop earning prestige and obligations for him. One escape valve, though, prevented the inflated economy from bursting: the destruction of "coppers," hammered and decorated sheets of raw metal nearly three feet long that the Indians had obtained from Whites. A copper was like a bank note of very high denomination. At first it represented several thousand blankets. But as the demand for the scarce coppers grew, it rose in value again and again, until each was worth blankets almost beyond calculation. One Kwakiutl copper purchased originally for four hundred blankets rose to a value of twenty-three thousand blankets (worth about $11,500 in the early years of this century).

A contender for rank ultimately found himself in a position whereby the only way he could humiliate a wealthy rival was to destroy one of the precious coppers. The act was equivalent to wiping out all the debts owed to him. It was an incredible price to pay, but the man who made such a dramatic gesture no doubt rose meteorically in rank.✝

THE RISE AND FALL OF CHIEFDOMS

The chiefdom possessed potential for expansion because of its own internal growth, and because it could absorb additional people through conquest and even through the desire of a nearby tribe to become part of the redistribution system. Records exist of bands and tribes that voluntarily joined Northwest Coast chiefdoms, undoubtedly because they recognized the economic benefits. Such growth was of advantage to the chiefdom, for it usually incorporated a group that inhabited a different sort of environment and could bring new products into the redistribution system. In all the Northwest Coast chiefdoms, there was a tendency to expand up to the limits of their topographical boundaries of fjords, mountains, dense forests, or the sea itself.

Anthropologists have disputed the part that warfare may have played in this expansion. The point was made in previous chapters that bands and tribes never fight for additional living space or to increase their population, as they lack the complex social organization to integrate the conquered peoples into their own societies. Chiefdoms, however, easily assimilate conquered peoples and occupy their lands, and that is why true warfare appears for the first time at this level of social organization. Northwest Coast warfare was not the skirmish and the ambush of the Iroquois or the coups ceremony of the Plains Indians. Rather, Northwest Coast wars were expeditions organized to exterminate or capture the enemy and to win his lands and wealth. Records exist of bitter and prolonged wars for the purpose of occupying territory—such as the Tlingit driving Eskimo bands off Kayak Island, and the Haida forcing the Tlingit to withdraw from parts of Prince of Wales Island.

Yet, as the chiefdom grows it contributes to its own decline. Usually it becomes so large that it no longer can redistribute goods efficiently. In that case, the citizens whose voluntary compliance is the cornerstone of the economic system may decide to leave it. When a man gets to be number 987 in the ranking system, sooner or later it occurs to him to join with Mr. 986 and some of the other lesser figures to form a chiefdom of their own. They are so far removed from the central authority that their departure is scarcely noticed. Nor could the chief force them to remain within the redistribution system, for a chief lacks police power to carry out his wishes.

The expansion and fragmentation of chiefdoms on the Northwest Coast were of such common occurrence that they are probably characteristic of this level of social organization. Usually some excuse was given for the break-up: warfare, a revolt by malcontents, a dispute over succession to the office of chief, and so on. Often, though, clear and obvious abuses in the office of the chief were the real causes. The chief, the specialist who directed redistribution, consumed a disproportionate amount of the production because of his many wives, his rank-conscious kinsmen, his private shamans, and his personal artisans. Whatever the reason, sooner or later the chiefdom fragmented into smaller groups, and the whole process of waging wars of territorial expansion began again. But any new Northwest Coast chiefdom was as unstable as the old. Every chiefdom is fated to collapse eventually, because it lacks one essential: the use of *legal* force, which does not exist until the level of the Aztec state is reached.

Natchez: People of the Sun

THE FRENCH ROMANTICS

Of the many glittering chiefdoms in southeastern North America, none outshone those that belonged to the Muskogean language family in Georgia, Alabama, Mississippi, and parts of Louisiana and Tennessee. The Muskogeans once numbered well upward of 50,000 people and included such groups as the Chickasaw, the Choctaw, the Creek, and the Seminole. Of them all, the grandest were the Natchez (since this is a French word, although of uncertain meaning, it is pronounced as if written *natchay*). The Natchez occupied at least nine villages, one of which was inhabited by the chief and was therefore known as the Great Village, in the vicinity of the present-day city of Natchez, Mississippi. Although there is considerable dispute about their aboriginal population, they are thought to have numbered about 4,500, and possibly a good deal more than that.

Their sedentary village life was based on agriculture, and maize was its base. The names for the thirteen months into which they divided the year indicate that they relied upon a variety of other foods as well, both wild and cultivated: Deer, Strawberries, Little Corn, Watermelons (probably introduced by the Spaniards), Peaches (possibly obtained from English settlements on the Atlantic coast), Mulberries, Great Corn, Turkeys, Bison, Bears, Cold Meal, Chestnuts, and Nuts. In addition, wild rice was sown on the banks, and seeds were gathered from wild plants; and a large wolflike dog, which helped hunters to tree turkeys and bears, was itself sometimes used for food. Clearly, the environment and the economy of the Natchez provided one of the essentials for the formation of a chiefdom: a wide diversity of foods that could be directed to a central authority for redistribution.

The Natchez were probably the people about whom de Soto, when he marched through their lands in 1542, reported that they dominated all their neighbors. The Natchez, devout worshipers of the sun, heard de Soto's claim that he was the sun's younger brother, but they were more skeptical than the Indians of Mexico who at first welcomed the Spaniards as gods. The Natchez asked that de Soto prove his claim by using his powers to dry up the Mississippi River. Unable to present such credentials, the survivors of de Soto's expedition were harassed by fleets of Natchez canoes during their escape back to Mexico down the Mississippi River. The Natchez do not again appear in history until 1682 when La Salle visited one of their villages. After that, their decline was swift: The French crushed them in a series of wars and sold the survivors into slavery.

In the short time that they permitted them to survive, the French were strangely fascinated by the Natchez. Perhaps the reason was that of all the Indians the French had seen from Canada to the West Indies, they regarded the Natchez as closest to the standards, ideals, and even morality of the Court of Versailles. Poetic metaphor described King Louis XIV as *le Roi Soleil*, "the sun king" of all France, but the Natchez seemed to have brought the metaphor into reality in their social and political system. "The sun is the principal object of veneration to these people," wrote Maturin Le Petit, a Jesuit priest, reporting on his visit to the Natchez in 1699, and "as they cannot conceive of anything which can be above this heavenly body, nothing else appears to them more worthy of their homage. It is for the same reason that the great chief of this nation, who knows nothing on earth more dignified than himself, takes the title of brother of the Sun, and the credulity of the people maintains him in the despotic authority which he claims."‡ Le Petit was particularly impressed by the high temple mounds the Natchez had built in order, he said, that the earthly sun and the heavenly sun could converse: "Every morning the great chief honors by his presence the rising of his elder brother, and salutes him with many howlings as soon as he appears above the horizon . . . Afterwards raising his hand above his head and turning from the east to the west, he shows him the direction which he must take in his course."

THE GREAT SUN

The chief of the Natchez, known as the Great Sun, was an intensification of the characteristics of the chief seen in the Northwest Coast. In fact, the entire Natchez society was as completely a chiefdom as it was possible to be without evolving to the next level of the state. The Great Sun and the most important nobles, known simply as Suns, were treated with extreme deference. The people always gave way before them and never turned their backs when withdrawing from these exalted presences. Only a few select elders and the Great Sun's wives might even enter his cabin. He was carried about on a litter moved at a fast pace by relays of eight men who, without breaking step, passed it from one team to another. The noted French explorer Charlevoix was impressed by the Great Sun's power and stated that he "acknowledges no superior but the Sun, from which he pretends to derive his origin. He exercises an unlimited power over his subjects, can dispose of their goods and lives, and for whatever labors he requires of them they cannot command any recompense."

As the redistributing agency, the Great Sun possessed an authority that would have been envied even by a Northwest Coast chief. He redistributed not only food and raw materials, but also manpower. Le Petit reported that "the French, who are often in need of hunters or of rowers for their long voyages, never apply to anyone but the great Chief. He furnishes all the men they wish, and receives payment, without giving any part to those unfortunate individuals, who are not permitted even to complain." The Frenchman's admiration for the authority possessed by the Great Sun was no doubt colored somewhat by the Frenchman's own authoritarian political system of the time; for, despite appearances, the Great Sun was not a complete despot. He could on a whim order the execution of anyone who displeased him, yet in matters of general concern to the chiefdom he was very much limited by a council of elders.

The Great Sun served as the symbol and rallying point for the entire chiefdom. When a male child destined to inherit the title of Great Sun was born, nobles and commoners alike brought forth their children from whom the Great Sun's future retainers were chosen. And when the Great Sun died, the funeral rites were spectacular. His wives, guards, and other retainers were expected to die also; and the rest of the population vied for the privilege of accompanying the Great Sun into the afterworld. About four days after death his body was borne in pomp toward the temple. Those who had volunteered to accompany him into death swallowed a concoction of tobacco that caused them to lose consciousness, and they were promptly strangled by their relatives. Then the cabin of the Great Sun was burned, and the fires in the village were extinguished. After several months his bones were exhumed, separated from any flesh that remained, and placed in a basket within the temple. Several temple guardians were also strangled at this second burial.

The Natchez chiefdom was a theocracy, pure and simple, and both secular and sacerdotal authority were embodied in the Great Sun. His large cabin was built atop a mound; nearby stood a similar mound, crowned by the temple. "All around it runs a circle of palisades on which are seen exposed the skulls of all the heads which their Warriors had brought back from the battles," reported Le Petit. The two mounds were located close to each other, Le Petit believed, to enable the Great Sun and the celestial sun "better to converse together." Inside the temple were the bones of the Great Sun's ancestors, and there burned the symbol of his authority, the eternal fire.

Only the Great Sun and a few priestly officials appointed by him were

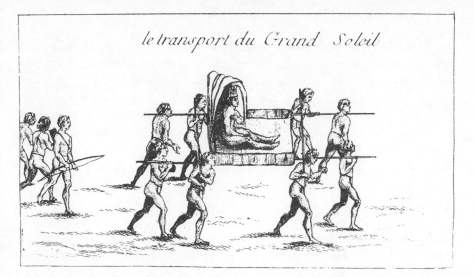

le transport du Grand Soleil

The Great Sun of the Natchez, who is being carried to the harvest festival by a relay of litter-bearers, was sketched by the French explorer Du Pratz in the early 1700's.

permitted to enter the temple, but Le Petit had either gained entrance or obtained a good description of its interior, for he observed: "Their Religion in certain points is very similar to that of the ancient Romans. They have a temple filled with Idols, which are different figures of men and of animals, and for which they have the most profound veneration . . . These are figures of men and women made of stone or baked clay, the heads and the tails of extraordinary serpents [probably rattlesnakes], some stuffed owls, some pieces of crystal, and some jaw bones of large fish." He also added that the Natchez had obtained a glass bottle from the French and that they guarded it inside the temple as a very precious object.

RULER AS SUPREME PRIEST

The cult of the sun represented the official religion of the chiefdom. It was sanctioned by the chief himself and its priesthood was stamped with his official approval. Its theology was quite complex, but it was based on a supreme deity who lived in the sky and was closely connected with the sun (he may indeed have been identical with it, but the early French reports are confused on this point). The Natchez believed that in the distant past the son of this deity had descended to earth and brought civilization to them as his own chosen people, giving them those laws, customs, ceremonies, and arts that made them powerful over their neighbors. Then this deity had retired into a stone that was ever afterward preserved in the principal temple; he left the actual governing of his people to the Great Sun. One third of the space in the cabin built atop the temple mound was devoted to this stone; the rest of the cabin housed the hampers filled with the sacred bones of former Great Suns.

The French priests and explorers reported that every evening and every morning the Great Sun came to the temple to worship the idols, and then announced to the people what the idols had foretold. Here, too, the Great Sun brought as offerings the first fruits of the harvest, clearly showing that the ideas of redistributor and supreme priest had become entwined, as happened also in the chiefdoms of Polynesia. A perpetual fire was maintained in the temple by special guardians, who were punished by death if they allowed it to go out. This fire could not be profaned for any earthly purposes, even for cooking the Great Sun's meals, for it burned solely in honor of the celestial sun. Fire caused by lightning also was revered greatly as a manifestation of the sun, and a bolt that destroyed a temple was regarded as a certain sign of divine wrath. In that event, the deity had to be placated, and so women threw their infants into the flames.

The priesthood represented a specialized profession in most chiefdoms of the Southeast, from the Natchez all along the coastal plain to the Powhatan of Virginia. Such priests were in charge of temples and ossuaries, and their training to carry out the complicated rites and ceremonies required many years. The priesthood naturally opposed those freelance manipulators of the supernatural, the shamans, but shamanism could no more be extirpated from the Natchez chiefdom than superstition has been eliminated from modern society. Anyone, for example, who had been struck by a bolt of lightning and lived to tell about it was thought to have gained thereby the power to cure disease. Shamans were, however, neutralized by being given harmless official duties. It was their function, for example, to bless the tobacco pills that were swallowed before strangulation.

The Natchez had a very clear concept of the afterworld, and it appeared most attractive to them. They therefore went willingly to their deaths, either as companions to their deceased Great Sun or as warriors. "They believed in the immortality of the soul, and when they leave this world they go, they say, to live in another, there to be recompensed or punished," reported Le Petit.

The rewards to which they look forward consist principally in feasting, and their chastisement in the privation of every pleasure. Thus they think that those who have been the faithful observers of their laws will be conducted into a region of pleasures, where all kinds of exquisite viands will be furnished them in abundance, that their delightful and tranquil days will flow on in the midst of festivals, dances, and women; in short, they will revel in all imaginable pleasures.

But those who had violated the laws or the traditions had a different sort of world to look forward to, one where they

will be cast upon lands unfruitful and entirely covered with water, where they will not have any kind of corn, but will be exposed entirely naked to the sharp bites of mosquitoes, that all Nations will make war upon them, that they will never eat meat, and have no nourishment but the flesh of crocodiles, spoiled fish, and shell-fish.

CASTE VERSUS CLASS

Among the Northwest Coast Indians, each man was ranked in a class by himself, but the Natchez possessed distinct hereditary classes. At the top, of course, was the Great Sun himself, who was the eldest son of White Woman (descent was matrilineal). His next younger brother was designated Little Sun, and he also held the post of Great War Chief. All the remaining brothers bore the titles of Suns. Beneath the topmost Suns were the Nobles, then the Honored People—and finally, at the bottom of the class system, the Stinkards. (In polite Natchez society no member of the nobler classes ever called someone "Stinkard" to his face, in the same way that southern Whites of good breeding today never call a Negro "nigger" to his face, although the word may trip easily from their tongues behind his back.)

The Natchez class system has occasionally been regarded as a caste system, but such was not the case at all. A caste system rigidly isolates people, but the remarkable fact about the Natchez class system was that it did just the opposite. Every member of the three noble classes had to marry a Stinkard. Furthermore, marriage alliances were made only in certain combinations, and the offspring of these combinations almost always belonged to a different class from their father. To be born a Sun, one needed a Sun mother and a Stinkard father. To be born a Noble, one's mother had to to be a Noble and therefore married to a Stinkard. But a male Sun had to marry a Stinkard woman, and so his son fell a notch, being a mere Noble instead of a Sun like his father. The Stinkard class itself was perpetuated by two kinds of unions: either marriage between an Honored father and a Stinkard mother, or marriage between two leftover Stinkards who had not been able to make a match with someone in the nobility.

To us, familiar with the rules of succession to European thrones, this complex system may seem preposterous. Even though the Great Sun was supreme, with each generation his male line regressed one step in class. His son was a Sun who was forced to marry a Stinkard woman—and so their offspring, the Great Sun's grandson, dropped down to the Noble class. When it came time for this Noble grandson to marry, he also had to choose a Stinkard woman, and so the great-grandson was born a mere Honored. Finally, the great-great-grandson of the Great Sun was reduced to the class of a lowly Stinkard. Another peculiarity of this class system was that the Stinkard class was constantly being depleted because of the drain of furnishing marriage partners to the nobility. You can easily calculate that more Stinkards were lost to the nobility than were being created by the single marriage combination of an Honored man and a Stinkard woman. The Natchez would eventually have lost all their Stinkards to the upper classes did not some compensating mechanism exist. This mechanism was the conquest by the Natchez of neighboring peoples who were then added to the Stinkard class.↕

In the female line, White Woman was the mother of the Great Sun. Her eldest daughter, the sister of the reigning Great Sun, succeeded to the title of White Woman at her death. This daughter's eldest son would therefore become the next Great Sun, and her eldest daughter the next White Woman. In that way the title of Great Sun remained in the female line— while with each generation the male line of the Great Sun sank lower until his great-great-grandson was reduced to the Stinkard class. This male line could bounce back to the nobility if the Stinkard great-great-grandson managed to marry a Sun woman; but never again could any male descendant of a Great Sun become another Great Sun.

As in the Northwest Coast chiefdoms, the noble classes were set apart by sumptuary laws and customs. Within each Natchez village, the location, the size, and the richness of furnishings of the dwellings reflected the differences in class. All children, of both sexes and of all classes, were entitled to tattoo a simple mark across the face. But as they rose in rank later on they could add to it tattoos of sun symbols, serpents, and other patterns. The entire body of a person of very high rank or of a distinguished warrior was covered with a bewildering array of patterns. In the matter of dress, only men of the higher classes could wear breechclouts dyed black; all other men wore white ones. Only Sun women were permitted to adorn their hair with diadems made from the feathers of swans. There was much conspicuous consumption and display among the higher classes, and all of it came out of the productive labors of the entire community. The sumptuary laws, though, served notice on the masses that the chief, his close nobility, and his priests maintained a vested interest in the surplus.

Despite the rigidity of the marriage rules and the hereditary class system, opportunities for advancement nevertheless did exist. In fact, there was much more social mobility among the Natchez than among the Northwest Coast Indians. The broadest avenue for advancement lay in warfare. Through his prowess and warlike exploits, even a Stinkard might become an Honored; and if he lifted himself out of the Stinkard class, then his wife rose with him. As soon as a Stinkard performed his first great deed in war and was advanced to the class of Honored men, he received a new name, and new tattoo marks attested to his rise. It was much more difficult, though, to make the jump from Honored to Noble, for the warrior had either to take twenty scalps or to obtain ten captives. The early French reports are not clear whether it was possible for a warrior to move up more than a single notch in his lifetime; it appears he was not.

THE LAST OF THE MOUND BUILDERS

Anthropologists do not agree about the origins of the Natchez and several other southeastern cultures. Many of the hallmarks of these cultures are strikingly similar to other chiefdoms found around the borders of the Caribbean Sea, the Gulf of Mexico, and the South Atlantic coastal plain. Some of these similarities are a political organization based on a chief and the practice of carrying him on a litter; a religious system based on temple mounds, a specialized priesthood, idols, and a perpetual fire; a war system that rewards exploits with changes in name and elevation in rank or class.

Some of these similarities can be explained by similar responses by groups to the same environment, by tendencies inherent in the chiefdom organization itself, and by sheer accident. Many of the specific culture elements, though, were undoubtedly due to diffusion. The Indians of the Caribbean possessed seaworthy dugouts, and the early explorers reported seeing the Indians far out at sea. Bartholomew Columbus, for example, in 1502 met Maya dugouts on their way back to Yucatán after trading in

Beheading of a captive by a warrior is shown in a sculpture that dates from the Late Mississippian. The Natchez were probably among the last survivors of this Mound Builder culture that was overwhelmed by Whites.

Central America. The Arawak crossed from South America to settle many islands in the West Indies and part of Florida as well. The Carib Indians even made three-masted dugouts. Many other Indian groups in Mexico and Central America—among them the Mosquito, Sumo, Paya, Jicaque, Cuna, Guaymi, and Cabecar—are known to have possessed sturdy craft and to have made voyages across the inland sea of the Caribbean.

Diffusion does not fill all the gaps in knowledge about the Natchez. It appears probable that the Natchez and some other chiefdoms in southeastern North America represented a lingering into historical times of the great Mound Builder culture which arose about A.D. 500 along the Mississippi River and its tributaries. But this glittering culture that had taken hundreds of years to evolve disappeared with amazing rapidity after the arrival of the Whites. The Indians suffered the usual depopulation due to the introduction of European diseases, but most of the deaths in the southeastern chiefdoms were the result of colonial rivalry between France and England. Both countries exerted strong influence there and they were determined to fight it out between themselves—down to the life of their last Indian pawn.

Exactly thirty years after the first French missionary visited them in 1699, the Natchez made their final desperate attempt to fight back. They attacked a French trading post and massacred about two hundred Whites. Retaliation was brutal, and within only two years the French and their Choctaw allies had utterly crushed the Natchez. Most of the Natchez were slaughtered, and about four hundred captives (including the Great Sun) were sold into slavery in Santo Domingo in the West Indies. A few miraculously escaped and took refuge with the Chickasaw, Creek, and Cherokee. The sacred fire of the Natchez that was intended to burn as long as the sun shone was forever extinguished. Remarkably, in 1940 two old people of Natchez ancestry were discovered living among the Cherokee, and they still spoke the old language.‡ When they died, nothing remained of the Natchez culture. Though Natchez blood still flows here and there in the veins of some Chickasaw, Creek, or Cherokee, the one memorial of that culture is the name of a dank city beside the Mississippi River.

THE STATE

XI

Aztec: Study in Total Power

THE RISE TO RESPECTABILITY

The native peoples of Mexico who made Cortés so avaricious with their wealth in gold, horrified him by the enormity of their human sacrifices, and impressed him by their military domination of much of Middle America are known variously as the Aztec, as the Tenochca, and as Colhua Mexico. Their names changed as their fortunes rapidly waxed. At first they were named after what they maintained was their northern homeland, a probably mythical place called Aztlán.* All that is known for certain about their origins is that they were a branch of the Uto-Aztecan peoples, and they were related to the impoverished Digger Indians of Nevada and some of the wealthier Pueblo Indians of New Mexico. After they had won a foothold in central Mexico, they were called Tenochca in honor of the patriarch who founded their capital city of Tenochtitlán, the present site of Mexico City. When they married into a revered and ancient lineage, the Colhuacán (pronounced Kool-wah-KHAN), they came to be known as Colhua. That was the name the people of the West Indies kept repeating to Columbus when he asked who lived to the west of the islands. In their final years, just before their conquest by Cortés, they became known as Colhua Mexica (that is, descendants-of-Colhuacán and rulers-of-Mexico). The origin of the word "Mexica" has been much disputed, but several authorities agree that it probably meant "The Navel of the Moon."

The Aztec represent one of history's great epics in social climbing—and

* In the Nahuatl language, most names are pronounced with every consonant sounded. In the cases that might give difficulty, pronunciations are indicated, and accent marks show where the stress should be.

an example of how one people can evolve from band to tribe to chiefdom and finally to state in only three or four centuries. Much of this evolution is documented in accounts by Spanish explorers and priests, and especially by the written records of the Aztec themselves. As in any dictatorship, the Aztec were obsessed with writing down their view of history; unfortunately most of these books were destroyed by the Spaniards, who considered them heathenish, but enough survive to provide a broad picture of Aztec life and history.

The history of these lowly hunters begins after the breakdown of the Classic civilizations of central Mexico and the final collapse in the twelfth century of the mighty Toltec of Tula, about forty miles north of Mexico City. A period of chaos followed as various groups sought to stake out territories for themselves. Five important new states were established by the middle of the twelfth century, the most illustrious of which was Colhuacán, whose rulers were descended directly from the royal line of Tula. At about that time many bands and tribes invaded the area, seeking land, and among the latecomers were the people who said they had wandered about after leaving Aztlán, guided by the image of their chief god, Huitzilopóchtli ("Hummingbird-on-the Left" and pronuounced Wheat-zeal-oh-POTCH-tlee), both a war god and a representative of the sun.

The Aztec could not at first find a place in crowded central Mexico, but eventually they were taken on as serfs and mercenary soldiers by the lordly Colhuacán. Their populations began to increase as they stole wives from their neighbors. As in a William Faulkner novel of social climbing in Yoknapatawpha County, the lowly Aztec went to the lordly Colhuacán, not only asking for but actually receiving a Toltec princess as a wife for their chief. They no doubt thought they were paying a unique compliment to the Colhuacán when in 1323 they sacrificed her, in the belief that she would then become a war goddess. The horrified Colhuacán expelled the Aztec from their lands.

And so the Aztec, no longer a hungry band of hunters but a people grown wise after their service in Colhuacán, set out once again. They traveled to the southwestern borders of the lakes that once surrounded Mexico City, where they found two unoccupied, marshy islands. They believed themselves to be a chosen people to whom it had been prophesied that they would found a mighty city at the place where they saw an eagle sitting upon a cactus and devouring a snake. There, on a deserted island wanted by no one, they beheld such a sight. By about 1345, under their chief Tenoch, they had already made remarkable progress in reclaiming the land. The swamps were drained; the islands were filled in and connected;

The warriors of Tula invaded the Maya of Yucatan some time after the tenth century and built at Chichén-Itzá a replica of their own capital city. It is in an excellent state of preservation and has been reconstructed with care, allowing us to visualize what Tula must have looked like in all its glory before the Aztec arrived in central Mexico. The photograph at the top left shows the giant pyramid, called El Castillo by the Spaniards. It apparently was dedicated to the worship of the sun, for each of the four stairways has 91 steps, making a total of 364 steps, plus the single step to the upper platform, which adds up to the 365 days in the solar year; in addition, each side of the pyramid has 52 panels, which equals the number of years in the Toltec cycle. The next photograph shows the entrance to the Temple of the Warriors where human sacrifices were made. Huge columns in the form of the serpent god Quetzalcóatl supported the roof, and in front was a reclining statue of Chac, the Maya god of rain. The bottom left photograph shows a portion of the circular observatory where the Maya astronomers made their sightings; the outside of the building was adorned with masks of the rain god. The top right photograph illustrates the extravagant stonework that decorated many of the buildings, with a riot of intertwined masks, serpents, human figures, and hieroglyphic inscriptions.

the lands were brought under cultivation. And building was begun on Tehochtitlán, one of the most magnificent cities ever erected on any continent. At this time the Aztec were still basically tribal in their social and political organization, with a few of the more complex characteristics of the chiefdom. But they seized on every opportunity to learn and to change, for they were a borrowing culture that offered little, but appropriated freely from others.

By 1428 the Aztec were ready. They totally crushed their rivals and became the mightiest state in Mexico. They were smart enough to put themselves completely into the hands of a shrewd court adviser, who immediately instituted the reforms that gave the Aztec the grandeur they believed was their destiny. His first step was to burn the books of the conquered peoples, because none of them had bothered to take proper notice of the people of Tenochtitlán. He instituted a policy of war to gain both tribute and captives for sacrifices. By terror and by diplomacy, the other peoples of central Mexico were soon forced to accept the fiction that these Aztec or Tenochca, these Colhua, these Mexica—whatever you called them—were the only true heirs of the great Toltec tradition.

The eighth ruler of the Aztec, Ahuítzotl (Ah-WHEAT-zotl), was coronated in 1486. By the time of his death in 1502 he had conquered most of the peoples southward to Guatemala and northward to the borders of the deserts; he ruled much of Mexico from the Gulf to the Pacific Ocean. He also brought about a cultural flowering similar to the one Augustus brought to ancient Rome. New aqueducts carried water from the mainland to the island capital; giant causeways, engineering marvels, were built to span the lakes. The fabulous Great Temple (on the site of Mexico City's Zócalo and the National Palace) was erected—and dedicated by the sacrifice of twenty thousand captives. The crafts and literature were encouraged, and many new schools established. While overseeing the construction of dikes to prevent flooding of the city, Ahuítzotl was accidentally hit on the head and killed. He was succeeded by his nephew, the philosopher-king Moctezuma II, who helped Aztec culture light up Mexico —and who saw its blaze extinguished by Cortés. (The usual spelling Montezuma is incorrect; the most exact English rendering would be Motecuhzoma, but Moctezuma is accepted by most specialists.)

THE VALLEY OF MEXICO

The heartland of the Aztec, and of several earlier great civilizations in Mexico, was the central area known as the Valley of Mexico. Actually it is not a valley at all, but a 3,000-square-mile basin in the highlands, completely surrounded by mountains. As this basin has no outlet, water flowing into it from the mountains once formed, during the dry winter season, five shallow lakes, which merged into a single large lake in the wet summer. The Spaniards first diverted the water out of the lakes in 1608 by digging a canal that let it flow to the Gulf of Mexico; the waters were almost completely drained by another tunnel constructed in about 1900. All that remains today are shallow Lake Xochimilco (Show-she-MEEL-ko) to the southeast of Mexico City and the puddle of Lake Texcoco (Tesh-KO-ko) to the northeast. As a result, the modern Mexico City is sinking back into the soft earth that underlies it.

Most of the valley is arid, and the summer rains fall in an erratic pattern. Complicating the problem even more was that the evaporation of the water in the lakes left behind a residue of salt, as happened also at Great Salt Lake in Utah. Obviously, to control the Valley of Mexico, the Aztec first had to control the water resource. They were able to flourish on the marshy islands because they used a unique method of cultivation known as the chinampa system. They did not invent it—it may be as old as two thousand years—but they developed its potential as a form of intensive agriculture that fed the growing populations of their city.

Chinampas are narrow strips of land—about three hundred feet long and between fifteen and thirty feet wide—almost completely surrounded by canals. They produce several crops a year and remain amazingly fertile century after century. They once were extremely widespread in the valley, but today they are reduced to only a few areas, one of them the "floating gardens" of Xochimilco, a leading tourist attraction of Mexico City.

The methods of chinampa farming in Aztec times were probably much the same as those practiced now. The farmers reach their chinampas on flat-bottomed canoes, from which they work them. Before each new planting the farmer scoops the rich mud from the bottom of the canals, loads it on his canoe, then spreads it on the surface of the chinampa. As crop after crop is grown, the height of the chinampa gradually rises. The farmer then lowers it once again by excavating the mud from the top, which he uses to build a new chinampa elsewhere. Each chinampa produces about seven crops a year—usually two of maize, and five others chosen from among beans, chili peppers, tomatoes, amaranth, and vegetables introduced from Europe, such as lettuce, carrots, cabbages, beets, and onions.

The chinampas enabled the Aztec to grow mighty and to erect a fabulous capital city. When Cortés reached Tenochtitlán, it was still growing rapidly, and it already had a population of 200,000 to 300,000 people—several times that of London in the same period. All the wondrous cities seen on the march from the Gulf of Mexico had not prepared the Spaniards for the sight of Tenochtitlán rising out of the waters of Lake Texcoco. Cortés declared it to be "the most beautiful city in the world," and he compared it to Venice. The most perceptive and reliable chronicler of the Cortés expedition, Bernal Díaz del Castillo, conveys the astonishment of his first glimpse of the city in November 1519:

We saw so many cities and villages built in the water and other great towns on dry land and that straight and level Causeway going towards Mexico [the city of Tenochtitlán], we were amazed and said that it was like the enchantments they tell of in the legends of Amadis, on account of the great towers and cues and buildings rising from the water, and all built of masonry. And some of our soldiers even asked whether the things we saw were not a dream. It is not to be wondered at that I here write it down in this manner, for there is so much to think over that I do not know how to describe it, seeing things that we did that had never been heard of or seen before, not even dreamed about.↕

He goes on to describe the palaces "wonderful to behold" and constructed with exotic woods. He describes a walk through orchards and a garden, "which was such a wonderful thing to see," and the great variety of trees and flowers, each with its own sweet scent. But a note of sadness, of an Eden willfully destroyed, also pervades his description:

Chinampa system is shown on an Aztec map—part of which has been damaged— of Tenochtitlán. Each house appears to have had six to eight plots associated with it, and the main canals are indicated.

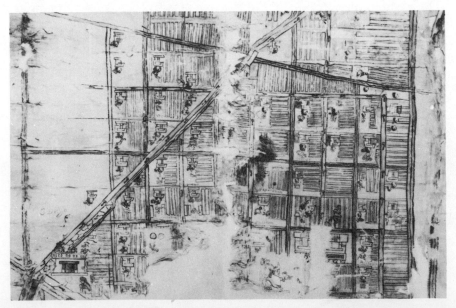

Map of Tenochtitlán, published in 1524 to illustrate Cortés' dispatches, clearly depicts much of the city planning and architecture of the capital city of the Aztec. Note the central temples and great pyramid, the large number of private dwellings, the causeways connecting the city to the mainland, the busy commerce of Lake Texcoco, and even the outlying cities.

I say again that I stood looking at it and thought that never in the world would there be discovered other lands such as these, for at that time there was no Peru, nor any thought of it. Of all these wonders that I then beheld today all is overthrown and lost, nothing left standing.

THE CONQUEST BY CORTÉS

Only five years after Moctezuma II became ruler in 1502, one of the fifty-two-year cycles of the complex Aztec calendar came to an end. The Aztec always feared the end of a cycle as a time fraught with peril, but in 1507 the fears seemed justified: Soothsayers reported that the omens for the following cycle were bad. During the next decade, portents of doom followed one another and brought increasing terror: A huge comet illuminated the sky; mysterious fires occurred in the Great Temple; the waters of the lakes flooded the capital city; strange sounds of crying in the night were heard. Moctezuma ordered anyone having a dream about the fate of the empire to hasten to him, and he sent his soldiers to search the city for such people. The mighty ruler who had been able to command tribute from most of Mexico was now paying tribute to his own citizens for their dreams. But none of the dreams he bought satisfied him, and so he committed the most pathetic act of all: He massacred the dreamers.

Moctezuma's trouble was that he was a philosopher-king, similar to some emperors of Rome before its fall. He knew too much and he thought too much about the supernatural and about myth. He was familiar with the ancient books of the Toltec, which foretold the return someday from the east of the cast-out god Quetzalcóatl (Kate-zal-KO-atl), the "Plumed Serpent." Moctezuma concluded that the portents meant he was destined to preside over the destruction of Mexico. He finally resigned himself to his fate.

His worst fears were confirmed in 1519 when a young adventurer named Hernán Cortés landed near Vera Cruz with an army of 508 soldiers, 16 horses, and 14 pieces of artillery. A few months later Cortés beached his ships and headed westward for the interior, setting out to conquer the millions of central Mexico. He was driven to such apparent foolhardiness not by a romantic spirit of adventure nor to win lands for his monarch, as some historians would have it, but by simple lust for gold. At that time every European dreamed of gold, sought it in abandoned caves, even sold their souls to the devil for it. Cortés frankly told one of the first Mexican nobles he met that he had come across the seas to their country because of sickness: "The Spaniards are troubled with a disease of the heart for which gold is the specific remedy."‡

The details of the conquest by Cortés have been told in full by Díaz del Castillo, by Prescott in his *Conquest of Mexico,* and by Cortés himself. In brief, the mighty Aztec empire disintegrated almost as soon as Cortés landed; the bewildered Moctezuma consulted his omens while the invaders approached closer and closer to Tenochtitlán. The original 508 Spanish soldiers were reduced to about 400, but their ranks had been swelled by thousands of Indian allies who flocked to the banner of Cortés in the hope that he would free them from their Aztec oppressors. Cortés did not even have to fight his way into the capital city; he was invited in by Moctezuma, who resignedly put himself in the hands and at the mercy of Cortés.

Ultimately a battle did take place, and Cortés had to flee Tenochtitlán. At that time Moctezuma died, and no one knows for certain if he died of a disease, was murdered by Cortés, or was assassinated by his own people. His successor died of smallpox within four months, and he in turn was succeeded by Cuauhtémoc (Kwow-TAY-mock) who led the fight against the Spaniards. Cortés, reinforced by fresh Spanish troops, and with tens of thousands of Indian allies, marched back to Tenochtitlán. The Aztec fought valiantly, from street to street and across the rooftops, while the canals flowed with the blood of an estimated 120,000 of their people. They had at last learned that Moctezuma had been wrong. These people were not gods but only plunderers like themselves.

The Aztec opportunity for victory, though, had passed. His people starving after eighty-five days of siege and his soldiers massacred, Cuauhtémoc surrendered on August 13, 1521. Cortés, true Spanish knight that he was, received this eleventh, last, and undoubtedly noblest of the Aztec emperors with much pomp and flattering courtesy. He had him ignominiously hanged three years later. Today, all that remains of what was once the most magnificent city in the world is some sculpture and the rubble of its temples—"wonderful to behold"—buried under the foundations of modern Mexico City. Shortly after the conquest, a native witness of the downfall of the city wrote the following poem in Nahuatl, the language of the Aztec:

> *The waters are red as if stained,*
> *And when we drink it is as if we drank salt water.*
> *Meanwhile we laid low the adobe walls*
> *And our heritage was a net of holes.*
> *Shields protected it,*
> *But even shields could not preserve its solitude!* . . .
> *We have chewed salty couch grass,*
> *Lumps of adobe, lizards, mice, the dust of the*
>   *earth, worms.*⇕

THE AZTEC STATE

To understand the rise of the Aztec and their precipitous decline, one has to realize they displayed every characteristic of an orderly and well-administered state—yet it was an illusion. In their extraordinarily rapid rise to statehood the Aztec had not rid themselves completely of some characteristics of the less complex levels of band, tribe, and chiefdom. They were plagued by these remnants in the body politic, as man is occasionally plagued in his own body by a useless remnant of an earlier stage in evolution, the vermiform appendix. Relics of more simple kinds of institutions persisted in all levels of Aztec society.

The Aztec state differed in several important respects from the less complex chiefdom. The Northwest Coast chiefs and the Great Sun of the Natchez commanded great deference; but they also were severely limited, in one way especially. A chief could lead other men into battle, and he was more powerful than anyone else in his society. But he lacked the *exclusive* right to use force. Whatever force he might employ was not the only force that existed in his society: Lineages might feud with each other; a group of warriors might set out independently to raid a neighboring chiefdom; a kinship group might inflict punishment on some offender. In a state, on the other hand, no one can use force but the state itself—that is, the ruler and his legally sanctioned delegates such as the police and the army. Feuding in a state is an unspeakable crime that is punished severely, for its very presence means that someone besides the state is making use of force. Once a society has separated one group of people—those empowered to administer force—from the rest of the population, it can separate them in other ways as well; and political classes arise. The Natchez had classes that ranged from Sun down to Stinkard, and there were individuals of different rank in the Northwest Coast chiefdoms; but these were only *social* classes and ranks that had no political significance. Number 625 at the potlatch was equal to number 125 before the law.

There was a difference between the Aztec state on the one hand and Babylon, Egypt, and Rome on the other. The difference was that the latter were successful empires—that is, they incorporated diverse cultures and different ethnic groups into one civil system. The Aztec, on the other hand, were more like marauders than colonizers. In some ways they resembled the Assyrians of the ancient Middle East, who also had a rapid rise and a precipitous decline. Time after time, the Assyrians swept out of the hills to plunder the rich cities of the Levant, then retired into their stronghold after exacting promises of tribute. Similarly, the Aztec armies sallied forth to quell disturbances, to protect trade routes, to plunder, and to exact tribute—and they also failed to alter deeply the basic makeup of the societies they conquered. They might arrange a political marriage between their own ruling line and that of a subject king, and they often substituted their own gods for those of the conquered peoples. But they did not permanently incorporate the vanquished territories. Instead, they left behind them an unchanged social system and a lingering hatred, which Cortés was quick to understand and to exploit. The Aztec state was still integrating itself and as yet had little talent for integrating others, as the Romans had. They were, after all, still amateurs at statecraft, and they had already come very far in a short time.

Another problem arose in the Aztec state, and it becomes more acute in the even more complex industrial society. Unless an Aztec individual were exceptionally gifted, he could not participate in the state's important activities. The state might offer a hundred ways of earning a living, but his probably seemed to be among the least important. There was room for only a few honored persons at public functions; he watched from afar and was jostled by crowds of other unhonored individuals like himself. In a state renowned for the high fashion of its rulers, the Aztec commoner went around threadbare. The more complex the society, the better is its capacity to enrich each member; but in practice it becomes increasingly difficult for the individual to receive his rewards. He is reduced to an onlooker, a bystander, while all around him momentous decisions are being made by others. His only opportunity consists of vicarious participation: He can identify with nationally known athletes or the man from his village who has made good in the big city. A lower-class Aztec probably did just that, and he obtained a feeling of participation from observing the pomp of Moctezuma's court at Tenochtitlán. In Aztec society, as in most modern ones, those who produced most of the wealth were denied its satisfactions. Such a condition could never exist in an Eskimo band, for every member of the Eskimo society is aware of the necessity for his full participation. When he is unable to participate because of age or ill health he often asks a relative to kill him, or he will commit suicide.

CLASS AND CLAN

The class system of Tenochtitlán was of extraordinary complexity, in large part because it was combined with territory, settlement patterns, economic specialization, and kinship. Territorially, the city was divided into four quarters, the *campans*, or "great neighborhoods," as the Spaniards called them. Each of the four *campans* was divided into several *calpulli*, or "small neighborhoods," and there were twenty of them in the entire city. Each of the *calpulli*, in turn, consisted of smaller kinship units known as *tlaxilacalli* (tlash-eel-ah-KAHL-lee) or "streets." Finally, the *tlaxilacalli* were divided into individual family plots consisting of several chinampas. Such an arrangement was undoubtedly regimented, and it lacked the freedom of movement from neighborhood to neighborhood characteristic of a modern city; but it was an excellent way to administer and govern a large population.

Imposed upon this territorial system was a class system. The hereditary nobility were the policy makers, and they lived on their own lands, which were not part of the *calpulli* system. The vast majority of the population belonged to the class of commoners who were organized into the twenty *calpulli*. The *calpulli* appear originally to have been clans founded by the first settlers of Tenochtitlán, and all members of the same *calpulli* claimed descent from a common ancestor. Each *calpulli* had its own temple, and the most important ones also had military schools for their youths. The men of the same *calpulli* served as a unit in warfare under their own leader. The members as a group paid tribute to the nobility, and they worked the lands that belonged to them. So each *calpulli* was at the same time a landholding corporation and a settlement group, as well as a real or fictitious kin group.

At first look, the *calpulli* clan system appears basically egalitarian, as were the clans in a tribe like the Iroquois, but that is not so. Everyone was ranked within his *calpulli* according to his closeness to the fictitious founder of the clan. So it was inevitable that each *calpulli* had certain aristocratic families who ran it; after the death of a chief, the new chief came from the same family. In the same way that the entire *calpulli* paid tribute to the state, the lesser ranking members of each *calpulli* paid tribute to the higher ranking members. Furthermore, some of the twenty *calpulli* were better than others; and of the four *campans* into which the city was divided, certain neighborhoods were better than others. Therefore, a man who came from the most aristocratic family within the most important *calpulli* in the best of the four *campans* was a person to be reckoned with.

Another social class was the *mayequauh* (mah-YEE-kwow), or "right hands." These were the laborers, drawn from the conquered peoples. They were usually the original owners of the conquered lands and they were bound to it, every bit as much as was a Russian serf under the czars: An Aztec inherited his "right hands" along with the land. Nevertheless, they were free men in every other way except in their obligations to the land, and they could even own property. But they did not enter into the *calpulli* system.

There were, in addition, several other classes. As the Aztec military conquests increased, the rulers created a nobility in addition to the hereditary nobility. These were the "knights" or the "Sons of the Eagle"—an outlet for the more ambitious members of the *calpulli*. Becoming a "Son of the Eagle" was a reward for service to the state, and such recognition both afforded social mobility to the worthy and prevented discontent. Creating such "knights" was somewhat like Britain's present-day Honors List, which allows an ambitious statesman, actor, or brewer to put "Sir" before his name, but does not entitle him to pass that honor on to his son.

Finally, the professional merchants, the *pochteca,* had a special place in the class system because of their services to the state. These long-distance traders brought back from Central America and the North American Southwest exotic products for the delectation of the nobility—feathers of the quetzal bird, turquoise, jaguar skins, feather coats, cacao beans, precious metals—but they were more than mere traders. They served also as spies who reconnoitered foreign lands in advance of the Aztec armies, and they probably also served as a fifth column just before the invasion. As reward for such service, they were organized into their own *calpulli* and had their own deities, emblems, and ceremonies, much as a guild in medieval Europe had certain privileges. They administered their own laws in their own courts, and they were governed by their own officers. As a further concession, they were permitted to pay tribute to the state in the form of trade goods rather than in products of the land.

The position of the *pochteca* among the Aztec just before Cortés was in some ways similar to that of the rising mercantile class in Europe in the Middle Ages. As in Europe, the *pochteca* were privileged beings who moved from one city-state to another with political immunity; Aztec armies protected their trade routes, and molesting a *pochteca* was often an excuse for war. There were also several commercial sanctuaries or "open ports" where traders from competing societies could meet freely and bargain. There was even resistance to them from the nobility, as occurred also in Europe. In the years just before the conquest, the Aztec nobility managed to curb the growing power of the *pochteca.* They were, for example, barred from attaining the rank of officer in the army; some were even put to death and their wealth appropriated by the nobles. Nevertheless, within a century or two, had the Spanish conquest not intervened, they undoubtedly would have succeeded in becoming crystallized as a merchant middle class, as happened in Europe.

The one person in the state who was in a class by himself was, of course, the ruler. The Spaniards, reared under an absolute monarch, were impressed by what they thought was Moctezuma's power beyond any limits. They were impressed by an illusion, for the reverence paid to Moctezuma obscured the fact that he lacked a solid base of power. He was treated as a semidivine personage, and even the highest noble did not dare to look him in the face; before entering Moctezuma's presence, the mightiest nobles garbed themselves in the meanest clothing. Moctezuma was borne in a litter on the shoulders of nobles. When he deigned to place his feet on the ground, nobles rushed to cover the path ahead of him with cloth so that he would not have to touch the rude earth. During mealtimes he was shielded from view by a screen as he chose from the several hundred dishes offered for his selection.

Díaz del Castillo was overawed by the luxury in which Moctezuma lived, and particularly by his palace—magnificent in construction—and the rooms filled with "the great number of dancers kept by the Great Moctezuma for his amusement, and others who used stilts on their feet, and others who flew when they danced up in the air." The palace also had a royal zoo that housed animals from all over Middle America, and a private sideshow of monstrosities of nature, including people with every known physical deformity. The Spaniard was overawed when he contemplated the royal garden:

We must not forget the gardens of flowers and sweet-scented trees, and the many kinds that there were of them, and the arrangement of them and the walks, and the ponds and tanks of fresh water where the water entered at one end and flowed out of the other; and the baths which he had there, and the variety of small birds that nested in the branches, and the medicinal and useful herbs that were in the gardens . . . There was as much to be seen in these gardens as there was everywhere else, and we could not tire of witnessing his great power.↕

WARRIORS AND PRIESTS

Two things kept the Aztec state going, or so the Aztec believed: the tribute in food and raw materials from conquered people, and the staggering number of sacrificial victims. Both needs could be filled in only one way, by war, and no other society in North America ever attained such a degree of militancy. Every man was expected to bear arms. Not even priests were exempt, although they were permitted to fight in their own units. Each of the city's four *campans* contained its own arsenal, which was always stocked and ready for immediate mobilization. War was extolled, and he who was permitted to die on the battlefield for Huitzilopóchtli considered himself fortunate indeed, as stated in an Aztec song:

> *There is nothing like death in war,*
> *nothing like the flowery death*
> *so precious to Him who gives life:*
> *far off I see it: my heart yearns for it!*↕

Wars were fought in deadly earnest, and they were surrounded by a mystique that makes an Islamic holy war seem pedestrian indeed. The Aztec conceived of war as a re-enactment on earth of a titanic battle that was waged in the skies, the Sacred War of the Sun, which every day had to fight off evil forces to make its way across the sky.

The demand for tribute was much less mystical, as is demonstrated by the Aztec records of tribute exacted from the conquered peoples. The Spaniards destroyed most of the Aztec books, but they were practical men also, so they preserved the tribute lists in Moctezuma's archives as a guide to what they could extort from the Aztec provinces. These records reveal that in just one year there flowed into Tenochtitlán an incredible tribute: fourteen million pounds of maize, eight million pounds each of beans and amaranth, two million cotton cloaks, in addition to quantities of war costumes, shields, feathers, precious stones, and many other items. Some of this haul was undoubtedly for the use of the nobles, and the food was used for feeding the Aztec populace. But much of it no doubt went to pay the artisans and others who rendered service to the palace and to supply the *pochteca* with goods to barter for other luxury items.

Aztec religion was of unbelievable complexity, and it was based on the machinelike repetition of cyclic rituals. The Solar Year was composed of eighteen months of twenty days each, with five highly dangerous days coming before the beginning of the following Solar Year. Each month had special ceremonies in which every Aztec was obligated to participate; the ceremonies were closely tied up with the primitive cycle of the agricultural year, the planting and watering and harvesting of various crops. Numerous other cycles were at work also, such as the Almanac Year of 260 days, in which each day, week, and month was associated with a particular god or goddess. Even each day was broken down into "hours" somewhat longer than our sixty minutes, and each of the thirteen daylight "hours" and the nine night "hours" had its own deity assigned to it.

Aztec religion seems obsessed with rhythms and cycles, but it is not much different from the "cyclic group rites" that have appeared in most of

Aztec calendar stone, thirteen feet in diameter and weighing more than twenty tons, was made from a huge block of stone quarried on the mainland and dragged across the causeway. It symbolizes the entire Aztec universe and the history of the world, and would require many pages to explain in detail. In the center is the sun, set within the symbols for the previous eras, the dates of which are given in hieroglyphs on the four arms around the sun. The twenty day names encircle the central symbols, and beyond them are the sun's rays and various star symbols. The two great fire serpents that form the outer rim probably were intended to symbolize time.

the world's higher civilizations and that are correlated with the rhythms of nature. The American today lives in an age of technology in which very few people farm—and even those few farms are mechanized—but he still observes a religious calendar that is a carryover of the annual changes in agricultural activities in the Mediterranean world. Americans who have inherited the religious traditions of the Christians of the eastern Mediterranean do not find it strange that a messiah should be born at the time of the winter solstice, when the sun is farthest away from earth and is about to return. Nor do they find it strange that in the spring, when nature is renewed in the Near East, the Hebrews should have set out from Egypt to found a new nation and the messiah should be resurrected.

The modern American is insulated from the agricultural cycle by his technology, and so was an Aztec because of the year-round production of his chinampas. The question arises why the Aztec continued to observe outmoded cyclic rites, and why we do also. The answer usually given is that the cyclic nature of agriculture makes for a convenient way to remember to perform the rites due the gods. That answer must be rejected in the case of the Aztec at least, for they possessed numerous custodians of their various secular and sacred calendars, and were so priest-ridden by a hierarchy of religious officials that they had no need to worry about neglecting to perform any sacred obligation.

An explanation must be sought elsewhere, and one can be found if these cyclic group ceremonies are regarded as "rites of intensification."‡ As societies evolve and become more complex, their concern with matters of subsistence usually slackens, for the ordinary citizen becomes farther and farther removed from the source of his food. All most Americans know about the beefsteak that arrives on their dinner tables is that someone in Chicago or Kansas City at some indefinite time in the past must have slaughtered an animal, and after passing through many hands a piece of meat reached the shelf in the neighborhood market. Such a person's food supply is different from that of his ancestors, who tilled the soil by the sweat of their brows and knew the source of each piece of fruit and every kernel of grain.

Similarly, as a group changes in its relation to its subsistence, other changes take place in relationship to the old order, to ways of doing things, and to the established institutions. That is really what Faulkner is talking about in his epic fictional history of Yoknapatawpha County. The conservative Aztec ruler or head priest saw the same changes occurring in Tenochtitlán as Faulkner saw in Mississippi. All Faulkner as an artist could do was to protest in words against the loss of older and simpler values of life, but the priests of the Aztec could take definite action. They instituted rites of intensification that reinforced recollections of the old ways of doing things. These rites were agents of conservatism that brought about conditioned responses to the ancestral values to which the individual had been trained. These rites were no different from the observance of Succoth by a Jewish family today living in American suburban society. Succoth is an eastern Mediterranean harvest festival, which, based on a solar cycle of twenty-eight years, celebrated the blessings brought by the sun. In every way but one—the moral values it teaches—it is totally obsolete for American suburban society.

The Aztec rites were in the hands of an elaborate hierarchy, similar in its rigid organization and power to the priestly hierarchies of ancient Egypt and Mesopotamia. As in these cultures also, shamans were absent, or their influence was insignificant. Instead, the Aztec relied almost exclusively on priests. Priests are quite different from shamans. Priests exercise no supernatural powers of their own but are merely those people selected by society to become experts in the performance of sacred ritual. Shamans are born and not made, but priests most assuredly are made by long and arduous training. Whenever shamanism appears in a state it represents a threat to orthodoxy, and everything possible is done to suppress it. The Catholic Church, right up through the time of the Reformation, expended considerable energy in denouncing and burning "false prophets" and "heretics," who were really shamans impelled by an inner religious feeling rather than by orthodox training.

The United States in recent years has witnessed a resurgence of shamanistic cults among all classes and all races. Storefront salvationists prosper in Harlem, and snake handlers in Appalachia; there are psychedelic prophets who advocate hallucinogenic drugs, revivalistic preachers who capitalize on the medium of television, prophets of a strange new cybernetic age, and mystical seers who bring suburban matrons a revelation from Tibet. All these people, despite the evident sincerity of most of them, are really religious entrepreneurs or shamans. They are in opposition to the professionals, the clergy, who received specialized instruction in seminaries, who were ordained in a way sanctioned by society, and who perpetuate orthodoxy. The revival of shamanism in the United States is probably symptomatic of the weakening of orthodox religion's ability to regulate social behavior and to maintain social values—and of the lack of any stirring new philosophy or ethic to replace the vacuum left by traditional religions.

The Aztec religion supported five thousand priests in Tenochtitlán alone and maintained a tight grip on ritual, the calendar and astronomy, scholarship, and both secular and religious education. The cosmogony the priests taught depicted man as living on the verge of doomsday, and the world as barely escaping from cataclysm after cataclysm. The end of each fifty-two-year cycle was particularly threatening, because that was the time when the gods might withhold the privilege of continued life. The fires in all the temples were extinguished, and the citizens mutilated themselves, fasted,

The ritual of human sacrifice demanded stone vessels for the storing and burning of hearts. Such vessels were gouged out of lava rock, then lavishly decorated or sculptured to refer to the gods for whom the sacrifices were made. This one represents the ocelot.

and prayed. As soon as the priests thought they detected a propitious omen in the skies, the breast of a living victim was slit open and a new fire started in his heart. From this fire, all the fires in the temples, and then in the homes, were relighted. The world was believed safe, more or less, for another fifty-two years. There were also five days of dread at the end of each Solar Year, as well as all sorts of dangers connected with cycles of longer and shorter duration.

The anxiety common to all of these dangers was the possible extinguishing of the Sun—by a flood, by the sky falling upon the earth, or by being blown out by a great wind. The Aztec regarded themselves as the people chosen to protect the Sun against such constant dangers—and they did it by their valor, their sobriety, and their sexual continence. They also had to nourish it and keep the contending forces of the heavens in balance by offering up human sacrifices in numbers almost beyond counting.

On their march inland toward the Aztec capital, the Spanish soldiers, as brutal a lot of adventurers as had ever been assembled under one banner, were shocked by the enormity of the human sacrifices they saw. Díaz del Castillo reported on what he saw in just one city: "I remember that in the plaza where some of the oratories stood, there were piles of human skulls

Aztec brazier represents the rain god Tláloc to whom great numbers of small children were sacrificed. As recently as the summer of 1967 a Nahuatl Indian, who spoke no Spanish, was arrested for offering a human sacrifice to this god to bring rain to his drought-stricken fields.

so regularly arranged that one could count them, and I estimated them at more than a hundred thousand. I repeat again that there were more than one hundred thousand of them."‡ The Spaniards quickly realized that the huge ceremonial pyramids that abounded everywhere were really altars for human sacrifice. At the top of each pyramid lay a huge stone with a depression to hold the heart and a rill for the blood to run off down the steps. The victim was held spread on his back while a priest made an incision under the rib cage and ripped out the heart. Most captives were sacrificed in this way, but there were variations, including gladiatorial sacrifice and the roasting of a victim until he was near death before tearing out his heart. Huge numbers of small children were sacrificed to the rain god Tláloc; the Aztec believed that the more the children cried with terror, the more pleased that god would be.

Human sacrifice was also practiced elsewhere in Middle America, but no other people outdid the Aztec in its intensity. Various attempts have been made to explain why sacrifice reached such extremes among the Aztec. Some scholars have tried to justify the sacrifices by comparing them to wars and inhuman acts that still ravage the world today, but such an argument is beside the point. Psychologically oriented anthropologists have suggested that the explanation was a bloodthirsty Aztec "personality"—an insupportable view, for no one has ever proved that the personality of individuals creates the culture. Nor is there much validity in the belief by some that sacrifice reached such extremes because of the famines that occurred in the fifteenth century; there were simpler ways for the Aztec to relieve a famine than killing off populations, the most obvious being to increase the tribute they demanded or to conquer more lands.

The problem can be explained in its own terms rather than in those of psychology or history. Once the Aztec religion initiated the practice of human sacrifice to forestall the cataclysms awaiting the people, it was trapped in a circle of events. Sacrificial victims could be obtained only through war, yet war could be waged successfully only by sacrificing victims; in order to obtain victims to ensure successful war, the Aztec first had to wage war. It was a circle that expanded to include increasingly greater sacrificial offerings.

Human sacrifice never occurs in societies beneath the level of the chiefdom, because in simple societies almost everyone is in a relationship to everyone else through marriage alliances, sodalities, or economic partnerships. A Zuni would not sacrifice Mr. X because it might turn out that Mr. X was married to his grandmother's sister's son's daughter. Nor would the Eskimo be so foolish as to sacrifice those kin and partners he may someday need to help fill his belly or to help him avenge an insult. Only as societies become increasingly complex does the awareness of kinship lessen; only then does man become inclined to sacrifice one of his own kind or an animal surrogate. Human sacrifice has appeared in complex societies around the world, but in Eurasia the practice seems to have centered in the Mediterranean world and surrounding areas. It was widespread in Mesopotamia, and it existed among the ancient Hebrews before the symbolic substitution of a ram for the sacrifice of Isaac; it occasionally appeared in ancient Greece. In the few centuries preceding the collapse of the Roman Empire it reached monumental proportions.

THE DEATH OF THE SUN

The cataclysm that had been foretold for so long finally did come. In 1521 the sacred fires were forever extinguished and the Spanish priests began to baptize the peoples of Mexico. There were so many millions of Indians,

Xipe (pronounced Shee-pay), the "Flayed God," was worshiped with human sacrifices from whom the priests removed the skin, which they then wore around their own bodies for twenty days. This stone carving, which is in nearly perfect condition, has the date of 1507, as the Aztec calendar calculated it, on its back.

and the supply of holy water was so limited, it is said the priests used their own saliva. The collapse of the Aztec empire was total and final, and the Spaniards met almost no resistance after they killed the last Aztec ruler in 1524. Historians have long plagued themselves by wondering how only five hundred Spaniards managed to conquer an empire that put brave and well-armored warriors into the field by the hundreds of thousands. But even the brief view of the Aztec social and political structure given in this chapter reveals that it was vulnerable to the sort of attack made by someone like Cortés. No single weakness led to the Aztec downfall, but rather the cause was the total kind of society the Aztec had erected. Using hindsight, one can only wonder why the conquest took Cortés as long as two years. The Aztec defeat was inevitable because of the following factors:

LACK OF AZTEC SOCIOPOLITICAL INTEGRATION. The Aztec had not yet achieved an integrated empire, and vanquished neighbors were always ready to rise in rebellion. Further, the Aztec—who displayed such organizational ability in their class system, the priesthood, and the army—were remarkably poor administrators of the conquered territories. They gave the vanquished every excuse for lingering hatred. The Aztec exploited them unmercifully for tribute and sacrificial victims, without giving them any of the benefits of Aztec culture. Cortés stumbled into a land that was already seething with intrigue and rebellion, ready to betray the Aztec oppressors.

POOR MILITARY TACTICS OF THE AZTEC.   Marvelously organized, numbering warriors almost beyond counting, lavishly equipped with efficient weapons and quilted armor that the Spanish soldiers regarded as superior to their own, well trained and desiring immolation on the battlefield, the Aztec war machine nevertheless had many weaknesses. It could not sustain a campaign after the initial attack, because the absence of beasts of burden made it impossible to bring up supplies, and the hostility of the conquered peoples made it difficult to live off the country. Despite their class of professional soldiers, the Aztec had developed no war strategy other than spying by merchants, followed by a surprise attack. They were ignorant of a common European tactic that would have afforded them immediate victory over the Spaniards: Split an enemy's forces into smaller units; then destroy these piecemeal. Mass-attack tactics by the Aztec were of no use, because the Aztec could bring only a portion of their overwhelming numbers into contact with the small number of Spaniards at any one time. In contrast, the small Spanish army was a marvelously efficient instrument. Generations of Spaniards had been bred to battle in the Moorish Wars between 711 and 1492, and in other conflicts in Europe as well. They had learned about primitive war through their conquests in Africa and in the West Indies. Cortés' army was small enough to live off the land, and so it required no logistical support.

RELIGIOUS PARALYSIS OF THE AZTEC.   The Aztec religion conceived of the world as operating in numerous intermeshed cycles. Because the massive machinery that ran the cycles operated largely beyond man's control, the Aztec had the constant anxiety that such machinery might someday break down. The portents of evil in the decade or so before the arrival of Cortés seemed to indicate that just such a thing was happening; and the inevitable result was paralysis.

SOCIAL PARALYSIS OF THE AZTEC.   The Aztec were overorganized. Every star in the heavens had its place, and so did every individual on earth. The educational system trained youths to obey orders without question, and the religious training demanded unquestioning faith. When the war chiefs were killed or captured, no mechanism existed for replacing them, and no lower echelon Aztec warrior stepped forward to take the leadership. An Aztec commoner who had been trained all his life to obey could not suddenly learn to command.

LIMITATIONS ON THE POWERS OF THE RULER. Moctezuma may have appeared semidivine and authoritarian, but he was limited in his powers, and one of these limitations proved disastrous for him. He might have ordered an attack as soon as the Spaniards landed at Vera Cruz. Immediate action was within his power, but he lacked the power to make long-range decisions alone. Once he failed to react instantly, he was committed to extended discussions and group decisions with his chief advisers, high priests, and war leaders. As the Spaniards slowly made their way across central Mexico toward Tenochtitlán, Moctezuma's ability to act alone and to make decisions became less and less. Finally, once the Spaniards reached the city, he was so benumbed by conflicting advice that he calmly handed himself over to Cortés as a hostage.

AZTEC LACK OF FOLLOW-THROUGH IN VICTORY. After the death of Moctezuma and the uprising against the Spaniards by the people of Tenochtitlán, Cortés was forced to retreat from the city in a rout in which he lost three quarters of his men. Instead of following up their advantage and destroying the Spanish remnants, the Aztec behaved as they always had after a victory: They plundered the corpses and searched for wounded Spaniards to offer as sacrifices. That gave Cortés valuable time to regroup and to await the reinforcements that aided him in his decisive victory the following year. Cortés was really fighting a different kind of war. At the very end, when the Aztec leaders expected to bargain with the conquerors in their usual way about the amount of tribute the Aztec would have to pay, they were unprepared for total war—the cannons that battered their homes, the ruthless destruction of their lives, their gods, their cherished beliefs.

All the above explanations are based solely on conditions within the Aztec state and in Mexico at the time. No attempt has been made to explain the Aztec collapse by recourse to outmoded arguments about the superiority of the Spaniards in leadership, armaments, morale, or race. Cortés was a competent leader, but any other leader of average ability probably would have conquered the Aztec just as easily—not because of the superiority of the Europeans but because of the intrinsic social and political weaknesses of the Aztec culture itself.

PART TWO

THE
LONG
MIGRATION

The Peopling of North America

THE CONTINENT THAT HAD NEVER KNOWN MAN

Previous chapters have discussed some of the different kinds of Indian groups that the explorers and later the settlers encountered. From the very first the explorers wondered who these people were and how they had arrived in North America in the first place. Despite the Indians' exotic customs and their unusual dress—or lack of it—the explorers were convinced that the Indians belonged to the nations of humankind. Pope Julius II solemnly declared that the Indians were descended from Adam and Eve—but that did not halt the speculations about how they had reached the New World. One popular theory of the time held that the Indians were the children of Babel cast into a primitive existence because of their sins. The belief that the Indians were descended from the Ten Lost Tribes of Israel had its vogue and then fell into disrepute, although the Church of Jesus Christ of Latter-Day Saints (Mormon) believes it to this day. Cotton Mather, the Puritan divine, attributed the Indians' arrival in America, as he attributed so much else, to the devil who willfully led them there to prevent their salvation. A partial list of peoples proposed as the Indians' ancestors, who either migrated to North America intentionally, or whose ships were blown off course, includes ancient Egyptians, Trojans, Greeks, Carthaginians, Etruscans, Tartars, Chinese Buddhists, Indian Hindus, Mandingos of Africa, ancient Irish, Welsh, Norse, Basques, and Huns.‡

No need exists, however, to account for the origin of the American Indian by miraculous events or by wayward fleets of ships across the

Atlantic or Pacific. The real story of the peopling of North America is fantastic enough, and it represents one of the sagas in the history of man.

As the land mass of the North American continent gradually took the shape we know today, the life it nurtured also became increasingly more familiar. Today Alaska and Siberia, at their closest point, are separated by fifty-six miles of fogbound, choppy water. But until about a million years ago the two continents were solidly joined by land, and a variety of animals crossed from one continent to another—the ancestors of horses, camels, opossums, wild dogs, weasels—as well as many kinds of birds. A million years ago, on the other hand, moose, elk, musk ox, mountain sheep, bears, wolves, foxes, bison, and many other groups of mammals familiar in North America today still had not made the crossing from Siberia to Alaska. Also notably absent was early man, who was beginning to spread through Eurasia. At that time warping in the crust of the earth around the Arctic caused the land connection to sink into the Bering and Chukchi seas. The two continents became effectively separated.

Previous to discoveries made in only the past few decades, no clear idea existed of how men and Asiatic mammals had reached North America. The explanation, however, has been found in recent research about the Pleistocene epoch, commonly called the Ice Age, which began about 1,500,000 years ago.‡ The Pleistocene was ushered in by great climatic fluctuations; eventually, four successive ice sheets advanced and then re-treated, and the most recent retreat is still going on. At their greatest thrust, the sheets buried about thirty-two percent of the land area of the globe. The spreading ice meant drastic changes for all living things. Ancient forests were mowed down as if they were clusters of matchsticks; the courses of rivers were altered, and some of them were so thoroughly dammed by ice packs that they turned into enormous lakes; huge basins, such as those now filled by the Great Lakes, were gouged out of the land.

It is remarkable that man should have evolved and spread during the ice ages. This weak biped, still shaky on his hind legs, had no fur to protect him against the cold climate; he lacked fangs, and his clawless hands were no match for such ice-age mammals as the sabertooth and the long-tusked mammoths and mastodon; he was too slow to pursue most game. During most of his slow evolution, he was an opportunistic feeder on whatever he could collect. His meager pickings included seeds and roots, carrion, insects such as locusts and termites; he killed rodents and lizards with primitive weapons. Yet, as ice sheet succeeded ice sheet, man continued to develop and to spread across the steppes of Asia. He had left the sheltered forests and was adapting to the cold of the grasslands. His highly developed brain enabled him to outwit prey, to nullify cold with clothing, to produce weapons that overcame the size, speed, and fangs of large mammals.

The Pleistocene saw the emergence, and the triumph, of man. By the middle of the most recent ice advance, which began about 65,000 years ago, and lasted until about 10,000 years ago, *Homo sapiens* had become firmly established in Siberia. He was an accomplished manufacturer of tools and weapons, a builder of semisubterranean shelters, a tailor of clothing made from animal hides, a wonderer about the supernatural. The development of a technology to hunt the ice-age mammals resulted in a sudden spurt in human populations in Eurasia. Since a lone hunter could not kill one of the huge beasts unaided, cooperation and simple political organizations must have arisen. For all this, though, man still had not cultivated any plants or domesticated any animal except possibly the dog; he had not yet invented the bow and arrow or the boat. Nor had he yet reached North America, still locked in the ice age.

OVER THE LAND BRIDGE

Man was able to reach the New World because the ice sheets locked up, in the form of glacial ice, immense amounts of the planet's water supply and in that way lowered the level of the sea. That ice sheets can store vast quantities of water is demonstrated by the glaciers that remain today in Greenland and the Antarctic; were they to melt abruptly, they would pour back into the sea enough water to raise its level by about 300 feet and thus inundate many of the world's major cities. Geologists do not agree about the exact depths to which the sea fell at various times in the Pleistocene, but during the last ice advance it probably dropped between 150 to 300 feet. A lowering of the sea by 300 feet would have allowed a land bridge to emerge that was 1,000 miles wide, wider even than the north-south span of present-day Alaska. A lowering by only 150 feet would have exposed a land bridge nearly a third as wide. The land bridge endured, off and on, for some tens of thousands of years, until a sudden rise in temperature throughout the world about 10,000 years ago accelerated the melt of the ice and poured water back into the sea. The land bridge was inundated, and it has remained flooded to this day.

Since the bridge was exposed whenever the ice sheets were at their maxima, one might think that at these times the land bridge must have been impassable because of the ice. But that is not so. During part of the last glacial advance, when the ice extended as far south as what are now the Ohio, the Missouri, and the Columbia rivers, most of Alaska and western Canada escaped the ice, and so did much of Siberia. No one can explain this fact for certain, but it appears to have been caused by low precipitation around Bering Strait at that time; with little rain and snowfall, there would have been enough ice to cover only the mountain ranges. So, during a large part of the Pleistocene, until the most recent ice sheet finally began melting about ten thousand years ago, Siberia and Alaska were linked by dry land. The width of the land bridge changed in rhythm with the advances and retreats of the white blanket, becoming more exposed as glaciation reached its maxima, becoming narrower and even disappearing altogether during the interglacial melts when the sea rose again. In effect, the connection between Siberia and Alaska was a slowly opening and closing drawbridge.

When the land bridge was exposed, it blocked off the cold Arctic waters, allowing the warm Pacific air to temper the northern climate. Much of the land bridge was a rolling plain glistening with lakes and ponds; large grazing mammals found pasturage on its vegetation, a luxuriant growth of tall grasses or the tangle of dwarf birch, willows, alders, heaths, and mosses found today on the tundra of northern Canada.‡ Such conditions were exceedingly favorable for the herds of large ice-age mammals that, in search of food and living space, crossed from one continent to another. A wealth of mammals, many now extinct, reached North America: large camels that resembled the two-humped kind still found in Asia; ground sloths; a big-horned bison that stood seven feet high at the hump and whose horn spread was as much as six feet; a beast somewhat similar to a large moose; several kinds of musk ox, and the mammoths shaggy with reddish-brown hair. Also crossing to North America was the horse, an animal that had evolved in North America and then spread to Eurasia before becoming extinct in the New World. At the end of the ice age the horse became extinct for the second time in North America, and none were found on this continent until they were brought across the Atlantic by the Spaniards in the sixteenth century.

The portal that admitted man to the New World is now known to have been the Bering Strait land bridge. Early man did not cross via the Aleutian Islands, even though on a map this chain appears to thrust out a connecting link to Asia. The great depth of the water west of the island of Attu rules out the Aleutians, and so does the fact that they, unlike most of Alaska, were heavily glaciated. Nor is there any evidence that any other primate (whether monkey, ape, or Neanderthal) in the direct line of man's evolution ever crossed the land bridge before *Homo sapiens* himself did so. He crossed on dry land over a bridge exposed by the fall of the sea—not braving the swirling snows or picking his way from iceberg to iceberg, as was once believed. (Of course, latecomers who arrived more recently than ten thousand years ago could at times have crossed the fifty-six-mile gap of Bering Strait on the winter ice; even more recent migrants, the Aleuts and the Eskimo, made the crossing in boats.) Nor can you read into this migration from one continent to another any sermon on the innate adventurousness of the human spirit; man quite unwittingly crossed to Alaska, merely following the aimless herds of mammals that he hunted for food.↕

The probable outlines of the Bering Strait land bridge are shown during the last ice age when the sea fell 75 feet (stippled), 150 feet (light gray) and 300 feet (medium gray) below present levels. (The darkest gray indicates the open sea.) The water locked up as ice in the glaciers allowed a bridge to emerge that was sometimes wider than Alaska itself.

No one knows for certain when the very first hunters crossed the Bering land bridge, and the prospects of finding precise evidence in the future are poor. Not only has the sea risen once more and covered the land bridge, but in some places nearly a hundred feet of sediments have drifted to its bottom, further hiding the evidence. It is certain, though, that man has been in North America for a very long time indeed. About eleven thousand years ago the migrants from Asia reached land's end. Unmistakable signs of human occupancy have been found dating from that time in Fell's Cave at the southern tip of South America. The actual crossing, of course, probably was much earlier, for it may have taken thousands of years for the trickle of generation after generation to span that distance from Siberia.

The earliest unanimously accepted evidence for the presence of man in North America, exclusive of Alaska, is dated about 13,000 years ago. To pinpoint the actual crossing from Siberia, a few thousand more years could be added to allow for the migration south from Bering Strait. Many sites in both North and South America suggest that the arrival of at least some bands of men may have been very much earlier. Charcoal samples—from what are thought to have been hearths—at Lewisville, in northeastern Texas, have given radiocarbon dates of more than 38,000 years. The validity of this site, however, depends on whether the charcoal samples were from man-made fires or from fires started accidentally by lightning and spontaneous combustion. A spear point was also found near the crude tools, but its presence is suspected to have been an elaborate prank. Nevertheless, many archeologists continue to regard this site as one of the most exciting and important discoveries ever made in the Americas.‡

A difficulty in proving that man reached North America as early as perhaps forty thousand years ago is that at that time he may not have developed the technology to make the spear points that provide indisputable evidence of his presence. Signs other than spear points have been discovered that *may* point to the earlier presence of man: carbon from possible campfires, various pieces of stone that appear to be crude scrapers and choppers, tiny flakes that seem to mark some sites as tool workshops. Archeologists often disagree about this evidence: Some claim that the stones may not be artifacts at all but only accidental fashionings of nature, such as stones rubbing against each other in a stream bed; the hearths may be from lightning-caused fires. Nevertheless, such signs of the first dawn of man in the New World have been found in so many places that many archeologists now believe there might be some truth in them after all. There are sites lacking spear points in the Baja California peninsula,

California, Nevada, Arizona, Texas, and Wyoming that have been dated at upward of 30,000 years ago.‡ (Dating of archeological sites is a most difficult art; a brief outline of the various techniques is given in Notes and Sources on pages 301–303.)

PATHS ACROSS THE CONTINENT

The remains of the Paleo-Indians, as the early hunters up to about 7,000 years ago are called, are always associated with the bones of the mammals that flourished at the end of the last ice age. All of these now-extinct species—early horses, big-horned bison, camel, mammoth, mastodon, and others—shared several characteristics important to man's success in the new continent. They all fed on grass; they traveled in herds in open country and so were visible at great distances; and each supplied a large amount of food in a single package. Their passage also left plainly marked trails that led to water and to protected valleys, to salt licks and to mountain passes. Even the White explorers later relied on the trails left by millions of bison across North America: Daniel Boone followed a bison trail in laying out his Wilderness Road across the Cumberland Gap, and many railroad beds through mountains followed routes pioneered by bison.

Early man no doubt followed their trails from the very first, which would have led to his crossing of the Bering Strait land bridge. His route in North America is not as yet completely known, but it probably followed the northern foothills of the Alaskan ranges before turning southward. The foothill route offered the advantages of being drier than the mucky lowland tundra and of affording vantage points to sight game; it is no accident that almost all early sites so far discovered in Alaska and northwestern Canada are located on the flanks of mountains. (Some of the bands also appear to have crossed the land bridge in the Seward Peninsula area, then followed the Yukon River upstream.) With no competition from other men and with an abundant food source, the populations of the bands of Paleo-Indians must have increased rapidly in Alaska. Such a buildup of population pressure no doubt forced bands on the fringes into new areas; when these bands, in turn, increased in numbers, there were additional expansions into new territories. At various times an ice-free corridor to the interior of the continent opened up around the Mackenzie valley. The Mackenzie, in turn, led to the eastern flank of the Rocky Mountains and to the Great Plains, the axis from which the primary dispersal of the Paleo-Indians took place.‡

Today the plains are an arid tableland, monotonously level and broken only by badlands. But toward the end of the last ice age the plains were threaded with rivers and dotted with lakes and marshes; tall grasses grew that fed large mammals, an abundance probably such as the world had never seen before or is likely to see again. By traveling southward along the mountain flanks, early man had the best of two environments: the grasslands of the plains with their herds, and the sheltered valleys of the foothills. No special instinct told him to head southward. In fact, his ancestors had traveled generally northward to reach the Bering land bridge from Siberia. The only direction he followed was that of the game trails that lured him on at random; no doubt some bands even followed game trails that wandered back to Asia. One trail merely led to another, and beyond the present one there was always the horizon promising more food, water, and perhaps a milder climate. Some bands branched off to the east by following river valleys, and to the west through passes in the Rocky Mountains that had not been glaciated; and some kept steadily southward until they reached the tip of South America.

THE EARLIEST BIG-GAME HUNTERS

From the time that man arrived in the New World until after the melt of the ice sheets about ten thousand years ago, two basic ways of life existed: big-game hunting in the Great Plains and eastern forests, and collecting wild plants and small game primarily west of the Rocky Mountains. In actual practice, judging from what we know of surviving primitive hunters, the big-game people probably obtained a sizable amount of food from plants as well. There were, of course, slight regional variations, such as different methods in the working of tools, but on the whole these early cultures were remarkably uniform. Of these two early orientations toward obtaining food, that of hunting big game was the most widespread, and much more information has been unearthed about it.

Possibly the oldest known site of the big-game hunters was discovered in 1936 when a student at the University of New Mexico was exploring caves in the Sandia ("Watermelon") Mountains near Albuquerque. He came upon one cave that showed signs of occupancy by Pueblo Indians and thought it worth further investigation. Archeologists from the university crawled into it for several hundred yards and discovered the claw from an extinct ground sloth, evidence that the cave had been occupied for many thousands of years before the modern Pueblo Indians used it. As the archeologists dug downward into the rocky debris they found layers showing that generation after generation of early men had lived atop the rubble of the one before.

The bottommost layer revealed clearly the presence of early man—scraps of flint, bones of mammoths and bison that had been shattered as if to extract the marrow, charcoal deposits from fires. Among the shattered bones, the archeologists found flint knives and scrapers, presumably used for working skins, and, most important, flint spear points. These Sandia points, as they have come to be known, were crudely chipped, but they are very distinctive: Most of them have a rounded shoulder on one side of the base, which probably made it easier to attach the point to the shaft.

As with numerous other sites, there has been dispute about the dating of Sandia, with dates ranging between a conservative 12,000 years of age to an extreme of 25,000 years. Sandia points are well documented from only a few other places not very far from Sandia cave itself, although claims have been made for other sites in Oregon and Ontario.‡

The next oldest Paleo-Indian hunting culture was considerably more widespread and uniform. This culture is known as Llano (also referred to as Clovis because it was first discovered near Clovis, New Mexico). The primary indicator of the Llano is its distinctive spear point, the Clovis Fluted. It is thin, usually between three and four inches long, and about a third as wide. It was rather crudely made, with only scant retouching of the edges or smoothing of the base. But it did have a flute, a narrow channel that extended part way from the base to the point.

Clovis Fluted points, and assemblages of other artifacts usually associated with them, have been found at numerous camps or butchering sites, most of which date about 12,000 years ago on the plains and 14,000 years ago in parts of Alaska. These Clovis points have been found in every one of the forty-eight contiguous states and southward into Mexico; so uniform was the culture across the continent, particularly east of the Rockies, that a site in Massachusetts is scarcely distinguishable from another Llano site in, say, Colorado. Practically every find of Clovis points has been associated with the bones of mammoths, although occasionally bones of horses and big-horned bison are found as well, indicating that these people specialized in hunting mammoths. The large number of immature mammoths at several sites indicates that the hunters were skilled in cutting young mammoths off from the herd's formidable adults. And it is clear, too, that these Llano hunts often were cooperative, for a single mammoth excavated in Arizona had eight fluted points embedded in it.‡

The next major culture after the Llano was the well-known Folsom, named after the community in New Mexico where it was first discovered. The accidental discovery of ancient points in 1925 by a cowpuncher who was tracing some lost cattle was an important event: It was the first major support given those archeologists who had been ridiculed for their claims of man's great antiquity in North America. Nineteen points were found here, most of them embedded in the remains of the big-horned bison; numerous Folsom points have since been discovered elsewhere, and they all date at between nine thousand and eleven thousand years ago. Even to the untutored eye of the amateur, these are beautifully fashioned. First, a piece of flint approximately three inches in length was flaked to the general shape. Then a flake, which sometimes reached from the base very nearly to the tip, was chopped away on each face to make long grooves. Finally the maker retouched the edges by removing tiny chips; he then ground the base smooth.

Considerable dispute has arisen about the reason for the elaborate fluting on Folsom points. Some archeologists believe that it made attachment to the lance easier; others, that it lightened the weight of the point so that it could be thrown farther. A third theory is that it had the same function as the grooves on a bayonet, allowing a greater flow of blood from the wound. Still another theory is that the grooves were merely an artistic flourish, just as the fine retouching around the edges probably gave no other benefit than esthetic satisfaction.‡ (Our accent on function appears to be a modern idea; many primitive peoples expend much more effort in making their tools than is called for by mere utility.) The theory that the fluting made attachment to the lance easier seems the most probable. Evidence for this is that the lower edges of the points are usually dulled, as if the maker wanted to be sure a sharp edge did not cut through the taut sinews used to haft the point to the shaft.

As in the case of Sandia and Llano, there is an unfortunate lack of information about the Folsom people themselves. Their butchering techniques are known, but not how they lived and what they may have believed in. Inference can go only so far; that is why archeologists are grateful for small favors. One such was handed them in 1966 when a University of New Mexico graduate student discovered just outside of Albuquerque what may be the oldest habitation site known in the New World—and is assuredly the most important Folsom site unearthed to date because of the number and variety of artifacts found there. At this Rio Rancho site, as it is known, at least two Folsom lodges were discovered. Each lodge was circular and about fifteen feet in diameter; it was built of a framework of

STAGES AND CULTURES	APPROX. DATES	PRIMARY GAME HUNTED	PROJECTILE POINTS
PLANO	9,500 TO 7,000 YEARS AGO	Pronghorn Antelope / Modern Bison / Big-Horned Bison	
PLAINVIEW	10,000 TO 7,500 YEARS AGO	Big-Horned Bison	
FOLSOM	11,000 TO 9,000 YEARS AGO	Big-Horned Bison	
LLANO	15,000 (?) TO 11,000 YEARS AGO	Mammoth	
SANDIA	25,000 (?) TO 12,000 YEARS AGO	Mammoth / Camel / Big-Horned Bison / Horse	
PRE-PROJECTILE STAGES	38,000 (?) TO 20,000 (?) YEARS AGO	Dire Wolf / Horse / Mammoth / Sabertooth	No Undisputed Projectile Points / SCRAPERS

small poles and apparently covered by bison skins. The hearths for cooking were placed outside. Implications about the daily life of Folsom man will not be available for several more years; the rest of the artifacts must be unearthed and analyzed, and the site studied more carefully.↕

A culture known as Plainview that flourished for a time after Folsom shows still further improvements in hunting technique. Near Plainview, Texas, the remains of one thousand big-horned bison were unearthed. These animals represented the mass slaughter of a herd that obviously had been stampeded over a bluff into the valley. The animals at the bottom were found to have no points in them; they must have been the leaders of the herd, killed by the fall and the weight of the other bison on top of them. But the bison that were at the rear and fell on top of the heap were probably only stunned. These were dispatched by the flint points found embedded in their bones. The Plainview points much resemble the basic outlines of Folsom points, but they lack the fluting.

The position of Plainview in the chronology of the Paleo-Indian hunters is not yet agreed upon, but it does seem clear that most of the sites so far discovered were butchering stations rather than settlements. This fact implies wandering, or at least mobile populations oriented toward hunting. Very little is known of these people aside from the tools they used to kill the bison and prepare the skins; only occasionally have paint palettes, beads, and decorated stone disks (probably used for ornament) been found. But the discovery of the Plainview sites is important in one respect: It reveals the great antiquity of the hunting method of stampeding bison over cliffs, a method still being used by the Plains Indians in the middle of the last century. The Lewis and Clark expedition, for example, reported more than one hundred bison carcasses left to decay after Indians drove a herd over a precipice. The Plainview people effectively dispel the romantic illusion that early man was innately a conservationist who killed only as much as he needed for food. His very method of hunting—the stampede—necessitated the slaughter of many animals to obtain only a few for food.

Plainview and a number of other cultures after Folsom are believed to have been transitional to the next major culture based on a hunting economy. First associated with Yuma County, Colorado, and with Eden Valley, Wyoming, where many spear points typical of it were discovered, this culture is now usually given the name Plano; most of the sites date between 7,000 and 9,500 years ago. This was a time of change on the continent as the climate became drier and the luxuriant carpet of grasses grew sparse. Mammoths, horses, and camels were dying out, and even the big-horned bison was giving way to the species we know today. The primary prey in which Plano points have been found is still the big-horned bison, but at some sites there are also modern bison, pronghorn antelope, and even deer.

THE GREAT EXTINCTION

The first faint trail of the Paleo-Indian hunters is picked up in the misty past, more than 20,000 years ago, but by about 7,000 years ago it had dwindled, to be replaced by a variety of new technologies and economies. During that tremendous span of time the many techniques of big-game hunting were perfected and they spread far. The bones of ice-age mammals and the variety of weapons and tools used to kill and butcher them has left an impressive record from Alaska to Cape Horn of the Paleo-Indian's ability to exploit his environment.

The hunting economy finally disappeared because of a change in the very factor that had brought it into existence in the first place—the climate. At the end of the last ice age the climate in interior North America was generally cool and moist, and numerous shallow lakes were bordered by luxuriant vegetation. The people who made the Llano and Folsom points lived under these ideal hunting conditions, and so did most of the Plano people. But as the ice began its rapid melt about ten thousand years ago, the climate started to change in a major way. As temperatures rose and the cloud cover diminished, there was an increase in the evaporation rate of the water that lay on the land. With the northward retreat of the cold air masses, precipitation probably was reduced as well. Slowly at first, and then at an accelerating rate, the plant cover thinned out, and the great herds declined drastically. The limitless abundance came to an end some seven thousand years ago, the date of the last Paleo-Indian sites based on big-game hunting. After that, the hunting of large mammals was limited largely to a few wet areas in the plains and was based solely on the modern species of bison.

The last ice age closed dramatically with the melting of huge blocks of ice, the pouring of water into freshets that swelled into torrents—and it closed also with one of the greatest extinctions of mammals the planet has ever known. Beginning about 12,000 years ago, and continuing over the next 6,000 years, the mammals' extinction in North America was of nearly the same magnitude as the dying out of the dinosaurs some 65,000,000 years earlier. Some of the better known mammals and their approximate dates of disappearance are: woolly mammoth, 10,000 years ago; various forms of tapir and ground sloth, 9,500 years ago; giant ground sloth and big-horned bison, 8,500 years ago; horse, camel, giant armadillo, and Columbian mammoth, about 7,500 years ago. The La Brea tar pits at Los Angeles, California, strikingly demonstrate how extensive this extinction was: The remains of thirty-five kinds of mammals that lived 15,000 years ago have been unearthed there; but 9,000 years later not one of them still survived in North America.

It might be supposed that these extinctions were due simply to the severe climate changes at the end of the last ice age. But the explanation must be more complex than that. All the mammals that became extinct had already survived several previous expansions and retreats of the ice, with their attendant climate changes, throughout the Pleistocene. Although some mammals died out in other parts of the world, the major extinctions occurred in North America. The camel and the horse died out in North America, but both survived in Eurasia despite the melting of the ice there; tapirs and ground sloths disappeared from North America, but both endured in South America. Obviously something was different about the conditions in North America, and that difference appeared only at the last ice age.‡

In North America there was only one addition to the environment that had not been present in previous interglacial times: man, armed with fire and possessor of a sophisticated hunting technology. The extinction of ice-age mammals was less severe in Africa and in Eurasia, possibly because man and mammals had been together on those continents for more than a million years and the mammals had had time to adapt to the ways of man. Also, Africa had already gone through its great extinction some 50,000 years ago when twenty-six groups of large mammals had disappeared—at a time when a human culture that specialized in hunting with large stone axes had spread over that continent. South America suffered no equivalent extinction, probably because the human populations were not large enough to decrease significantly the mammal populations. Undoubtedly the climate change placed the mammals of North America under great stress; but the final tipping of the balance toward extinction may have been the toll taken by the Paleo-Indian's hunting economy.

The question has often been asked how the small human population in North America would have been able to kill off tremendous numbers of mammals—and the answer can be found in some of the ecological laws that govern animal populations. Every species of animal in the world requires a minimum population to survive. Cormorants, for example, will not breed successfully if their populations on their nesting grounds fall below a density of three nests per ten square feet. The fifty breeding pairs of heath hens that survived for a time on Martha's Vineyard, off Cape Cod, were below the critical minimum for their species—and owing to the inability of this small population to breed successfully, the species became extinct in 1932. In Siberia, it has been found that the optimum number of reindeer making up a herd is between three and four hundred because of complex relationships between the reindeer, blood-sucking insects, and the food plants. Undoubtedly the extinction of the ice-age mammals began with the enormous losses their populations suffered because of the changing climate. Then the Paleo-Indian hunters had to kill comparatively few of the mammals to reduce their numbers beneath the critical minimum necessary for survival.

Although the ice-age hunters were comparatively few, the inroads they made into mammal populations were out of all proportion to their numbers. Early man concentrated around waterholes and streams; as the land became more arid, the huge beasts had to go to those watering places where man himself was lying in wait. There are piles of mammal bones at Folsom and Plano sites, and they are not accidental, for a graveyard of mammoths no more existed than did the mythical one of the African elephant. Rather, the bones tell a story of repeated slaughter by Paleo-Indian hunters along the watercourses.↕

Although there are technical distinctions between the Sandia, Llano, Folsom, and Plano cultures, it is clear that they all were part of one broad cultural stage of ice-age hunters. The ice-age mammals were the major food supply for these Paleo-Indians, and, to capitalize on that resource, they perfected a technology that spread across North America, and into South America as well. The kills of big game had allowed the Paleo-Indians to increase their numbers; the mammals afforded skins for shelter and for clothing during the climatic vagaries at the end of the ice age. The abundance, though, had also limited man's incentive to move into less bountiful regions, to experiment with living in deserts or along seacoasts, to harvest the continent's incredible variety of small mammals, birds, fishes, and plants.

As the great herds began to disappear like the melting ice, man was thrown back to an earlier stage in his development. Once again he became a collector of whatever foods he could find—small mammals, carrion, insects, and the seeds of wild plants. While some bands were still hunting the last of the mammoths and big-horned bison, others were experimenting with the environment. The great hunting cultures of the ice age, which had spread from the Pacific to the Atlantic, and nearly from pole to pole, gave way in prominence to a diversity of local cultures, born of the slow process of trial and error. These Archaic people, as they are called by archeologists, specialized in nothing, but they were versatile in attempting everything.

PREADAPTED CULTURES EMERGE

In a remarkable diversity of environments—the rich pine woods of the Southeast, the cold northern forests, the arid West—the Archaic people invented fish spears, snares for trapping rodents and birds, darts for bringing down small game, baskets for collecting roots, stones for grinding seeds. Most important, manos (the round milling stones, resembling rolling pins, that are held in the hands) and metates (the shallow base stones) for grinding plant food became increasingly common as time went on. Their appearance was a clear indication that as the numbers of Pleistocene mammals dwindled, at least some people were supplementing their food supply with plants. Settlement patterns changed also, as man colonized the seacoasts and rivers where he obtained fish, shellfish, plants, and small game. Life became considerably more sedentary, and the numbers of people seem to have increased markedly. Different ways of exploiting different environments resulted in the budding off of new cultures and the growth of new kinds of institutions to make them effective.

To modern man, possessor of an advanced technology, it may not appear very important whether people kill a large mammal or a variety of smaller animals for food—any more than it matters whether one orders steak or chicken for dinner. But at the early stages in cultural development the differences are crucial. The food of collectors comes in smaller packages than that of the big-game hunters; different methods of hunting, transporting, storing, distributing, and preparing the food have to be developed. Instead of merely cutting off steaks from a single mammoth and perhaps drying strips for future use, new techniques of storage and transport must be devised. Instead of an array of spear points, a new technology of snares and weirs has to be developed to capture small land animals and fishes.

It would be an extreme oversimplification to visualize a continent full of Paleo-Indian hunters who, when their prey animals declined, promptly switched over to the Archaic way of making a living. While these hunters were perfecting their specialty they had overshadowed the other, far different Archaic economies that were developing. When the series of climate changes began after the melt of the ice, resulting in changes in the plant and animal life of the continent, the Archaic cultures had already emerged sufficiently to take advantage of the changed conditions. In short, they were *preadapted* to the changes.

Preadaptation is a well-known principle in biological evolution.‡ The structures of all living things are enormously complex, possessing many features that at a certain stage in development might have no apparent use, but which arose as the random companion of the evolution of other parts of the organism. Let some change take place in the environment   climate, an abundance of a new kind of food or the shortage of an old kind, competition by other species—and this random feature might be the very thing that would enable the organism to adapt to the changed conditions. An example is the accidental preadaptation of paired fins and lungs in certain fishes; after a long series of small changes, the fishes lived on land, breathed air, and ultimately evolved into amphibians.

The same sort of preadaptation occurs in human cultures as well. There often is no rational explanation why one group of people does something in a particular way, seemingly without any increased efficiency. For a time anthropologists regarded the quaint customs of primitives as survivals from some more ancient way of life, much as the sacrum at the base of spine may be a vestigial organ. But in most cases such eccentric human ways look back to nothing; they arose by accident, or accompanied other changes in the culture. However, this insignificant eccentricity may someday be extremely important in adapting to new conditions. The archeological record shows clearly that there were eccentric ways of life during the times of the ice-age hunters. Had conditions in North America not changed after the retreat of the ice and in this way brought them into prominence, little would be known of them. But the adaptations did exist, and conditions did change— and so, in the story of man upon this continent, they assume paramount importance.

THE DESERT CULTURE AND THE EASTERN ARCHAIC

After the melt of the ice the Archaic way of life became continent-wide in two forms: the Desert culture of the western part of the continent, and the Eastern Archaic culture. From the deserts of the Southwest and the Great Basin westward to the Pacific Ocean, the land was largely arid and devoid of the large mammals that had enabled the specialized hunting cultures to arise. Instead, the Desert culture was oriented toward plants—the collecting of small seeds and roots for food, the use of plant fibers for baskets and footwear. No matter where it existed, the Desert culture possessed certain hallmarks. Most characteristic are the baskets for transporting and storing grain, and the manos and metates used to grind seeds, fruit, roots, and even insects. At Danger Cave, Utah, the typical pattern of the Desert culture appears to have flourished as much as 9,500 years ago, at about the same time as the Llano and Folsom cultures were flourishing on the Great Plains.

The Desert people exploited every possible food resource in their inhospitable land, using nets, snares, and grinding stones; they must have existed on a precarious edge between survival and extinction. The discovery of a number of caves they occupied in Nevada, Utah, Arizona, and Oregon has given a clear picture of their tools and their way of life. The caves are small and were only intermittently occupied, indicating that the people lived in small groups and wandered much of the year in search of food. For thousands of years after the Desert culture emerged, scarcely any basic changes took place in the pattern of food collecting as a way of life. And in some places in California and the Great Basin, the Desert way of life persisted virtually unchanged until the arrival of the Whites. It was, however, this Desert culture, with its accent on plants, that later provided the substratum upon which the agricultural cultures of the Pueblo and the Mexican empires were erected.

Since the Eastern Archaic was not primarily dependent on plants, it is more difficult to define than the Desert culture. For many archeologists it is simply a long period of time during which local environments were skillfully exploited in a multitude of ways. More than ten thousand Eastern Archaic sites are already known, and there is only one common denominator: In each of them, man came to terms with what the habitat offered. Archaic peoples utilized antlers and bones to manufacture fishhooks, spears, and harpoon heads; some learned to work copper for tools and ornaments; they had a variety of projectile points for all kinds of game.

One of the oldest Eastern Archaic sites, dating back more than nine thousand years, is the Modoc Rock Shelter, a cave in the Illinois bluffs that overlooks the Mississippi River southeast of St. Louis. The bottommost, and therefore the oldest, layer of artifacts and refuse in the cave reveals a simple culture that was quite different from the culture of the ice-age hunters who flourished at about the same time. The Modoc Shelter reveals no bones of mammoth or big-horned bison; instead, the people who lived there hunted deer, elk, raccoon, and opossum. Hunters of mammoth and bison had to be prepared to follow the wandering herds on the game trails, but the mammals hunted by the inhabitants of Modoc all tended to remain in the same locality. So the Modoc hunters had a year-round food supply without having to wander far from their natural shelter in the bluffs. The river provided a wealth of other food: fishes, turtles, snails, and mussels. It is significant that more than half of the fish bones found in the oldest levels of the cave were those of catfish, the slow-moving inhabitants of the quiet backwaters of rivers. The technology of the early Modoc people probably was not sufficiently advanced to capture any faster-moving fish.

Grinding stones are virtually absent in these bottom layers at Modoc, showing that the primary food source in the early Archaic was still small animals. By about 8,200 years ago, plant foods were being increasingly relied upon, for the mano and the metate are clearly present in layers dating to that time. Deer was still a mainstay of the diet, only now it was hunted more efficiently with light spears hurled by an atlatl (spear thrower). The variety of tools begins to widen: Bone was used to make awls, and flint to manufacture drills; ornaments were made of shell and pendants of worked stone. The food base had broadened to include the migrant ducks and geese, which must have abounded in the ponds and along the reedy riverbanks, much as they still do today. The bones of dogs appear, showing that they had become domesticated companions of man, and possibly a source of food as well. Anyone who looks closely at the Modoc culture of some 8,000 years ago must inevitably feel the shock of recognition, for here is the familiar world of the Woodland Indian of early American history.‡

The Eastern Archaic emerges as an Arcadian time in the history of man in North America, during which he utilized his resources to the fullest, yet still lived in harmony with his environment. In fact, J. R. Caldwell,‡ a specialist in the archeology of eastern North America, has lauded the Archaic people for what he calls their "primary forest efficiency"—their adaptation to many kinds of environments in which only the surplus food resources were cropped as they became seasonably available. Their wide-ranging use of the environment was quite remarkable: By the time explorers reached the Great Lakes area, the descendants of this Archaic people were using 275 species of plants for medicine, 130 for food, 31 as magical charms, 27 for smoking, 25 as dyes, 18 in beverages and for flavoring, and 52 others for various purposes.‡ No animal or any particular group of animals was singled out for exploitation; the Eastern Archaic peoples practiced what is today known as multiple-use conservation.

BEGINNINGS OF AGRICULTURE

Agriculture developed in the Near East perhaps as long ago as eleven thousand years, but it did not begin until a few thousand years later in the New World. New World agriculture assuredly arose independently of the Old World, for the first crops cultivated in the Near East were wheat, barley, and rye—and these plants did not exist in primeval North America. New World agriculture was not only different from that practiced in the Old World; in many ways it was superior as well. Indians cultivated a wider variety of plants than did Europeans at the time of the discovery of North America, and they used horticultural techniques that were in many cases more advanced. The intimate connection that the Indians achieved between man and domesticated plants is demonstrated by maize. Old World wheat or rye can survive in the wild as a weed, but no form of New World maize has ever been found growing in the wild; every maize plant that grows anywhere today is a domesticated variety. So completely has maize been domesticated that it would promptly become extinct were man to stop growing it, for it does not possess any way for its seeds, the kernels, to be dispersed. Equally remarkable was the Indians' skill in utilizing the great number of poisonous plants: They devised a way to squeeze out the deadly poison from manioc, known as tapioca in the United States, leaving the starch.

The most widespread and important crop, however, was maize, grown throughout the area bounded by southern Canada and Chile. Because it was the foundation upon which the higher cultures of the New World were built, it was important for anthropologists to learn the date and place of its domestication. But there seemed little hope of ever discovering the steps in the domestication of wild maize. Many fruitless searches were made in Central and South America, and many theories were put forth that were later discredited. Then in 1960, the exploration of numerous caves in the Tehuacán valley, south of Mexico City, finally settled many of the questions. The archeologists digging down into the rubble unearthed twenty-eight levels of human occupancy, a complete record of human history from about twelve thousand years ago until approximately the time Cortés conquered Mexico in 1521. No other archeological region in the world has ever afforded such a clear picture of the rise of a civilization step by step.

The remains of plants and animals depicted the changing environments and man's constantly realigned relations to them. And above all, the excavations have supplied the answers to how, where, and when maize was domesticated in the New World.

Between about 12,000 and 9,200 years ago, the caves were occupied by small bands of nomadic families, collectors of wild plants and hunters of small animals such as rabbits and birds. Then a subtle shift in emphasis took place: Plants were used increasingly as food. Not much later, between 8,700 and 7,000 years ago, the people still relied upon wild varieties of chili peppers and beans, but they also began to grow domesticated squash and avocados. By about 7,200 years ago wild maize appeared. Each ear was no larger than a man's thumbnail and the plant itself was probably no more conspicuous than many kinds of weeds growing today along road-sides and on abandoned fields. But, with man's aid, maize had the potential to grow larger and to evolve into a plant with long rows of seeds on large cobs.

The cave inhabitants were relying heavily upon agriculture by about 5,400 years ago: Nearly a third of their food came from domesticated plants. The first permanent settlements appeared, and the groundwork for civilization was laid. By 3,500 years ago, archeologists found evidence of complex village life, pottery, elaborate religious rituals, and the intricate social organization that all these things imply. And by 2,000 years ago, large-scale irrigation works were being constructed;‡ tomatoes and peanuts were added to the long list of domesticated plants, and turkeys were domesticated; specialized occupations arose in religion, art, and govern-ment; there was evidence of a far-flung trade. This civilization culminated about 1,000 years ago in the high culture of the Mixtec, who ruled until they were conquered by the Aztec shortly before the arrival of Cortés. And so the story of Tehuacán over the past 12,000 years demonstrates the gradual evolution of small, nomadic bands of collectors and hunters into a complex and despotic high civilization based on agriculture.‡

Using oversimplified data from the Near East, social scientists in the past spoke glibly of an "agricultural revolution," during which time man's population suddenly soared, cities were founded, and the many trappings of civilization appeared. Recent archeological discoveries from the Near East cast doubt on this interpretation, and the thousands of years it took for agriculture to develop at Tehuacán assuredly show that it is not true. The food-production *revolution* turns out to be a slow *evolution,* a long period of experimentation rather than a sudden burst. Although signs of plant domestication appear around Tehuacán as early as 8,700 years ago, settled village life did not begin until about 3,500 years later, pottery not until 5,000 years later, and a population spurt not until 5,500 years after the initial domestication of plants. In fact, it was not until about 3,000 years ago that what might be called a high civilization arose.‡

TRANSPACIFIC CONTACTS?

The Tehuacán caves demonstrate how cultures gradually change, how new ideas and techniques emerge out of the old. They refute those archeologists who are quick to attribute changes in a culture to new migrations of people, either across the Bering Strait or across the Pacific. These archeologists in the past pointed to several innovations in the Archaic that they felt were imported from Asia. One such innovation was agriculture, but Tehuacán now offers indisputable evidence that many crops were domesticated in Mexico, and that the techniques of agriculture developed independently of the Old World. Similarly, the building of earthen burial mounds was long attributed to Asia, but now most archeologists are convinced that the mounds were a logical outgrowth of the Archaic's increasing concern with burial and the afterlife.

Nevertheless, remarkable similarities do exist in tools, myths, art, technology, and even customs between various North American Indians and peoples in Asia. There is, for instance, an atlatl from the North American plains that is exactly the same in design as some spear throwers found among Australian aborigines. Quite an impressive list of similar cultural items could be drawn up, including stone clubs from California and New Zealand, bells from Arizona and China, musical panpipes from California and Burma.

These resemblances cannot be denied; but many of them can be explained by two well-known scientific laws. One is convergence, a principle more clearly understandable in biological than in anthropological terms. It means simply that around the world various plants and animals look alike, not always because they are related, but because they have become adapted to the same environments. Cacti are widespread in the deserts of the New World, but they never grew in the Old World until modern man spread them there accidentally. The African deserts are instead the home of euphorbias—an entirely different group of plants, but also spiny, succulent, and adapted to arid conditions—which look enough like cacti to confuse even some horticulturists. Convergence occurs in culture also. Two human societies not related and far distant from each other, but subject to the same potentials and conditions, may arrive at the same way of doing things. In the forests of the Amazon, where wood and plant poison are available, Indians developed the blowgun; living in much the same sort of environment, with wood and plant poison similarly available, the Semang of Malaysia independently invented the blowgun.

The second scientific law is the principle of limited possibilities.‡ Only a limited number of sounds can be made by human lips. In the aboriginal California language known as Yuki, the sound *ko* means "go" and *kom* means "come." There are no other similarities between Yuki and English, and it would be absurd to dream of a connection between the languages. There are only a limited number of ways in which a human can depict his sex organs in a fertility symbol. Menstruation can be surrounded with one of the ten or twenty different kinds of mysteries the human mind has managed to concoct about it, but the number of possibilities soon runs out. So it is inevitable that occasionally similarities will appear in widely separated societies that have no other connection.

The highly publicized voyage made by Thor Heyerdahl westward across the Pacific from South America in the balsa raft *Kon-Tiki* was undertaken to prove his theory that American Indians populated the Polynesian Islands and southeastern Asia. Among the dubious pieces of evidence put forth by Heyerdahl for such a Transpacific migration is this example of linguistic acrobatics: A pre-Incan group of Indians in South America had a god known as Kon-Tiki or Illa Tiki, and the Polynesians today have a god known as Tiki. Heyerdahl neglects to mention that a tribe in Africa, one he does not maintain had any connection with South American Indians, is called Tiki Tiki by its neighbors, and undoubtedly the sound *tiki* occurs in other unrelated languages as well.‡

Probably most of the resemblances between Asian and American Indian cultures can be attributed to the principles of convergence or limited possibilities. But there still remain some facts that cannot be explained away so easily. The law of probability is stretched to the breaking point if it is used to explain how Asians and Mexican Indians could have independently and accidentally worked out exactly the same complex rules for the game of pachisi. Nor can chance explain not only how a bundle of panpipes from the Solomon Islands of the Pacific came to look like a bundle from the New World, but also how both societies hit upon tuning their instruments to the same pitch and using the same scale.

The significance of such similarities, however, is uncertain. At this time, archeologists seem more inclined to accept some Transpacific contacts than they were a few decades ago, and old reports and artifact collections are being reexamined. The essential point, though, is not whether contacts between Asia and the New World took place across the Pacific, but rather to what extent they influenced the native cultures of North America. In most cases the contacts were only of minor importance because they occurred in comparatively recent times—*after* the native American cultures were already pointed in certain directions. New ideas and techniques are carried by people, and migrations of people across the Pacific would have been difficult until Asians invented seagoing ships. New Zealand is much closer to Asia than are the Americas, yet the Polynesians did not settle New Zealand until a mere seven hundred years ago. By the time that Polynesians were on the move across the Pacific, the major patterns of North American culture had already developed. So the first argument against the importance of Transpacific contacts is that in many cases they occurred too late to shape the native cultures that had already emerged in North America. A second argument is that it really is unimportant, when looking at the evolution of cultures, whether pottery or writing came to the New World across the Pacific. As a matter of fact they both possibly did, but much more important are the ways in which the already evolving cultures utilized or modified or even rejected them.

A third argument in favor of the independent evolution of the native Indian cultures is a peculiar characteristic of all cultures: They are much more likely to accept a change in a minor aspect of culture, such as a toy, than in something as major as a food crop. If prehistoric contact existed across the Pacific between Asia and the New World, then it had remarkably little effect on anything so important as agriculture. Out of the many thousands of plants that are grown for food or fiber, only four are shared by the Old World and the New: gourd, cotton, sweet potato, and coconut. Plant geographers are convinced that the sweet potato originated as a New World plant, and the coconut is not significant because it is spread by ocean currents and not by people. So out of the multitudes of plants grown in the Old World, only two, cotton and gourd, in theory could have been brought to the New World by Transpacific contacts. It is much more likely, though, that they spread around the world before the continents drifted apart and before man evolved. Similarly, the Maya of Mexico and Guatemala *may* have received the lotus-blossom decorative motif from a Transpacific contact perhaps several hundred or even a thousand years ago. But if they did, then why did they not also borrow from Asians the arch, of much greater value?

The final argument is that many extraordinary and complex inventions undoubtedly originated in the New World. They include the many aspects of plant domestication and horticulture, the hammock, the tobacco pipe, an intricate ventilating and cooling system for ceremonial chambers, the enema, the hollow rubber ball, the surgical practice of trepanning, the toboggan, and numerous other things that were brought back to the Old World after Columbus. If Indians could invent all these, why could they not also have invented independently other things known also in the Old World?↕

Of all the cultural items that may have diffused from Asia, the one that seems most likely is pottery. The earliest pottery found anywhere in the New World dates from about five thousand years ago in the area around Valdivia on the coast of Ecuador. Its distinctive designs and decorations did not exist any place else in the world except in the Jomon culture on Kyushu, the southernmost island of Japan—and the dates for that kind of pottery in both places are approximately the same. Anyone who sees the shards is impressed with how impossible it is to tell the Valdivian ones from the Jomon. But to explain the remarkable similarity requires a strenuous suspension of disbelief.

The archeologists who made this startling discovery have hypothesized that a Japanese fishing vessel was caught offshore in a typhoon and blown so far out to sea that it could not return home. The fishermen somehow survived many months of floating the more than eight thousand nautical miles to Ecuador; rain supplied them with fresh water and they tapped the sea's abundance for food. They made a landfall on the coast of Ecuador where Indians belonging to a completely different culture and linguistic family accepted them. Not only did these Japanese know how to fish; they also had learned from their wives the complex art of making pottery. And, this hypothesis concludes, they found apt pupils in the Valdivia people of Ecuador. On the face of it, such a sequence of fortuitous events is incredible; yet no archeologist has found an alternate way to explain what Japanese pottery is doing on the coast of Ecuador, nor to explain how such sophisticated pottery appeared suddenly in Ecuador without any record of previous amateurish attempts.↕

The origins of pottery in Ecuador seem to have been explained, yet this fact is not really crucial to any examination of the evolution of North American cultures. The end of the Archaic is marked by innovations in all aspects of culture, not just in pottery alone, and it would be foolish to attribute such a flowering of innovations solely to imports of ideas from Asia. It is hardly believable that the numerous specializations that arose among the various Indian groups were due to alien technologies cast up on the North American shore. Rather it is more reasonable to take the view of J. R. Caldwell that the Archaic culture itself possessed a great "reservoir of innovators" who accounted for the increasing specialization of the cultures.

THE FLOWERING OF DIVERSITY

During the three thousand years that preceded the discovery of North America, the fabric of Indian culture grew increasingly rich and varied. Scores of sites have been found for every one that existed in the Archaic, and these more recent sites differ considerably among themselves. Cultures everywhere were diversifying, specializing.

Until recently, most archeologists looked upon the agricultural cultures of the southwestern deserts that arose after the Archaic as mere variations on the same theme.✝ It is now known, though, that such a picture of uniformity is an illusion. Several major specializations arose that were quite distinct in their origins. For example, in southern Arizona, centered on the Gila and Salt rivers and their tributaries, the Hohokam ("those who have vanished," in the present-day Pima Indian language) arose nearly four thousand years ago. There are numerous differences between the Hohokam and other cultures of the southwestern deserts, but most note-worthy is the development by the Hohokam of a far-flung system of irriga-tion works, the earliest of them dating from some two thousand years ago at Snaketown, south of Phoenix. Rather than merely incorporating agricul-ture into an existing pattern of collecting seeds, as did other desert peoples, the Hohokam liberated themselves from their environment. On the major rivers they built dams that redirected the flow of water into canals, some of them thirty feet wide in places and extending for more than twenty-five miles.✝ The Hohokam were receptive to new ideas, primarily from Mexico. They made exquisite jewelry and distinctive pottery; they built pyramids and ball courts and used rubber balls imported from Central America; they appear to have used astronomy to calculate planting dates. Possibly the first etchings with acid were the remarkable works of art created on marine shells by the Hohokam. But about A.D. 1100 their distinctive way of life disappeared; the Hohokam survive today only as the Pima and Papago Indians of southern Arizona.

Another great culture that emerged from the Desert Archaic foundation was the Anasazi ("the ancient ones," in the language of the Navaho, who later occupied much of their territory).✝ Of all southwestern cultures, the

Mummy Cave at Canyon de Chelly National Monument in Arizona shows the sweep of Pueblo settlement from the early pit houses at right to the multistoried dwellings at left. The site was abandoned before the end of the thirteenth century and the area evacuated.

Anasazi are the best known: Mesa Verde in Colorado, Chaco Canyon in New Mexico, and Canyon de Chelly in Arizona are but three of the hundreds of cliff dwellings in the area where Utah, Colorado, New Mexico, and Arizona meet. The Anasazi received their distinguishing culture traits not from Mexico but from the southeastern United States; the type of maize they grew was southeastern, and so was the pottery they made. Their architecture is the most distinctive among all the southwestern cultures: Huge apartment houses at Pueblo Bonito, New Mexico, for example, contained eight hundred rooms. The Anasazi developed irrigation (although not so extensively as the Hohokam), and their skills in weaving, basketry, pottery, making household utensils, and masonry architecture

were rarely equaled north of Mexico. With surplus food and relative
stability, they developed an exceedingly rich ceremonial and artistic life.
The pomp of their religious festivals can be inferred from the size of their
dance courts or plazas; the dances surviving to this day among the Pueblo
Indians of Arizona and New Mexico, impressive as they are, are but faint
shadows of an exuberant Anasazi religious life.

The Anasazi culture came to an abrupt end about A.D. 1300. The great
villages were evacuated, and the populations migrated to their present
locations at pueblos on Arizona mesa tops or along the Rio Grande River
near Santa Fe and Albuquerque. Many explanations have been offered for
this sudden exodus. Archeologists have attributed it to warfare between the
pueblos, to raids by the Ute and Apache Indians who began filtering into
the Southwest from the north about that time, or to the great drought that
began in 1276 and lasted until 1299.‡ All of these explanations no doubt
are partially true—particularly the indications of warfare, for all of the
later pueblos were designed with such ingenious safeguards as removable
ladders. But too little consideration may have been given to changes in the
environment. The rainfall pattern altered in the two centuries before the
abandonment of the pueblos. The river channels on which the Indians
depended for water for their crops probably cut deeper into the land,
leaving the irrigation ditches high and dry. The Indians did not know the
principles of the siphon or the pump, and so they could not lift the water

*Plan of Pueblo village is clearly revealed at the Tuoynyi ruin in Frijoles Canyon
near Los Alamos, New Mexico. Note the central plaza and the circular ceremonial
chamber, or kiva.*

to the level of their fields. The loss of these lands for agriculture was probably aggravated by the increasing unreliability of the rainfall.‡

THE EASTERN WOODLANDS

At approximately the same time as the southwestern cultures were emerging out of the Desert culture, some 3,500 to 4,000 years ago, the Eastern Archaic was changing markedly in two ways: the manufacture of crude pottery and an increased attention to burial observances. Many archeologists believe that both represent the rise of a new culture pattern, known as the Woodland.‡ The Woodland culture flowered between 2,000 and 1,200 years ago in the area that now includes southern Ohio, northern Kentucky, and northwestern West Virginia. This flowering, called the Adena culture, was exceedingly rich: Clusters of burial mounds surrounded the bodies of eminent personages, who were entombed with offerings and with the bodies of those presumed to have been their retainers. Mound rose atop mound as new burials were made and earth added, until some of the piles reached heights of seventy feet. A complex of several mounds usually was surrounded by an earthen wall as much as five hundred feet in diameter. The sheer size of the mounds and the richness of the grave offerings point to a complex religious life and also to the chiefdom's complex political organization.

A remarkable fact about the Adena culture is that it achieved political complexity, social classes, a large population, rich pottery, and elaborate ornamentation—all without the major influence of agriculture. The Adena sites have yielded remains of squash and sunflower, but no maize; the subsistence pattern is the typically Archaic one of exploiting all aspects of the environment by hunting and gathering. Adena must have represented to the simpler cultures around it the potentialities of the Woodland way of life, much as ancient Rome must have represented to Gaul the potentialities of the Pax Romana.

Adena was but the prelude to the most remarkable, influential, and extensive culture to arise north of Mexico after the Archaic. It is named Hopewell after the owner of a Ross County, Ohio, farm, which had on it large earthworks, a village site, and burial mounds. Hopewell fused Adena, Archaic, and other elements. It was centered in southern Ohio and Illinois, but eventually it dominated much of the Adena area itself and extended its influence as far away as Minnesota, New York, Florida, and Louisiana. Although some uncertainty exists about the exact dates for

Hopewell, there is no doubt that it had already appeared about 2,250 years ago, and that in a few places Hopewell and Adena existed side by side until about A.D. 300.

Hopewell should technically not be called a culture—that is, a distinct kind of society with its own social, political, and technological ways of doing things. Rather, Hopewell consisted of many different societies with their own customs—but all bound together by two things. One was a cult of the dead, and the other was an economic bond. The cult of the dead consumed enormous amounts of materials for use as grave goods, and their procurement involved tapping widely separated areas of the continent.

Hopewell was on a much grander scale than Adena; the burial mounds were considerably larger, and the tomb offerings much richer. The earthworks extended for miles in patterns of octagons, squares, and circles; one earthwork enclosure in Ohio surrounds an area of four square miles. The offerings to the dead were munificent: One site alone yielded 48,000 pearls from freshwater shellfish. The exotic raw materials transported along the trade routes were fashioned by Hopewell artisans into some of the most finely wrought objects ever to appear in the Americas. Copper (from the borders of Lake Superior) and mica (from the Appalachians) were worked into delicate ornaments; obsidian (from the Rocky Mountains) was used to make elaborate ceremonial knives; alligator teeth and large conch shells (from Florida and the Gulf of Mexico) were used as beads and incorporated into clothing as decorations; several kinds of stone (from quarries in Minnesota and Wisconsin) were carved into tobacco pipes shaped like animals.

To judge by the extent of the earthen works, a tremendous labor force must have been recruited—and that implies a large, sedentary population. Anthropologists know from the study of other primitive societies that a strong central government must have been necessary to coordinate a large population. A powerful central authority seems confirmed by the burials of important personages, and by the vast tribute in goods rendered unto Hopewell by its simpler Woodland neighbors. A cult of the dead implies also a permanent priesthood. The very fact that so much ceremonial art was produced, and that it was of a uniformly high order of excellence, means that a specialized artisan class must have been subsidized by the priesthood.

Some archeologists have attributed the Hopewell cult, particularly the burial mounds, to diffusion from the Vera Cruz area of Mexico. But the tradition of heaping mounds of earth on the dead extends back three thousand years in North America; furthermore, the earliest of these mounds are found in Ohio and Illinois, not in places close to Mexico. These earliest mounds were rounded, whereas the Indians of Mexico built theirs in a pyramidal shape. The lavish mortuary rites and the placing of valued objects with the dead also have precursors in the Eastern Archaic burial practices and need not have been derived from Mexico.

By about A.D. 500 the Hopewell cult was in decline everywhere. This decline was once attributed to a dwindling population, but new information reveals that the population at the Hopewell sites during their last decades was actually higher than during the previous several centuries. The probable explanation seems to be that Hopewell's social and political institutions could not carry the load of increased populations. The institutions had developed at much lower levels of populations, and for a long time they answered all of the people's needs. But as populations increased markedly, and the Hopewell society became considerably more complex, these institutions were inadequate for the new problems that arose. One new problem was a period of unrest in eastern North America. The archeological record gives evidence of warfare and raiding: At just one typical site dating from the final period, the skeletons of seventy-eight percent of the males show that they met violent deaths. After about A.D. 500 the Hopewell people stopped building ceremonial centers in open valleys and sought out hilltops that could be defended.

There was, though, no way to defend the cult of the dead, and it was doomed; grave goods could no longer be obtained through trade because of the unsettled conditions. When the unifying feature of the Hopewell cult—the economic bond that procured the grave goods—disappeared, then the entire cult necessarily had to disappear also. A few burial mounds stocked with meager offerings were built about A.D. 750, but they are the last—and after that date the once-powerful Hopewell no longer existed.↕

THE MOUND BUILDERS

With the disappearance of the flamboyant Hopewell cult, the Woodland cultures settled back into the monotony that had marked the Archaic. There was one major exception: Along the Mississippi and other river systems of the south there emerged about A.D. 500 a culture that equaled Hopewell in its richness. This Mississippian culture, as it is called, was the immediate antecedent of the sophisticated southeastern chiefdoms—the Choctaw, Chickasaw, Natchez, and others—that so impressed early explorers such as

The Mound Builder culture, which spread across the Southeast and was still extant when the Spaniards arrived, produced outstanding art, as demonstrated by this gorget cut from the shell of a giant conch. The figure on the left may be a panther or a bear; the one on the right is undoubtedly an eagle in all its fury.

de Soto. Although the focus of the Mississippian was from Ohio southward to Louisiana and from Tennessee westward to Arkansas, its zone of influence reached out as far as the Great Plains and New York.

Numerous questions about the Mississippian are still unanswered, even though it arose as recently as a thousand years before the discovery of North America, and even though an abundance of sites have been uncovered. Archeologists do not agree, for instance, about its origin: Some attribute it to the migration of ideas from Mexico or Central America. It is indeed true that some of the Mississippian's sophisticated art—pottery, textiles, and ornaments worked from shell, wood, copper, and stone— much resembles Middle American art. But even more of the art had its

Mask carved from a single piece of wood is one of the finest prehistoric cere-
monial objects ever recovered from the Mound Builder cultures of the Southeast.
The original painted decorations have largely disappeared, and the shell inlays are
missing from the ear lobes, but its power remains. The mask was probably used
in the Deer Dance, which persisted until historic times.

roots in Adena and Hopewell. Current thinking treats the Mississippian as
an indigenous culture, an outgrowth of the Hopewell cults in the south,
blended with Mexican elements that arrived comparatively late.

The most imposing characteristic of the Mississippian is the pyramidal
mound, built not to cover a burial but to serve as a foundation for a temple
or a chief's house. Apparently centers of these mounds were built without
any uniform plan. Some were carefully laid out, with pyramidal mounds
grouped around a central plaza, but others consisted of a loose string of
conical mounds, reminiscent of Hopewell. Dwellings were often near the
ceremonial structures, but in some places they were distant from the
mound. Some centers were very small, comprising only two or three
mounds, whereas Cahokia, at East St. Louis, Illinois, had more than eighty-

five mounds and a village area that extended for six miles along the Ohio River. One of the largest Cahokia mounds was about one hundred feet high, and its base covered sixteen acres. The immensity of the labor involved would be awesome even in these days of bulldozers, but was much more so for the Mississippian people, who did not possess wheeled vehicles or beasts of burden. The mounds were constructed solely by human laborers who carried every clod of earth in baskets. Several specialists have attempted to estimate the number of laborers and the span of years involved to build Cahokia; they agree only that it must have taken thousands or tens of thousands of people working for a few hundred years. The Mississippian population must have been extraordinarily dense: At least 383 villages bordered the Mississippi River in the short distance of about seven hundred miles between where the Ohio and Red rivers enter it. And there were thousands of other villages up and down the Mississippi, on its tributary streams, and along other river systems.‡

In presenting this brief survey of the archeological roots of the Indian cultures first encountered by explorers, it has been necessary to leave open many questions about their rise, diversification, and fall. At their various stages of evolution, the aboriginal Indian cultures were presented with only a limited number of possibilities. Certain kinds of societies—the small band, the large band, the tribe, the chiefdom, the state, and variations of them—made certain choices about religion, law, government, and art more often than not. These choices, of course, were not consciously made, nor was a vote taken by the group. The choices either worked for the society or they did not. And they were often the only adaptive choices the societies could make.

Before proceeding to examine the swift destruction by Whites of the Indian cultures that had taken tens of thousands of years to build, let us see what light physical anthropology and linguistics can shed on the cultural evolution of man in North America.

XIII

The Generations of Adam

THE MISSING SKELETONS

A camp of Folsom men and butchering sites of other Paleo-Indians have been found; their projectile points and other weapons and tools have been unearthed, and so have the bones of the various animals they preyed on. Tens of thousands of artifacts have been discovered—but few of the bones from the hands that made them. The anthropologist needs to know more about early man than the spear points he made or the animals he hunted. Did he look primitive, with heavy brow ridges and underslung jaw, or did he resemble the modern Indian? Most important, do the biological changes of man in North America substantiate the story of his cultural evolution as seen by archeology?

There is a real scarcity of Paleo-Indian skeletons, partly because the populations of early man were low in comparison with the millions of mammals that left their bones in the earth. Also, early man may not have practiced ritual burial in the New World, although he sometimes did in the Old, and the skeletons may have merely decayed. The real explanation, though, is that a number of skeletons of ancient man were located, but because of a misconception they were ignored and even destroyed. The misconception was the belief on the part of many anthropologists that the skeletons of early man would have a primitive appearance and reveal a people with heavy brow ridges, stooped posture, and gangly arms. In other words, they were expecting to find a Neanderthaloid or some sort of New World ape man. And while these anthropologists were upholding the idea that only what looks ancient is old, many skeletons of early man in North America were overlooked because they appeared to be merely the burials of modern Indians.

THE EVIDENCE OF THE SKULLS

Upward of twenty-five skulls of undisputed antiquity are now known, and all of them date back to before the end of the last ice age; one skull found near San Diego, California, may be as old as 29,000 years, according to recent carbon-14 dating.‡ Preserved at Tepexpan, northeast of Mexico City, for example, is a slice of life out of the last ice age. At least twelve thousand years ago (and possibly as long ago as sixteen thousand years) an Indian drowned there along the swampy edge of a large lake. His skeleton was found lying on its face under the silt that accumulated above him, and near by were two large mammoths that had also become mired in the mud, perhaps the very ones he had been hunting. Another skull is that of a woman found in 1953 near Midland, Texas, in a layer beneath the stone tools of Folsom man and the remains of his quarry, the big-horned bison. Therefore, Midland woman is older than the Folsom culture, which flourished in that area about ten thousand years ago. Several attempts have been made to arrive at a date for Midland woman by radioactivity and other techniques, but there has been no agreement among the various methods; estimates range from ten thousand to twenty thousand years in age.

The skull fragments of Midland woman were painstakingly put back together again, and several interesting facts emerged. She had a long skull with delicate features; her brow ridges were light; her teeth and jaw were small. There is nothing "primitive" about her; she is just what would be expected of a *Homo sapiens* ancestor of the modern Indian. Those anthropologists who were looking for some robust, beetle-browed Neanderthal type were simply looking for the wrong kind of man. Dressed in modern clothing, the Paleo-Indians would appear no different from a cross section of humanity seen on a New York City street. Not one of the early skulls possesses the Classic Mongoloid characteristics seen today in some Chinese, Koreans, Mongols, and Eskimos: wide flat faces, heavy jaws, shovel-shaped front teeth. Nor might any of the skulls be mistaken for a European Neanderthal. All are unmistakably modern and of the same species as ourselves.

The skulls confirm the dates given by archeology for the arrival of man in the New World. Had these earliest skulls resembled Neanderthal man, a much greater antiquity for man in North America would have to be argued for. So even though the number of skulls available for study is meager, a conclusion emerges: Man is a comparative newcomer on the continent; he has been here for only 25,000 years or so out of the nearly 2,000,000 years in which he and his ancestors have existed on the planet.

These skulls also offer conclusive evidence that the ancestors of the Indians came from Asia. Skulls have been unearthed in recent years in several widely separated parts of China. They all date from the same general time period as the North American skulls. Were any of these Chinese skulls placed in a collection of early North American ones, they would not stand out as unusual. They look exactly like those of Indians, and, like the skulls of American Indians, they are only slightly Mongoloid. That means that neither the Chinese nor the American Indian skulls resemble the Classic Mongoloids who arose about fifteen thousand years ago as adaptations to cold environments. The ancestors of the American Indian therefore must have arrived in North America before the Classic Mongoloid type evolved. (On the other hand, the earliest Aleut skull of about four thousand years ago is clearly Classic Mongoloid, and so are the oldest Eskimo skulls.) Presumably both the early Chinese and the American Indians represented a general Mongoloid race that was overrun by the specialized, cold-climate Classic Mongoloid type; the older race survived only because representatives of it had migrated to the New World, as well as to parts of Asia. The inescapable evidence of the Asian skulls is that varieties of modern man akin to the American Indian existed in eastern Asia in the late Pleistocene, and that they served as the reservoir from which the first Americans flowed out across the Bering Strait land bridge.‡

THE AMERICAN RACE

As the early explorers traveled the length and breadth of North America they encountered Indians who varied greatly from place to place. Many people picture the typical Indian as resembling the portrait on the buffalo nickel or as a brave riding across the plains in technicolor, but the explorers reported Indians of many sizes and colors. Indians range from tall and thin to short and fat; their complexions are dark brown, red, yellow, even white; their hair is straight or wavy, black or brown. Such disparity, though, is only an illusion. The American Indian actually represents one of the most homogeneous populations on earth. It used to be thought that numerous migrations of many different kinds of people took place to the New World. Nowadays, many anthropologists believe that there were only two major migrations: the Eskimo, Aleut, and Athabaskans (of north-western Canada and the Southwest); and everyone else.‡ And probably no human population that has ever expanded over such a large area has re-mained so uniform. The early men who arrived in America represent one of the world's major isolated populations, one that invaded a new area and found no other human populations with which to interbreed. Except for the late-arriving Eskimo, Aleut, and Athabaskan populations, the genes of the early Americans were not mixed with those of other peoples.

There is no way in which modern man can cover up the evidence of genetic traits such as blood type, head shape, fingerprints, and so forth; these clues to race are influenced neither by environment nor by diet. With the exception of the Eskimo and the Aleut, the blood groups of aboriginal Americans are remarkably uniform, so much so that the Indians have been placed by at least one anthropologist in a separate race, distinct even from the Asian Mongoloids.‡ The American Indian is unique because his particular cluster of several blood types and other physical traits is not found in the same combinations in other races around the world. The incidence of such traits as red-green color blindness and the presence of hair on the middle segments of the fingers is very low. American Indians almost never become bald or have gray hair, even in extreme old age, and their skin tans readily. They have a high frequency of arches rather than whorls in their fingerprints.‡ Unimportant as these and other characteristics may seem, they provide the conclusive evidence that sets the American Indian apart from all other human populations.

The divergence of the early migrants into a number of obviously different Indian populations can be explained only by the four possibilities recognized today by geneticists. These are mixture, mutation, random genetic drift, and natural selection. Mixture can be dismissed, since no other humans had ever existed previously in North America. Similarly, mutations—accidental changes in the genes that govern heredity—do not enter directly into the explanation. Mutations are simply a source of some-thing new in a population. Whether or not they will have importance depends upon the remaining two factors: random genetic drift and natural selection.

Random genetic drift is an accidental change in the proportions of various genes in a population due to wars, famine, migration, or anything else that causes a fraction of an originally large population to become the new breeding unit. A small group of people is almost certain to differ genetically from the large population of which it was formerly a part. If this small population then breeds among its own members, the differences between it and its parent population become accentuated even more.

To visualize how genetic drift works, imagine an original breeding population to be represented by one hundred brown and one hundred white mice, each of which is capable of reproducing only its own color. Then separate at random fifty mice from the colony of two hundred. The mathematical probability is that more of one color than another will be chosen—let us say twenty brown and thirty white. These fifty mice now represent the small migrant population that split off from the original population of two hundred mice who were divided equally between brown and white. Obviously, even at the very outset the migrant group is different: It is sixty percent white instead of only fifty percent. Then, after each mouse in the splinter population has reproduced its own color, make another selection of fifty mice. Since there are more white mice than brown, the chances are that once again more white mice will be selected.

In fact, once the composition of the first-generation group favors the white mice, the chances are that after further selection the numbers of brown mice will decrease until they finally disappear from the migrant population. The migrants will then be completely different from the original population: Instead of only fifty percent of the mice being white, all the mice—one hundred percent—will be white. Such an experiment with mice is only a dramatization of the much more complex changes that occur in splinter populations of humans. A breeding population as small as that given in the mice example is not at all unusual among humans. The breeding populations of some Eskimo groups number no more than ten, and small breeding populations were probably very much the rule during most of man's tenure in North America.

The effect of a mutation appearing in such a small breeding population is dramatic, in contrast to its appearance in a large population. A mutation in the population of Modern America does not spread rapidly, nor is it likely to be lost; it usually maintains a low frequency in this large gene pool. But in a very small population, such a mutation can easily be lost through chance—if, for example, the three people who carry it are killed in a skirmish. Or, on the other hand, the mutation might spread rapidly through a small breeding population if the three people who do *not* have it are killed.

The second important cause of the diversity of the Indian population is natural selection: Organisms possessing beneficial characteristics survive in relatively larger numbers and leave more offspring than do those organisms of the same species that do not possess them. Food, for example, can act as a selective agent. When one kind of food is abundant, it favors the reproduction of the organisms that know how to use it over other organisms not experienced in its use. A disease is selective because it favors those possessing an immunity to it. But the greatest natural-selection filter of all to aboriginal man was the North American continent itself—ten million square miles of tundra, forest, grassland, desert, each with its own climates and environmental stresses. Each Indian population in its habitat was exposed to the workings of natural selection, and was influenced for good or ill by it.

So genetic theory also confirms the evidence of artifacts unearthed by archeologists. The vastness and the variety of North America are sufficient to account for the diversity in the color, size, and stature of the Indian; this diversity resulted primarily from natural selection working upon small populations that had felt the effect of random genetic drift. There is no need to postulate invasions of large numbers of people from across the Pacific or Atlantic oceans.

HALF A THOUSAND TONGUES

The science of linguistics has also helped to reconstruct the long road the ancestors of modern-day Indians traveled in North America. At the time of the discovery of the New World, the explorers found a Babel of tongues. In North and South America more languages were spoken—about 2,200 of them—than in all of Europe and Asia at that time.‡ Despite what some early explorers and European scholars believed, there never was such a language as "American Indian"—meaning, presumably, one common language with only local dialects. There were dialects in plenty—that is, mutually intelligible variations of a mother tongue—but there were also numerous distinct languages as different as English is from Swahili. Rather than one common language that linked the Indians of North America, about 550 distinct languages were spoken, and nearly every language comprised numerous dialects. A second misconception was that a language had to be written to rank as a full-fledged language. In North America, a truly written language developed only in Mexico, yet most Indian groups were able to communicate a rich unwritten tradition of poetry, oratory, and drama.

Pictograph writing: Even those Indians who did not develop a written literature, as did the Aztec and the Maya of Mexico, used several kinds of notation and memory devices. This wooden box was used by the Ojibway Indians of the western Great Lakes to store ceremonial eagle feathers. Pictograph designs on the cover served as reminders of the songs to be sung at the ceremonies. They could not be read by the uninitiated, any more than Chinese can be read by an American without instruction.

Scholars who based their studies on the reports of the early explorers once thought that in the primitive life of the Indian might be found clues to the beginnings of man's power of speech. But a study of American Indian languages has clearly revealed that they were no more primitive than European languages, nor were they any more limited in their vocabularies. A sample dictionary of the English language for use by those with an education beyond the high-school level contains about 45,000 words. (Shakespeare, in the rich imagery of all of his plays and poems, used about 24,000 words, and the King James Bible used about 7,000.) The number of words recorded in the Nahuatl language of Mexico is 27,000; in Maya, 20,000; in Dakota, 19,000—and undoubtedly linguists missed most of the subtleties that make our dictionaries so bulky. Even Darwin was in error in scarcely crediting primitive peoples with speech. He thought barely human the speech of the natives of Tierra del Fuego, at the southern tip of South America, who are among the most primitive peoples on earth. But a study of one of these people, the Yahgan, has revealed a vocabulary of at least 30,000 words.‡

Some thousands of languages of primitive peoples around the world have been studied, and no "primitive" language has been found anywhere. All languages are able to express whatever their cultures require of them, whether it be a concrete name for a kind of bird or an abstract word to explain the creation of the universe. Conversation is one of man's principal amusements. Primitive peoples delight in it, and a good speaker often achieves high status; among peasant populations, as in Ireland, conversation still ranks as *the* social occupation. Some languages have a more complicated grammar than English has, some less; but on the average, the languages of primitive peoples are more complicated than English.

Languages are remarkably stubborn in the face of upsetting events. Wars, new religions, cultural upheavals, or a change in economic systems usually do not affect the language. The French language survived the French Revolution, and Welsh has successfully resisted 1,500 years of pressure and political domination by Englishmen. Ancient Egypt was conquered by the Hyksos, the Assyrians, the Persians, the Greeks, and the Romans, but the people continued to speak Egyptian. Only after the Arabs not only conquered Egypt but also instituted a new religion did the language finally change, in that way achieving what four thousand years of conquest had been unable to do. Even so, Coptic, a dialect of the ancient Egyptian language, has survived among Christians in Egypt. Similarly, Nahuatl, Maya, and numerous other aboriginal languages are still widely spoken in Mexico today, despite more than four centuries of enforced migration, disease, starvation, and atrocities by Whites determined to extirpate these cultures.

Languages, of course, do change somewhat over a period of time. English has gone through some striking alterations since the writing of *Beowulf,* and even since *Hamlet.* Linguists possess the written evidence for these changes; but even if they lacked such evidence, they could still piece together the history of the English language by studying its rules, its structure, and its relation to other languages. For example, the German word *Tanz* means "dance," and *Trank* means "a drink." An examination of many other German words beginning with "T" reveals that they are replaced in English by the letter "d." Similarly, the German "D" is replaced in English by "th," as in *Donner,* "thunder," or in *Dank,* "thanks." The science of linguistics has been able to demonstrate that the words *foot, pes, pous,* and *Fuss*—English, Latin, Greek, and German for the same thing—are derived from an ancestral word common to them all.

American Indian languages can be analyzed in much the same way. Languages are quite regular and consistent in their changes, and it is very rare that a sound will change in one word only. Rather, that sound will change in the same way in all words where it appears. Linguistic rules such as this have been applied to the Indian language family known as Algonquian, which numbers speakers from the Atlantic to the Pacific and includes, among others, the Penobscot, Delaware, Ojibway, Menomini, Cheyenne, Blackfoot, Arapaho, and Yurok. By comparing a considerable number of words from the various Algonquian languages, and by studying the changes that took place from one language to another, linguists have reconstructed the Proto-Algonquian language that was the ancestor of the modern Algonquian language family.

Most of the changes that occur in a language are in the vocabulary. By inventing a new noun such as "radioactivity," the English vocabulary has been enriched but the language itself has not changed. And even though "belike" is now obsolete, the English language has not changed in any major way since the time when the word was in common use. The sounds of a language are much less subject to change than the vocabulary, and the over-all plan of the structure of the language changes scarcely at all. These principles apply equally to unwritten languages, for it is only Western civilization's sense of superiority that leads it to maintain that unwritten languages change more rapidly than do written languages. During the past four centuries Spanish, for example, has changed much more than Nahuatl, the language of the Aztec state and its survivors today.

DATING BY LANGUAGE

The anthropologist cannot dig up dead languages in the same way as he unearths spear points. That he can measure the rate of change, however, and that a study of the ancient relations between languages can afford clues to cultural evolution, is a premise that has occupied the energies of several anthropological linguists since about 1950. Glottochronology, as their method is called, when perfected, will provide a time scale that corresponds to archeological methods for dating the past. The method of glottochronology has been, first, to compose a list of basic words that occur in almost every language, those spoken in both the complex industrial society and the nonliterate one. These words refer to things and situations that are not linked to any particular kinds of culture and are unchanging: low numerals, pronouns, colors, categories of animals and plants, parts of the body, extremes of temperature, and so forth. Some of the words in the basic list that appear in every known language any place on earth are:

I, we, one, two, all, many, man, woman, fish, bird, tree, seed, root, skin, flesh, blood, bone, ear, eye, nose, mouth, tooth, tongue, foot, drink, eat, hear, sleep, walk, fly, sun, moon, water, mountain, night, hot, cold, red, green, big, small.

Words such as these have a much slower rate of change than the rest of a vocabulary. For example, while "automobile," "airplane," and "rocket ship" were entering the English language the basic word "walk" was still retained, and it is likely to be retained for a long time to come no matter what new methods of transportation are invented in the future. Nevertheless, even the basic words are eventually lost to the vocabulary, and they seem to drop out at a steady rate. The study of thirteen language families showed there was relatively little difference between them in the rate of loss: Every thousand years a language loses about nineteen percent.

So the next step in the development of glottochronology was to compare the basic words that have survived in two related languages. A skilled linguist can quickly spot their many cognates—that is, the words they share that were derived from a shared mother tongue. If the two daughter languages have a large number of cognates, then they are linguistically close, whereas those with only a small number of cognates diverged much longer ago. The linguistic distances between hundreds of North American Indian languages have now been determined.

For example, the three languages X, Y, and Z in the past branched off from a common ancestral tongue. But since X and Y share more cognates, then Z must have split off long before X and Y separated from the mother tongue and then from each other. The approximate date when these splits took place can be estimated by the use of the formula stated above: A language loses nineteen percent of its basic words every thousand years. A thousand years after they diverged, language X will still retain eighty-one percent of its basic words, and so will language Y. Two languages do not usually lose the same basic words, so each language will still retain a percentage—that is, eighty-one percent—of what the other loses. By computation, when comparing two languages, they share sixty-six percent of the basic words after each thousand years. If fewer than sixty-six words are retained, then the linguist concludes that more than a thousand years have elapsed; if more than sixty-six words are retained, then less time has passed. The premise of glottochronology, then, is that the rate of change in a language is predictable, as it is for certain radioactive elements. And if the premise is sound—as it appears to be—it constitutes a new tool analogous to radiocarbon dating.

A specific example of how glottochronology works is seen in a study of the Eskimo-Aleut language family. The Greenland Eskimo and the Yukon Eskimo of Alaska have a sixty-six-percent correspondence in their vocabularies of basic words. The conclusion of glottochronology, then, is that these two Eskimo branches have been separated for only a thousand years; this same period of separation has been confirmed by archeological methods of dating. With Eskimo and Aleut, however, the percentage of shared words is considerably smaller, and so the conclusion is that the two languages have been separated for a much longer time. Glottochronology arrives at a date of separation for Eskimo and Aleut of about four thousand years—much the same span of time as that determined by archeology.

Analysis of the aboriginal languages of North America has led to the conclusion that the numerous tongues spoken at the time of the European discovery required at least fifteen thousand to twenty thousand years to diverge. This figure necessarily is only an estimate, for glottochronology is still in need of refinements. Yet linguistics offers an approximate date for the peopling of North America that does not vary too widely from the evidence of archeology and physical anthropology.‡

MAN AT THE MERCY OF HIS LANGUAGE

Linguistically speaking, man is not born free. He inherits a language full of quaint sayings, archaisms, and a ponderous grammar; even more important, he inherits certain fixed ways of expression that may shackle his thoughts. Language becomes man's shaper of ideas rather than simply his tool for reporting ideas. An American's conventional words for directions often limit his ability to read maps: It is an apt youngster indeed who can immediately grasp that the *Upper* Nile is in the *south* of Egypt and the *Lower* Nile is in the *north* of Egypt. Another example: English has only two demonstrative pronouns ("this" and "that," together with their plurals) to refer either to something near or to something far away. The Tlingit Indians of the Northwest Coast can be much more specific. If they want to refer to an object very near and always present, they say *he; ya* means an object also near and present, but a little farther away; *yu* refers to something still farther away, while *we* is used only for an object so far away that it is out of sight. So the question arises whether even the most outspoken member of American society can "speak his mind." Actually, he has very little control over the possible channels into which his thoughts can flow. His grammatical mind was made up for him by his culture before he was born.

The way in which culture affects language becomes clear by comparing how the English and Hopi languages refer to H_2O in its liquid state. English, like most other European languages, has only one word—"water" —and it pays no attention to what the substance is used for or its quantity. The Hopi of Arizona, on the other hand, use *pahe* to mean the large amounts of water present in natural lakes or rivers, and *keyi* for the small amounts in domestic jugs and canteens. English, though, makes other distinctions that Hopi does not. The speaker of English is careful to distinguish between a lake and a stream, between a waterfall and a geyser; but *pahe* makes no distinction among lakes, ponds, rivers, streams, waterfalls, and springs.

A Hopi speaker, of course, knows that there is a difference between a geyser, which spurts upward, and a waterfall, which plunges downward, even though his vocabulary makes no such distinction. Similarly, a speaker of English knows that a canteen of water differs from a river of water. But the real point of this comparison is that neither the Hopi nor the American uses anywhere near the possible number of words that could be applied to water in all of its states, quantities, forms, and functions. The number of such words is in the hundreds and they would hopelessly encumber the language. So, to prevent the language from becoming unwieldy, different kinds of water are grouped into a small number of categories. Each culture defines the categories in terms of the similarities it detects; it channels a multitude of ideas into the few categories that it considers important. The culture of every speaker of English tells him that it is important to distinguish between oceans, lakes, rivers, fountains, and waterfalls—but relatively unimportant to make the distinction between the water in a canteen in his canoe and the water underneath the same canoe. Each culture has categorized experience through language in a quite unconscious way—at the same time offering anthropologists commentaries on the differences and similarities that exist in societies.

The possibility of such a relationship between language and culture has been formulated into a hypothesis by two American linguists, Sapir and Whorf. According to Sapir, man does not live in the midst of the whole world, but only in a part of it, the part that his language lets him know. He is, says Sapir, "very much at the mercy of the particular language which has become the medium of expression" for his group. The real world is therefore "to a large extent unconsciously built up on the language habits of the group . . . The worlds in which different societies live are distinct worlds, not merely the same world with different labels attached."◊ To Sapir and Whorf, language provides a different network of tracks for each society, which, as a result, concentrates on only certain aspects of reality.

According to the hypothesis, the differences between languages are much more than mere obstacles to communication; they represent basic differences in the "world view" of the various peoples and in what they understand about their environment. The Eskimo can draw upon an inventory of about twenty very precise words for the subtle differences in a snowfall. The best a speaker of English can manage are distinctions between sticky snow, sleet, hail, and ice. Similarly, to most speakers of English, a seal is simply a seal, and they have only that one word to describe it; if they want to say anything else about the seal, such as its sex or its color, then they have to put an adjective before the word "seal." But the Eskimo has a number of words with which to express various kinds of sealdom: "a young swimming seal," "a male harbor seal," "an old harbor seal," and so forth. A somewhat similar situation exists in English with the word "horse." This animal may be referred to as "chestnut," "bay mare," "stallion," and other names that one would not expect to find in the vocabulary of the horseless Eskimo.

The Eskimo, of course, is preoccupied with seals, a primary food source for him, whereas some speakers of English seem to be taken up with the exact particulars of the domesticated horse. The real question is: Do these different vocabularies restrict the Eskimo and the speaker of English, and do they force the speakers of different languages to conceptualize and classify information in different ways? Can an Eskimo look at a horse and in his own mind classify it as "a bay mare"? Or, because he lacks the words, is he forever blind to the fact that this kind of animal exists? The answer is that with a little practice an Eskimo can learn to tell apart the different kinds of horses, just as an American can learn about the various seals, even though the respective languages lack the necessary vocabularies. So vocabulary alone does not reveal the cultural thinking of a people.

But does the *totality* of the language tell anything about the people who speak it? To answer that, look at the English verb "grab." An English speaker says, "I grab it," "I grabbed it," "I will grab it," and so on. Only the context of the situation tells the listener what it is that is being grabbed and how it is being done. "I grab it" is a vague sentence—except in one way. English is remarkably concerned about the tense of the verb. It insists on knowing whether I grab it now, or grabbed it some time in the past, or will grab it at a future time. The English language is preoccupied with time, and so is the culture of its speakers, who take considerable interest in calendars, record-keeping, diaries, history, almanacs, stock-market fore-casts, astrological predictions, and always, every minute of the waking day, the precise time.

No such statement as "I grab it" would be possible in Navaho. To the Navaho, tense is of little importance, but the language is considerably more discriminating in other ways. The Navaho language would describe much more about the pronoun "I" of this sentence; it would tell whether the "I" initiated the action by reaching out to grab the thing, or whether the "I" merely grabbed at a horse that raced by. Nor would the Navaho be content merely with "grab"; the verb would have to tell him whether the thing being grabbed is big or little, animate or inanimate. Finally, a Navaho could not say simply "it"; the thing being grabbed would have to be described much more precisely and put in a category. (If you get the feeling that Navaho is an exceedingly difficult language, you are correct. During World War II in the Pacific, Navaho Indians were used as senders and receivers of secret radio messages because a language, unlike a code, cannot be broken; it must be learned.)

Judging by this example and by other linguistic studies of Navaho, a picture of its speakers emerges: They are very exacting in their perception of the elements that make up their universe. But is this a true picture of the Navaho? Does he perceive his world any differently from a White Ameri-can? Anthropological and psychological studies of the Navaho show that he does. He visualizes himself as living in an eternal and unchanging universe made up of physical, social, and supernatural forces, among which he tries to maintain a balance. Any accidental failure to observe rules or rituals can disturb this balance and result in some misfortune. Navaho curing cere-monies, which include the well-known sandpainting, are designed to put the individual back into harmony with the universe. To the Navaho, the good life consists of maintaining intact all the complex relationships of the universe. It is obvious that to do so demands a language that makes the most exacting discriminations.

Several words of caution, though, about possible misinterpretations of the Sapir–Whorf Hypothesis. It does not say that the Navaho holds such a world view because of the structure of his language. It merely states that there is an interaction between his language and his culture. Nor does the hypothesis maintain that two cultures with different languages and differ-ent world views cannot be in communication with each other (the Navaho and the White American are very much in communication today in Arizona and New Mexico). Instead, the hypothesis suggests that language is more than a way of communicating. It is a living system that is a part of the cultural equipment of a group, and it reveals a culture at least as much as do spear points, kinship groups, or political institutions. Look at just one of the clues to culture that the Sapir–Whorf Hypothesis has already provided: Shortly after the hypothesis was proposed, it was attacked on the basis that the Navaho speak an Athabaskan language and the Hopi a Uto–Aztecan one, yet they live side by side in the Southwest and share a culture. So, after all, asked the critics, what difference can language make in culture? Instead of demolishing the hypothesis, this comparison actually served to reveal its value. It forced anthropologists to take another look at the Navaho and the Hopi. As the hypothesis had predicted, their world views are quite far apart—and so are their cultures.

The Sapir–Whorf Hypothesis has alerted anthropologists to the fact that language is keyed to the total culture, and that it reveals a people's view of its total environment. Language directs the perceptions of its speakers to certain things; it gives them ways to analyze and to categorize experience. Such perceptions are unconscious and outside the control of the speaker. The ultimate value of the Sapir–Whorf Hypothesis is that it offers hints to cultural differences and similarities among peoples, which is the concern of this book.

PART THREE

SOCIETIES UNDER STRESS

XIV

The End of the Trail

FIRST ENCOUNTERS

Much has been written about the genocide practiced by Whites upon Indians by warfare and by the deliberate spread of smallpox; by physically removing large populations to desert wastes and by psychologically breaking their spirit; by destroying their bison to empty their stomachs and by tearing apart their cultures to empty their hearts of any hope. It is not the purpose of this book to add to that vast literature. But in order to understand the total experience of primeval man in North America—and also to understand the last two chapters of this book, which explore what happens to cultures as they disintegrate—something must be said about the changing relations between Whites and Indians.

The first record of an encounter with Indians is by Columbus; he described the Arawak Indians who inhabited the Caribbean islands as "a loving people, without covetousness . . . Their speech is the sweetest and gentlest in the world."‡ But in their haste to exploit the new abundance of the Americas, the Spaniards set the loving and gentle Arawak to labor in mines and on plantations. Whole Arawak villages disappeared through slavery, disease, and warfare, as well as by flight into the mountains. As a result, the native population of Haiti, for example, declined from an estimated 200,000 in 1492 to a mere 29,000 only twenty-two years later.‡

The earliest contacts between the Indians and the Whites were inquisitive, yet wary, on both sides. Some Europeans at first were not certain that the Indians were true human beings: King Ferdinand of Spain approved

243

the importation of White women into the West Indies to prevent the Spaniards from mating with native women "who are far from being rational creatures." Nor were the Indians certain what to make of the Whites. A Spanish chronicler of the time reported that Indians in the Caribbean islands drowned any Whites they could capture. They then stood guard over the corpses for weeks—to determine if the dead were gods, or if they were subject to putrefaction like other mortals. The contrasting attitudes of King Ferdinand and the Indians point up the basic difference in expectations between the two cultures. The Whites treated the Indians like animals; the Indians suspected the Whites might be gods. Both were wrong, but the attitude of the Indians was more flattering to mankind.‡

Wherever the Whites penetrated, the Indian populations went into drastic decline, and probably no one will ever know for sure what the primeval population of the New World was. Traditional estimates have been unduly conservative. Until recently, it was firmly believed that fewer than a million Indians lived north of Mexico in 1492; but recent research shows that North America was by no means so sparsely settled when the Whites arrived. Traditional estimates acknowledged that Mexico was more densely occupied, and figures ranged from about three million people in the area between the Rio Grande River and Costa Rica up to fifteen million people inhabiting Mexico alone. In recent years old evidence has been re-evaluated and new evidence has come to light, with the result that there has been a steady tendency among anthropologists to raise these figures considerably. Several recent attempts to estimate the total native population of Mexico just before the Spanish conquest, using a variety of techniques that have been cross checked, give a figure between thirty million and about thirty-seven million. And estimates now number the Indian and Eskimo population between the Rio Grande River and the Arctic from 9,800,000 to 12,500,000.‡ The early explorers found a continent that was densely inhabited in its many environments by a wide variety of Indian groups.

The extent of the Europeans' destruction of Indian numbers and cultures is attested to by the long roll of groups that have become extinct, and by the pitifully few survivors, many of mixed blood. The Aleut, who inhabit the Aleutian Islands of Alaska, numbered upward of 20,000 people before they came into contact with White trading ships. Today a few thousand survive, living in scattered villages at river mouths, and their decline continues. For the Indian populations in the area comprising the forty-eight contiguous United States, the low point was reached in 1850 when the number probably fell to less than 250,000. Since then the Indians have made a remarkable comeback—in numbers, if not in social and economic gains. The 1960 census puts the Indian population at 551,669, but this does not take into account the several hundred thousand others of mixed blood who do not wish to be classified as Indians. In addition, a total of approximately 225,000 Indians and Eskimos have been registered by various Canadian agencies.

Many people have wondered what it was that caused the Indian population to plummet so drastically. Part of the answer can be found in murder, starvation, and disease—and part also in the physical and emotional stress to which the Indians were submitted by Whites. The effects of stress on human populations still are not completely understood, but it is known beyond doubt that these effects are deleterious. World War II provided clear evidence. About 25,000 American soldiers became prisoners of the Japanese; they were much more inhumanely treated than the American prisoners in European camps. The Japanese abused them mentally and physically, and sapped them of all human dignity; more than a third of the Americans died in prison whereas less than one percent of the American prisoners in Europe died. Six years after their liberation from the Japanese camps, a group of former prisoners was studied. Their death rate was twice that of males of the same age, race, stature, and so forth who had not been imprisoned—but the causes of their deaths were not related directly to imprisonment. Twice the anticipated number had died of cancer; more than four times the expected number succumbed to gastrointestinal diseases; nine times the norm died of tuberculosis. There is no reason to believe that American Indians—herded into crowded reservations, torn from their families, sumitted to indignities—suffered any less from the effects of stress.↕

THE NOBLE RED MAN AND
THE BLOODTHIRSTY SAVAGE

Two contrasting images of the Indian—as Noble Red Man and as Bloodthirsty Savage—have prevailed in the minds of Whites in the past five hundred years, and feelings have tended to shift back and forth between the two. Columbus brought home six Indians to show to Queen Isabella, and, dressed in full regalia and decorated with war paint, they quickly became the curiosities of Spain. In England, Sir Walter Raleigh brought Chief Manteo to visit Queen Elizabeth; she was so delighted with the

Indian that she dubbed him Lord of Roanoke. An Indian craze took hold in Elizabethan England, and Shakespeare complained about it in *The Tempest* when he wrote: "They will not give a doit [a small coin equal to about half a farthing] to relieve a lame beggar, they will lay out ten to see a dead Indian."

After the initial confusion as to what to make of these inhabitants of the New World, certain philosophers—principally French—entertained a romantic view. Europeans had often thought that somewhere in the world must dwell a noble race, remnants of that golden age before man became corrupted by civilization. As reports of Indians filtered back to Europe, a distinguished French philosopher of the late sixteenth century, Michel de Montaigne, took the trouble to talk with explorers, to read all the travelers' chronicles, and even to meet three Indians who had been brought as curiosities to the Court of Versailles. He concluded that the Noble Savage had at last been found, for the Indian "hath no kind of traffic, no knowledge of letters, no intelligence of numbers, no name of magistrate, nor of politics, no use of service, of riches, or of poverty; no contracts, no successions, no partitions, no occupation but idle, no apparel but natural, no manuring of lands, no use of wine. The very words that import a lie, falsehood, treason, covetousness, envy, detraction, were not heard among them."‡ Montaigne presented an idealized notion about the aborigines of the New World that foreshadowed the Noble Savage of Jean Jacques Rousseau.

By the seventeenth century, observers had reached the firm conclusion that American Indians were in no way inferior to Whites, and many writers took special pains to salute the Noble Red Man. The Jesuit missionary Bressani, who served in Canada from 1645 to 1649, reported that the inhabitants "are hardly barbarous, save in name. There is no occasion to think of them as half beasts, shaggy, black and hideous." He goes on to comment on the Indian's tenacious memory, his "marvelous faculty for remembering places, and for describing them to one another." An Indian, Bressani states, can recall things that a White "could not rehearse without writing."‡ Another Jesuit enthusiastically corroborates him by stating that Indians "nearly all show more intelligence in their business, speeches, courtesies, intercourse, tricks and subtleties, than do the shrewdest citizens and merchants in France."‡

The Noble Red Man captivated Europe, but for those colonists living a precarious life along the fringes of the New World, the widespread opinion was that the Indians were of an inferior race. That did not prevent the colonists from believing, at first, that the Indian might seek salvation, and that civilization, European-style, could be conferred as a blessing upon him. Only a few years after the permanent settlement of Virginia, some fifty missionaries arrived to begin the massive task of converting the heathen. The Indians, for their part, did not respond with alacrity to the idea of adopting a culture that to them, in many cases, seemed barbarous indeed. Furthermore, they increasingly resented encroachments by Whites upon their lands: As early as 1622 the Indians of Virginia rose against the colonists and killed about 350 of them.

The Puritans in New England were not immediately presented with an Indian problem, for diseases introduced earlier by trading ships along the coast had badly decimated the Indian population. Yet when the Pequots resisted the migration of settlers into the Connecticut Valley in 1637, a party of Puritans surrounded the Pequot village and set fire to it. About five hundred Indians were burned to death or shot while trying to escape; the Whites devoutly offered up thanks to God that they had lost only two men. The woods were then combed for any Pequots who had managed to survive, and these were sold into slavery. Cotton Mather was grateful to the Lord that "on this day we have sent six hundred heathen souls to hell."

The Puritans failed miserably in their dealings with the Indians of New England, with scarcely a glimmer of kindness to illuminate black page after black page of cruelty and humiliation. There were many reasons why the Puritans were so much less successful with Indians than were the Spaniards or the French or even other Englishmen. The Puritans insisted upon a high standard of religious devotion that the Indians were unable or unwilling to give. The Puritans lacked any way to integrate the Indians into their theocracy, for they did not indulge in wholesale baptisms (as they charged the French did), nor were any Puritans specifically assigned to missionary tasks. The heart of the matter, though, is that conversion of the heathen was not one of the compelling motives—or justifications—for the Puritan settling of New England, as it was for the Spaniards in the Southwest. The contempt with which Puritans regarded Indians is revealed in this order from the General Court of the Colony of Massachusetts Bay in 1644:

It was ordered that noe Indian shall come att any towne or howse of the English (without leave) uppon the Lords day, except to attend the publike meeteings; neither shall they come att any English howse uppon any other day in the weeke, but first shall knocke att the dore, and after leave given, to come in (and not otherwise) . . . ↕

The desire of Whites to occupy Indian lands, and the constant rivalry between French and English traders for the furs gathered by the Indians, led to many skirmishes and several bloody wars, all of which involved Indians on both sides. The Whites were determined to fight it out with each other—down to the last Indian. These battles culminated in the French and Indian War of 1763, which represented a disaster to many Indian groups in the northeastern part of the continent. In May, 1763, an Ottawa warrior by the name of Pontiac fell upon Detroit and captured the English forts, one after the other. Lord Jeffrey Amherst, who commanded the British military forces in North America at the time, debated with his subordinates the relative advantages of hunting Indians down with dogs or infecting them with smallpox. Dogs were not available, so officers distributed among the Indians handkerchiefs and blankets from the smallpox hospital at Fort Pitt—probably the first use of biological warfare in history. Clearly, a sharp turn away from the admiration for the Noble Savage had taken place.

The Indian came to be regarded as a stubborn animal that refused to acknowledge the obvious blessings of White civilization. The idea of the Bloodthirsty Savage took hold, and the same relentless pattern was repeated—across Pennsylvania, Ohio, Virginia, and Kentucky, across the whole western frontier as the new United States came into being. Hugh Henry Brackenridge, a modest literary figure of the young nation, stood for the changed attitude when he wrote in 1782 of ". . . the animals, vulgarly called Indians." Rousseau's Noble Savage was laid to rest when John Adams stated in 1790: "I am not of Rousseau's Opinions. His Notions of the purity of Morals in savage nations and the earliest Ages of civilized Nations are mere Chimeras." Even that man of enlightened homilies, Benjamin Franklin, observed that rum should be regarded as an agent of Providence "to extirpate these savages in order to make room for the cultivators of the earth."

THE GREAT REMOVAL

Following the War of 1812, the young United States had no further need for Indian allies against the British, and as a result the fortunes of the Indians declined rapidly. By 1848, twelve new states had been carved out of the Indians' lands, two major and many minor Indian wars had been fought, and group after group of Indians had been herded westward, on forced marches, across the Mississippi River.

As in other inhumane and deceitful chapters in the history of the United States, the justifications of God and civilization were invoked. To Senator Thomas Hart Benton of Missouri it was all very simple: The Whites must supplant Indians because Whites used the land "according to the intentions of the Creator." Some spoke of the benefits to the Indian of removing him from contact with Whites, which would give him the time to assimilate at his own pace the blessings of civilization. A senator from Georgia, hoping to expedite the removal of Indians from his state to what later became Oklahoma, glowingly described that arid, treeless territory as a place "over which Flora has scattered her beauties with a wanton hand; and upon whose bosom innumerable wild animals display their amazing numbers."

Such statements do not mean that the Indians lacked defenders, but the intensity of the indignation was in direct proportion to a White's distance from the Indian. On the frontier, the Indian was regarded as a besotted savage; but along the eastern seaboard, where the Spaniards, Dutch, English, and later the Americans had long since exterminated almost all the Indians, philosophers and divines began to defend the Red Man. In response to Georgia's extirpation of her Indian population, Ralph Waldo Emerson protested: "The soul of man, the justice, the mercy that is the heart's heart in all men, from Maine to Georgia, does abhor this business." Presidents such as Jefferson, Monroe, and Adams, who came from the East, occasionally displayed some scruples about the treatment the Indian was receiving. Thomas Jefferson, though, was hoodwinked, or else he deluded himself, when he wrote shortly before his death of the civilization Whites had brought to the Indian:

Let a philosophic observer commence a journey from the savages of the Rocky Mountains, eastwardly towards our seacoast. These he would observe in the earliest stage of association living under no law but that of nature, subsisting and covering themselves with the flesh and skin of wild beasts. He would next find those on our frontiers in the pastoral state, raising domestic animals to supply the defects of hunting. Then succeed our own semi-barbarous citizens, the pioneers of the advance of civilization, and so in his progress he would meet the gradual shades of improving man until he would reach his, as yet, most improved state in our seaport towns. This, in fact, is equivalent to a survey, in time, of the progress of man from the infancy of creation to the present day.‡

But President Andrew Jackson had been reared on the frontier and he was utterly insensitive to the treatment of the Indians. He denounced as an "absurdity" and a "farce" that the United States should bother even to negotiate treaties with Indians as if they were independent nations with a right to their lands. He was completely in sympathy with the policy of removal of the Indians to new lands west of the Mississippi. He exerted his influence to make Congress give legal sanction to what in our own time, under the Nuremburg Laws, would be branded as genocide. Dutifully, Congress passed the Removal Act of 1830, which gave the President the right to extirpate all Indians who had managed to survive east of the Mississippi River. It was estimated that the whole job might be done economically at no more than $500,000—the costs to be kept low by persuasion, promises, threats, and the bribery of Indian leaders. When U.S. Supreme Court Justice John Marshall ruled in favor of the Cherokee in a case with wide implications for protecting the Indians, Jackson is said to have remarked: "John Marshall has made his decision, now let him enforce it."

During the next ten years, almost all the Indians were cleared from the East. Some like the Chickasaw and Choctaw went resignedly, but many others left only at bayonet point. The Seminole actively resisted and some retreated into the Florida swamps, where they stubbornly held off the United States Army. The Seminole Wars lasted from 1835 to 1842 and cost the United States some 1,500 soldiers and an estimated $20,000,000 (about forty times what Jackson had estimated it would cost to remove all Indians). Many of the Iroquois sought sanctuary in Canada, and the Oneida and the Seneca were moved westward, although fragments of Iroquois tribes managed to remain behind in western New York. The Sac and Fox made a desperate stand in Illinois against overwhelming numbers of Whites, but ultimately their survivors also were forced to move, as were the Ottawa, Potawatomie, Wyandot, Shawnee, Kickapoo, Winnebago, Delaware, Peoria, Miami, and many others who are remembered now only in the name of some town, lake, county, or state, or as a footnote in the annals of a local historical society.

All in all, an estimated seventy thousand Indians are believed to have been resettled west of the Mississippi, but the number may have been closer to one hundred thousand. No figures exist, though, as to the numbers massacred before they could be persuaded to leave the East, or on the tremendous losses suffered from disease, exposure, and starvation on the thousand-mile march westward across an unsettled and inhospitable land.

THE CHEROKEE

Some of the Indians who were forced west of the Mississippi might with justification be regarded as "savages," but this cannot be said of the

Cherokee. About 1790 the Cherokee decided to adopt the ways of their White conquerors and to emulate their civilization, their morals, their learning, and their arts. The Cherokee made remarkable and rapid progress in their homeland in the mountains where Georgia, Tennessee, and North Carolina meet. They established churches, mills, schools, and well-cultivated farms; judging from descriptions of that time, the region was a paradise when compared with the bleak landscape that the White successors have made of Appalachia today. In 1826 a Cherokee reported to the Presbyterian Church that his people already possessed 22,000 cattle, 7,600 houses, 46,000 swine, 2,500 sheep, 762 looms, 1,488 spinning wheels, 2,948 plows, 10 saw mills, 31 grist mills, 62 blacksmith shops, and 18 schools. In one of the Cherokee districts alone there were some 1,000 volumes "of good books."‡ In 1821, after twelve years of hard work, a Cherokee named Sequoya (honored in the scientific names for the redwood and the giant sequoia trees in California, three thousand miles from his homeland) perfected a method of syllabary notation in which English letters stood for Cherokee syllables; by 1828 the Cherokee were already publishing their own newspaper. At about the same time, they adopted a written constitution providing for an executive, a bicameral legislature, a supreme court, and a code of laws.

Before the passage of the Removal Act of 1830, a group of Cherokee chiefs went to the Senate committee that was studying this legislation, to report on what they had already achieved in the short space of forty years. They expressed the hope that they would be permitted to enjoy in peace "the blessings of civilization and Christianity on the soil of their rightful inheritance." Instead, they were daily subjected to brutalities and atrocities by White neighbors, harassed by the state government of Georgia, cajoled and bribed by federal agents to agree to removal, and denied even the basic protection of the federal government. Finally, in 1835, a minority faction of five hundred Cherokee out of a total of some twenty thousand signed a treaty agreeing to removal. The Removal Act was carried out almost everywhere with a notable lack of compassion, but in the case of the Cherokee—civilized and Christianized as they were—it was particularly brutal.

After many threats, about five thousand finally consented to be marched westward, but another fifteen thousand clung to their neat farms, schools, and libraries "of good books." So General Winfield Scott set about systematically extirpating the rebellious ones. Squads of soldiers descended upon isolated Cherokee farms and at bayonet point marched the families off to what today would be known as concentration camps. Torn from their

Sequoya, the son of a white trader and a Cherokee woman, was a cripple who excelled as both mechanic and artist, as well as an intellectual giant who invented a system of syllabary notation for the Cherokee language. Starting in 1821, thousands of Cherokee learned to read and write their language. After the forcible removal of the Cherokee to the Arkansas Territory, Sequoya joined his people there. Still restless, his ideals undiminished by privation, he set out to visit Indians of various language stocks in a fruitless quest for a common Indian grammar. He also hoped to find a group of Cherokee who, according to tradition, had crossed the Mississippi and disappeared some place in the West. It was during this last quest that he took sick in the Sierra of Mexico in about 1843 and died. Several years later, an Austrian botanist who admired the American Indian felt that the coast redwood should be named after a Red man, so he called it Sequoia sempervirens or "ever-living Sequoia." Later, when the closely related giant sequoias of the California mountains were discovered, they were named Sequoia gigantea. The name of one of the greatest intellects the Indians produced would be totally unfamiliar to most Whites had not two trees in California been named in his honor.

homes with all the dispatch and efficiency the Nazis displayed under similar circumstances, the families had no time to prepare for the arduous trip ahead of them. No way existed for the Cherokee family to sell its property and possessions, and the local Whites fell upon the lands, looting, burning, and finally taking possession.

Some Cherokee managed to escape into the gorges and thick forests of the Great Smoky Mountains, where they became the nucleus of those living there today, but most were finally rounded up or killed. They then were set off on a thousand-mile march—called to this day "the trail of tears" by the Cherokee that was one of the notable death marches in history. Ill clad, badly fed, lacking medical attention, and prodded on by soldiers wielding bayonets, the Indians suffered severe losses. An estimate made at the time stated that some four thousand Cherokee died en route, but that figure is certainly too low. At the very moment that these people were dying in droves, President Van Buren reported to Congress that the government's handling of the Indian problem had been "just and friendly throughout; its efforts for their civilization constant, and directed by the best feelings of humanity; its watchfulness in protecting them from individual frauds unremitting." Such cynicism at the highest level of government has been approached in our own time by the solemn pronouncements by President Lyndon B. Johnson about the Vietnam War.

One man who examined the young United States with a perceptive eye and who wrote it all down in his *Democracy in America,* Alexis de Tocqueville, happened to be in Memphis during an unusually cold winter when the thermometer hovered near zero. There he saw a ragged party of docile Choctaw, part of the thousands who had reluctantly agreed to be transported to the new lands in the western part of what was then the Arkansas Territory. Wrote de Tocqueville:

It was then the middle of winter, and the cold was unusually severe; the snow had frozen hard upon the ground and the river was drifting huge masses of ice. The Indians had their families with them, and they brought in their train the wounded and the sick, with children newly born and old men upon the verge of death. They possessed neither tents nor wagons, but only their arms and some provisions. I saw them embark to pass the mighty river, and never will that solemn spectacle fade from my remembrance. No cry, no sob, was heard among the assembled crowd; all was silent. Their calamities were of ancient date, and they knew them to be irremediable.‡

De Tocqueville was a discerning observer of the methods used by the Americans to deal with the Indians, and he described with restrained outrage how the Indians were sent westward by government agents: ". . . half convinced and half compelled, they go to inhabit new deserts, where the importunate whites will not let them remain ten years in peace. In this manner do the Americans obtain, at a very low price, whole provinces, which the richest sovereigns of Europe could not purchase." Reporting that a mere 6,273 Indians still survived in the thirteen original states, he predicted accurately the fate of the Indians in their new homes across the Mississippi:

The countries to which the newcomers betake themselves are inhabited by other tribes, which receive them with jealous hostility. Hunger is in the rear, war awaits them, and misery besets them on all sides. To escape from so many enemies, they separate, and each individual endeavors to procure secretly the means of supporting his existence.

Long before the science of anthropology and the study of what today is politely called "culture change," de Tocqueville understood how an entire culture might become raveled like some complexly woven fabric:

The social tie, which distress had long since weakened, is then dissolved; they have no longer a country, and soon they will not be a people; their very families are obliterated; their common name is forgotten; their language perishes; and all traces of their origin disappear. Their nation has ceased to exist except in the recollections of the antiquaries of America and a few of the learned of Europe.

The great removal was not the panacea that its advocates in Congress had maintained, in the names of God and civilization, it would be. Families had been separated, and many Indians had died en route. The new lands were much less hospitable to farming than those the Indians had been forced to evacuate, and the different game animals required new skills to hunt. To make matters worse, there was the hostility of the Plains Indians, who had been inveigled into giving up some of their lands to make room for the eastern Indians. The Plains Indians asserted that the bison had been driven away by the newcomers, and clashes between various groups became increasingly common. The Chickasaw, who had dutifully agreed to removal, said they could not take up the land assigned to them because of their fear of the "wild tribes" already inhabiting it. The United States government no more honored its obligation to protect the Indians in their new territory than it had honored any of its previous obligations toward them. In 1834 fewer than three thousand troops were available along the entire frontier to maintain order and to protect the newcomers against the Plains tribes. The result was that the very Indians whose removal had been ordered ostensibly to pacify and to civilize them were forced once more to take up their old warrior ways to defend themselves. So the result of the great removal was that once again, as in earlier years of competition between French and English, Indian was pitted against Indian for the benefit of the Whites.

THE LAST STAND

The plight of the Indian west of the Mississippi River was only a sad, monotonous duplication of what had happened east of it—warfare, broken treaties, expropriation of land, rebellion, and ultimately defeat. No sooner were the eastern Indians dropped down on the plains than the United States discovered the resources in the West, and miners and settlers were on the move. Emigrant trains rumbled across the plains, and once again the aim of the frontiersman was to get the Indian out of the way. A Kansas newspaper summarized the general feeling about Indians in the middle of the last century: "A set of miserable, dirty, lousy, blanketed, thieving, lying, sneaking, murdering, graceless, faithless, gut-eating skunks as the Lord ever permitted to infect the earth, and whose immediate and final extermination all men, except Indian agents and traders, should pray for."‡ The "final extermination" was hastened by epidemics that swept the West and sapped the Indians' power to resist the Whites. A mere hundred Mandan out of a population of sixteen hundred survived a smallpox epidemic (they are extinct today); the same epidemic, spreading westward, reduced the total number of Blackfoot Indians by about half. The majority of Kiowa and Comanche Indians were victims of cholera. The Indians would have been crushed by Whites in any event, but smallpox and cholera made the job easier.

Up to 1868, nearly four hundred treaties had been signed by the United States governments with various Indian groups, and scarcely a one had remained unbroken. By the latter part of the last century, the Indians finally realized that these treaties were real-estate deals designed to separate them from their lands. In the last three decades of the nineteenth century, Indians and Whites skirmished and then fought openly with ferocity and barbarity on both sides. Group by group, the Indians rose in rebellion only to be crushed—the southern Plains tribes in 1874, the Sioux in 1876, the Nez Percé in 1877, the Cheyenne and Bannock in 1878, the Ute in 1879, and the Apache throughout much of the 1880's, until Geronimo finally surrendered with his remnant band of thirty-six survivors. These wars represented the final spasms of a people who had long before been defeated logistically and psychologically. General William Tecumseh Sherman attributed the final victory of the United States Army to the railroads, which were able to transport his troops as far in one day as they had been able formerly to march in a month. General Phil Sheridan, on the other hand, had urged the destruction of the bison herds, correctly predicting that when they disappeared the Indians would disappear along with them; by 1885 the bison were virtually extinct, and the Indians were starving to death on the plains. One way or another, the Indian Wars finally ended; and with the enforced peace came an economic recession in the West, for the United States government had spent there about one million dollars for every Indian killed by 1870.

For nearly three centuries the frontier had lived under both the myth and the reality of the scalping knife and the tomahawk, and now the Bloodthirsty Savage was nearly gone. The Whites were in full control of the Indian situation, and the remnants were shifted about again and again, as many as five or six times. All of which led the Sioux chief Spotted Tail, grown old and wise, to ask the weary question: "Why does not the Great White Father put his red children on wheels, so he can move them as he will?"‡

In the eastern part of the country after the Civil War, a concern for the plight of the Indian replaced concern for the Negro. The sincere efforts of humanitarians were immediately seized upon by opportunists who developed a plan to use the Indian as a means of plundering the public coffers. A well-intentioned movement had gained support to give the remnant Indian populations the dignity of private property, and the plan was widely promoted in the halls of Congress, in the press, and in the meetings of religious societies. As a result, Senator Henry L. Dawes of Massachusetts sponsored the Dawes Allotment Act of 1887; he hoped it might salvage something for the Indians, who, he felt, would otherwise lose everything to voracious Whites. When President Grover Cleveland signed the act, he stated that the "hunger and thirst of the white man for the Indian's land is almost equal to his hunger and thirst after righteousness."‡ The act provided that after every Indian had been allotted land, any remaining surplus would be put up for sale to the public.

The loopholes with which the Dawes Act was punctured made it an efficient instrument for separating the Indians from this land. The act permitted Indians to lease their allotments, and many did so, ignorant of their true worth. Gullible Indians were persuaded to write wills leaving their property to White "friends." After this ploy became widespread, there was a suspicious increase in the number of Indian deaths from undetermined causes; in some cases murder was proved. The plunder was carried on with remarkable order. The first lands to go were the richest— bottom lands in river valleys, or fertile grasslands. Next went the slightly less desirable lands, such as those that had to be logged before producing a bountiful crop. Then the marginal lands were taken, and so on, until all the Indian had left to him was desert that no White considered worth the trouble to take. At this time the Indian birth rate had become higher than the mortality rate, and so there were more and more Indians on less and less land. The Indians did what they had always done: They shared the little they had and went hungry together. Between 1887, when the Dawes Act was passed, and 1934, out of the 138 million acres that had been their meager allotment, all but 56 million acres had been appropriated by Whites. The Bureau of Indian Affairs examined these remaining lands and concluded that 14 million acres were "critically eroded," 17 million acres "severely eroded," and 25 million acres "slightly eroded." Of the 56 million acres of land the Indians managed to hang on to, not a single acre was judged uneroded by soil conservationists.

The victory over the Bloodthirsty Savage—reduced in numbers, deprived of lands, broken in spirit, isolated on wasteland reservations—was complete except for one final indignity. That was to Americanize the Indian, to eliminate his last faint recollection of his ancient traditions—in short, to exterminate the cultures along with the Indians. There was not much Indian culture left to eradicate, but at last zealous Whites found something. Orders went out from Washington that all male Indians must cut their hair short, even though many Indians believed that long hair had supernatural significance. The Indians refused, and the battle was joined. Army reinforcements were sent to the reservations to carry out the order, and in some cases Indians had to be shackled before they submitted.

Most of the attention of the Americanizers was concentrated on the Indian children, who were snatched from their families and shipped off to boarding schools far from their homes. The children usually were kept at boarding school for eight years, during which time they were not permitted to see their parents, relatives, or friends. Anything Indian—dress, language, religious practices, even outlook on life (and how that was defined was up to the judgment of each administrator of the government's directives)—was uncompromisingly prohibited. Ostensibly educated, articulate in the English language, wearing store-bought clothes, and with their hair

The encounter between an Indian and a White bureaucrat is shown bitterly satirized in these early twentieth-century carvings by a Salish Indian of the Northwest Coast. The artist said that the figures tell the story, all too typical, of the starving "Suppliant Indian" who goes to the "Indian Agent" for help. The agent looks very severe as he reprimands him with a long lecture on how he should have saved his money. Reluctantly, the agent gives the Indian some paper scrip that entitles him to flour and potatoes.

short and their emotionalism toned down, the boarding-school graduates were sent out either to make their way in a White world that did not want them, or to return to a reservation to which they were now foreign. The Indians had simply failed to melt into the great American melting pot. They had suffered psychological death at an early age.

This is the point at which to halt the story of the changing relationships between Whites and Indians, for to all intents and purposes the Indian civilization disappeared early in the twentieth century. The conquest has been complete: The Indian was remade in the White's image or else safely bottled up on reservations. It is for another book by someone else to describe the plight of the Indian in American society today—his median family income of about $30 a week, his average age at death a mere 43 years, his infant mortality rate about twice that of his White neighbors. And of the Indian infants that survive, one study shows that about 500 of every 1,700 will die in their first year of "preventable diseases."‡

In the story of the American Indian, there is much room for compassion and charity, but the Indian experience is not unique. It has been repeated endlessly wherever one people conquered another. It was already an old story in ancient Egypt and Mesopotamia, among the Hebrews and the Canaanites and the Philistines. In modern times, it has been reenacted almost wherever Eurasian colonialism penetrated. Nor has the story ended, for even today the Japanese are still faced with the problem of what to do with their native people, the disappearing Ainu, the Indonesian leaders are trying to Indonesianize their Dyaks, and the Filipinos to Filipinize their Negritos.

Borrowed Cultures

THE DEBT TO THE INDIAN

When two cultures collide something is bound to happen, and world history has shown that the responses cover a wide range. Even though the ancient Romans conquered Greece and were the dominant group both in numbers and in power, they acknowledged the superiority of its culture; and as a result, the civilization of the Romans became Hellenic through and through. Their latter-day descendants, the Italians who began to immigrate to the United States after about 1850, were similarly absorbed by another culture, only this time they were in the minority and they went into the American melting pot.

The change produced in one culture by its encounter with another is called "acculturation." Rarely is the exchange of culture traits an equal one, and never does one culture emerge entirely untouched; the encounter almost always results in an increased similarity between the two cultures, leaving one of them dominant. In some cases, assimilation proceeds so far that it is virtually complete except for a single element that separates one group from the rest—as, for example, the refusal of the otherwise assimilated Jews in pre-Hitler Germany to convert to Christianity. On the other hand, one culture may be overwhelmed physically, but not assimilated by the other. That is what most often happened to the American Indian.

Yet, culturally, the Indian appears to have won out over his White conquerors. About half the states have Indian names, and so do thousands of cities, towns, rivers, lakes, and mountains. Americans drink hootch, meet in a caucus, bury the hatchet, have clambakes, run the gantlet, smoke the peace pipe, hold powwows, and enjoy Indian summer; the epithet "skunk" that the frontiersmen hurled so freely at the Indian is itself derived from an Indian word, as are many others in the English language. The march of settlers westward followed the same trails that the Indians had trod, eventually developing them into today's network of concrete highways. Whites learned from the Indian how to hunt, how to farm, and even how to survive in the New World.

Within a century or so after the discovery of America, more than fifty new foods had been carried back to the Old World, including maize, turkey, white potato, pumpkin, squash, the so-called Jerusalem artichoke, avocado, chocolate, and several kinds of beans. (Potatoes and maize now rank second and third in total tonnage of the world's crops, behind rice but ahead of what is probably man's oldest cultivated grain, wheat.) The European has turned for relief to drugs and pharmaceuticals the Indians discovered: quinine, ephedrine, novocaine, curare, ipecac, and witch hazel. Moccasin-style shoes are patterned after Indian footwear; canoes, after their birchbark craft; apparel worn at ski resorts is copied from Eskimo clothing. Many historians believe that the Constitution of the United States and those of several state governments were partly influenced by the democratic traditions of Indian societies. The noted psychoanalyst Carl G. Jung once stated that he discerned an Indian component in the character of some of his White American patients—if true, a demonstration of how subtly the culture of the conquered can invade the very personalities of the conquerors.↕

SQUAW MEN

One rarely mentioned aspect of the encounter between Indians and Whites was the appeal that the Indian societies held for generation after generation of Whites. No sooner did the first Whites arrive in North America than a disproportionate number of them showed they preferred Indian society to their own. Within only a few years after Virginia was settled, more than forty male colonists had married Indian women, and several English women had married Indians. There was only one reason why the colony of Virginia instituted severe penalties against going to live with Indians: Whites *were* doing just that, and in increasing numbers. In fact, the word "Indianize"—in its meaning "to adopt the ways of the Indians"—originated as far back as the seventeenth century when Cotton Mather was led to inquire: "How much do our people Indianize?" They did so to a great extent. Throughout American history, thousands of Whites enthusiastically exchanged breeches for breechcloths.

Indianization impressed Michel Guillaume Jean de Crèvecoeur, who wrote in 1782 in his *Letters from an American Farmer:* "It cannot be, therefore, so bad as we generally conceive it to be; there must be in the Indians' social bond something singularly captivating, and far superior to be boasted of among us; for thousands of Europeans are Indians, and we have no examples of even one of those Aborigines having from choice become Europeans."‡ De Crèvecoeur touched precisely the sore spot that so bewildered Whites. Why did transculturalization seem to operate only in one direction? Whites who had lived for a time with Indians almost never wanted to leave. But almost none of the "civilized" Indians who had been given the opportunity to savor White society chose to become a part of it. And the White squaw men persisted in their determination, even though they were subjected to legal penalties, as well as to great contempt from other Whites.

Numerous attempts have been made to explain Indianization. Some people have speculated that civilization forms merely a thin veneer over man's basic bestiality, that he reverts to the primitive at the first opportunity. Yet Indian society, with its complicated relationships between a welter of households, families, kin groups, sodalities, moieties, ranks, and classes, was even more structured than the contemporary White society. Other people have simply regarded Whites who gave up the blessings of civilization and Christianity as renegades and backsliders—or, in psychological terms, rebellious personalities. But the reasons why particular individuals chose to Indianize do not illuminate anything about why whole groups of people behaved that way. Nor does this problem relate solely to the American Indian. Some of the first missionaries sent to the South Seas from London, in the eighteenth century, threw away their collars and married native women.

There were special aspects of Indian society that made it possible for so many thousands of Whites to be incorporated into it. One of the things that amazed the earliest explorers, almost without exception, was the hospitality with which Indians received them. When the Indians later learned that the Whites posed a threat, their attitude changed, but the initial contacts were idyllic. That was particularly true of those Indian societies at the band and tribal levels, although even the chiefdoms of the West Indies warmly greeted Columbus. Hospitality and sharing were characteristic of all Indian societies.

Another pertinent way in which Indian society differed was in the matter of adoption. If a prisoner of war was not reserved for torture, he was usually adopted by a family to replace a lost husband or a dead child. The adopted person was thoroughly integrated into all aspects of the Indian society he had joined. He had the same rights and obligations as any native-born member. He was expected to become a part of the kinship system, the clans and moieties, the ceremonial and warrior societies. He had new parents, new kin, new allegiances. Such total adoption explains the complaints of many of the squaw men, typically stated by one of them: "When you marry an Indian girl, you marry her whole damn tribe!"

Clearly, the pattern of Indianization had already been established among Indians themselves long before the Whites arrived; it required no major readjustment to adopt Whites, as in the past Indians had been adopted. So thoroughly were adoptees integrated into the complex social structure of the Indian society that even Whites who had originally gone unwillingly as captives of the Indians refused to be ransomed. These captives had been integrated in the fullest way and given a definite role to play. A White could become an extremely important person in Indian society. When thirty cases of captive Whites, fifteen men and fifteen women, were analyzed by an anthropologist, he found an unusually high percentage of social success; three or four of the men had become chiefs and about the same number of women had become the wives of chiefs.↕

The Indians' willingness to receive squaw men is demonstrated by the numerous cases of Negroes who joined Indian tribes. The Indians in the southern states learned slavery from the Whites, but they adapted it to their own kind of culture. For one thing, they wanted slaves as prestige items, even though in most cases slaves did not earn their keep. This was in contrast to the Whites, who valued slaves solely for their mechanical utility in harvesting the bounty of the New World. More important, the Indians altered the institution of slavery somewhat to create a role in society for the slave, who had been a nonperson among the Whites.

The truth is not that the escaped Negro was running away from "civilization" to return to his primitive ways, as White apologists have stated, but that he was running *into* a society that was much more structured. He chose to be a slave under Indian masters because they gave him something that the Whites denied him: the opportunity to exist, even as a chattel, inside a rigid social structure. The Negro, in turn, was valuable to the Indian, for he brought with him skills he had learned from his White masters. Negro slaves among the Indians possessed a degree of social mobility, and there are cases on record of their rising to high office and status. It is believed that Osceola, the great Seminole leader, was part Negro.

The question naturally arises why transculturalization did not work the other way. Why did not Indians enter White society, particularly in view of the numerous attempts made by Whites to "civilize" them? The answer is that the White settlers possessed no traditions and institutions comparable to the Indians' hospitality and sharing, adoption, and complete social integration. Indians who associated closely with Whites soon found themselves confronted by a social system in which they might on occasion be courteously and even kindly treated; they might be educated and given clothes; yet no White family found it in the tradition of Western civilization to adopt an Indian as an equal member of the family group. The Whites who educated Indians did so with the idea that the Indians would return to their own people as missionaries to spread the gospel, not that they might become functioning parts of White society.‡

Voluntary assimilation, known as Indianization in the Americas, is one response that has occurred at other places and in other times when two cultures collided. An unusual manifestation of it is when the whole dominant culture takes up the ways of the conquered. That does not happen very often, but it did occur when the Hyksos conquered Egypt about 1700 B.C. and when the Romans conquered the Greeks in the second century B.C. The Hyksos adopted Egyptian manners, dress, and language; they apparently did not interfere with the Egyptian religion, but rather accepted it as their own; the Egyptian social and political systems continued without alteration. Similarly, the Romans became almost completely Hellenized, incorporating many Greek elements into their religion, taking the art and literature of the Greeks for models, and adopting their social customs and their system of education to such a degree that Greek tutors became fashionable.

Perhaps the most spectacular example of voluntary assimilation is Hawaii, which in 1819 abolished its religion and many other aspects of its culture, including an extraordinary number of taboos. At the same time the Hawaiians substituted, again voluntarily, what they considered was the best of everything they had learned about Western civilization from Captain Cook and other explorers, whalers, and traders in the previous forty years. Some divines are inclined to regard this as one of Christianity's finest moments, but actually the first missionary did not reach the islands until five months *after* the fact, at which time the islanders adopted the new religion to fill the vacuum left by the one they had abandoned.

Again and again around the world, assimilation has worked best when it was not forced. The ancient religion of the Hawaiians came to a voluntary end at the behest of Chief Kamehameha II, with the consent of his principal advisers and his mother. No White ordered, or even suggested, the action he took. At almost no time in the history of the United States, though, were the Indians afforded similar opportunities for voluntary assimilation. There was already such a history of bloodshed, duplicity, and bitterness that in the rare cases where such opportunities did exist, the Indians would have been out of their minds to take advantage of them.

ACCULTURATION WITHOUT ASSIMILATION

When two cultures meet, their adjustments do not inevitably have to result in total assimilation. People can still cling to the old ways and retain a goodly number of their customs. In fact, the dominant culture may encourage them to do so for their quaintness and tourist appeal, as demonstrated by the Franco dictatorship in Spain, which encourages regional dances and costumes yet demands total conformity in the religious and political areas of culture. Despite the Americanization movement, many immigrant groups managed to salvage something of the old country in their new homes in North America: the Friends of Italian Opera, German beer halls, the Saint Patrick's Day parade, the United Jewish Appeal.

Along the border between the United States and Mexico two very different facets of European culture are divided by a political boundary, yet they have influenced each other while maintaining their own identities. The Mexican influence on the United States side of the border is seen in Spanish names for cities (Santa Fe, El Paso) and for topographical features (arroyo, sierra); much of the architecture, including even government buildings, is Mexican-inspired; restaurants serving Mexican food are widespread, and many homes are furnished with Mexican pottery and textiles; most Americans in the area pride themselves on speaking at least some Spanish. A similar situation prevails on the opposite side of the border, where American-made gadgets are very much in evidence, and where Mexicans go to restaurants that serve American-style food. Even the uneducated Mexicans speak a good deal of English, and they pride themselves on knowing how to get along with the gringos.

Acculturation has taken place across the border, yet Mexicans and Southwesterners are very different in the totality of their cultures. The interaction between the two groups has further been complicated by the presence of Indians on both sides of the border. Most of these Indians have learned to speak either Spanish or English or both, in addition to their native languages, and have made adjustments to both cultures. The Pueblo Indians, in particular, have kept their social organization and religion intact, and they have salvaged a good deal of their material culture as well, by a form of passive resistance. Yet, on the surface they seem to have accepted White ways: They speak both Spanish and English; most have converted to Christianity; they drive American automobiles and trucks; they eat Mexican-style food.

When today's remnants of Indian societies are examined closely, it is seen how well some have worked out a compromise with their White conquerors—acculturation without assimilation. They use United States currency and banks, speak English to Whites, furnish their American-style homes with American-made goods, subscribe to American magazines, own television sets or radios that receive programs prepared by the dominant White society. They have accepted almost all of the material aspects of White American society. But at the Shawnee reservation in eastern Oklahoma, for example, one can see that, even though deprived economically and crowded onto marginal lands, the Indians have managed to snatch what is important to them out of their general defeat. By a steady intransigence, the Shawnee have maintained their own identity in the face of the White majority. Perhaps the Shawnee found it easier than some other Indian groups, because they were already experienced in the problems of acculturation long before being herded onto reservations. Even before the conquest by Whites, they had taken to roaming and thus had come into contact with other Indians of different languages and customs. The trail of the Shawnee leads from their earliest recorded home, now parts of Tennessee and South Carolina, through Pennsylvania, Ohio, Indiana, Missouri, and Texas, before the Whites finally placed them on a reservation in Oklahoma. In the face of constant exposure to outside influences, they survived by developing an antiassimilation attitude. Their small numbers survived culturally because they rejected oppressive parts of the White culture at the same time that they accepted unimportant parts.

THE NAVAHO

In contrast, the Navaho represent one of the world's best examples of a culture that tends to borrow rather than to reject. Their population today stands at nearly one hundred thousand, and they far outnumber any other group of Indians in the United States; their reservation of more than fifteen million acres in Arizona and New Mexico far surpasses all others in size. Although by the standards of White America they are impoverished, compared with most other Indians in North America they must be considered wealthy. Their economic prospects, too, are brighter than those of most Indians, for mineral wealth has been found on their lands and they are aggressively pursuing more efficient agriculture and the introduction of small industries. The tribal council at Window Rock, Arizona, has installed a computer to help it keep track of the tribe's one million dollars in income each month, much of it from oil and mineral leases.

From the time of their earliest appearance as a people, the Navaho have successfully borrowed from other cultures—Pueblo, Spanish, Mexican, and White American. They were able to do this because they arrived in the Southwest from the north with only a simple cultural framework—but they could fit into it any aspects of other people's culture that might be useful to them. Furthermore, they were so impoverished culturally that they had nothing to lose and everything to gain by borrowing. Remains of Navaho dwellings—called hogans—found in New Mexico have been dated no earlier than between 1491 and 1541. Unless someday earlier remains of hogans are found, the only possible conclusion is that the Navaho were every bit as much newcomers to the Southwest as were the Spaniards.

Contact between two very different cultures—the sedentary Pueblo farmers and the seminomadic Navaho hunters—took place along a broad front in Arizona and New Mexico. In their long trek southward, the Apachean people who were to become the Navaho had encountered many different Indian groups; now suddenly they were confronted with town dwellers, agriculturists who had conquered the desert. To the sophisticated Pueblo Indians, the Navaho must have seemed little better than barbarians.

Unlike the Whites, the Pueblo Indians never undertook any program to "civilize" their new neighbors. They defended themselves against Navaho attack, but they did not consciously try to coerce the Navaho into accepting their own culture. Left free, the Navaho could borrow whatever they considered useful in Pueblo culture. Had they been forced, as Whites later attempted to coerce the Indians, then the Navaho might have reacted differently: They might have resisted all culture change.

The first historical, rather than archeological, record of the existence of the Navaho does not occur until 1626, in a report written by a Spanish priest. But the report confirms that the Aztec culture was not alone in evolving rapidly. The report shows that within only a hundred years or so after arriving as hunters and gatherers in the Southwest, the Navaho had already become expert in agriculture. The priest separates the Navaho from all their other relatives among the Apache who, he declares, "live by the hunt." Instead, he refers to them as "Apaches del Nabaxu" (*Navaho* is the Spanish corruption of a Pueblo word that means "big planted fields"). He goes on to describe the Navaho as "very skillful farmers" who had already learned how to store their surplus maize.

After the Spaniards settled the Southwest, the Navaho began another burst of cultural borrowing—or, more accurately, stealing. Spanish ranches and villages were so depleted of horses—not to mention sheep—that by 1775 the Spaniards had to send to Europe for 1,500 additional horses. After the Pueblo Rebellion against the Spaniards was put down in 1692, many Pueblo took refuge with their Navaho neighbors—and taught them how to weave blankets, a skill for which the Navaho are still noted, and to make pottery. During this time the Navaho probably absorbed many Pueblo religious and social ideas and customs as well, such as ceremonial paraphernalia and possibly the Pueblo clan system.

By the time the United States took possession of the Southwest in 1848, after the Mexican War, the Navaho had become the dominant military force in the area. Their population had grown from about four thousand in 1740 to more than fifteen thousand in 1848. The Navaho had also nearly completed their borrowing from the Pueblo, Spanish, and Mexican cultures. In addition to the items already listed, they had enlarged their agricultural inventory by growing wheat, melons, peaches, and other Old World crops, as well as the native maize and beans. Their architecture now included ceremonial hogans, and three other types of hogans as well. The shaman no longer was merely the inspired visionary he had been when the Navaho were only at the band level; he had become the diagnostician of sickness and prescriber of the types of ceremonies to be employed for the cure. The role of the carefully educated Navaho "singer" became important in those ceremonies that had borrowed sand paintings, prayer sticks, masks, and altars from the Pueblo Indians.

The American soldiers who marched into Santa Fe had no trouble with the Mexicans, but the Navaho stole several head of cattle from the herd of the commanding general himself, not to mention thousands of sheep and horses from settlers in the vicinity. The Americans launched numerous punitive expeditions against the Navaho, who signed treaty after treaty and broke every one of them, for army officers did not realize that the headman of one Navaho group was powerless to control any other group. For their

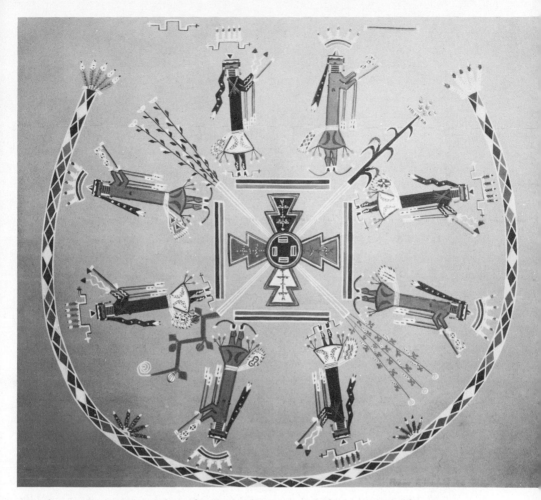

Navaho sand painting used in the Hail Chant, one of the many Navaho cere-monials, illustrates a complex mythology. It shows the figures of Rainbow Boy and Rainbow Girl at their different positions as they walk around the central lake, which has cloud symbols on four sides. Four holy plants grow out of the central lake. At the open eastern portion of the rainbow rope, lightning and rainbow guards are stationed. This is but a small indication of the intricate mythology contained in this one painting.

part, the Navaho headmen probably did not understand that when they signed a treaty it was expected that they would control every other Navaho group as well as their own. Finally, in 1863, Colonel Kit Carson was ordered to clear the country of Navaho Indians and to resettle any survivors at Fort Sumner in eastern New Mexico, where they could be "civilized." Carson's strategy was the same as that applied against the Plains Indians a little later: He destroyed the Navaho food base by systematically killing their livestock and by burning their fields. Carson's "Long Knives" (his soldiers, so named by the Indians because of their bayonets) also cut off the breasts of Navaho girls and tossed them back and forth like baseballs.

Within less than a year Carson's strategy had been eminently successful. A few Navaho bands managed to hold out in the remote mesas and canyons, but the people as a whole had been starved into submission: The survivors, begging for food, surrendered to the Whites. Ultimately, about 8,500 Navaho made what they still call the "Long Walk" to captivity at Fort Sumner, three hundred miles away. After they had been there for four years, the Navaho signed a peace treaty that entitled them to a reservation of about 3,500,000 acres, much less land than they had held previously. (This reservation has been enlarged from time to time to its present 16,000,000 acres, but its size has not kept pace with the population growth from not quite 15,000 in 1868 to about 100,000 today.)

Although the Fort Sumner experience failed to Christianize the captive Navaho, it did succeed in altering the culture in one important respect: From that time on, the Navaho Indians ceased to be raiders. Now the finishing touches were applied to Navaho culture. The first trading post opened on the new reservation in 1871, and by 1890 there were thirty-nine such posts. The Navaho's experience with traders was much more congenial than it was with the government agents who tried to get them to cut their hair, or with the missionaries who gave them a vision of damnation when they had already had fear enough of ghosts. The trader taught them the potentialities of a new kind of economic life. Silver-working, which apparently some Navaho had learned while imprisoned at Fort Sumner, was encouraged by the traders, and so was the weaving of blankets. Through the trading post, and later through wage labor, the Navaho were drawn into the White American market economy. Pickup trucks have replaced the wagons that replaced the horses that replaced the aboriginal dogs. Male attire is now cowboy Southwestern, although the Navaho women have been more conservative in retaining the velveteen blouse and calico skirt first worn at Fort Sumner. Factory-made utensils and tools have replaced Navaho pottery, baskets, and wooden and stone implements.

Clearly, today's Navaho is tremendously different from the culturally impoverished wanderer who invaded the Southwest some five hundred years ago. Time after time, as the Navaho came into contact with Pueblo, Spaniard, Mexican, and White American, he borrowed from their cultures what he needed. Yet, he remained a Navaho—independent, proud, adjusting to continual changes in his way of life. By no means are Navaho Indians simply imitation Whites.

The Navaho learned the most from the Pueblo, who never tried to civilize them. In contrast, the brutal policy of Kit Carson and the humiliating experience at Fort Sumner basically changed Navaho culture in only one respect: It switched from a partial dependence upon raiding to a market economy. And the Navaho willingly accepted from the trader what he could never be forced to accept from the missionary or government agent. The Navaho clearly demonstrate the errors made by Whites in their encounters with Indians, and also the mistakes Eurasians in general made with other primitive peoples around the world. Among the Navaho, the greatest and most durable culture change has come about as a result not of coercion, but of being presented with a cultural model which they were free to accept or reject.‡

The same is true also of many other primitive societies. The potlatch, for example, became for some Northwest Coast Indians a symbol of defiance to White authority. The Canadian Indian Act of 1885 expressly forbade the potlatch and provided for imprisonment up to six months for anyone guilty of engaging in the ceremonial. Passage of the act was the signal for the golden age of potlatching to begin among the Southern Kwakiutl; outwitting the Indian agent and the Canadian police gave the traditional feast added zest. In 1952 a revised Indian Act rescinded the prohibition, and potlatching once again became legal in Canada. Only a handful of old men bothered to attend a potlatch given later that year, whereas if the old law had remained in effect a large turnout would have been expected.‡

NAVAHO AND ZUNI WAR VETERANS

The Navaho and the Zuni share many cultural elements and live alongside each other in western New Mexico. Both are at the tribal level, the physical environment of their lands is much the same, and their histories have been entwined for nearly five centuries; yet their cultures have remained distinct. This was vividly demonstrated by the different ways in which the Navaho and Zuni responded to World War II, and also by the ways each group treated the returned veterans.

In the case of the Zuni, 213 men went into the armed forces during the war years. Many more Zuni were eligible to be drafted, but the council of high priests petitioned the draft board for deferment of men holding religious offices. When that was granted, the Zuni priests then requested

Navaho Kachina Maiden reveals the Navaho as seen through the eyes of the Hopi, a neighboring Pueblo tribe in Arizona. Note the satirical touches of the heavily rouged cheeks; the hair elaborately combed into a bun; the abundance of jewelry around the neck, on the belt, and on the hands; as well as the typical Navaho blouse, skirt, and leggings.

the exemption of almost every eligible male, for the priests claimed that every male belonged to some priesthood or else took part in an important ceremony. When the draft board agreed to defer only Zuni "high priests serving for life," the Zuni responded by creating new religious positions and reviving extinct ceremonies, some of which had not been performed for nearly forty years.

The Navaho displayed none of the reluctance of the Zuni to go off to war. Approximately 3,600 Navaho served, and about 800 of these were voluntary enlistments. Many more Navaho were willing to serve, but they had an extremely high rejection rate because of illiteracy and poor health. Nor were any cases known in which Navaho officials attempted to obtain exemptions. On the contrary, delegates to the tribal council made speeches stating how pleased they were that their boys were going into the army. The departure of the Navaho men from their communities was even ritualized by the performance of the ceremony known as the Blessing Way.

At Zuni, when the veterans returned no fuss was made over them; in fact, they were treated with great suspicion and subjected to gossip, rumor, and ridicule. When one Zuni veteran wanted to establish a branch of the American Legion, a malicious rumor started that he was planning to use dues money for his personal enrichment. The anxieties of the veterans resulted in a sharp increase in drunkenness and restless behavior. Within a few years, though, most of them had been reintegrated into Zuni life (the thirty-three who refused to conform left the village). The veterans married, rejoined religious societies, and dutifully returned to work in the fields. On the other hand, the Navaho veterans were welcomed back with enthusiasm and by the performance of many ceremonials. Instead of resistance to the knowledge and experiences the young men had received, the Navaho generally were proud that their boys had learned to speak English so well. There was enthusiasm when, for example, the Veterans Administration offered to start an agricultural training program. The veterans represented merely another step in the history of the Navaho as a borrowing culture.

What was there in the two cultures that made the Navaho welcome the opportunity to serve in the war while the Zuni remained steadfastly resistant both to the war and to the veterans? Part of the answer can be found in the simple facts of different settlement patterns. The Navaho live on their reservation as scattered families that frequently shift residence, largely because theirs is a livestock economy. So when the Navaho veteran returned, he had only to adjust to his own family and to his neighbors. In contrast, the Zuni village is compact. The Zuni veteran returned not just to his own isolated family but also to a tight web of household, lineages, clans, kivas, and societies in which he had to find his place once again. Because of the physical closeness of people in Zuni, gossip and ridicule could be brought into action immediately as weapons of social control.

Secondly, the reactions of the two societies might have been predicted from the differing kinds of acculturation they had undergone. The Navaho had always freely borrowed cultural items, and World War II represented another opportunity for them to examine White ways close up. Some veterans were even encouraged to live off the reservation among Whites, so they could bring back more of this precious new information. In contrast, the Zuni are examples of what has been called "antagonistic acculturation." They adopted the material and external trappings of the Whites without adopting White goals; in fact, most of the trappings were adopted so as better to resist White culture. As Zuni changed physically in the last century from a compact terraced pueblo to a more modern village of stone and adobe houses, antagonism to White culture increased, for it was obvious that Whites were making inroads with their technology. Many Zuni considered the incursions of White technology a threat to their religion, and they responded by becoming more secretive and more determined to maintain the traditional ways. So instead of regarding the veterans as returned heroes, they looked upon them as suspects who might subtly introduce new ways that they learned while living among Whites. When one veteran dressed in a business suit, he was ridiculed for trying to act like a White man.

The final explanation lies in the contrasting histories of the two cultures in the matter of warfare. Offensive warfare was an important feature of Navaho life until the internment at Fort Sumner in 1864. But Zuni warfare had been largely defensive, and they had been forced to give it up almost two centuries earlier, after the Spanish beat down the Pueblo Rebellion in 1692. Also, the Navaho exalted the warrior for his individual exploits. Even in aboriginal times, though, the Zuni warrior enjoyed little prestige because the people believed that his success depended largely on the prayers of the priests who stayed at home. The Zuni veteran brought back no cultural booty, but only the danger of infecting his people with more White ways. He was entitled to no celebrations.✇

XVI

The Hopes of the Oppressed

REVIVALISTIC MOVEMENTS

A culture that is in the process of being swamped by another often reacts defensively by physically grappling with the outsiders. But it may wage a cultural war as well. Such defensive reactions have been given various labels by anthropologists: nativism, revivalism, revitalization, and messianism. All are deliberate efforts to erect a better culture out of the defeat or decay of an older one. They may be as fanciful as the attempt in Ireland at the end of the last century to revive the moribund Irish Gaelic form of the Celtic language in the face of British rule. Or, in the case of some minority groups in the United States exposed to Americanization, the defensive reaction may consist of ethnic get-togethers, at which foods from the old country are eaten, native costumes worn, folk dances performed, and the language of the homeland spoken.

The reactions of primitive peoples overpowered by Eurasian colonial empires have usually been much more extreme. Their lands appropriated, their social system ripped apart, their customs suppressed, and their holy places profaned—they tried to resist physically, but they were inevitably defeated by the superior firepower and technology of the Whites. As hopelessness and apathy settled over these people, the ground was prepared for revivalistic and messianic movements that promised the return of the good old days. North America has been the scene of many dozens of these movements, in one place after another erupting sporadically and then dying down. And they resulted almost every time in bloodshed and additional defeats, which produced further disillusionment to spark the next revival.

The Indians, as well as other peoples who came under colonial rule, have more recently experienced the same sort of acculturation that took place among the Jews and early Christians in the ancient Near East. There are strong parallels between the hope for salvation among the Jews and the hopes of Indians who followed native prophets, between the early Christian martyrs and the Indian revolts against United States authority, between the Hebrew and the Indian prophets. Particularly fascinating, and it is a story not often told, is the way in which the Jews and early Christians have served as models for oppressed peoples from primitive cultures far from the Near East. Almost wherever the White missionary has penetrated, primitive peoples have borrowed from his bible those elements in which they saw a portrayal of their own plight; and most often this has been an identification with the Jews. The roots of many nativistic movements—among such groups as the Maori of New Zealand, the Kikuyu of Kenya, the Bantu of South Africa, and the Ghost Dancers of North America—can be found in the appeal that the story of the Jews held for these people. Because of such identification, some primitive peoples have claimed descent from one of the ten lost tribes of Israel. In their yearning to escape from servitude, they have found a model in Moses, whose name is a popular cognomen among many colonial peoples. They regard the arrest and execution of a native on charges of being a rebel against White authority in the same terms as the trials undergone by the Hebrew prophets or the passion of Jesus.↕

THE FIRST PHASE: RECOVERY OF LOST CULTURES

The succession of revivalistic and messianic movements that took place among the American Indians used to be looked upon merely as stubborn resistance by Indian heathens to the obvious blessings the Whites wanted to bestow. But anthropological studies have shown it was not that simple. All the Indian revivalistic movements fall into two phases. One, which will be discussed in this section, attempts the recovery of an old and lost culture; the other attempts to accommodate itself to Whites.↕

As their cultures began to disintegrate under military and cultural assault by Whites, the Indians yearned to restore a way of life that was fast disappearing. Such a situation was particularly favorable for the rise of prophets who promised the disappearance of the White intruders and the retrieving of the past. In 1680 the Pueblo Indians, led by a prophet named Popé who had been living at Taos, expelled the Spaniards. Catholic priests were slaughtered in their missions and their bodies piled high on church altars. About one fifth of the total Spanish population of 2,500 was killed outright, and the rest fled to El Paso, Texas. Everything of Spanish manufacture or ownership—not only churches, houses, furniture, and art, but even swine and sheep—was destroyed. The god of the Spaniards was declared dead, and the old religious ways came out into the open again. But Popé's attempt to become complete dictator over all the Pueblo Indians was clearly an impossible fantasy since they were organized only on the tribal level, and tribes are extremely fragile. The Pueblo confederation broke apart and the people warred among themselves. In 1692 the Spaniards marched back in victory.

The Pueblo Rebellion was primarily a revolt against alien authority, but the next major Indian uprising, which took place in 1762, was clearly messianic. A Delaware Indian prophet appeared in Michigan and preached a doctrine that he said had been revealed to him in a vision. He called for the cessation of strife by Indian against Indian, and a holy war against Whites to be carried on only with bows and arrows. Foolishly, in his rejection of all White culture, he rejected also the use by Indians of White firearms, which might have tipped the balance in his favor. This prophet (whose name no one ever bothered to record) inflamed the Indians around the Great Lakes, and finally a practical man, an Algonkian named Pontiac, arose to lead them. He formed a confederation and attacked English forts all along the Great Lakes until he was ambushed and his forces utterly defeated. But his unsuccessful holy war festered like a wound. Forty years later the Shawnee Prophet (whose Indian name translates as "The Rattle"), twin brother of Chief Tecumseh, repeated the promises of the Delaware Prophet: liberation of Indians and extirpation of the Whites. Indians from many dozens of tribes and bands sent emissaries to the Shawnee to listen to his teachings, and they returned home to excite the entire frontier.

Tecumseh established the greatest Indian alliance that ever existed north of Mexico. He and his emissaries visited almost every band, tribe, and chiefdom from the headwaters of the Missouri River in the Rocky Mountains to as far south and east as Florida. Indians everywhere were arming themselves for the right moment to attack the Whites when, in 1811, Tecumseh's brother, the Shawnee Prophet, launched a premature attack at Tippecanoe, on the banks of the Wabash. In the battle that ensued, the Indians were defeated by General William Henry Harrison, who later was elected President of the United States under the slogan of "Tippecanoe and Tyler, Too." Tecumseh rallied his remaining forces and joined the British in the War of 1812. He fought bravely in battle after battle, but in 1813 his 2,500 warriors from the allied tribes were defeated decisively, once again by General Harrison, in Ontario. He was killed, but his followers spirited away his body, and for years thereafter the frontier was plagued by rumors that he would soon return. He never did, and the prophecy of his brother had been dramatically disproved by White bullets.

There is a sequel, ironic and tragic, to the story of the Shawnee Prophet. One of his followers, named Kanakuk, became a prophet among the Kickapoo, but his teachings were entirely different. Instead of being an advocate of war against Whites, he called upon the Kickapoo to abjure killing, lying, the use of liquor, and all other sins; their reward, he said, would be the discovery of new green pastures where they could settle in peace. But these proposals did not save his people from being forced out of their small area of land in Missouri and onto another in Kansas that was both smaller and less green. There, in 1852, he died of smallpox. His band of faithful, convinced that he would rise again on the third day, gathered in a close group around his body—in spite of all medical warnings about the dangers of infection. The cult, almost down to the last follower, was wiped out by smallpox.

DREAMERS

The Dreamers originated among the Indians who lived along the lower reaches of the Columbia River in Oregon and Washington. This cult, too, sought recovery of the lost culture, but it differed from the previous revivalistic movements in that it had strong Roman Catholic overtones. Smohalla ("Preacher") was born about 1820 in the Rocky Mountains and was educated by Roman Catholic missionaries. He proclaimed a cult largely influenced by Catholic doctrine; he also became known as a great shaman and worker of miraculous cures. But about 1860 he was challenged by another shaman—named Moses, ironically enough—who left him bleeding and presumed dead on the banks of a river.

He was carried downstream by rising flood waters, and a White farmer rescued him. Once he had recovered from his ordeal, Smohalla wandered through the Southwest and into Mexico. When he returned finally to his own people, he maintained that he had actually been dead and that the Great Spirit had conversed with him. The Great Spirit told Smohalla how disgusted he was that the Indians had forsaken their native religion for that of the Whites. Smohalla's miraculous return was sufficient proof for many that the Great Spirit had chosen him as a messenger of revelation to the Indian people.

Because he went into frequent trances, Smohalla became known as the Dreamer, and so his followers were known collectively as Dreamers. Upon awakening from one of his trances, he would report to them the visions he had had; out of these visions he pieced together a remarkable cosmogony. In the beginning, the Great Spirit created the earth, the animals, and all living things, including mankind. The first men he created were Indians, followed next by Frenchmen, then priests, Americans, and finally Negroes —which was pretty much Smohalla's opinion about the hierarchy of the portion of mankind he knew. Therefore the earth belonged to those first men, the Indians, who must take care not to defile it as the Whites had. "You ask me to plow the ground!" said Smohalla. "Shall I take a knife and tear my mother's bosom? You ask me to cut grass and make hay and sell it and be rich like white men! But how dare I cut my mother's hair?" Smohalla's preaching posed a major obstacle to the United States government at a time when its official policy was to force all Indians to become farmers.

Inspired by the teachings of Smohalla, Chief Joseph of the Nez Percé in Idaho rebelled in 1877. Before he was trapped only thirty miles short of refuge in Canada, he had consistently outwitted and outfought a superior United States Army across a thousand miles of Rocky Mountain terrain. It was also one of the most honorable of the Indian wars—at least on Chief Joseph's side; for, although he forbade his warriors to scalp or to torture, the Whites massacred his women and children. Finally, with most of his warriors dead, his people starving, freezing, and maimed, Chief Joseph walked toward the White generals, handed his rifle to them, and said: "I am tired of fighting . . . My people ask me for food, and I have none to give. It is cold, and we have no blankets, no wood. My people are starving to death. Where is my little daughter? I do not know . . . Hear me, my chiefs. I have fought; but from where the sun now stands, Joseph will fight no more forever."

Despite the promises contained in the surrender agreement, the United States Army did not permit the survivors to return to their lands. Instead, they were sent to the malarial bottomlands of the Indian Territory, where the six of Chief Joseph's children who had managed to survive the rebellion all died of disease, along with most of his band. Chief Joseph and those few who remained alive were then allowed to walk, in winter, to a new reservation in northern Washington, fifteen hundred miles away.

They were given no supplies of clothing or food for the trip. Despite Chief Joseph's defeat, and the defeat of several other Indian leaders who were inspired by Smohalla, the cult of the Dreamers survived for some time thereafter. It even had a minor resurgence in 1883 in response to the increasing frustration brought by the building of the Northern Pacific Railroad.

THE GHOST DANCE

The climax of the many revivalistic movements was the Ghost Dance of 1890. It first appeared about 1870 among the Northern Paiute who lived on the California–Nevada border. The Union Pacific Railroad had recently completed its first transcontinental run, and no doubt that inspired the vision of the prophet Wodziwob that a big train would bring back his dead ancestors and announce their arrival with an explosion, an idea probably inspired by the steam whistle. He proclaimed that a cataclysm would swallow up all the Whites but miraculously leave behind their goods for those Indians who joined his cult. Also, a heaven on earth would be created, for at that time the Great Spirit would return to live with the Indians. These miracles were to be hastened by ceremonial dancing around a pole and by singing the songs that Wodziwob had learned during a vision. But no benefits ever resulted from these dances, and they were abandoned.↕

The Ghost Dance that erupted twenty years after Wodziwob, in 1890, resulted from the intertwining of several strands, one of which was the founding in 1831 by Joseph Smith of the Latter-Day Saints of Jesus Christ (Mormons). He prophesied that a New Jerusalem would arise in the desert, where all those with faith would gather, including the lost tribes of Israel. After the Mormons settled in Utah, it became part of their belief that the Indians represented the remnants of the Hebrew tribes taken into captivity by the Assyrians some 2,500 years earlier. The Mormons sent emissaries to the Indians, whom they dubbed Lamanites, inviting them to join the Mormon colonies and to be baptized. Joseph Smith was also supposed to have prophesied in 1843 that when he reached his eighty-fifth year—that is, in 1890—the messiah would appear in human form.

The various threads now begin to come together. The Indian prophet Wodziwob had an assistant, and the assistant had a son who became known as Wovoka the prophet. In that year awaited by the Mormons—1890—Wovoka appeared and preached the Ghost Dance religion. The Mormons found it perfectly understandable that in the promised year the messiah should appear first among the Indians rather than among Whites, for the Indians were the descendants of Jews and thus possessed priority.

James Mooney, who is responsible for most of our information about the Indian revivalistic and messianic movements, never doubted the sincerity of Wovoka. Mooney talked with him at length in 1892 and appraised him as being the usual sleight-of-hand shaman but by no means a fraud. Wovoka never claimed to be the messiah awaited by the Mormons (although his followers did). He personally made no attempt to spread his teachings, and in fact he never even left Walker Lake, Nevada. Wovoka had led an obscure life until he suddenly fell into a trance during a solar eclipse. When he awoke, he reported that God had taken him by the hand and shown him all the dead Indians happy and young again. God then told Wovoka about a dance that the people must perform to bring the dead Indians back to life again, for the dance generated energy that had the power to move the dead. The dance was spread quickly both by Paiute missionaries and by other Indians who came to visit Wovoka. His teachings took hold among many Paiute and related Shoshonean groups, but not among Indians in California and Oregon, who had already been immunized by the failure of the first Ghost Dance of Wodziwob in 1870. The Pueblo theocracy, of course, rejected it.

Ethnographers have puzzled over why the Ghost Dance of 1890 made almost no impression at all among the Navaho, who are usually regarded as emotional, and who had been subjected to much the same deprivation, defeat, starvation, disease, and forcible removal as the other Indian groups that enthusiastically adopted the Ghost Dance. There is no doubt that news of the Ghost Dance was carried to the Navaho by Paiute missionaries and that they were familiar with all its teachings, yet they totally rejected it. A goodly number of explanations have been offered. Some anthropologists have argued that the Navaho are skeptical by nature, whereas others state that the Navaho were comparatively wealthy in livestock at the time and no longer undergoing the stress of deprivation.

One aspect of Navaho culture, its religion, does suggest a valid explanation. The most significant element in the Ghost Dance complex was the promised return of the dead Indians. Ghost Dance missionaries tried to win over the Navaho by stating that at that moment the Navaho ancestors were on their way back to the reservation. If there is a single aspect of Navaho religion that clearly separates it from that of the surrounding Pueblo Indians, it is the Navaho's fear of the dead and of ghosts. What to other Indians was welcome news—the return of their ancestors—

Ghost Dance shirt was worn during the last desperate attempt by the Plains Indians to forestall the White conquest of their culture, as well as of their lands and lives. This Sioux shirt shows the mystic designs that were supposed to have protected the wearer against White bullets. Each man painted his own shirt after having a vision of the particular designs that would protect him.

to the Navaho represented a calamity. Even though the Navaho undoubtedly desired the Ghost Dance's promises of the disappearance of the Whites and the restoration of the old ways of life, they were also frightened that the teachings about ghosts might be true.↨

After the Ghost Dance spread across the Rockies to the Plains tribes it ran amok. The Cheyenne and the Arapaho in Oklahoma started dancing immediately. The fervor attacked other Plains tribes virulently, particularly the Sioux, who were at that time the largest and most intransigent of them all. The Sioux had been forced to submit to a series of land grabs and to indignities that are almost unbelievable when read about today. At the very time that news of the Ghost Dance reached them, they were being systematically starved into submission—by the White bureaucracy—on the little that was left of their reservation in South Dakota. The spark to ignite the

Sioux was also present in the person of their White-hating leader, Sitting Bull, a veteran of Custer's last stand in 1876.

The Sioux sent delegates to speak to Wovoka, who advised them to work hard and to make peace with the Whites. By the time the messengers reported back to the Sioux, though, Wovoka's advice had become corrupted and his teachings distorted by confusion with earlier and more violent nativistic movements. The Sioux's version of Wovoka's teachings was that dancing would not only bring back the ancestral dead and the herds of bison, but also exterminate the Whites by causing a landslide. And, best of all, the Indians would be invulnerable to White firepower, for their "ghost shirts"—dance shirts fancifully decorated with designs of arrows, stars, birds, and so forth—were capable of warding off bullets.

Interestingly enough, the Ghost Dance took its most virulent form on the Rosebud Sioux reservation; and the Rosebud population has continued to this day to harbor strong feelings against the authority of the United States government. (For example, on April 15, 1967, when approximately a quarter of a million people marched on the United Nations to protest the Vietnam War, the only Indian group to send a large delegation was the Rosebud Sioux.) From Rosebud, the Ghost Dance spread like a prairie fire to the Pine Ridge Sioux and finally to Sitting Bull's people at Standing Rock. The Sioux rebelled; the result was the death of Sitting Bull and the massacre of the Indians (despite their ghost shirts) at Wounded Knee in 1890. As quickly as it had set the plains aflame, the Ghost Dance was extinguished.

Only a few months after the massacre at Wounded Knee, while the Sioux were still confused and embittered by their defeat, a deranged White man visited their reservations. He declared himself to be the messiah and he predicted the millennium when the star-pansy flowers bloomed that spring. When the star pansies did bloom and the millennium did not come, the Sioux disillusionment was complete. The last hope of a return to the old days was replaced by resignation to whatever future trials the Whites had in store for them.

A further irony is that the Ghost Dance spread rapidly for only one reason: White culture. English, as the only language common to the various tribes, was the means by which Wovoka's teachings were communicated among the Indians. And the Indians who spread word of the new movement were able to get from place to place quickly because they took advantage of the rapid transportation provided by the White man's railroads.

The Ghost Dance movement of 1890 died at Wounded Knee, and with it died something else. The Ghost Dance represented the last futile attempt by the American Indians to retrieve the old ways, to save their fast-disappearing culture. From that time on, Indians turned to movements that sought accommodation with Whites.

THE SECOND PHASE: ACCOMMODATION

The Indians' hope of bringing back the old days had proved an illusion, but the second response—adaptation to an alien White world—was rooted in firmer ground. Perhaps the earliest of the accommodation movements was that founded in 1799 by a Seneca named Handsome Lake. Whites called his cult the "New Religion" of the Iroquois, but its name translated into English really meant "Good Tidings" or "Good Message." It combined traditional Iroquois beliefs with those of the Quakers, among whom Handsome Lake had been reared, and it quickly spread from the Seneca to the rest of the Six Nations.

The contorted frozen body of a Sioux leader lies on the field at Wounded Knee. He was one of some three hundred Sioux men, women, and children waiting to surrender, who were massacred in 1890 by the United States Army cavalry.

Handsome Lake was regarded as a prophet at a time when Iroquois fortunes seemed on the rise again after a period of hopelessness. The American Revolution had divided the allegiance of the Six Nations, causing them to fight among themselves; Jesuit missionaries had instigated mass migrations of these people to Canada; their population had been further diminished by warfare, disease, and rampant alcoholism, and they had been deprived of most of their lands. By the time of Handsome Lake, though, they had faced the reality of the White conquest, and they were putting the pieces back together again. They had made peace with the new American republic, and they believed themselves to be protected by their solemn treaties with it. That Thomas Jefferson while President had called the religion of Handsome Lake "positive and effective" gave the Iroquois a new sense of security, as well as pride in the high esteem Whites had for their prophet.

The Quaker influence is evident in Handsome Lake's teachings. He renounced witchcraft and instead emphasized introspection, compassion for those who were suffering, and good deeds even in thought. He believed in silent prayer and the confession of sins, and he recommended the White man's bible as a good guide for any Iroquois to follow through life. Although Handsome Lake accepted the idea of monotheism, which was easily grafted onto the Iroquois concept of a Great Spirit, he rejected the New Testament; and Jesus played no role in his religion. Wherever the two pieces could be fitted together, traditional Iroquois festivals and beliefs were combined with Christian rituals. For example, the Iroquois had a feast resembling the Eucharist to mark the New Year, at which time a white dog was sacrificed to the Great Spirit. The place of worship looked like a church but was called a longhouse, thus recalling the traditional Iroquois dwelling and the hallmark of the Iroquois League.‡

PEYOTISM

The most vigorous Indian religion today, Peyotism, seeks spiritual independence. Peyotism teaches accommodation to a White world, and even more, it gives the Indian a method of cultural emancipation. Peyotism can be understood only against the background of the Ghost Dance. The Ghost Dance was final and disastrous proof to the Indian that the Whites were in North America to stay; the Peyote cult has tried to emancipate the Indian without the same violence. The Ghost Dance made its unfulfillable promises at a time when the Indians were ready for rebellion; the Peyote cult spread when the Indians were ready to admit defeat. The Indian no longer had to be concerned with fighting off the United States Army. He now had to wage a subtler war in which the White was trying to exterminate Indian culture and substitute his own. The problem that Peyotism, or any other messianic movement, had to solve was how to coexist with Whites yet remain spiritually independent. The result was that Peyotism borrowed freely from Western civilization in order to salvage what it considered important in paganism.

Peyote is a small cactus, unusual in that it has no spines, whose rounded top is cut off and eaten. It contains stimulants related to strychnine and sedatives related to morphine. But since there is no proof that it is habit-forming, it cannot be classified as a true narcotic—much to the dismay of the United States Bureau of Indian Affairs, which would welcome an excuse to stamp out its use. In 1951 a group of anthropologists published a statement intended to counteract the government's efforts to have peyote declared illegal. They stated, after partaking both of the plant and of the rites connected with its use: "It does not excite, stupefy or produce muscular incoordination; there is no hangover; and the habitual user does not develop an increased tolerance or dependence. As for the immorality that is supposed to accompany its use, since no orgies are known among any Indian tribes of North America, the charge has as much validity as the ancient Roman accusations of a similar nature against the early Christians."✠ The hallucinations are usually in the form of color visions, often described as elaborate and beautiful designs that change shape constantly as with a kaleidoscope. Sound sensations are somewhat less frequent: Users have described hearing the sun rise with a roar and fly across the sky with the accompanying sound of drums.

The recent history of the use of peyote is fairly well known. It grows in northeastern Mexico, and it is always sought in the wild, never having been domesticated. It was eaten in Mexico before the arrival of the Spaniards, although its use increased as the Spanish regime became more and more oppressive. The first clear evidence of the use of peyote by the Indians of the United States was after an Apache band visited Mexico in 1770, but for the next seventy-five years or so its use north of the Rio Grande remained negligible. As the Plains culture disintegrated after the middle of the last century the use of peyote spread northward in the wake of defeat and despair. In this century it has spread to the Great Lakes and to the plains of Canada. It also jumped east of the Mississippi River, carried there by Indians who had learned its use while they were forced to live on reservations in Oklahoma.

A peyote fan is held in this self-portrait of Trinidad Archuleta, a Taos Indian, who wears a Plains Indian War Dance costume. Many Plains Indians live at Taos, the pueblo closest to them, and there has been considerable intermarriage and cultural exchange. The use of the hallucinogenic cactus peyote, which is particularly widespread among the Plains Indians, is much more prevalent at Taos than at any other pueblo. The portrait was painted nearly fifty years ago.

The ritual use of peyote has been organized into a full-fledged religion, incorporated as the Native American Church, which is the primary native religion among more than fifty Indian bands, tribes, and chiefdoms in the United States. It is definitely Christian in orientation, but what Indians call "the road of peyote" is a road quite independent of Christianity. For example, it opposes attempts by any Christian sects to impose their official canon on the Indians. As in most messianic movements among primitive peoples, the Judaic-Christian God is more acceptable than Jesus, since he is associated with the oppression by Whites in the name of Christianity. The Indian feels that eating peyote is his exclusive way of partaking of the Holy Spirit, in much the same way that some Christians partake of the wine of the Eucharist. Peyotism is totally a Pan-Indian movement, an accomplishment in itself when one recalls the warfare between Indian groups in aboriginal times. Some Peyote churches welcome Negroes to their services, but only a thoroughly trusted and sympathetic White may attend.

The question arises as to why peyote spread in just the way it did, why some Indians took it up enthusiastically and why others rejected it. Peyote was checked in its spread west of the Great Basin by the presence there of another hallucinogenic drug, Jimson weed, to which potential users of peyote were already committed. Peyotism became most firmly entrenched among the Plains Indians, a people who had always sought the emotional experience of a vision and who were searching for a way out of their despair at the end of the last century. In contrast, peyote has scarcely been used by the Pueblo Indians, although an exception is Taos, the most northeasterly of the pueblos and the one that is closest in culture to the Plains tribes. For one thing, Pueblo culture has traditionally emphasized priestly ritual rather than individual emotionalism. Further, the Pueblo did not suffer the great shocks of displacement, defeat, and a changed way of life that the Plains tribes did.↕

In decades to come, enterprising sociologists will probably re-examine the anthropological literature on peyote, seeking leads as to why students at certain colleges in the 1960's became enthusiastic users of hallucinogenic drugs, such as LSD, while other students did not. They will undoubtedly note a correlation between the use of drugs and the size of the university where individual students find themselves oppressed by the administration and lacking personal contact with the faculty. It is probably no accident that the hippie cult has also favored the wearing of Indian headbands and beads. And no doubt the sociologists will find many similarities in social stress between Plains reservation life in the 1890's and American college life in the 1960's.

MESSIAHS: INDIAN AND OTHERS

Several decades ago, reproductions in miniature of a sculpture called "The End of the Trail," which depicted a doleful Indian horseman, were commonly seen in White American living rooms. They seemed to signify the final victory over the vanishing Red man. In the years since, the Indian has not only refused to vanish, but has, thanks to the various messianic movements, managed to find a way to survive in a White world and to salvage a part of his native culture.

The scene of messianic movements has now switched from North America to other frontiers of the world—to South America, to Africa and Asia, and to the islands of the Pacific. Since the Second World War, with much of the world in turmoil, with the emergence of new nations and the spread of White influence, new messianic movements have sprung up vigorously, even within the context of such well-established religions as Islam, Buddhism, and Taoism. The dozens of messianic movements that have arisen among North American Indians can shed light on how and why they originate, the course they take, and the response Whites make to them.↕

Every messianic movement known to history has arisen in a society that has been subjected to the severe stress of contact with an alien culture—involving military defeat, epidemic, and acculturation. The bewildered search for ways to counteract the threat may actually increase the stress, arousing anxiety over whether new solutions will be any better than the old. Once doubts arise about any aspect of the ancestral cultural system, there is yet increased stress due to fear that the entire cultural system may prove inadequate. At this point, the culture as a whole begins to break down, manifested by widespread alcoholism, apathy, disregard of kinship obligations and marriage rules, and intragroup violence.

Such behavior comes at the very time when the culture is least able to cope with it, and so the intensity of the stress increases still more. Ultimately, the inadequacy of the culture becomes apparent even to the most conservative of its members, and the culture may deteriorate to such an extent that it literally dies. The birth rate drops and the death rate rises; the society no longer possesses the will to resist, and it is fallen upon by predatory neighbors; the few survivors scatter and either gradually die out or are absorbed by other groups. The collapse may be forestalled or even averted if a revitalization or messianic movement arises that is acceptable to the culture. Such a movement depends upon the appearance of a particular personality at a certain precise time in the disintegration of the culture.

Almost every messianic movement known around the world came into being as the result of the hallucinatory visions of a prophet. One point must be emphasized about the prophet of the messianic movement: He is not a schizophrenic, as was so long assumed. A schizophrenic with religious paranoia will state that he is God, Jesus, the Great Spirit, or some other supernatural being. The prophet, on the other hand, never states that he is supernatural—only that he is or has been in contact with supernatural powers. (Of course, after his death, his disciples tend to deify him or at least to give him saintly status.)

Invariably the prophet emerges from his hallucinatory vision bearing a message from the supernatural that makes certain promises: the return of the bison herds, a happy hunting ground, or peace on earth and good will to men. Whatever the specific promises, the prophet offers a new power, a revitalization of the whole society. But to obtain these promises, the prophet says that certain rituals must be followed. These rituals may include dancing around a ghost pole or being baptized in water, but usually numerous other duties must be attended to day after day. At the same time that the prophet offers promises to the faithful, he also threatens punishment and catastrophe, such as world destruction or everlasting damnation. The prophet now declares the old ways dead and shifts attention to a new way or to a revised conception of an old part of the culture. To spread the word of what he has learned from his visions, he gathers about him disciples and missionaries.

The various prophets known to world history differed in their preaching methods, just as the American Indian prophets differed from each other. Some prophets spoke emotionally to large crowds, whereas others addressed themselves to small groups and left it to their disciples to carry the message. Some, like the Qumran sect that copied out the Dead Sea scrolls, appealed to a religious elite of particularly devout people, whereas others concerned themselves only with the downtrodden and exploited who shall inherit the earth.

What most impresses the people around the prophet is the personality change he has undergone during this time. In most cases, he lived in obscurity until he suddenly emerged as a prophet; the Indian prophets became cured of previous spiritual apathy, and those who had been alcoholics gave up the habit. The sudden transformation in personality may be due to changes produced in the body under physical and emotional stress, although more research on this point is needed. It is known, though, that individuals vary a great deal in the reaction of their metabolisms to stress. That alone would explain why, when stress reaches a certain intensity in the culture, only certain individuals feel called forth to become prophets while most do not. In any event, the prophet has emerged in a new cultural role, and his personality is liberated from the stress that called his response into being in the first place. Immune to the stress under which his brethren still suffer, he must to them appear supernatural.

The disciples who gather around the prophet also, like him, undergo a revitalizing personality change—as did Peter, to name one very familiar example. The prophet continues his spiritual leadership, but the disciples take upon themselves the practical tasks of organizing the campaign to establish the new movement. They convert large numbers of people, who in turn also undergo revitalizing personality transformations. If the messianic movement has been allowed to survive to this point by the oppressive, dominant culture that called it into being in the first place, a vital step must now be taken. The prophet must emphasize that he is only the intermediary between the converts and the supernatural being whose message he has been spreading. This step is essential, for it ensures the continuity of the new movement after its founding prophet dies. The prophet puts the converts and the supernatural being into close touch with each other by calling for certain symbolic duties the faithful must perform toward the supernatural being, such as eating peyote or partaking of bread and wine.

The new movement often has to resist both the oppressive alien culture and the opposition of factions within itself. The successful messianic movement meets this resistance by resorting to any one of a number of adaptations. It may change its teachings, as did the early Christians who gradually gave up Jewish rituals, such as circumcision. It may resort to political maneuvering and compromise. Most messianic movements, though, make the disastrous mistake that almost all Jewish and American Indian messianic movements did: They choose to fight. Islam alone succeeded by force of arms, whereas the success of the early Christians was their choice of universal peace as their weapon.

Once the messianic movement has won a large following, a new culture begins to emerge out of the death of the old—not only in religious affairs but in all aspects of economic, social, and political life as well. An organization with a secular and a sacerdotal hierarchy arises to perpetuate the new doctrine. The religion in that way becomes routinized in a stable culture. All routinized religions today (whether they be the Native American Church, Mohammedanism, Judaism, or Christianity) are successful descendants of what originated as messianic movements—that is, one personality's vision of a new way of life for a culture under extreme stress.

These steps apply equally to the messianic movement in Soviet Russia, even though it denies belief in the supernatural. Czarist Russia in 1917 was a society under extreme stress, disintegrating both on the war front and at home; in the previous decade it had suffered a humiliating defeat by the Japanese. There was unrest, and repressive measures were stern. A prophet, Lenin, arose; and he made a miraculous return from exile in Switzerland in a railroad car that traversed enemy territory. He preached his vision of Utopia, and he referred constantly to a revered, almost supernatural being named Karl Marx. The missionary fervor excited Lenin's close followers, and they in turn won adherents even among their former enemies in society. One element of the population in particular—the economically downtrodden—was appealed to, and it was promised a reward here on earth. But first these people had to perform certain rituals: convert to the new doctrine of Marx–Lenin; change the economic way of life; publicly confess errors, even if such confession resulted in martyrdom. After the prophet's death, a political organization of key disciples (Stalin, Trotsky, and others) continued his teachings and prepared a complex doctrine that admitted of no revisionism or deviation. The prophet himself was deified after death, as demonstrated today by the people paying homage at Lenin's tomb to the embalmed cadaver that, miraculously, is not heir to the flesh's corruption.

A SOCIETY FOR THE PRESERVATION OF CULTURES

When, in 1832, the mighty leader of the combined forces of the Sac and Fox, Chief Black Hawk, finally surrendered, he offered a grave warning:

The changes of fortune and vicissitudes of war made you my conqueror. When my last resources were exhausted, my warriors, worn down with long and toilsome marches, yielded, and I became your prisoner . . . I am now an obscure member of a nation that formerly honored and respected my opinions. The pathway to glory is rough, and many gloomy hours obscure it. May the Great Spirit shed light on yours, and that you may never experience the humiliation that the power of the American government has reduced me to, is the wish of him who, in his native forests, was once as proud as you.↕

Black Hawk's warning to a young and confident nation was hardly noticed. But I quote these words at a time in which the might of the United States is being ground down in an inhumane and hopeless war in the Vietnam jungles. At home its society is being subjected daily to increased stress as the environment is befouled, the resources are squandered, and the population soars. The times are clearly out of joint when people are still starving to death in the mightiest nation ever seen on earth, when the Negro American is still culturally disenfranchised after a century of political freedom, when citizens have lost touch with an impersonal government.

The United States today is beset on all sides by difficulties and hard decisions, by changes that reverberate throughout the whole society. It is small solace for a politician to hear that the troubles of state are nothing new, that Folsom man may have coped with a few of them and the Aztec assuredly had to cope with many. For it has been a leading thought in this book that the experiences of man over more than 25,000 years on this continent can hold up a mirror to Modern America. To understand the changes shaking religious orthodoxy in America today, it is necessary to understand messianism and how religious practices have evolved in different kinds of social organizations. To comprehend the discontent in American cities today, we have to understand the complex web that binds an individual to his society; and the experience of the Indians is revealing here also. The quest for hallucinations on college campuses can be understood better in the context of the vision quest by American Indians. And so through the inventory of culture—knowledge, belief, art, law, morals, and custom—much else can be learned from the living test tube of the Indian experiment in North America.

Yet we have allowed these cultures to die, and the ancestors of some of us intentionally eradicated them. There is something here that sense and sensibilities rebel against. Today's American bemoans the extermination of the passenger pigeon and the threatened extinction of the whooping crane and the ivory-billed woodpecker; he contributes to conservation organizations that seek to preserve the Hawaiian goose, the sea otter of the Aleutian Islands, the lizard of the Galápagos Islands.

But who ever shed a tear over the loss of native American cultures? Who laments the Pequot of Connecticut, the Beothuk of Newfoundland, the Mandan of the plains, the bands of Baja California, all now extinct? Who would recollect the Delaware Indians if their name were not also that of a state? Who now cares that in 1916 Ishi, the last Yahi Indian of California ever to tread the earth, died in a museum of anthropology in San Francisco?↕ No Society for the Preservation of the Yahi was ever established, nor was a dollar ever raised to conserve the cultures of the Kickapoo and the Peoria Indians. Millions of dollars have been expended to excavate and transport to museums the tools, weapons, and other artifacts of Indians —but scarcely a penny has been spent to save the living descendants of those who made them. Modern man is prompt to prevent cruelty to animals, and sometimes even to humans, but no counterpart of the Humane Society or the Sierra Club exists to prevent cruelty to entire cultures.

All over the world today primitive cultures are disappearing and at an accelerating pace. The Tasmanians are already gone forever. The Yahgan of Tierra del Fuego, studied by Darwin, are virtually extinct, and every year sees fewer Arunta in Australia and Negritos in the Philippines, fewer Aleuts in Alaska and Ainu in Japan, fewer Bushmen in South Africa and Polynesians in Hawaii. Even should peace come immediately to Vietnam, its culture has already been destroyed by the same means by which Americans also destroyed the Indian cultures—military assault, famine, disease, and pacification.

Little is being done to preserve the numerous cultures that have so much to tell modern man. Our imaginations have been unable to devise anything better than the treatment today of the hundred or so Kalapalo Indians of the Amazon Basin who still remain on earth. They have been herded onto a state preserve where they are kept like rare whooping cranes or bighorn sheep. To do nothing now is to let our children lament that they never knew the magnificent diversity of mankind because our generation let disappear those who might have taught them.

Aboriginal custom of sharing endures today, as seen in recent Rosebud Sioux funeral ceremony in which the deceased's belongings are spread out for neighbors to share. Similarly, the poor Indians of the late nineteenth century, starved into submission by Whites, shared the little they had before starving together.

Notes and Sources

CHAPTER I

Much of the material in this chapter is based on the writings of Service (1962, 1963, 1966), Steward (1955, 1956), and White (1949).

Page 3 *The Journal of Christopher Columbus* (1960), New York: Clarkson N. Potter, p. 24.

Page 4 Service (1963), p. 116.

Page 6 As outlined in *Ancient Society* (1877).

Page 7 The most recent attempt, and one of the most ambitious, is by Darcy Ribeiro (in press: *The Civilization Process, Stages of Sociocultural Evolution*), which proposes a series of technological revolutions that cause societies to pass from Archaic to Regional and then to World Civilizations, with numerous steps in between. One problem with Ribeiro's theories is that many of these revolutions actually turn out to be long evolutionary sequences.

Page 10 The Cheyenne example, as well as other examples of great importance to an understanding of cultural evolution, can be found in Meggers (1960).

Page 11 *Patterns of Culture* was published in 1934. See my other disputes with Ruth Benedict on pages 89–92 and 125.

Page 12 A delightful, and relatively moderate, presentation of the psychological viewpoint in anthropology is La Barre (1954).

Page 14 The Koryak example appears in La Barre (1954), pp. 242–243.

Page 15 The taxonomic classification of social organizations is based largely on the theories of Service and Steward. At the 1967 annual meeting of the American Anthropological Association, Service suggested an alternative classification into egalitarian and hierarchical societies, but it does not materially affect the classification presented here.

CHAPTER II

In connection with the ethnological chapters that follow, two books will be particularly helpful both for their summaries and for their extensive bibliographies: Driver (1961) and Spencer, Jennings, et al. (1965).

The most important sources for the Great Basin Shoshone are two works by Steward (1938, and particularly chapter 6 of 1955). See also O. C. Stewart (1939) and, among older studies, Lowie (1924). An historical approach is Trenholm and Carley (1964); a recent and very valuable study of one particular group is Kelly (1964).

Page 16   *Roughing It* by Mark Twain, Harper & Brothers edition, 1871, pp. 131–132.

Page 17   *Native Races* by H. H. Bancroft, The History Press, 1886, p. 440.

Page 18   *The Descent of Man* by Charles Darwin, 1871, chapter 3.

Page 19   An excellent comparison of the societies of apes and men can be found in Sahlins (1959).

Page 20   The item about the North African landing comes from Steward (1955), p. 102.

Page 24   The estimate for the dollar value of an American wife today is from Wolf (1966), pp. 13–14.

Page 25   The statistics on the prevalence of incest were reported at the 1967 convention of the American Psychological Association by R. O. Olive, chief psychologist at Ionia State Hospital, Michigan.

Page 25   The statement that Canada geese seem to be the only animals that possess incest avoidance comes from *Gluttons and Libertines* by Marston Bates, New York: Random House, 1967, p. 84.

Page 26   A. L. Kroeber (1948), section 167.

Page 26   Tylor (1888), p. 267.

Page 29   The statistics on production are from a personal communication from Marvin Harris, Department of Anthropology, Columbia University.

Page 32   Powell and Ingalls (1874), pp. 3, 21.

CHAPTER III

Basic sources for the Eskimo are Boas (1888), Jenness (1922), Weyer (1932), Spencer (1959), Birket-Smith (1959), Gubser (1965), and Oswalt (1967). For a view of the modern life of the Eskimo, see Hughes (1960), Van Stone (1962), and Chance (1966). For interesting insights rather than detailed information, Freuchen (1961) and Jenness (1929) are recommended. A nontechnical summary of Arctic archeology appears in Giddings (1967); see also Giddings (1954, 1960, 1964) and Collins (1964).

Page 34   The quote appears in Birket-Smith (1959), p. 14.

Page 34   Estimates of Eskimo populations vary greatly. The 73,000 figure comes from Chance (1966).

Page 35   Birket-Smith (1959), p. 8.

Page 37   Carpenter (1966), p. 206.

Page 43   Freuchen (1961), p. 154.

Page 44   Rasmussen (1927), p. 250.

Page 45   The source of this item about calypso is Greenway (1964), p. 203, a most wise and amusing book.

Page 45   An excellent discussion of legal mechanisms in Eskimo society appears in Hoebel (1954), pp. 67–99.

Page 46   The scatological verse and the incident of the old woman appear in Birket-Smith (1959), p. 151.

Page 47 An excellent brief discussion on communism in primitive societies appears in Service (1966), pp. 21–25.

Page 49 The material on witchcraft comes largely from Swanson (1960), chapter 8. Using only the Copper Eskimo as his example, he somewhat underestimates the importance of witchcraft in Eskimo society.

Page 50 Several psychological studies of the shaman have been made; a recent one is Silverman (1967).

Page 52 Weyer (1932) describes several curing ceremonies in detail and also presents much excellent material on Eskimo religion. See also the references to Eskimo religion in Norbeck (1961) and Howells (1948). A full discussion of shamanism in relation to American Indians is Park (1938).

CHAPTER IV

General sources for the Sub-Arctic bands are Steward (1955, particularly chapter 8), Jenness (1932, 1935), Speck (1940), and Leacock (1954).

Page 58 The Champlain quote is from *The Works of Samuel de Champlain,* edited by H. P. Bigger, Toronto, 1923, vol. 2, p. 171.

Page 58 Le Jeune's observations are in Thwaites (1906), vol. 5, p. 25.

Page 59 Quoted in Thwaites (1906), vol. 8, p. 57.

Page 60 Much of the material on territories is from Leacock (1954). A dissenting view, and what I feel is an atypical case, is Knight (1965).

Page 61 Hallowell's basic study on anxiety is 1941, but see also his 1955 and 1960 publications.

Page 61 The Parry Island example is from Jenness (1935), p. 110.

Page 63 For additional material on reincarnation, see the fascinating book by Swanson (1960).

Page 64 The material on the Penobscot totems is mainly from Speck (1940), pp. 203–211.

Page 64 The study of the Rainbow Division is by Linton (1924).

Page 65 An able critique of Freud's theory is A. L. Kroeber (1920).

Page 65 The Lévi-Strauss quote is from *Totemism* (1963), p. 89.

Page 66 Totemism has held a fascination for many minds. Lévi-Strauss upholds the theory presented here; the same work contains objective summaries and critiques of other theories.

CHAPTER V

For theoretical discussions of patrilocal (called patrilineal by Steward) bands, see Steward (1955, particularly chapter 7) and Service (1962, pp. 66–83). Some standard ethnologies on the southern California bands are Sparkman (1908), A. L. Kroeber (1908, 1931), Hooper (1920), Strong (1929), and Meigs (1939).

Page 69 The Tylor quote is from his *Anthropology,* reprinted Ann Arbor: University of Michigan Press, 1960, p. 249.

Page 71 Most of the material on the Serrano is from Strong (1929).

Page 73 Vagina-envy is discussed in Bettelheim (1954) and the kangaroo-envy theory was presented at the 1966 annual meeting of the American Anthropological Association and later published by Singer and De Sole (1967).

Page 73 Greenway's explanation is (1964), pp. 73–75.

Page 75 Much of the preceding material on Baja California cultural hybrids comes from Owen (1965). Note also the brief communication by Steward on pages 732–734 of the same issue.

CHAPTER VI

The Pueblo have probably inspired more anthropological studies than any other American Indians. The papers listed here include only those directly concerned with the aspects of Pueblo life discussed in this chapter. For a good recent review of the important Pueblo literature, though, see Dozier (1964). Parsons (1939), Underhill (1948), and Eggan (1950) are valuable for general studies of the Pueblo.

For theoretical aspects of tribal organization, see Service (1962), pp. 110–133, and Steward (1955), pp. 151–172.

For specific studies of the Zuni, see Stevenson (1901); Bunzel (1932); Benedict (1934), but of course with the caveats discussed in this chapter; Goldman (1937), with somewhat milder caveats; Roberts (1956). There is also a good brief summary in Spencer, Jennings, et al. (1965), pp. 295–318.

Page 83 The Mundurucú material is based on a study by Murphy (1956).
Page 83 Bunzel (1932), p. 480.
Page 89 A delightful analysis of Memorial Day is in *American Life* by W. L. Warner, Chicago: The University of Chicago Press, 1953, pp. 1–26.
Page 89 Goldfrank (1945 A).
Page 90 Ellis (1951).
Page 90 The facts about drunkenness are from Smith and Roberts (1954).
Page 90 Li An-che (1937).
Page 93 Norbeck (1961), p. 208, quotes portions of this account from *Scatologic Rites of All Nations* by J. G. Bourke, Washington, 1891.
Page 94 For the place of buffoonery in Indian religions, see Steward (1930), Parsons and Beals (1934).

CHAPTER VII

Morgan (1851) is essential for any understanding of the Iroquois, and Beauchamp (1905) is valuable. There also have been several important papers by Speck (among them, 1944 and 1955) and Fenton (1941, 1953). Two good books are by Hunt (1940) and Noon (1949).

Page 97   Quoted in Quain (1937), p. 240.
Page 100 Quoted in *Historical Sociology* by B. J. Stern, New York: Citadel Press, 1959, p. 167.
Page 102 This discussion of great men and great events owes a debt to the "Patterns" and "Cultural Processes" sections of A. L. Kroeber (1948) and to White (1949).
Page 103 The simultaneous interest in ape art by a number of zoologists is reported in *The Biology of Art* by Desmond Morris, New York: A. A. Knopf, 1962, p. 30.
Page 104 The material on Iroquois psychotherapy comes from Wallace (1958).
Page 106 Quoted in Thwaites (1906), vol. 13, pp. 59–79.
Page 107 As just one example, see *Genesis* 6:2. For comment, see *The Anchor Bible: Genesis,* translated and edited by E. A. Speiser, Garden City, N.Y.: Doubleday, 1964, p. 44.
Page 108 These and numerous other facts are found in a fascinating book: *A Dictionary of Angels* by Gustav Dourdson, Glencoe, Ill.: The Free Press, 1967.

Page 109   There are several good papers on the False Face society by Fenton (particularly 1940 A and 1940 B).

Page 110   *Observation on the Inhabitants, Climate, Soil . . .* by John Bartram, London, 1751, pp. 43–44.

Page 111   Morgan (1851), pp. 145–146.

CHAPTER VIII

The literature on the Plains Indians is unusually rich, and only highlights can be indicated here. Among general works are: Wedel (1941), Lowie (1954), and Laubin and Laubin (1957). Service (1963) has a good brief discussion on pp. 112–137. Readable historical material is found in Josephy (1961).

A pioneering work on the prehistory of the plains area is Strong (1940). For more recent studies, see Mulloy (1952), Wendorf and Hester (1962), and Wedel (1964).

The ethnology of particular tribes makes delightful reading, and the choice of books and papers is tremendous. For excellent brief discussions of Mandan, Teton Dakota, and Kiowa, see Spencer, Jennings, et al. (1965), pp. 337–383. The Mandan are discussed in depth by Bowers (1950). Three particularly good works on the Cheyenne are Grinnell (1923, 1956) and Hoebel (1960). For the Blackfoot: Wissler (1910, 1911), Goldfrank (1945 B), and Ewers (1955, 1958). For the Crow, Lowie (1935) and Ewers (1953); for the Comanche, Wallace and Hoebel (1952); for the Sioux, Hassrick (1964). A classic on the Omaha is Fletcher and La Flesche (1911).

Page 113   This quote and subsequent ones from the Coronado expedition are from *Eyes of Discovery* by John Bakeless, New York: Dover, 1961, pp. 92–93.

Page 115   An excellent summary of the effect of the horse on many Indian cultures is Roe (1955). See also Ewers (1955).

Page 124   Hagan (1961), p. 15, is the source for the origin of scalping.

Page 124   The extinction of the Beothuk is described in Hodge (1906), p. 142.

Page 125   *The Study of Man* by Ralph Linton, New York: Appleton-Century, 1936, p. 463.

Page 125   Freud's letter on the causes of war is in *Character and Culture*, vol. 9 in *The Collected Papers of Sigmund Freud*, New York: Collier Books, 1963, p. 141.

Page 126   Two excellent papers on Plains warfare are by Newcomb (1950, 1960). See also Mishkin (1940) for the importance of economic factors. Various theories of primitive warfare in general can be found in Turney-High (1949).

Page 130   For a discussion of the vision quest in several cultures, see Underhill (1948).

CHAPTER IX

A vast literature exists about the Northwest Coast chiefdoms, but there is very little of a general nature aside from Drucker (1955), which offers a brief but able summary, and to which much of this chapter is indebted. A valuable collection of papers, some of which are cited below, by many specialists is McFeat (1966). A brief summary of several northern and central chiefdoms is in Spencer, Jennings, et al. (1965), pp. 168–212. General works on Northwest Coast art are Davis et al. (1949), Inverarity (1950), Holm (1965), and Hawthorn (1967). Outstanding among studies of particular chiefdoms are: Drucker (1951) and Service (1963), pp. 207–228 for the Nootka; Boas (1909) and Drucker and Heizer (1967) for the Kwakiutl; Garfield (1939) for the Tsimshian; McIlwraith (1948) for the Bella Coola; Swanton (1909) for the Haida; Colson (1953) for the Makah; de Laguna (1960) for the Tlingit.

Page 135   For theory in the preceding section and elsewhere in this chapter, see Service (1962), pp. 143–177.

Page 137   Material on the workings of the Tsimshian chiefdom and a fuller explanation of the system can be found in Garfield (1939), particularly pp. 182–184.

Page 138   Drucker (1939), p. 58.

Page 140   The source for the discussion of adultery and rank is Oberg (1934).

Page 146   The question of Oceanic and other influences on the totem pole is discussed in Quimby (1948).

Page 151   Anything so intriguing as the potlatch understandably has been the subject of a vast literature and many differing viewpoints. Most of the books listed above discuss one or another aspect of it; it is discussed specifically by Barnett (1938), Codere (1951, 1956), Suttles (1960), and Drucker and Heizer (1967). Drucker and Heizer take issue with many other interpretations of the potlatch. They emphasize that the chief was not great because he gave grand potlatches, but rather gave them because he was great. It was not so much his pleasure as his duty.

CHAPTER X

For the Natchez, the basic source, which pulls together a tremendous amount of historical and ethnological information, is Swanton (1911). Everything published since is merely a footnote to this important piece of scholarship. See the same author (1946) for the Natchez in the context of other southeastern cultures. Le Petit's valuable account of the Natchez can be found in Thwaites (1906), vol. 68.

Page 155   Le Petit and other contemporary sources are abundantly quoted in Swanton (1911). All quotes in this chapter are either from that source or from Thwaites (1906).

Page 160   The question of the Stinkards and their replenishment is discussed, along with other interesting facts about the class system, in Hart (1943) and Quimby (1946).

Page 163   The story of the two survivors is told in Swanton (1946), p. 160.

CHAPTER XI

The definitive volume in English devoted exclusively to all aspects of Aztec life is Vaillant (1962). But it was published originally in 1944 and was only slightly revised posthumously in 1962; it should, for all its excellence in many ways, be read with caution because much of it is out of date. Another recent and readable account is Soustelle (1961). An excellent book that covers the entire sweep of Mexican civilization is Coe (1962)—a work to which I am indebted for both information and interpretation. Two other books on major Mexican cultures that are highly recommended are Wolf (1959) and Bernal (1963). (There exists, in addition, a voluminous literature in Spanish, German, and other foreign languages, which is not listed in my Bibliography; many of these works, though, are listed in the bibliographies of the above volumes.)

For specific information on Aztec art, see chapters in the above volumes as well as Covarrubias (1957). For Aztec religion, see the very attractive volume by Caso (1958) as well as Séjourné (1960) and León-Portilla (1963). For the history of the conquest by Cortés, no better source exists than the eyewitness account by Díaz del Castillo (reprinted 1956). There is a good short chapter on the Aztec in Spencer, Jennings, et al. (1965), pp. 467–486. For the archeological background, see the books listed above by Wolf (1959), Vaillant (1962), Coe (1962), and Bernal (1963)—plus Armillas (1964), Willey (1966), and Millon (1967).

Page 170 This quote and the next are from Díaz del Castillo (1956), pp. 190–191.
Page 172 Quoted by Wolf (1959), p. 161.
Page 173 Quoted in Séjourné (1960), p. 4.
Page 178 Díaz del Castillo (1956), p. 214.
Page 179 Quoted by Coe (1962), p. 168.
Page 181 Called such by Chapple and Coon (1942), pp. 507–508.
Page 184 Díaz del Castillo (1956), p. 119.

CHAPTER XII

Basic sources for knowledge about the earliest men in North America are: Macgowan and Hester (1962), pp. 1–188; Spencer, Jennings, et al. (1965), pp. 7–56; Jennings and Norbeck (1964); Wormington (1957); Sellards (1952); Willey (1960 A, 1960 B, 1966); Mason (1962); Haynes (1964, 1966). An important, but probably overly conservative, summary is Griffin (1967). In addition, Spaulding (1955) and Caldwell, (1958, 1962) are very valuable. Two good primers on the techniques of archeology are Gorenstein (1965) and Deetz (1967).

Page 191 A longer list appears in Wauchope (1962), p. 3.
Page 192 The date of more than 1,500,000 years ago is more than 500,000 years earlier than was until quite recently supposed. Some of the reasons for pushing the date back can be found in Ericson, Ewing, and Wollin (1964). The definitive source on the Pleistocene is Wright and Frey (1965).
Page 194 A good recent general account of the land bridge is Hopkins (1967); see also his earlier 1959 paper as well as the valuable ones by Haag (1962) and Chard (1958). For a recent study of vegetation on the land bridge, see Colinvaux (1967).
Page 195 Few people suspected even a part of the truth about the origins of the American Indian. Only several decades after Columbus discovered the New World, a Spanish priest, José de Acosta, thought that somewhere in the northern part of North America would ultimately be found a portion of the continent that was "not altogether severed and disjoined" from the Old World (Macgowan and Hester, 1962, p. 12). Two centuries after that, Thomas Jefferson, in his Notes on the State of Virginia, put forth the concept of an Asian cradle for the Indian and a crossing via Bering Strait.
Page 196 One in particular who believes in the great antiquity of this site is Krieger (1964), pp. 43–45.
Page 197 For more on preprojectile-point cultures, see Krieger (1962).

The entire question of archeological dating is complex and technical. There are two main methods for very ancient material: the geological and the radioactive. The first of these relies upon the extensive knowledge geologists have accumulated about the Pleistocene. As the ice advanced and retreated, major climatic changes occurred that affected all life in the vicinity. So when a geologist detects the bones of certain animals predominating at one level of a site, he may be able to infer a particular climate and therefore a particular glacial or interglacial period. Pollen grains preserved in the deposits also are valuable clues, for they reveal the character of the vegetation and hence the climate. Each plant species has a distinctive pollen grain, which is remarkably durable and may be preserved in lake sediments for many thousands of years. Because the kinds of trees and other plants in a given region vary with changes in climate, the variation from level to level in the ratio of different pollen grains in a dried lake bed reflects local climate changes. The approximate age of Indian artifacts found in or under certain pollen series can in this way be estimated, but exact dating must be done by other methods.

The geological study of rivers has been of some use, since the terraces along riverbanks were the result of high and low water at various times, and these changing volumes of water were due to glacial events. Lake beds also can be revealing, as wind, water, or glacial melt can cause annual deposits of sediments in distinct layers that vary in thickness and composition. Each layer is known as a varve, and in some localities there may be hundreds of varves, one atop the other. The position and depth of artifacts in the varve series can in this way indicate approximate age.

Geological methods, though, give only *relative* dates; they state that a campfire at a particular site burned after such and such a time and before some other time—but they cannot date the century, or even the millennium, of the fire. For *absolute* dating, back at least to 55,000 years ago, the archeologist uses the radioactive methods discovered by Willard F. Libby in the late 1940's. Radioactive dating is based on the principle that several mildly radioactive substances have always been formed in the earth's atmosphere by the action of cosmic rays. Carbon-14, for instance, is present in all living matter, since every plant or animal absorbs it from its environment until it dies. Dr. Libby stated that, after death, the carbon-14 stored in plant or animal tissue disintegrates at the same very slow and fixed rate every place in the world. (Contrary to these early convictions, recent findings show that the production of carbon-14 is not unvarying at all times and all places. It usually varies by less than two percent, but at certain times in the past it may have varied by as much as twenty percent.)

For example, an ounce of carbon-14 will disintegrate to only half an ounce after 5,730 years, with a margin of error of eighty years. That half ounce will become a quarter of an ounce in 11,460 years; only a sixty-fourth of the original ounce of carbon-14 will be left after about 34,380 years. So to arrive at an absolute date for the sample, all that was needed was to develop laboratory techniques to determine the original store of carbon-14 absorbed by the plant or animal when it was alive. In this way, charcoal from the campfire found at an early-man site often can show quite accurately when these artifacts were in use. An animal bone carved by early man might give the atomic laboratory the facts it needs to date the time when the animal died and therefore ceased absorbing carbon-14 from the atmosphere. There are, though, several limitations to the method. Certain parts of plants or animals often do not concentrate enough carbon-14 while alive to provide a reliable sample for the laboratory, or they may concentrate it in varying amounts. Second, a sample can become contaminated: Water trickling into a site might have leached out some of the carbon-14 and therefore made the sample appear older than it actually is; or the subsequent penetration of a root into the sample might have had the contrary effect. Such hazards to accuracy are being offset by more refined techniques and by using multiple samples. When several samples all give dates clustering around the same time, and there is nothing in the geological lay of the land to dispute this approximate date, then the average of several radiocarbon dates is accepted as a reasonably accurate pinpoint in time.

A good brief summary of dating techniques is Heizer (1953). A definitive study of the numerous dating techniques known about is Brotherwell and Higgs (1963).

Page 197   A possible route is outlined by Griffin (1960).
Page 199   Little of a scientific nature about Sandia man has been published since the early discoveries. For a popular account by the archeologist involved, see Hibben (1960).
Page 199   A good review of the facts about Clovis appears in Haynes (1966).
Page 200   See Wormington (1957), p. 29, for various fluting theories.
Page 202   Information about the Rio Rancho, New Mexico, site comes from personal communications from Lewis Binford and Frank Hibben.
Page 204   For more on extinction, see Newell (1963).
Page 205   Paul Martin of the University of Arizona Geochronology Laboratory has been a leader in upholding the theory of early man as the cause of the North American extinction. Among his numerous publications, see 1961, 1966, and 1967.
Page 207   For a discussion of preadaptation in biological evolution, see Simpson (1953), pp. 188–198.
Page 209   The best summary of Modoc is Fowler (1959).
Page 209   Caldwell's valuable study is his 1958 papers.
Page 209   For the variety of plants utilized around the Great Lakes, see Yarnell (1964).
Page 211   There is no space here to go into the fascinating subject of irrigation societies, but it is discussed in detail by Wittfogel (1957). A cautionary footnote, though, is provided by Flannery et al. (1967).
Page 211   For the origins of corn and the Tehuacán caves, see MacNeish (1964 A, 1964 B) and Mangelsdorf et al. (1964).
Page 212   More information on agricultural evolution is in Coe and Flannery (1964).
Page 213   The earliest exposition, and still one of the best, of convergence and limited possibilities in anthropology is Goldenweiser (1913).
Page 213   Wauchope (1962), pp. 103–115, explodes many of the claims of the Kon-Tiki expedition.
Page 215   The whole question of Transpacific contacts is complex and in contention. A leading exponent of such contacts has been Ekholm (1955, 1964).

Page 215   A very readable account of the Ecuadorian discovery is in Meggers and Evans (1966). The scientific report by Meggers, Evans, and Estrada (1965) contains numerous illustrations of Valdivian and Jomon pottery.

Page 216   Some general sources on the Southwest are McGregor (1965) and Reed (1955, 1964).

Page 216   For Hohokam canals, see Woodbury (1960).

Page 216   Among the numerous excellent studies of the Hohokam and the Anasazi are: Haury (1950), Judd (1954), Reed (1954, 1955, 1964), and Jennings (1956).

Page 218   It is possible to be exceedingly exact about comparatively recent archeological dates in the Southwest because of a technique known as dendrochronology—that is, dating ruins by the study of the growth rings in their wood. Most trees that grow in areas of erratic rainfall, such as the Southwest, add rings of new growth in varying widths each year. For example, a period of three years of drought followed by one year of heavy rainfall shows a pattern of three very narrow rings and one wide ring outside of them. A two-hundred-year-old tree cut down today would reveal a pattern of wide and narrow rings covering exactly two hundred years. Also the inner (and therefore oldest) rings in this same tree would overlap the pattern of the outer rings of another log found in an adobe house that had been, say, cut in 1775. And the inner rings of this 1775 log would similarly overlap the pattern found on beams still older that had been used to build Pueblo Indian dwellings. In this way, master charts of ring patterns that go back to 59 B.C. have been drawn up for various areas of the Southwest.

When an archeologist excavates a ruin in the Southwest, he is likely to find logs and pieces of wood incorporated into the construction. All he has to do is to slide his sample along the master chart until he finds the place where the patterns of wide and narrow rings match. Then he knows that the outside ring of his sample will tell him the exact year in which that tree was cut down, and presumably also that date tells him when construction began. A side benefit of tree-ring dating is that it gives very precise information about the amounts of rainfall for each year; the study of tree rings has given archeologists a clear picture of the severe drought in the Southwest from 1276 to 1299. Although in this region dendrochronology is an exceedingly useful tool, attempts to apply it in other parts of North America have failed. The reason is that in these other well-watered areas there is insufficient variation in tree-ring widths from year to year to form a distinctive enough pattern for dating.

An old but still generally useful paper is Haury (1935). More recent information is in Brotherwell and Higgs (1963), pp. 162–176.

Page 219   The view that changes in the land itself resulted in abandonment has been upheld with considerable logic by Schoenwetter (1962).

Page 219   For the Woodlands, see Caldwell (1958), Griffin (1952, 1967), and Sears (1964).

Page 221   Several points of view about Adena and Hopewell will be found in Caldwell and Hall (1964). See also Spaulding (1955), Webb and Baby (1957), Dragoo (1963), and Prufer (1964).

Page 224 The classic study of the Mississippian is Phillips, Ford, and Griffin (1951). See also Caldwell (1962).

CHAPTER XIII

A good brief article on physical anthropology in the Americas is T. D. Stewart (1960); also valuable are Newman (1953, 1962). Excellent readings on human evolution are Hulse (1963), Buettner-Janusch (1966), and Howells (1967, revised edition). For general background in linguistics, and for delightful reading in other fields of anthropology as well, consult Sapir (1963).

Page 226 The information on the San Diego skull is a personal communication from Lewis Binford.

Page 227 I am indebted for this conclusion to T. D. Stewart (1960), pp. 267–269.

Page 228 Neumann (1952) originally postulated eight different varieties of man in North America resulting from separate migrations. In 1960 he concluded that there were only two major migrations.

Page 228 Boyd (1950) has placed American Indians in a separate race, as have several other anthropologists.

Page 228 Information on genetic traits can be found in the basic sources on physical anthropology and evolution listed above and, in particular, in Mourant (1954).

Page 230 Facts on the number of languages, plus much else of interest, can be found in Voegelin and Voegelin (1944) and McQuown (1955).

Page 231 Mumford (1967) discusses the Yahgan and many other aspects of language; although provocative of thought, several of his conclusions are very much open to dispute.

Page 235 The literature on glottochronology is immense. The pioneering papers are Swadesh (1952) and Lees (1953). The question of validity is raised by Bergsland and Vogt, with comments by several specialists (1962). See also Hymes (1960). An excellent summary of the implications of glottochronology and other linguistic studies for knowledge about aboriginal man in America is Swadesh (1964).

Page 237 The quotation is from Sapir (1929). See also Whorf (1956). Various views of the Sapir-Whorf Hypothesis are contained in the papers in Hoijer (1954).

CHAPTER XIV

A brief and excellent discussion of Indian-White relations, representing an assault upon a nation's conscience, is Hagan (1961). Other valuable summaries are Pearce (1953), Fey and McNickle (1959), McNickle (1962), and Oswalt (1966). Primary sources are documented in Washburn (1964).

Page 243 *The Writings of Christopher Columbus,* edited by P. L. Ford, 1892, p. 165.

Page 243 The figures on the decline in populations in Haiti are from McNickle (1962), p. 10.

Page 244 These facts and observations come from Lévi-Strauss (1961), pp. 79–80.

Page 244 Revised population estimates are from Dobyns, Thompson, et al. (1966).

Page 245 The World War II study was reported by Alexander Alland, Jr., of

Columbia University at the 1967 annual meeting of the American Anthropological Association.

Page 246   Montaigne's comments are from "On Cannibals," chapter 31 of Book One of the *Essays* (Heritage Club edition).

Page 246   The Bressani quote is from Thwaites (1906), vol. 38, p. 257.

Page 246   The second Jesuit quote is from Thwaites (1906), vol. 29, p. 281. From here until the end of the chapter I am indebted to the following for so many quotations and facts that it would be impractical to cite individually: Fey and McNickle (1959), Hagan (1961), Washburn (1964), and chapter 12 of Spencer, Jennings, et al. (1965).

Page 247   Quoted in Washburn (1964), p. 183.

Page 249   Quoted in Smith (1950), p. 219.

Page 251   Fey and McNickle (1959), p. 30.

Page 253   The quotes from de Tocqueville are from the Knopf edition (1945), vol. 1, pp. 339–341.

Page 255   Quoted in Spencer, Jennings, et al. (1965), p. 498.

Page 256   Quoted in Hagan (1961), p. 121.

Page 256   Quoted in Hagan (1961), p. 141.

Page 259   Such a book has just appeared as this one is going to press. It is *The New Indians* by Stan Steiner, 1968, New York: Harper & Row—and it is highly recommended.

CHAPTER XV

Much valuable comment on acculturation will be found in sections 162–182 of A. L. Kroeber (1948). Two valuable symposium volumes on acculturation in several Indian societies are Spicer (1960) and Tax (1952 B). For a thorough documentation of the impact of Whites upon Indians in one specific area, the Southwest, see Spicer (1962). For the same sort of treatment for Mexico, see Tax (1952 A). Unfortunately, there was insufficient space in this chapter to discuss the problems of Indian-White and Indian-Negro mixed races, but this material is covered well by Berry (1963).

Page 261   Additional information on the debt of our culture to the Indian can be found in Driver (1961), chapter 26, and Hallowell (1957, 1959).

Page 262   The de Crèvecoeur quote is from the Dutton edition, 1957, p. 209.

Page 263   Swanton (1926).

Page 264   My discussion of Indianization is based largely on Hallowell (1963). See his excellent bibliography for further sources.

Page 271   Much of the material on the Navaho came from Vogt (1960). I am also indebted to several papers by Hill (1940 A, 1940 B, and 1948). See also Underhill (1956), and Kluckhohn and Leighton (1946).

Page 271   The potlatch example is from Drucker and Heizer (1967), pp. 27–34.

Page 274   The story of the Navaho and Zuni veterans is based on the study by Adair and Vogt (1949). See also Goldfrank (1952).

CHAPTER XVI

This chapter owes its primary debt to two books I enthusiastically recommend: Lanternari (1963) and Mooney (1896). Other important basic sources appear in the notes below.

Page 276 Among the primitive movements that have identified themselves with the Jews of biblical antiquity, none is more fantastic than the Hau-Hau movement among the Maori of New Zealand. In 1864 the Maori renounced their half-hearted conversion to Christianity and revolted against the British. They synthesized a new religion, based largely on borrowings from the Old Testament. Their supreme deity was called Jehovah, and the Maori stated that they were descendants of one of the lost tribes led into bondage by the Assyrians. Te-Ua, their prophet, regarded himself as the new Moses, and he was called "Tiu," which translates as "Jew" in Maori. Te-Ua declared New Zealand to be the new Promised Land and the Maori its chosen people; he predicted that Jehovah would speak to them directly from the top of a high pole they erected, just as he had once spoken to Moses on Mount Sinai. He foretold the day when the British would be ejected from the Maori lands, thereby ushering in the millennium. Then, he said, the Jews would travel from the Near East to New Zealand to unite with their long-lost Maori cousins.

In 1865 the rebellious Maori captured a British ship and imprisoned the crew, except for one Captain Levy who, being a Jew, was set free. Thereafter, any Jews who came to New Zealand were given haven, although all other Whites were killed. The Maori fought the British with the same fanaticism that the Jews had once shown against the Romans; and they were similarly defeated, although the movement lingered on in one form or another, with sporadic outbreaks, until 1892. Such identification with the Jews was by no means limited to the Maori, but was widespread throughout the Polynesian islands. (A fuller descripiton of the Hau-Hau movement appears in Lanternari, 1965, Mentor edition, pp. 200–210.)

Page 276 The primary source on the Indian movements that will be discussed in the rest of the chapter is Mooney (1896)—a work covering many Indian revitalization movements besides the Ghost Dance of 1890.

Page 280 For more on the Ghost Dance of 1870, see DuBois (1939) and Spier (1927). For some additional material on the 1890 dance, see Lesser (1933).

Page 282 This explanation was first, I believe, suggested by Hill (1944).

Page 285 For more on the Handsome Lake religion, see Deardorff (1951) and Wallace (1961).

Page 286 The statement on peyote is from La Barre et al. (1951).

Page 288 An extensive literature exists on peyote, in particular La Barre (1938, 1960), Slotkin (1956), and Aberle (1966).

Page 289 Much of the analysis that follows was aided greatly by Wallace (1956). Two important papers whose contents I could not discuss because of lack of space are by Nash (1955) and Hurt (1960). One of the few searching studies of the phenomenon of the messiah in many cultures is Wallis (1943).

Page 292 Quoted in Astrov (1962), p. 142.

Page 294 The story of Ishi has been told very well indeed by T. Kroeber (1961).

Bibliography

ABERLE, D. F. 1966. *The Peyote Religion Among the Navaho*. New York: Viking Fund Publications in Anthropology.

ADAIR, J., and E. VOGT. 1949. "Navaho and Zuni Veterans: A Study in Contrasting Modes of Culture Change." *American Anthropologist*, pp. 547–561.

ARMILLAS, P. 1964. "Northern Mesoamerica." In Jennings and Norbeck (1964), pp. 291–329.

ASTROV, M., editor. 1962. *American Indian Prose and Poetry (The Winged Serpent)*. New York: Capricorn Books.

BANK, T. P. 1958. "The Aleuts." *Scientific American*, November, 1958, pp. 112–120.

BARNETT, H. G. 1938. "The Nature of the Potlatch." *American Anthropologist*, pp. 349–358.

BEAUCHAMP, W. M. 1905. *History of the New York Iroquois*. Albany: N.Y. State Museum Bulletin.

BENEDICT, R. 1934. *Patterns of Culture*. Boston: Houghton Mifflin. (Reprinted New York: Mentor, 1946.)

BERGSLAND, K., and H. VOGT. 1962. "The Validity of Glottochronology." *Current Anthropology*, pp. 115–153.

BERNAL, I. 1963. *Mexico Before Cortez*. Garden City, N.Y.: Doubleday.

BERRY, B. 1963. *Almost White*. New York: Macmillan.

BETTELHEIM, B. 1954. *Symbolic Wounds, Puberty Rites and the Envious Male*. Glencoe, Ill.: The Free Press. (Revised edition New York: Collier Books, 1962.)

BIRKET-SMITH, K. 1959. *The Eskimos*. London: Methuen.

BOAS, F. 1888. *The Central Eskimo*. Smithsonian Annual Report. (Reprinted Lincoln: University of Nebraska Press, 1964.)

———. 1909. "Kwakiutl of Vancouver Island." *American Museum of Natural History Memoir*.

BOWERS, A. W. 1950. *Mandan Social and Ceremonial Organization*. Chicago: The University of Chicago Press.

BOYD, W. C. 1950. *Genetics and the Races of Man*. Boston: Little, Brown.

BROTHERWELL, D., and E. HIGGS. 1963. *Science in Archaeology*. New York: Basic Books.

BUETTNER-JANUSCH, J. 1966. *The Origins of Man*. New York: John Wiley & Sons.

BUNZEL, R. L. 1932. "Introduction to Zuni Ceremonialism." *Bureau of American Ethnology Annual Report*.

CALDWELL, J. R. 1958. "Trend and Tradition in the Prehistory of Eastern United States." *American Anthropological Association Memoir*.

———. 1962. "Eastern North America." In Willey and Braidwood (1962).

——— and R. L. HALL. 1964. *Hopewellian Studies*. Springfield: Illinois State Museum.

CARPENTER, E. 1966. "Image Making in Arctic Art." In *Sign, Image, and Symbol*, edited by G. Kepes. New York: Braziller, 1966, pp. 206–225.

CASO, A. 1958. *The Aztecs, People of the Sun*. Norman: University of Oklahoma Press.

CHANCE, N. A. 1966. *The Eskimo of North Alaska*. New York: Holt, Rinehart and Winston.

CHAPPLE, E. D., and C. COON. 1942. *Principles of Anthropology*. New York: Henry Holt.

CHARD, C. S. 1958. "New World Migration Routes." *Anthropological Papers of University of Alaska*, December, 1958, pp. 23–26.

CODERE, H. 1951. "Fighting with Property." *American Ethnological Society Monograph*.

———. 1956. "The Amiable Side of Kwakiutl Life." *American Anthropologist*, pp. 334–351.

COE, M. 1962. *Mexico*. New York: Frederick A. Praeger.

———. 1964. "The Chinampas of Mexico." *Scientific American*, July, 1964, pp. 90–98.

——— and K. V. FLANNERY. 1964. "Microenvironments and Mesoamerican Prehistory." *Science*, pp. 650–654.

COLINVAUX, P. A. 1967. "Bering Land Bridge: Evidence of Spruce in Late-Wisconsin Times." *Science*, pp. 380–383.

COLLINS, H. B. 1964. "The Arctic and Subarctic." In Jennings and Norbeck (1964), pp. 85–116.

COLSON, E. 1953. *The Makah Indians*. Minneapolis: University of Minnesota Press.

COON, C. 1953. "Climate and Race." In *Climate Change*, edited by H. Shapley. Cambridge, Mass.: Harvard University Press, 1953, pp. 13–31.

COVARRUBIAS, M. 1954. *The Eagle, the Jaguar, and the Serpent: Indian Art of the Americas*. New York: A. A. Knopf.

———. 1957. *Indian Art of Mexico and Central America*. New York: A. A. Knopf.

DAVIS, R. T., et al. 1949. *Native Arts of the Pacific Northwest*. Stanford, Calif.: Stanford University Press.

DEARDORFF, R. 1951. "The Religion of Handsome Lake." In *Symposium on Local Diversity*, Bureau of American Ethnology Bulletin, pp. 77–107.

DEETZ, J. 1967. *Invitation to Archaeology*. Garden City, N.Y.: Doubleday.

DÍAZ DEL CASTILLO, B. 1956. *The Discovery and Conquest of Mexico, 1519–21*. New York: Farrar, Straus and Cudahy.

DILLON, L. S. 1956. "Wisconsin Climate and Life Zones in North America." *Science*. pp. 167–176.

DOBYNS, H. F., H. P. THOMPSON, et al. 1966. "Estimating Aboriginal American Population." *Current Anthropology*, pp. 395–449.

DOLE, G. L., and R. L. CARNEIRO, editors. 1960. *Essays in the Science of Culture in Honor of Leslie A. White.* New York: Thomas Y. Crowell.

DOZIER, E. P. 1964. "Pueblo Indians of the Southwest." *Current Anthropology,* pp. 79–97.

DRAGOO, D. W. 1963. *Mounds for the Dead.* Pittsburgh: Carnegie Museum.

DRIVER, H. 1961. *Indians of North America.* Chicago: The University of Chicago Press.

DRUCKER, P. 1939. "Rank, Wealth, and Kinship in Northwest Coast Society." *American Anthropologist,* pp. 55–65.

———. 1951. "The Northern and Central Nootkan Tribes." *Bureau of American Ethnology Bulletin.*

———. 1955. *Indians of the Northwest Coast.* New York: McGraw-Hill. (Reprinted Garden City, N.Y.: Natural History Press, 1963.)

———, and R. F. HEIZER. 1967. *To Make My Name Good: A Reexamination of the Southern Kwakiutl Potlatch.* Berkeley: University of California Press.

DU BOIS, C. 1939. "The 1870 Ghost Dance." *University of California Anthropological Records.*

EGGAN, F. 1950. *Social Organization of the Western Pueblos.* Chicago: The University of Chicago Press.

———, editor. 1955. *Social Anthropology of the North American Tribes.* Chicago: The University of Chicago Press.

EISELEY, L. C. 1955. "The Paleo-Indians: Their Survival and Diffusion." In *New Interpretations of Aboriginal American Culture History.* Anthropological Society of Washington, D.C., 1955, pp. 1–11.

EKHOLM, G. 1955. "The New Orientation toward Problems of Asiatic-American Relationships." In *New Interpretations of Aboriginal American Culture History,* Anthropological Society of Washington, D.C., 1955, pp. 95–109.

———. 1964. "Transpacific Contacts." In Jennings and Norbeck (1964), pp. 489–510.

ELLIS, F. H. 1951. "Patterns of Aggression and the War Cult in Southwestern Pueblos." *Southwestern Journal of Anthropology,* pp. 177–201.

ERICSON, D. B., M. EWING, and C. WOLLIN. 1964. "The Pleistocene Epoch in Deep-Sea Sediments." *Science,* pp. 723–732.

EWERS, J. C. 1953. "Of the Crow Nation." *Bureau of American Ethnology Bulletin,* pp. 1–74.

———. 1955. "The Horse in Blackfoot Indian Culture." *Bureau of American Ethnology Bulletin.*

———. 1958. *The Blackfoot.* Norman: University of Oklahoma Press.

FARB, P. 1963. *Face of North America: The Natural History of a Continent.* New York: Harper & Row.

FENTON, W. N. 1940 A. "Museum and Field Studies of Iroquois Masks and Ritualism." *Smithsonian Report.*

———. 1940 B. "Masked Medicine Societies of the Iroquois." *Smithsonian Report,* pp. 397–430.

———. 1941. "Towanda Longhouse Ceremonies." *Smithsonian Institution Bulletin.*

———. 1953. "The Iroquois Eagle Dance." *Bureau of American Ethnology Bulletin.*

FEY, H. E., and D. MC NICKLE. 1959. *Indians and Other Americans.* New York: Harper & Brothers.

FLANNERY, K. V., et al. 1967. "Farming Systems and Political Growth in Ancient Oaxaca." *Science,* pp. 445–454.

FLETCHER, A. C., and F. LA FLESCHE. 1911. "The Omaha Tribe." *Bureau of American Ethnology Report.*

FOWLER, M. L. 1959. "Modoc Rock Shelter: An Early Archaic Site in Southern Illinois." *American Antiquity,* pp. 257–270.

FREUCHEN, P. 1961. *Book of the Eskimo.* Cleveland: World Publishing.

FREUD, S. 1918. *Totem and Taboo.* (Reprinted in new translation, New York: Norton, 1962.)

GARFIELD, V. E. 1939. "Tsimshian Clan and Society." *University of Washington Publications in Anthropology,* pp. 167–349.

GIDDINGS, J. L. 1954. "Early Man in the Arctic." *Scientific American,* June, 1954, pp. 82–88.

———. 1960. "The Archaeology of Bering Strait." *Current Anthropology,* pp. 121–138.

———. 1964. *The Archaeology of Cape Denbigh.* Providence, R.I.: Brown University Press.

———. 1967. *Ancient Men of the Arctic.* New York: A. A. Knopf.

GOLDENWEISER, A. 1913. "The Principle of Limited Possibilities in the Development of Culture." *Journal of American Folk-Lore,* pp. 259–281.

GOLDFRANK, E. S. 1943. "Historic Change and Social Character, a Study of the Teton Dakota." *American Anthropologist,* pp. 67–83.

———. 1945 A. "Socialization, Personality, and the Structure of Pueblo Society (with particular reference to the Hopi and Zuni)." *American Anthropologist,* pp. 516–539.

———. 1945 B. "Changing Configurations in the Social Organization of a Blackfoot Tribe During the Reserve Period." *American Ethnological Society Monograph.*

———. 1952. "The Different Patterns of Blackfoot and Pueblo Adaptation to White Authority." In Tax (1952 B).

GOLDMAN, I. 1937. "The Zuni of New Mexico." In Mead (1937).

GOODE, W. J. 1951. *Religion Among the Primitives.* New York: Crowell-Collier.

GORENSTEIN, S. 1965. *Introduction to Archaeology.* New York: Basic Books.

GREENWAY, J. 1964. *The Inevitable Americans.* New York: A. A. Knopf.

GRIFFIN, J. B., editor. 1952. *Archaeology of Eastern United States.* Chicago: The University of Chicago Press.

———. 1960. "Some Prehistoric Connections Between Siberia and America." *Science,* pp. 801–812.

———. 1967. "Eastern North American Archaeology: A Summary." *Science,* pp. 175–191.

GRINNELL, G. B. 1923. *The Cheyenne Indians.* New Haven, Conn.: Yale University Press. (Reprinted New York: Cooper Square, 1962).

———. 1956. *The Fighting Cheyennes.* Norman: University of Oklahoma Press.

GUBSER, N. J. 1965. *The Nunamint Eskimo.* New Haven, Conn.: Yale University Press.

HAAG, W. G. 1962. "The Bering Strait Land Bridge." *Scientific American,* January, 1962, pp. 112–123.

HAGAN, W. T. 1961. *American Indians.* Chicago: The University of Chicago Press.

HALLOWELL, A. I. 1941. "The Social Function of Anxiety in Primitive Society." *American Sociological Review,* pp. 869–881.

———. 1955. *Culture and Experience.* Philadelphia: University of Pennsylvania Press.

————. 1957. "The Impact of the American Indian on American Culture." *American Anthropologist*, pp. 201–217.

————. 1959. "Backwash of the Frontier." *Smithsonian Report*, pp. 447–472.

————. 1960. "Ojibwa Ontology, Behavior, and World View." In *Culture in History*, edited by S. Diamond. New York: Columbia University Press, 1960, pp. 19–52.

————. 1963. "American Indians, White and Black: The Phenomenon of Transculturalization." *Current Anthropology*, pp. 519–531.

HART, C. W. 1943. "A Reconsideration of the Natchez Social Structure." *American Anthropologist*, pp. 374–386.

HASSRICK, R. B. 1964. *The Sioux.* Norman: University of Oklahoma Press.

HAURY, E. W. 1935. "Tree Rings—The Archaeologist's Time-Piece." *American Antiquity*, pp. 98–108.

————. 1950. *Stratigraphy and Archaeology of Ventana Cave, Arizona.* Tucson: University of Arizona Press.

HAWTHORN, A. 1967. *Art of the Kwakiutl Indians and Other Northwest Coast Indian Tribes.* Seattle: University of Washington Press.

HAYNES, C. V. 1964. "Fluted Projectile Points: Their Age and Dispersion." *Science*, pp. 1408–1413.

————. 1966. "Elephant Hunting in North America." *Scientific American*, June, 1966, pp. 104–112.

HEIZER, R. F. 1953. "Long Range Dating in Archaeology." In Kroeber (1953), pp. 3–42.

————. 1964. "The Western Coast of North America." In Jennings and Norbeck (1964), pp. 117–148.

————, and M. A. BAUMHOFF. 1962. *Prehistoric Rock Art of Nevada and Eastern California.* Berkeley: University of California Press.

HERSKOVITS, M. J. 1955. *Cultural Anthropology.* New York: A. A. Knopf.

————. 1960. *Economic Anthropology.* New York: A. A. Knopf.

HIBBEN, F. C. 1960. *Digging Up America.* New York: Hill and Wang.

HILL, W. W. 1940 A. "Some Navaho Culture Changes During Two Centuries." *Smithsonian Miscellaneous Collections*, pp. 395–415.

————. 1940 B. "Some Aspects of Navaho Political Structure." *Plateau*, pp. 23–28.

————. 1944. "The Navaho Indians and the Ghost Dance of 1890." *American Anthropologist*, pp. 523–527.

————. 1948. "Navaho Trading and Trading Ritual." *Southwestern Journal of Anthropology*, pp. 371–396.

HODGE, F. W. 1906. "Handbook of American Indians North of Mexico." *Bureau of American Ethnology Bulletin.* (Reprinted New York: Pageant Books, 1960.)

HOEBEL, E. A. 1954. *The Law of Primitive Man.* Cambridge, Mass.: Harvard University Press.

————. 1960. *The Cheyennes: Indians of the Great Plains.* New York: Holt, Rinehart and Winston.

HOIJER, H., editor. 1954. *Language in Culture.* Washington, D.C.: American Anthropological Association Memoir.

————, et al. 1946. *Linguistic Structures of Native America.* New York: Viking Fund Publications in Anthropology.

HOLM, B. 1965. *Northwest Coast Indian Art.* Seattle: University of Washington Press.

HOOPER, L. 1920. "The Cahuilla." *University of California Publications in American Archaeology and Ethnology*, pp. 316–380.

HOPKINS, D. M. 1959. "Cenozoic History of the Bering Land Bridge." *Science,* pp. 1519–1528.
———. 1967. *The Bering Land Bridge.* Stanford, Calif.: Stanford University Press.
HOWELLS, W. W. 1948. *The Heathens.* Garden City, N.Y.: Doubleday.
———. 1967. *Mankind in the Making.* Revised Edition. Garden City, N.Y.: Doubleday.
HUGHES, C. C. 1960. *An Eskimo Village in the Modern World.* Ithaca, N.Y.: Cornell University Press.
HULSE, F. S. 1963. *The Human Species.* New York: Random House.
HUNT, G. T. 1940. *The Wars of the Iroquois.* Madison: University of Wisconsin Press.
HURT, W. R. 1960. "The Yankton Dakota Church: A Nationalistic Movement of Northern Plains Indians." In Dole and Carneiro (1960), pp. 269–287.
HYMES, D. H. 1960. "Lexicostatistics So Far." *Current Anthropology,* pp. 3–43.
INVERARITY, R. B. 1950. *Art of the Northwest Coast Indians.* Berkeley: University of California Press.
JENNESS, D. 1922. "Life of the Copper Eskimos." *Canadian Arctic Expedition Report. Vol. 12.*
———. 1929. *People of the Twilight.* New York: Macmillan. (Reprinted Chicago: The University of Chicago Press, 1959.)
———. 1932. *The Indians of Canada.* Ottawa: National Museum of Canada.
———. 1935. "The Ojibwa Indians of Parry Island, Their Social and Religious Life." *National Museum of Canada Bulletin.*
JENNINGS, J. D., editor. 1956. "The American Southwest: A Problem in Cultural Isolation." In Wauchope (1956), pp. 59–128.
———, and E. NORBECK, editors. 1964. *Prehistoric Man in the New World.* Chicago: The University of Chicago Press.
JOSEPHY, A. M., editor. 1961. *The American Heritage Book of Indians.* New York: Simon & Schuster.
JUDD, N. M. 1954. "The Material Culture of Pueblo Bonito." *Smithsonian Miscellaneous Collections.*
KELLY, I. T. 1964. *Southern Paiute Ethnography.* Salt Lake City: University of Utah Anthropological Papers.
KLUCKHOHN, C., and D. LEIGHTON. 1946. *The Navaho.* Cambridge, Mass.: Harvard University Press. (Reprinted Garden City, N.Y.: Natural History Press, 1962.)
KNIGHT, R. 1965. "A Re-examination of Hunting, Trapping, and Territoriality Among the Northeastern Algonkian Indians." In Leeds and Vayda (1965), pp. 27–42.
KRIEGER, A. D. 1962. "The Earliest Cultures in the Western United States." *American Antiquity,* pp. 138–143.
———. 1964. "Early Man in the New World." In Jennings and Norbeck (1964), pp. 23–84.
KROEBER, A. L. 1908. "Ethnography of the Cahuilla Indians." *University of California Publications in American Archaeology and Ethnology,* pp. 29–68.
———. 1920. "Totemism and Taboo: An Ethnological Psychoanalysis." *American Anthropologist,* pp. 48–55.
———. 1931. "The Seri." *Southwestern Museum Papers,* pp. 1–60.
———. 1939. "Cultural and Natural Areas of Native North America." *University*

of California Publications in American Archaeology and Ethnology. (Reprinted Berkeley: University of California Press, 1963.)

————. 1948. *Anthropology.* New York: Harcourt, Brace.

————, editor. 1953. *Anthropology Today.* Chicago: The University of Chicago Press.

KROEBER, T. 1961. *Ishi.* Berkeley: University of California Press.

LA BARRE, W. 1938. *The Peyote Cult.* New Haven, Conn.: Yale University Press.

————. 1947. "Primitive Psychotherapy in Native American Cultures: Peyotism and Confession." *Journal of Abnormal and Social Psychology,* pp. 294–309.

————, et al. 1951. "Statement on Peyote." *Science,* pp. 582–583.

————. 1954. *The Human Animal.* Chicago: The University of Chicago Press.

————. 1960. "Twenty Years of Peyote Studies." *Current Anthropology,* pp. 45–60.

LAGUNA, F. DE. 1960. "The Story of a Tlingit Community." *Bureau of American Ethnology Bulletin.*

LANTERNARI, V. 1963. *The Religions of the Oppressed.* New York: A. A. Knopf. (Reprinted New York: New American Library, Mentor Books, 1965.)

LAUBIN, R., and G. LAUBIN. 1957. *The Indian Tipi.* Norman: University of Oklahoma Press.

LEACOCK, E. 1954. "The Montagnais 'Hunting Territory' and the Fur Trade." *American Anthropological Association Memoir.*

LEEDS, A., and A. P. VAYDA. 1965. *Man, Culture, and Animals.* Washington, D.C.: American Association for the Advancement of Science.

LEES, R. B. 1953. "The Basis of Glottochronology." *Language,* pp. 113–127.

LEÓN-PORTILLA, M. 1963. *Aztec Thought and Culture.* Norman: University of Oklahoma Press.

LESSER, A. 1933. "Cultural Significance of the Ghost Dance." *American Anthropologist,* pp. 108–115.

LÉVI-STRAUSS, C. 1961. *A World on the Wane.* New York: Criterion Books.

————. 1963. *Totemism.* Boston: Beacon Press.

LI AN-CHE. 1937. "Zuni: Some Observations and Queries." *American Anthropologist,* pp. 62–76.

LINTON, R. 1924. "Totemism and the A.E.F." *American Anthropologist,* pp. 296–300.

LOWIE, R. H. 1924. "Notes on Shoshonean Ethnography." *American Museum of Natural History Anthropological Papers,* pp. 185–314.

————. 1935. *The Crow Indians.* New York: Farrar & Rinehart. (Reprinted New York: Holt, Rinehart and Winston, 1956.)

————. 1954. *Indians of the Plains.* New York: McGraw–Hill. (Reprinted Garden City, N.Y.: Natural History Press, 1963.)

MC FEAT, T., editor. 1966. *Indians of the North Pacific Coast.* Seattle: University of Washington Press.

MAC GOWAN, K., and J. A. HESTER. 1962. *Early Man in the New World.* Garden City, N.Y.: Doubleday.

MC GREGOR, J. C. 1965. *Southwestern Archaeology.* Urbana, Ill.: University of Illinois Press.

MC ILWRAITH, T. F. 1948. *The Bella Coola Indians.* Toronto, Ontario: University of Toronto Press.

MAC NEISH, R. S. 1964 A. "Ancient Mesoamerican Civilization." *Science,* pp. 531–537.

————. 1964 B. "The Origins of New World Civilization." *Scientific American,* November, 1964, pp. 29–37.

MC NICKLE, D. 1962. *The Indian Tribes of the United States.* New York: Oxford University Press.

MC QUOWN, N. 1955. "Indigenous Languages of Native America." *American Anthropologist,* pp. 501–570.

MANGELSDORF, P. C., et al. 1964. "Domestication of Corn." *Science,* pp. 538–545.

MARTIN, P. 1961. "The Last 10,000 Years." *Geochronology Laboratories of the University of Arizona Publication.*

———. 1966. "African and Pleistocene Overkill." *Nature* (London), 22 October 1966, pp. 339–342.

———, and H. F. WRIGHT, editors. 1967. *Pleistocene Extinctions: Search for a Cause.* New Haven, Conn.: Yale University Press.

MARTIN, P. S., G. I. QUIMBY, and D. COLLIER. 1947. *Indians Before Columbus.* Chicago: The University of Chicago Press.

MASON, R. J. 1962. "The Paleo-Indian Tradition in Eastern North America." *Current Anthropology,* pp. 227–284.

MEAD, M., editor. 1937. *Cooperation and Competition Among Primitive Peoples.* New York: McGraw-Hill. (Reprinted Boston: Beacon Press, 1961.)

MEGGERS, B. J. 1954. "Environmental Limitations on the Development of Culture." *American Anthropologist,* pp. 801–823.

———. 1960. "The Law of Cultural Evolution as a Practical Research Tool." In Dole and Carneiro (1960), pp. 302–316.

———. 1968. "Prehistoric New World Cultural Development." (In Press.)

———, C. EVANS, and E. ESTRADA. 1965. "Early Formative Period of Coastal Ecuador: The Valdivia and Machalilla Phases." *Smithsonian Contributions to Anthropology.*

———, and C. EVANS. 1966. "A Transpacific Contact in 3000 B.C." *Scientific American,* January, 1966, pp. 28–35.

MEIGS, P. 1939. "The Kiliwa Indians." *Ibero-Americana,* pp. 1–114.

MILLON, R. 1967. "Teotihuacan." *Scientific American,* June, 1967, pp. 38–48.

MISHKIN, B. 1940. "Rank and Warfare Among Plains Indians." *American Ethnological Society Monograph.*

MOONEY, J. 1896. "The Ghost Dance Religion and the Sioux Outbreak of 1890." *Bureau of American Ethnology Annual Report.* (Reprinted Chicago: The University of Chicago Press, 1964.)

MORGAN, L. H. 1851. *League of the Ho-De-No-Sau-Nee or Iroquois.* (Reprinted New York: Corinth Books, 1962.)

———. 1877. *Ancient Society.* (Reprinted New York: Meridian Books, 1963.)

MOURANT, A. E. 1954. *The Distribution of Human Blood Groups.* Springfield, Ill.: Charles C. Thomas, Publisher.

MULLOY, W. 1952. "The Northern Plains." In Griffin (1952), pp. 124–138.

MUMFORD, L. 1967. *The Myth of the Machine.* New York: Harcourt, Brace & World.

MURPHY, R. F. 1956. "Matrilocality and Patrilineality in Mundurucú Society." *American Anthropologist,* pp. 414–434.

NASH, P. 1955. "The Place of Religious Revivalism in the Formation of the Intercultural Community on Klamath Reservation." In Eggan (1955), pp. 377–442.

NEUMANN, G. K. 1952. "Archaeology and Race in the American Indian." In Griffin (1952), pp. 13–34.

———. 1960. "Origins of the Indians of the Middle Mississippi Area." *Proceedings of the Indiana Academy of Sciences,* pp. 69–72.

NEWCOMB, W. W. 1950. "A Re-examination of the Causes of Plains Warfare." *American Anthropologist*, pp. 317–329.

———. 1960. "Toward an Understanding of War." In Dole and Carneiro (1960), pp. 317–336.

NEWELL, N. D. 1963. "Crises in the History of Life." *Scientific American*, February, 1963, pp. 77–92.

NEWMAN, M. T. 1953. "The Application of Ecological Rules to the Racial Anthropology of the Aboriginal New World." *American Anthropologist*, pp. 311–327.

———. 1962. "Evolutionary Changes in Body Size and Head Form in American Indians." *American Anthropologist*, pp. 237–256.

NOON, J. A. 1949. *Law and Government of the Grand River Iroquois*. New York: Viking Fund Publications in Anthropology.

NORBECK, E. 1961. *Religion in Primitive Society*. New York: Harper & Row.

OBERG, K. 1934. "Crime and Punishment in Tlingit Society." *American Anthropologist*, pp. 145–156.

OSWALT, W. H. 1966. *This Land Was Theirs*. New York: John Wiley & Sons.

———. 1967. *Alaskan Eskimos*. San Francisco: Chandler Publishing.

OWEN, R. C. 1965. "The Patrilocal Band: A Linguistically and Culturally Hybrid Social Unit." *American Anthropologist*, pp. 675–690.

PARK, W. Z. 1938. *Shamanism in Western North America*. Evanston, Ill.: Northwestern University Press.

PARSONS, E. C. 1939. *Pueblo Indian Religion*. Chicago: The University of Chicago Press.

———, and R. L. BEALS. 1934. "The Sacred Clowns of the Pueblo and Mayo-Yaqui Indians." *American Anthropologist*, pp. 491–516.

PARSONS, T. 1966. *Societies: Evolutionary and Comparative Perspectives*. Englewood Cliffs, N.J.: Prentice-Hall.

PEARCE, R. H. 1952. "The 'Ruines of Mankind': the Indian and the Puritan Mind." *Journal of the History of Ideas*.

———. 1953. *The Savages of America*. Baltimore: Johns Hopkins University Press.

PHILLIPS, P. J., J. A. FORD, and J. B. GRIFFIN. 1951. *Archaeological Survey in the Lower Mississippi Alluvial Valley*: Cambridge, Mass.: Peabody Museum of Archaeology and Ethnology, Harvard University.

POWELL, J. W., and G. W. INGALLS. 1874. "Report on the Conditions of the Ute Indians." *Smithsonian Institution*.

PRUFER, O. H. 1964. "The Hopewell Cult." *Scientific American*, December, 1964, pp. 90–102.

QUAIN, B. H. 1937. "The Iroquois." In Mead (1937), pp. 240–312.

QUIMBY, G. I. 1946. "Natchez Social Structure as an Instrument of Assimilation." *American Anthropologist*, pp. 134–137.

———. 1948. "Culture Contact on the Northwest Coast Between 1785 and 1795." *American Anthropologist*, pp. 247–255.

———. 1960. *Indian Life in the Upper Great Lakes*. Chicago: The University of Chicago Press.

RASMUSSEN, K. 1927. *Across Arctic America*. New York: G. P. Putnam's Sons.

———. 1932. "Intellectual Culture of the Copper Eskimo." *Canadian Arctic Expedition Report*.

REED, E. K. 1954. "Transition to History in the Pueblo Southwest." *American Anthropologist*, pp. 592–597.

————. 1955. "Trends in Southwestern Archaeology." In *New Interpretations of Aboriginal American Culture History*, Anthropological Society of Washington, pp. 46–58.

————. 1964. "The Greater Southwest." In Jennings and Norbeck (1964), pp. 175–192.

ROBERTS, J. M. 1956. "Zuni Daily Life." *Notebook of Laboratory of Anthropology of University of Nebraska*.

ROE, F. G. 1955. *The Indian and the Horse*. Norman: University of Oklahoma Press.

SAHLINS, M. D. 1959. "The Social Life of Monkeys, Apes, and Primitive Man." In Spuhler (1959), pp. 54–73.

————. 1967. *Tribesmen*. Englewood Cliffs, N.J.: Prentice-Hall.

SAPIR, E. 1929. "The Status of Linguistics as a Science." *Language*, pp. 207–214.

————. 1963. *Selected Writings in Language, Culture, and Personality*. Berkeley: University of California Press.

SCHOENWETTER, J. 1962. "Pollen Analysis of Eighteen Archaeological Sites in Arizona and New Mexico." In *Chapters in Prehistory of Arizona*, edited by P. S. Martin, Chicago: Chicago Museum of Natural History.

SEARS, W. H. 1964. "The Southeastern United States." In Jennings and Norbeck (1964), pp. 259–289.

SEJOURNE, L. 1960. *Burning Water: Thought and Religion in Ancient Mexico*. New York: Grove Press.

SELLARDS, E. H. 1952. *Early Man in the New World*. Austin: University of Texas Press.

SERVICE, E. R. 1962. *Primitive Social Organization*. New York: Random House.

————. 1963. *Profiles in Ethnology*. New York: Harper & Row.

————. 1966. *The Hunters*. Englewood Cliffs, N.J.: Prentice-Hall.

SILVERMAN, J. 1967. "Shamans and Acute Schizophrenia." *American Anthropologist*, pp. 21–31.

SIMPSON, G. G. 1953. *The Major Features of Evolution*. New York: Columbia University Press.

SINGER, P., and D. DE SOLE. 1967. "The Australian Subincision Ceremony." *American Anthropologist*, pp. 355–358.

SLOTKIN, J. S. 1956. *The Peyote Religion*. Glencoe, Ill.: The Free Press.

————. 1965. *Readings in Early Anthropology*. New York: Viking Fund Publications in Anthropology.

SMITH, H. N. 1950. *Virgin Land: The American West as Symbol and Myth*. Cambridge, Mass.: Harvard University Press.

SMITH, W., and J. M. ROBERTS. 1954. *Zuni Law: A Field of Values*. Cambridge, Mass.: Peabody Museum of Archaeology and Ethnology, Harvard University.

SOUSTELLE, J. 1961. *The Daily Life of the Aztecs*. London: Weidenfeld & Nicolson.

SPARKMAN, P. S. 1908. "The Culture of the Luiseño Indians." *University of California Publications in American Archaeology and Ethnology*, pp. 187–234.

SPAULDING, A. C. 1955. "Prehistoric Cultural Development in the Eastern United States." In *New Interpretations of Aboriginal American Culture History*, Anthropological Society of Washington, D.C., pp. 12–28.

SPECK, F. G. 1940. *Penobscot Man*. Philadelphia: University of Pennsylvania Press.

————. 1944. *Midwinter Rites of the Cayuga Longhouse*. Philadelphia: University of Pennsylvania Press.

————. 1955. *The Iroquois.* Bloomfield Hills, Mich.: Cranbrook Institute.

SPENCER, R. F. 1959. "The North Alaskan Eskimo: A Study in Ecology and Society." *Bureau of American Ethnology Bulletin.*

————, J. D. JENNINGS, et al. 1965. *The Native Americans.* New York: Harper & Row.

SPICER, E. H. 1960. *Perspectives in American Indian Culture Change.* Chicago: The University of Chicago Press.

————. 1962. *Cycles of Conquest.* Tucson: University of Arizona Press.

SPIER, L. 1927. "The Ghost Dance of 1870 Among the Klamath of Oregon." *University of Washington Publications in Anthropology.*

SPUHLER, J. N., editor. 1959. *The Evolution of Man's Capacity for Culture.* Detroit: Wayne State University Press.

STEVENSON, M. C. 1901. "The Zuni Indians." *Bureau of American Ethnology Bulletin.*

STEWARD, J. H. 1930. "The Ceremonial Buffoons of the American Indian." *Michigan Academy of Sciences,* pp. 187–207.

————. 1938. "Basin-Plateau Sociopolitical Groups. *Bureau of American Ethnology Bulletin.*

————. 1955. *Theory of Culture Change.* Urbana, Ill.: University of Illinois Press.

————. 1956. "Cultural Evolution." *Scientific American,* May, 1956, pp. 69–80.

STEWART, O. C. 1939. *Northern Paiute Bands.* Berkeley: University of California Press.

STEWART, T. D. 1960. "A Physical Anthropologist's View of the Peopling of the New World." *Southwestern Journal of Anthropology,* pp. 259–271.

STRONG, W. D. 1929. "Aboriginal Society in Southern California." *University of California Publications in American Archaeology and Ethnology,* pp. 35–273.

————. 1940. "From History to Prehistory in the Northern Great Plains." *Smithsonian Miscellaneous Collections,* pp. 353–394.

SUTTLES, W. 1960. "Affinal Ties, Subsistence, and Prestige Among the Coast Salish." *American Anthropologist,* pp. 296–305.

SWADESH, M. 1952. "Lexicostatistic Dating of Prehistoric Ethnic Contacts." *Proceedings of American Philosophical Society,* pp. 452–463.

————. 1964. "Linguistic Overview." In Jennings and Norbeck (1964), pp. 527–556.

SWANSON, G. E. 1960. *The Birth of the Gods.* Ann Arbor: University of Michigan Press.

SWANTON, J. R. 1909. "Contributions to the Ethnology of the Haida." *The American Museum of Natural History Memoir.*

————. 1911. "Indian Tribes of the Lower Mississippi Valley and Adjacent Coast of the Gulf of Mexico." *Bureau of American Ethnology Bulletin.*

————. 1926. "Notes on the Mental Assimilation of Races." *Journal of Washington Academy of Sciences,* pp. 493–502.

————. 1946. "The Indians of the Southeastern United States." *Bureau of American Ethnology Bulletin.*

————. 1952. "The Indian Tribes of North America." *Bureau of American Ethnology Bulletin.*

TAX, S., editor. 1952 A. *Heritage of Conquest.* Glencoe, Ill.: The Free Press.

————, editor. 1952 B. *Acculturation in the Americas.* Chicago: The University of Chicago Press.

THWAITES, R. G., editor. 1906. *The Jesuit Relations and Allied Documents.* Cleveland: Burrows Brothers.

TRENHOLM, V. C., and M. CARLEY, 1964. *The Shoshonis.* Norman: University of Oklahoma Press.

TURNEY-HIGH, H. H. 1949. *Primitive Warfare, Its Practices and Concepts.* Columbia: University of South Carolina Press.

TYLOR, E. B. 1871. *Primitive Culture.* (Reprinted New York: Harper & Row, 1958, as *The Origins of Culture* and *Religion in Primitive Culture.*)

———. 1888. "On a Method of Investigating the Development of Institutions; Applied to Laws of Marriage and Descent." *Journal of the Royal Anthropological Institute,* pp. 245–267.

UNDERHILL, R. 1948. "Ceremonial Patterns in the Greater Southwest." *American Ethnological Society Memoir.*

———. 1953. *Red Man's America.* Chicago: The University of Chicago Press.

———. 1956. *The Navahos.* Norman: University of Oklahoma Press.

VAILLANT, G. C. 1962. *The Aztecs of Mexico.* Garden City, N.Y.: Doubleday.

VAN STONE, J. W. 1962. *Point Hope, An Eskimo Village in Transition.* Seattle: University of Washington Press.

VOEGELIN, C. F., and E. W. VOEGELIN. 1944. "Map of North American Indian Languages." *American Ethnological Society.*

VOGT, E. Z. 1960. "Navaho." In Spicer (1960), pp. 278–336.

WALLACE, A. F. C. 1956. "Revitalization Movements." *American Anthropologist,* pp. 264–280.

———. 1958. "Dreams and Wishes of the Soul: A Type of Psychoanalytic Theory Among the Seventeenth Century Iroquois." *American Anthropologist,* pp. 234–248.

———. 1961. "Cultural Composition of the Handsome Lake Religion." In "Symposium on Cherokee and Iroquois Culture," *Bureau of American Ethnology Bulletin,* pp. 143–157.

WALLACE, E., and E. A. HOEBEL. 1952. *The Comanches.* Norman: University of Oklahoma Press.

WALLIS, W. D. 1943. *Messiahs: Their Role in Civilization.* Washington, D.C.: American Council on Public Affairs.

WASHBURN, W., editor. 1964. *The Indian and the White Man.* Garden City, N.Y.: Doubleday.

WAUCHOPE, R., editor. 1956. "Seminars in Archaeology." *Society for American Archaeology Memoir.*

———. 1962. *Lost Tribes and Sunken Continents.* Chicago: The University of Chicago Press.

WEBB, W. S., and R. S. BABY. 1957. *The Adena People.* Columbus: Ohio Historical Society.

WEDEL, W. R. 1941. "Environment and Native Subsistence Economies in the Central Great Plains." *Smithsonian Miscellaneous Collections,* pp. 1–29.

———. 1963. "The Plains and Their Utilization." *American Antiquity,* pp. 1–16.

———. 1964. "The Great Plains." In Jennings and Norbeck (1964), pp. 193–222.

WENDORF, F., and J. J. HESTER. 1962. "Early Man's Utilization of the Great Plains." *American Antiquity,* pp. 159–171.

WEYER, E. M. 1932. *The Eskimos.* New Haven, Conn.: Yale University Press.

WHITE, L. A. 1949. *The Science of Culture.* New York: Farrar, Straus.

———. 1959. *The Evolution of Culture.* New York: McGraw-Hill.

WHORF, B. L. 1956. *Language, Thought, and Reality.* Cambridge, Mass.: The M.I.T. Press.

WILLEY, G. R., editor. 1956. *Prehistoric Settlement Patterns in the New World.* New York: Viking Fund Publications in Anthropology.

————. 1960 A. "Historical Patterns and Evolution in Native New World Cultures." In *The Evolution of Man,* edited by S. Tax, Chicago: The University of Chicago Press, pp. 111–141.

————. 1960 B. "New World Prehistory." *Science,* pp. 73–86.

————. 1966. *An Introduction to American Archaeology: North and Middle America.* Englwood Cliffs, N.J.: Prentice-Hall.

————, and R. BRAIDWOOD, editors. 1962. *Courses Toward Urban Life.* New York: Viking Fund Publications in Anthropology.

WISSLER, C. 1910. "Material Culture of the Blackfoot Indians." *American Museum of Natural History Anthropological Papers,* pp. 1–175.

————. 1911. "The Social Life of the Blackfoot Indians." *American Museum of Natural History Anthropological Papers,* pp. 1–64.

WITTFOGEL, K. A. 1957. *Oriental Despotism.* New Haven, Conn.: Yale University Press.

WOLF, E. 1959. *Sons of the Shaking Earth.* Chicago: The University of Chicago Press.

————. 1966. *Peasants.* Englewood Cliffs, N.J.: Prentice-Hall.

WOODBURY, R. 1960. "The Hohokam Canal at Pueblo Grande, Arizona." *American Antiquity,* pp. 267–270.

WORMINGTON, H. M. 1957. *Ancient Man in North America.* Denver: Denver Museum of Natural History.

WRIGHT, H. E., and D. G. FREY, editors. 1965. *The Quaternary of the United States.* Princeton, N.J.: Princeton University Press.

YARNELL, R. A. 1964. "Aboriginal Relationships Between Culture and Plant Life in the Upper Great Lakes Region." *University of Michigan Anthropological Papers.*

Index

Clothing: Eskimo, 35–36, 37; Great Basin Shoshone, 17
Clovis, 199, 203
Columbus, Christopher, 3, 4, 243, 245
Comanche, 77, 116, 127, 255
Communism: Eskimo communal property, 46; Marxist theory and Iroquois, 99–100; modern vs. primitive, 46–47
Composite bands: bases of, 55–56; economic controls, 56; environment and, 68; family and, 55, 62; leadership, 55–56, 59; reincarnation belief and, 61–62; Sub-Arctic, 55–56, 57
Composite tribes, 15, 119, 122
Convergence principle, culture and, 212–13
Copper Eskimo (Canada), 41
"Coppers," Northwest Coast, 150–51
Coronado, Francisco, 4, 77, 113, 115
Cortés, Hernan, 4, 164, 168, 169, 170, 186–88
Council of Sachems, Iroquois, 98–99, 104, 108
Coups: Cheyenne, 122; Plains Indians, 122–23; status and, 122, 123
Cree, 116, 117, 124
Creek, 153, 163
Crow, 116; societies, 120, 127; vision quests, 128
Cuauhtémoc, 173
Cult(s): of dead, 220–21; Dreamers, 278–80; Kachina, 84, 85, 87, 93; messianic, 206–7, 275, 276, 277–80; "New Religion" of Iroquois, 284–85; peyotism, 285–89; resurgence of shamanistic, 182; war, 92
Cultural evolution, 8–11; adaptation and, 13–14; behavior patterns and stage, 14; convergence principle and, 212–13; diffusion and, 212–16; great men and, 100–4; independent invention and, 102–3, 104, 213, 214–15; limited possibilities principle and, 213; Mexico, stages in, 210–12; North America for study, 7–9; preadaptation and, 207; theories on, 6–8, 212–16; See also Culture(s); Culture change
Culture(s): adaptive choice and, 224; borrowing and, 267, 268, 270–71; contacts between, 8, 9–11, 267, 268,

Culture (Cont.)
270–71, 289–90; cultural hybrids, 74–76; defined, 18–19; diffusion and, 161, 163; environment and, 38–40, 134; explanations for similarities and differences, 6, 11–15, 212–16, 216–19; extinction of, 293–94; great men and events and, 100–4; interactions between, 8, 9–11; invention acceptance by, 9–10, 22, 23; language and, 235–39; leisure and, 28; messianic movements and, 289–90; personality and, 11–12, 13, 185; preservation of, 292–94; revivalistic movements, 275–84, 289–92, 306–7; social organization and, 12–14; surplus production and, 28, 29, 118; transmission of Indian to Whites, 261–64; warfare explained by, 125–26; See also Acculturation; Cultural evolution; Culture change; and under specific topic
Culture change: biological explanation, 11; culture contact and, 260–61; defined, 117; horse and, 10, 31–32, 112, 115–18, 122, 126; mechanism of, 9–11; psychological explanation, 11–13; theories on, 212–16; See also Acculturation; Cultural evolution; and under specific group

Dakota, 116, 124, 231
Danger Cave (Utah), 208
Darwin, Charles, 18, 231
Dating, 301; dendrochronology, 304; Folsom, 226; geologic methods, 302; Hopewell, 219–20; language in, 233–35; major methods, 302–3; man in North America, 196, 226–27, 235; Navaho, 267–68; Plainview, 202; problems in, 197; radiocarbon, 196, 226, 320–23; Sandia cave, 199; skulls, 226–27
Dawes Allotment Act, 256, 257
Dead: cult of, 220–21; Navaho fear of, 281–82; Sioux funeral ceremony, 294
Debt slavery, 141–42
Delaware Indians, 97, 250, 277, 293
Dendrochronology, 304
Desert culture, 207–8, 219; Southwestern cultures from, 216–19